THE

MIGHTY

AND THE

ALMIGHTY

EDITED BY
NICK SPENCER

THE

MIGHTY

AND THE

ALMIGHTY

HOW POLITICAL LEADERS DO GOD

Biteback Publishing

First published in Great Britain in 2017 by
Biteback Publishing Ltd
Westminster Tower
3 Albert Embankment
London SE1 7SP
Introduction, selection and editorial apparatus copyright © Nick Spencer 2017

ISBN 978-1-78590-191-1

10 9 8 7 6 5 4 3 2 1

A CIP catalogue record for this book is available from the British Library.

Set in Adobe Garamond Pro

Printed and bound in Great Britain by
CPI Group (UK) Ltd, Croydon CR0 4YY

CONTENTS

Acknowledgements   vii

Contributors   ix

Introduction *by Nick Spencer*   xi

Margaret Thatcher (1979–90) *by Nick Spencer*   I

Ronald Reagan (1981–89) *by Nick Spencer*   II

Václav Havel (1989–92, 1993–2003) *by Natan Mladin*   27

Bill Clinton (1993–2001) *by Simon Perfect*   43

Nelson Mandela (1994–99) *by Paul Bickley*   63

John Howard (1996–2007) *by Clare Purtill*   77

Tony Blair (1997–2007) *by Andrew Connell*   87

Mary McAleese (1997–2011) *by Elizabeth Oldfield*   103

Viktor Orbán (1998–2002, 2010–) *by Joseph Ewing*   115

Vladimir Putin (2000–08, 2012–) *by Ben Ryan*   129

George W. Bush (2001–09) *by Hannah Malcolm*   141

Angela Merkel (2005–) *by Nick Spencer*   155

Ellen Johnson Sirleaf (2006–) *by Maddy Fry*   167

Gordon Brown (2007–10) *by Paul Bickley*   179

Kevin Rudd (2007–10) *by Andrew Connell*   191

Nicolas Sarkozy (2007–12) *by Ben Ryan*   205

Lee Myung-bak (2008–13) *by Henry van Oosterom*   219

Fernando Lugo (2008–12) *by Ben Ryan*   235

Barack Obama (2009–17) *by Simon Perfect*   249

Goodluck Jonathan (2010–15) *by Maddy Fry*   269

David Cameron (2010–16) *by Nick Spencer*   279

Tony Abbott (2013–15) *by Gillian Madden*   295

Theresa May (2016–) *by Nick Spencer*   307

Donald Trump (2017–) *by Nick Spencer*   321

Conclusion *by Nick Spencer*   337

ACKNOWLEDGEMENTS

The Mighty and the Almighty began life several years ago in the form of a productive conversation between Theos and Simon Mabon of Lancaster University. It ended up taking a different form and becoming the work of diverse hands, some of which had their first outing on www.theosthinktank. co.uk, others of which make their first appearance in this volume, but we remain grateful for those initial explorations.

We would also like to thank Tom Slade for his diligence in working through the book's footnotes and the team at Biteback for having captured the vision of a book that analysed how political leaders actually do God, rather than assumed it, as so many commentators seem to do.

Nick Spencer
Theos, 2017

CONTRIBUTORS

Paul Bickley is director of political programme at Theos and the author of *Building Jerusalem: Christianity and the Labour Party* (Bible Society, 2010).

Andrew Connell is a researcher and academic based in Cardiff. His interests include public policy, devolution, and the place of the church in public life. He is the author of *Welfare Policy under New Labour: The Politics of Social Security Reform* (I. B. Tauris, 2011).

Joseph Ewing is a former Theos researcher and is currently working in public affairs in the third sector.

Maddy Fry is a journalist and a former Theos researcher. She currently works as a policy researcher for the think tank Muslim Engagement and Development and is also writing a novel.

Gillian Madden is a former Theos researcher and is currently completing an MA in Christian leadership, with a particular focus on political theology and the identity of the local church.

Hannah Malcolm is a former Theos researcher and is now living and working at Hilfield Friary, Dorset.

Natan Mladin is a researcher at Theos. He is currently completing a PhD in theology and the arts at Queen's University Belfast, with a thesis that explores the doctrine of providence with the aid of theatre studies.

Elizabeth Oldfield is director of Theos and co-author of *More than an Educated Guess: Assessing the Evidence on Faith Schools* (Theos, 2013).

Henry van Oosterom is a former Theos researcher and is currently studying for a Master's in international security at the Paris School of International Affairs.

Simon Perfect is a researcher at Theos and also a teaching fellow at the School of Oriental and African Studies, where he teaches courses on Islam in Britain and Muslim communities in minority contexts.

Clare Purtill is a former Theos researcher and co-author of *Religion and Well-being: Assessing the Evidence* (Theos, 2016). She is currently working in Parliament for a Labour MP.

Ben Ryan is a researcher at Theos and the author of a number of reports, most recently *A Soul for the Union* (Theos, 2016). He is currently editing a book about the ethics of migration policy.

Nick Spencer is research director at Theos and the author of a number of books, most recently *The Evolution of the West: How Christianity Has Shaped Our Values* (SPCK, 2016). His next book is titled *The Political Samaritan: How Power Hijacked a Parable*.

INTRODUCTION

NICK SPENCER

We begin with a horror story.

It is a fringe meeting at the Labour Party conference, September 2015, Monday morning. The British Humanist Association, the UK's premier association of atheists and agnostics, is hosting its 'no-prayer annual breakfast'. This is a lot like the prayer breakfasts that are held annually in Westminster, Washington and many other political capitals, only somewhat smaller and without any prayer.

Breakfast has long gone by the time shadow business secretary Angela Eagle, soon to be a contender for leadership of the Labour Party (and therefore, in theory, the country), launches into an attack on Tim Farron MP. Mr Farron is the new leader of the Liberal Democrats, a party hunted to the point of extinction at the 2015 general election. As the leader of the nation's only other centre-left party, one might have expected Ms Eagle to attack Mr Farron for (some of) his policies or his political principles. But instead, her attack took a different line.

'At a time when we have a huge revival of fundamentalist religious belief,' she told them, 'we have a newly elected leader of the Liberal Democrats who is an evangelical Christian who believes in the literal truth of the Bible. He does. He just doesn't want to talk about it a lot because he knows how much it will embarrass his own party.'

Ms Eagle's vision was alarming, if a little sketchy on the details (if, after all, there has been a huge 'revival of fundamentalist religious belief' in the

UK, one can't help wonder where they all are on a Sunday morning). Still, she blew the dog whistle with vigour: 'revival', 'fundamentalist', 'evangelical', 'literal'; the choir to whom she was preaching must have shuddered. The prospect of a religious – a *seriously* religious – politician getting anywhere near the levers of power is, Eagle implied, petrifying. Her speech was a reminder, according to the *Guardian* diarist who attended and wrote about the event, that fundamentalism takes many forms.[1]

• • •

With no disrespect to the leader of the Liberal Democrats in the UK (who, for the record, does in fact speak openly about his Christian faith[2]), Mr Farron is rather unlikely to get anywhere near the levers of power. The Liberal Democrats' brief union with the Conservative Party in the 2010–15 coalition government ended in an appallingly messy divorce in which the senior partner got the house and most of the savings, and the junior one the contents of the garden shed and a sleeping bag. Even had they not been left with only eight (now nine) MPs, it is unlikely that any Liberal Democrat party leader will rush into political marriage again. In that regard, it was simply the energy with which Ms Eagle reviled Mr Farron's faith that was unusual. One wonders what she would have said of a parliamentarian who stood a genuine chance of office.

But if her vigour was unusual, the denunciation itself was not. British voters are familiar, some wearyingly so, with the idea that Christianity and politics do not mix. We all know what happens when they do: crusades, inquisitions, invasions, persecution. We free moderns should never forget that religious adversaries are always on the prowl, seeking someone to devour. The price of secular freedom is eternal vigilance, usually of religious people.

Nevertheless, it was the great secular hope that walls of separation, whether constitutionally or culturally erected, and the general decay of Christian belief in the West, would render any theo-political threat dormant, and such eagle-eyed vigilance redundant. Denunciations like that at the 'no-prayer breakfast' would become unnecessary because there would be too few Christians, either in power or in voting booths, for the theo-political menace to scare the secular horses.

The last forty years have turned out somewhat different. The rest of the world did not do what most Westerners expected it to, and secularise in the manner of its formal colonial powers. The emergence of politically confident Islam in the Middle East and south Asia; the continued strength of Catholicism in Central and South America, and its growth in Africa; the remarkable explosion of Pentecostalism in Central and South America and in sub-Saharan Africa; the extraordinary story of Christianity in South Korea, and its survival and then upsurge in China: none of this had been predicted. Different paths were taken and Western politicians found themselves operating in a world that is, as the sociologist Peter Berger has remarked, 'as furiously religious as it ever was, and in some places more than ever'.[3]

Worse, Western politics did not secularise, or more precisely did not secularise as fully and comprehensively as many were expecting. The upsurge in Christian engagement in US politics startled many from the late 1970s; Pope John Paul II played a seminal role in the end of communism in Europe, and even in the somewhat less religious countries of western Europe and Australia, churches remained a part of the political scene, often playing significant walk-on roles themselves. Moreover, as the stories in this volume indicate, Christian political leaders have hardly become less prominent over recent decades, and may, in fact, have become more so. Worse still, those Presidents and Prime Ministers were often open and unapologetic about their faith, and its political significance. It was the stuff of Angela Eagle's nightmares.

• • •

This book examines the faith of those leaders, twenty-four of them to be precise. While it can be read straight through it can just as profitably be dipped into and cherry-picked for figures who especially appeal to readers.

All but one of its subjects were happy to call themselves Christian, the exception being Václav Havel, whose writings on theism and ethics are so striking that they demand attention and inclusion, and all held highest office (all but one executive office). Nevertheless, for all their similarity in framing and focus, the chapters in *The Mighty and the Almighty* are subtly different. When a subject has a long and twisting life story, such as Nelson Mandela, more space is given to charting that. When a subject or their country is liable to be less familiar to a reader – Lee Myung-bak in South Korea, Fernando Lugo in Paraguay, or Ellen Johnson Sirleaf in Liberia, for example – the chapter offers more background and explanatory detail. A few chapters – well, the one on Havel – offer more space for discussion of the subject's writing and intellectual ruminations. For some, most commonly American Presidents, the cup of evidence runneth over; for others, often British Prime Ministers, we find ourselves gathering up the crumbs from under the political table. Because no two political leaders are alike – and, as we shall see, being a Christian political leader does little to alter such diversity – no two chapters on them are alike.

Of our subjects, the majority held or hold office in Western or 'developed' countries (the exceptions – Mandela, Sirleaf, Lugo and Goodluck Jonathan – provide interesting points of comparison), although not all those countries are 'Western' (e.g. South Korea) or indeed fully functioning democracies (e.g. Russia). Most of the leaders are (or were) openly and publicly Christian (although some were rather camera shy) but by no means all liked to claim a direct connection between their faith and politics. Some were more culturally Christian; some more comfortable with vicarious faith; others were explicit and confessional; a few were converts; several once contemplated a career in the Church; one, remarkably, had been a bishop. Many others – Tarja Halonen of Finland, Luiz Inácio Lula da Silva of Brazil, F. W. de Klerk of South Africa, Lech Wałęsa of Poland, Boris Trajkovski of Macedonia, John Bruton and Bertie Ahern of Ireland, Yulia Tymoshenko of Ukraine, José María Aznar of Spain, Helmut Kohl and Gerhard Schröder of Germany, Stephen Harper, Jean Chrétien and Justin Trudeau of Canada, even Robert Mugabe of Zimbabwe – might have been included but for reasons of space (and, in some instances, available source material).

As mention of the last of these names suggests, *The Mighty and the Almighty* is no work of apology or PR. Robert Mugabe might have been vigorously attacked by the Catholic hierarchy in Zimbabwe (at least recently) but he was educated as a Catholic, married in a Catholic church and calls himself a Catholic. He did not, alas, make the cut but Vladimir Putin, no less open about his devout faith (to Russian Orthodoxy) did. Neither is renowned as a paragon of democratic virtue. The purpose of *The Mighty and the Almighty* is not to discuss nice Christian politicians, or those politicians we would like to be Christian, or those Christian politicians with whom we agree (who, after all, is the 'we' here?). Rather it is intended to look at leading politicians – meaning those who have sat in the highest office – who have claimed some Christian faith, and to explore how they have squared the two; how, in effect, the Mighty (or at least those who professed a belief in him) have dealt with the Almighty when in office.

As any good pollster will tell you, twenty-four is a pretty low sample size, even when dealing with a 'universe' as small as this one. We must be careful about drawing firm conclusions about 'how politicians do God' from such a group. Nonetheless, some patterns and tentative conclusions do emerge and are discussed at the end of the book. Before that, however, *The Mighty and the Almighty* seeks to offer a series of theo-political biographies of men and women who have had more of an opportunity than most to shape the world in which we live. What role their Christian faith played in this shaping is explored in each chapter. Whether it is something about which we should be delighted, pleased, indifferent, sceptical or, like Angela Eagle, afraid is a question to which we shall turn.

NOTES

1. Simon Hattenstone, 'The cult of Jeremy Corbyn, the great silverback mouse', *The Guardian*, 29 September 2015, https://www.theguardian.com/politics/2015/sep/29/jeremy-corbyn-labour-conference-great-silverback-mouse (accessed 19 January 2017).

2. The author heard one such address at a public meeting in the Attlee Suite in Portcullis House in November 2016, to mark one year after the Commission on Religion and Belief report, in which Mr Farron was positively evangelical about his faith.

3. Peter Berger (ed.), *The Desecularization of the World: The Resurgence of Religion in World Politics* (Eerdmans, 1999), p. 2.

MARGARET THATCHER
(1979–90)

NICK SPENCER

Margaret Thatcher was Britain's most serious and explicitly religious Prime Minister since Stanley Baldwin, arguably since William Gladstone. The second child of devout Methodists, she was a preacher before she was a parliamentarian, a Christian before a Conservative, and convinced that political problems had spiritual roots. 'Economic problems never start with economics. They have much deeper roots in human nature,' she said in her first conference address as Conservative Party leader in 1975, an address of which she subsequently remarked, 'I was not going to make just an economic speech. The economy had gone wrong because something else had gone wrong spiritually and philosophically.'[1]

BIOGRAPHY

Margaret Thatcher was born above her father's grocer's shop in Grantham, Lincolnshire, on 13 October 1925. Her father, rather than her mother, with whom she claimed she had very little in common, was the dominant figure in her early life. Hardworking, austere, puritanical and civic minded, Alfred Roberts was a Methodist preacher, who inculcated in his daughter a spirit of self-reliance and independence. Margaret attended chapel four times on a Sunday, 'a religious environment which, by the standards of today, would seem very rigid'.[2] Although there was no doubting her sincerity or involvement, she latterly indicated that, for her, less Christianity would have been more, and she declined to impose on her own children anything like as demanding an observance – or, indeed, any Christian observance at all.[3]

Her Grantham upbringing was subsequently much mythologised, not least by Thatcher herself once she had become leader of the opposition. 'All my ideas about life, about individual responsibility, about looking after your neighbour, about patriotism, about self-discipline, about law and order, were all formed right in a small town in the Midlands, and I've always been thankful that I was brought up in a smaller community so that you really felt what a community could be,' she remarked.[4] However much exaggeration there might be in this, it is clear that her Methodist upbringing was formative – 'our lives revolved around Methodism,' she latterly remarked – and although tempered by marriage to the millionaire Denis Thatcher, and submerged by an early parliamentary career in a more patrician, Conservative milieu, it was the values of thrift, industry, self-reliance and probity that shaped and inspired her politics.[5]

She became a committed member of the Oxford University Wesleyan Society (OUWS) in her student days, attending study groups, and even preaching on the local circuit. Slowly, however, politics drew her attention and she gravitated from the OUWS to the OU Conservative Association. The connection remained close, however, as evidenced by an address to the local Free Church Council in Dartford, when standing for election there in 1951, which tied together patriotism, Christian decency and a religious calling to public service.

Thatcher transferred her denominational allegiance to low-church Anglicanism in the 1950s as she moved physically, emotionally and spiritually from Grantham, not least on account of her marriage to Denis, who was, to all intents and purposes, a non-believer. She never considered the denominational shift to be substantial, however, pointing out that Wesley always considered himself an Anglican, and maintaining her discernibly nonconformist social ethic long after she began attending the established church.

Margaret Thatcher was devout and there was never a whisper of a suggestion that her Christianity was put on for office or for the cameras. According to the rector of St Peter and St Paul, Ellesborough, the parish church nearest to the prime ministerial residence of Chequers, Thatcher attended more often in the first two years of her premiership than any other post-war Prime Minister. Moreover, in another sign of her religious integrity, she always refused communion when there, on account of the fact that, despite her move from Wesleyan Methodism, she was never confirmed an Anglican. Christian beliefs and commitments went all the way down and not even her sharpest critics ever accused her of spiritual superficiality. Indeed, if anything, their problem and criticism was precisely the reverse, that Thatcher took her particular spiritual commitments too seriously, too inflexibly and too absolutely for the political world.

'WE DO NOT LEGISLATE FOR SAINTS'

Thatcher insisted that Christianity did not dictate her politics. 'I never thought that Christianity equipped me with a political philosophy,' she told an audience at St Lawrence Jewry in 1978. However, she went on, 'it did equip me with standards to which political actions must, in the end, be referred'.

It is not entirely clear how we should read this statement, made as it was by an opposition leader seeking office. Many years later in the autobiographical account of her time as Prime Minister, she wrote how her 'whole political philosophy' was 'based' on 'what are often referred to as "Judaeo-Christian"' values.[6] She was clear throughout her political life that Christians could belong to either main party in the UK, though there was never any doubt which was the truer home for them.

That noted, Thatcher did try to strike a balance in her Christian political pronouncements. On those (relatively rare) occasions on which she spoke in some detail about Christianity, she stressed how she saw in the faith a *balance* between two competing doctrines. In her speech at St Lawrence Jewry she explained how there is a 'great Christian doctrine' that 'we are all members one of another'. This was expressed 'in the concept of the Church on earth as the Body of Christ', and from it 'we learn our interdependence' and the 'great truth that we do not achieve happiness or salvation in isolation from each other but as members of society'.[7] This is not the voice that people associate with Margaret Thatcher.

More familiar is the other 'great doctrine', that people are 'all responsible

moral beings ... infinitely precious in the eyes of their Creator', faced with
the 'choice between good and evil'. Although it was with these free, moral,
responsible beings that Thatcherism was better associated, she insisted to the
audience at St Lawrence Jewry that 'the whole of political wisdom consists in
getting these two ideas in the right relationship to each other'.

To critics, not least ecclesiastical ones, it was precisely this theological
balance that she failed to strike: recognising a tension between individual
and collective responsibility, and then ignoring it or pretending it was in
fact no tension at all. This can be seen in her 1977 Iain Macleod Memorial
Lecture, 'Dimensions of Conservatism', in which she attacked the 'socialist'
conviction that there was a choice between capitalism, which, 'based on
profit[,] embodies and encourages self-interest' and is therefore 'selfish and
bad', and socialism, which rejects the free market and therefore 'is based on
and nurtures altruism and selflessness'. This, she vigorously pronounced, was
'baseless nonsense in theory and in practice'. 'There is not and cannot possibly be any hard and fast antithesis between self-interest and care for others',
she told her audience, precisely for those reasons she would identify in her
St Lawrence Jewry lecture the following year. 'Man is a social creature, born
into family, clan, community, nation, brought up in mutual dependence',
this being a 'cornerstone' of Christian morality, as evidenced in the Golden
Rule. This command, to 'do as you would be done by', was predicated precisely on a 'concern' and 'responsibility for self'. Only by respecting and
honouring the self could one 'extend' the same to others. 'Our fellow-feeling
develops from self-regard.' Altruism (of the kind socialists expected and defended) might be admirable but it was neither realistic nor necessary, nor,
importantly, a *political* project. 'You may object that saintly people can well
have no personal desires, either material or prestigious; but we do not legis-
late for saints.'[8]

Thatcher's Christian politics was not as monolithic or red-in-tooth-and-
claw as critics (and indeed some allies) insisted. Her social, ecclesiastical and
theological upbringing in Grantham, however much mythologised, did leave
her with a sense that there was such a thing as corporate responsibility, as
'society'. Crucially, however, not only was this not the same as the state – a
point that Archbishop William Temple, with whom Thatcher profoundly

disagreed, was making in the 1920s – but, in Thatcher's mind, it was actively undermined by the state. Whereas for fellow parliamentarians such as Tony Benn, who shared a nonconformist hinterland (if absolutely nothing else) with Thatcher, the state would preserve, enable and encourage virtue, mutuality and responsibility, for Margaret Thatcher it did little other than hinder them.

Once again, there were subtleties here in her approach. However much she stood in the line of descent from late Victorian liberalism and deployed its rhetoric, she was no political Canute. 'The role of the state in Christian society is to encourage virtue, not to usurp it,' she told the St Lawrence Jewry audience, leaving open the possibility that the state did have some positive role to play.[9] She returned to this in a speech to the General Assembly of the Church of Scotland in 1988, one of the most theologically explicit speeches ever made by a sitting Prime Minister. 'Speaking personally as a Christian', she began by outlining three 'distinctive marks' of Christianity, three marks which, in good Christian fashion, were actually one:

> First, that from the beginning man has been endowed by God with the fundamental right to choose between good and evil ... second, that we were made in God's own image and, therefore, we are expected to use all our own power of thought and judgement in exercising that choice ... and third, that Our Lord Jesus Christ, the Son of God, when faced with His terrible choice and lonely vigil, chose to lay down His life that our sins may be forgiven.[10]

Thatcher's Christianity had, by 1988, lost some of its emphasis on the corporate nature and was, as she told a hapless John Humphrys, who had tried to catch her out in a pre-election radio interview the previous year, fundamentally about personal choice.[11] Yet even now, she went on to say how we must recognise that 'modern society is infinitely more complex than that of Biblical times', and that 'in our generation, the only way we can ensure that no one is left without sustenance, help or opportunity, is to have laws to provide for health and education, pensions for the elderly, succour for the sick and disabled'. It was clearly not that the state had no role in securing the

public good, even if that role was more tilted towards legislation and regulation than provision. However, she immediately went on to say, 'Intervention
by the state must never become so great that it effectively removes personal
responsibility.' The point at which state intervention became so great as to
interfere with this 'responsibility' was a great deal earlier for Thatcher than it
was for many other Christians, not least her critics in the Church of England.

Thatcher's Christianity, then, imbued her with an awareness of but profound scepticism towards the role of collective institutions in securing the
public good. But it also, crucially, formed in her an awareness of and profound sympathy towards the role of the individual in securing that good.
This was central to her political philosophy. If her theo-politics had deep
Christian roots anywhere, it was here. 'Our religion teaches us that every
human being is unique and must play his part in working out his own
salvation,' she told her audience at the Iain Macleod lecture.[12] 'The New
Testament is preoccupied with the individual, with his need for forgiveness
and for the Divine strength which comes to those who sincerely accept it,'
she said in a later speech at St Lawrence Jewry.[13]

Thatcher's anthropology depicted unique, created, fundamentally independent and responsible beings who, if they lived their lives according to
their Creator's intentions – working hard, spending and saving responsibly,
sustaining secure family lives, and participating in local community and
voluntary associations rightly – would ensure that they, their communities
and their society worked. This cashed out in the full range of her policies,
but it also bred a tension in her Christian politics that was as ironic as it was
irreconcilable.

Thatcher liked and spoke often about the UK being a Christian nation or,
when that term became sociologically contentious or politically inadvisable,
being a nation founded on and formed by 'Judeo-Christian values'. This was
no less sincere than her own personal faith. The choice and independence
she so powerfully advocated rested foursquare on strong moral foundations,
such as those she grew up with in Grantham. 'Freedom will destroy itself if it
is not exercised within some sort of moral framework, some body of shared
beliefs, some spiritual heritage,' she told St Lawrence Jewry in 1978, and for
Britain that framework was undoubtedly Christian. 'Christian religion ... is

a fundamental part of our national heritage ... we are a nation whose ideals are founded on the Bible.'[14]

Not surprisingly this led Thatcher to be heralded by many conservative Christians – not, note, Christian Conservatives: the distinction will become clear – as something of a saviour. Upset and resentful at the political, social and cultural liberalism that began to transform the nation in the 1960s, they sought, and in Thatcher believed they had found, 'one of us': someone who acknowledged, respected and strove to protect the nation's Christian foundations, identity and morals. Rhetorically she gave them much of what they wanted.

However, *her* commitment to *their* agenda was somewhat more questionable. Thatcher's voting record on the traditional social conservative issues was mixed. She had supported the decriminalisation of homosexuality and of abortion, but had opposed the Divorce Reform Act and spoken out against the liberalisation of obscene material. However, she rarely spoke in Parliament on any of these matters, and never took much active interest, at least until 1975 when she became leader of the opposition. She had no strong attachment to the National Viewers' and Listeners' Association, the organisation spearheaded by Mary Whitehouse that was most prominent in voicing socially conservative concerns through the 1970s and 1980s, although this is certainly not to claim she was indifferent to those concerns. The health of the family was a particular issue for her and she set up the Family Policy Group (FPG) in 1981, for example. However, the fact that, according to John Sparrow in the Cabinet Office, the FPG was briefed to generate initiatives to reverse the 'collectivist beliefs and attitudes ... ingrained in large numbers of the population' and restore 'the spirit of individual responsibility, confidence and self-reliance' suggests that Thatcher's understanding of 'family' was informed more by her wider ethical and economic concerns than by the more traditional language and ideas of the social conservatives.[15]

This pinpoints the tension. The *Daily Mail* journalist Mary Kenny remarked of Thatcher's moral universe that 'the individual and the libertarian values are in conflict with the family much more than those of a socialist ethic.'[16] Thatcher would, of course, have disputed that but the fact that the point may be made of more than simply family values is significant.

Thatcher's one parliamentary defeat was over the Shops Bill in 1986, when a remarkable coalition of Christians, one-nation conservatives, small traders and trade unionists worked together against it. The vigorous debate around the issue of Sunday trading often highlighted the tension – many called it outright hypocrisy – of Thatcher's position, as she sought to enable a market extension that would have horrified her father and the Victorian Methodist culture that formed him (and her). An aged Harold Macmillan, making a final appearance in the House of Lords, warned (rightly) that the bill was 'another step in the secularisation of our people'. More personally, the former Methodist preacher and Labour MP Ron Lewis asked, 'Is she, as the head of the government, going to besmirch her father's memory by bringing in legislation that will help consign the sanctity of the Sabbath day to the scrapheap?'[17] That was a sharp question but sharp precisely because it was accurate.

Much the same point could be made about Thatcher's programme to de-regulate credit across the nation. This could be, and was, morally defended as liberating people and giving them more responsibility over their own financ-es and lives. But it didn't take a financial genius to work out that easy credit would invariably lead to a culture of debt, and given that Alfred Roberts described debt as the 'curse of mankind' in a 1936 speech, it is equally easy to lay the charge of hypocrisy, or at least self-contradiction, at his daughter's door.[18] There are indications that she was aware of this, or at least alert to the problematic and paradoxical consequences of trying to achieve Victorian, Judeo-Christian ends through the means of liberalisation and deregulation. Thatcher was, it is said, uncomfortable with many of the visible extravagances of capitalism and in private reportedly raged against the excesses of bankers. Frank Field MP once asked her about her greatest regret in office, to which she replied, 'I cut taxes and I thought we would get a giving society and we haven't.'[19] Her former head of communications, Harvey Thomas, observed that 'she thought like a grocer's daughter … [and] couldn't understand the culture she had created'.[20]

However much this was the case – and opponents may justly point out that there was no shortage of critics, not least the established Church, which warned her regularly and loudly about the culture she was creating – this problem was not epiphenomenal, a merely secondary or incidental issue that happened to appear as an accident of her main policies. It was bred deep in the bone of Thatcherism and, arguably, of Thatcher's political Christianity.

CONCLUSION

Margaret Thatcher offers a fascinating and, in modern British history, unprecedentedly broad and deep case study of the combination of Christianity and politics. Steeped in the Christian faith, intelligent, thoughtful, sincere, authentic, Margaret Thatcher's Christianity shaped her politics genuinely and profoundly. It was not as severe or blunt as many assume but nor was it nuanced or balanced. It played aggressively to the political right but in doing so was beset by fault lines that gave sustenance to her many critics, foremost among whom was the Church of England.

Eliza Filby, Thatcher's spiritual biographer, wrote in the introduction to her book *God and Mrs Thatcher* that 'the religious faith of leaders is not to be underestimated. It can drive some to war, others to peace; some left, others right.'[21] This may be so, but it is never easy, even in a case as public and discussed as Margaret Thatcher's, to say how far her religious faith moved and motivated her. We have no counterfactual case study of a woman free of the influence of Alfred Roberts, Methodism and pre-war Grantham against which to compare the UK's first female Prime Minister. That recognised, few would doubt that Christianity, albeit flavoured by the circumstances of upbringing, the political context of the moment and Thatcher's own fierce personal convictions, informed her politics in deep and momentous ways.

NOTES

1. 'Speech to Conservative Party conference', 10 October 1975, Margaret Thatcher Foundation website, http://margaretthatcher.org/document/102777 (accessed 19 January 2017); Margaret Thatcher, *The Path to Power* (London: HarperCollins, 1995), pp. 305–6.
2. 'Speech at St Lawrence Jewry', 30 March 1978, Margaret Thatcher Foundation website, http://margaretthatcher.org/document/103522 (accessed 19 January 2017).
3. 'I did not insist that they went to church. I think that was probably because I'd had so much insistence myself.' Quoted in Eliza Filby, *God and Mrs Thatcher* (London: Biteback Publishing, 2015), p. 67.
4. 'Radio interview for IRN (Conservative leadership election)', 31 January 1975, Margaret Thatcher Foundation website, http://margaretthatcher.org/document/102602 (accessed 19 January 2017).

5. Thatcher, *The Path to Power*, p. 5.

6. Margaret Thatcher, *The Downing Street Years* (London: HarperCollins, 1993), p. 509.

7. 'Speech at St Lawrence Jewry'.

8. 'Speech to Greater London Young Conservatives (Iain Macleod Memorial Lecture: "Dimensions of Conservatism")', 4 July 1977, Margaret Thatcher Foundation website, http://margaretthatcher.org/document/103411 (accessed 19 January 2017).

9. 'Speech at St Lawrence Jewry'.

10. 'Speech to General Assembly of the Church of Scotland', 21 May 1988, Margaret Thatcher Foundation website, http://margaretthatcher.org/document/107246 (accessed 19 January 2017).

11 Humphrys's question, 'Prime Minister, what is the essence of Christianity?', was intended, he said, to trick her into 'mumbl[ing] something about morality or love'. 'Choice,' she replied. See John Humphrys, *Devil's Advocate* (London: Arrow, 2000), pp. 261–2. Humphrys reflects in his book that he was subsequently persuaded by her answer: 'Later I realised exactly what she meant and, dammit, she was right. The whole point of Christianity is that you have a choice between doing good and doing evil. If you end up in Heaven, that's because you made the right choice; if you end up in Hell, it's your fault.'

12. 'Speech to Greater London Young Conservatives'.

13. 'Speech at St Lawrence Jewry', 4 March 1981, Margaret Thatcher Foundation website, http://www.margaretthatcher.org/document/104587 (accessed 19 January 2017).

14. 'Speech to General Assembly of the Church of Scotland'.

15. Filby, *God and Mrs Thatcher*, p. 133. The irony of a state initiative being deployed by an anti-statist party to help restore a moral autonomous culture was remarked on at the time.

16. Quoted in Filby, *God and Mrs Thatcher*, p. 219.

17. See Filby, *God and Mrs Thatcher*, pp. 229–32.

18. Ibid., p. 343.

19. Quoted ibid., p. 348.

20. Ibid., p. 336.

21. Ibid., p. xxiii.

RONALD REAGAN (1981–89)

NICK SPENCER

INTRODUCTION

Ronald Reagan's election as fortieth President of the United States in November 1980 was to mark as significant a shift in American politics as Margaret Thatcher's did in Britain. The new President's public image was, in many ways, the polar opposite to his British counterpart: California and Hollywood as opposed to Grantham and Methodism. Yet there was a clear ideological bond between the two politicians, and when they first met in 1975, a close personal chemistry was also in evidence. Reagan sought to reform America as Thatcher did the UK and in his case Christianity was to play an even more significant role.

EARLY YEARS

Ronald Wilson Reagan was born on 6 February 1911 in Tampico, Illinois, the son of John Edward Reagan (Jack), a first-generation Irish immigrant, and Nelle Clyde Wilson Reagan. Although Nelle was a Protestant, the Reagans had been married in a Catholic church in 1904 largely on account of Jack's heritage. He, however, showed little interest in Ronald or his brother Neil's spiritual upbringing (and not much in their general upbringing), struggling with finances and drink throughout their childhood, and regularly moving the family in search of work. Reagan lived in five different towns and twelve rented apartments before his teen years.

It was Nelle, and the church, that were to prove his rock. Nelle had a live and active faith, leading prayer meetings, teaching in the Sunday school, directing the choir, working with the Women's Missionary Society and chairing the Committee on Missions. Highly biblically literate, it was her Bible on which Reagan swore his oath of allegiance when he assumed the presidency in 1981.

When the family finally settled, Reagan attended a Disciples of Christ church in Dixon, Illinois, a denomination whose beliefs and commitments bore close resemblance to Reagan's later politics: providence, progress and a nationalistic spirit that could equate the country's interest with God's will and occasionally explained America's mission 'in prophetic, millennialistic terms'.[1] 'I was raised to believe that God has a plan for everyone and that seemingly random twists of fate are all part of his plan,' Reagan later said.[2]

Fortified by his mother and the church, Reagan's teenage faith was further edified by his pastor, Ben Cleavar, to whom he was particularly close and whose daughter he dated, and a good smattering of evangelical books, in particular the novel *The Printer of Udell's*, reading which was like a spiritual experience for the young man, and which prompted him to get baptised. Thereafter, Reagan taught in the Sunday school and was vice-president of the Hi-Y Club, a social club associated with the Young Men's Christian Association. The Disciples of Christ gave Reagan his first experience of public speaking, and many assumed he was on his way to being a minister. He left Dixon in 1928 for Eureka College, a liberal arts school established by the Disciples of Christ in 1850 to provide a Christian education, where he studied economics and sociology, from which point his media career took off.

TO THE WHITE HOUSE

Reagan started as a sports announcer at WOC radio in Davenport, Iowa, before progressing to WHO radio in Des Moines, where his profile gradually grew nationally, and thereafter to Hollywood in the late 1930s, where he signed with Warner Brothers and became a star. By the early 1950s, his movie career was on the wane and he was hired by General Electric as a travelling spokesman, a position he held until 1962 when his political interests began to take centre stage.

Reagan had begun life as an FDR Democrat but disaffection with high tax rates (more than 90 per cent for the highest rate in the 1950s) and burgeoning welfare spending pushed him, by the later 1950s, into the arms of the Republican Party, claiming that the Democrats left him rather than the other way round. Although already a national figure in his own right, his first major political speech was delivered in 1964 for Barry Goldwater, who was running as a Republican candidate against Lyndon Johnson for the presidency. This so-called 'Time for Choosing' speech lambasted communism and the big state and announced the American public's 'rendezvous with destiny'. It was hugely successful, although more for Reagan than for Goldwater. Two years later, he stood successfully for the governorship of California, which he held from January 1967 to January 1975, whence he ran for President for the first time.

After his youthful fervour, Reagan's practical involvement in the church had faded somewhat (again, not unlike Thatcher's), and although he joined the Hollywood Beverly Christian Church in 1930s, his attendance there was sporadic. His faith and religious commitments remained, however, and were made evident from his earliest days in public office. 'It is inconceivable to me', he said minutes into the 1967 inaugural address, 'that anyone could accept this delegated authority without asking God's help,' going on to say:

> Someone back in our history, maybe it was Benjamin Franklin, said if ever someone could take public office and bring to that public office the precepts and teachings of the Prince of Peace, he would revolutionise the world and men would be remembering him for 1,000 years. I don't think anyone could follow those precepts completely. I'm not so presumptuous as to think I can – but I will try very hard.[3]

Reagan told the broadcaster David Frost that Christ was the historical figure he most admired,[4] and he was repeatedly clear about his need for prayer. The sentiments did not win him the Republican Party nomination in 1976, let alone the presidency, but they signalled a new voice in top-rank American politics, saturated in Christian faith and not afraid to use it. In 1976, the American public chose Jimmy Carter, a born-again Southern Baptist, many believing that they were going to get undiluted, born-again Baptist

Christianity. His resolute failure to satisfy them, combined as it was with an unprecedented loss of American self-confidence, paved the way for Reagan's ebullient, optimistic and rhetorically polished faith to move into the highest office four years later.

REAGAN'S RHETORIC

It was perhaps his theo-political rhetoric that constituted Ronald Reagan's biggest single impression on US politics.

Reagan accepted the Republican nomination before a huge crowd in Detroit on 17 July 1980. At one point, almost stammering, he admitted to his audience, 'I— I have— I have thought of something that is not part of my speech. And I'm worried over whether I should do it.' He took time before divulging his secret, building the suspense still further. 'I'll confess that I've been a little afraid to suggest what I'm going to suggest.' He paused. 'I'm more afraid not to.' He then asked the audience, and the nation, 'Can we begin our crusade, joined together, in a moment of silent prayer?' The moment lasted fully thirteen seconds until the would-be President broke it with his final words of the night: 'God bless America.' The reaction was rapturous, in Detroit and beyond.

In their study of how twentieth-century Presidents used religion rhetorically, David Domke and Kevin Coe showed how, from the administration of Franklin D. Roosevelt until that of Jimmy Carter, around half of White House addresses to the nation invoked God, the high points being Roosevelt himself and Harry Truman, both invoking God about 60 per cent of the time, and the low points being Richard Nixon and Carter, at about 30 per cent. With Reagan, this figure shot up to 96 per cent.[5]

The same story can be told of the number of times God was invoked within these presidential addresses. This hovered at one to two per address between 1933 and 1981, but then increased to an average of three with Reagan. Even more tellingly, in what Domke and Coe call 'high state occasions', inaugurations and State of the Union addresses, the increase went from between one and three invocations on average to six with Reagan. God was summoned not only in more speeches but more often within speeches, and especially within big speeches.

Precisely the same pattern emerged with invocations of 'faith', and words like 'mission' or 'crusade'. The proportion of presidential speeches with entreaties for God's help and general requests for divine favour oscillated between 10 per cent and 40 per cent between Roosevelt and Gerald Ford, fell to under 10 per cent for Carter, but then rose to over 90 per cent with Reagan.[6] Perhaps most tellingly, prior to Reagan taking office, the phrase 'God bless America' had been used only once in a national address, by Nixon on 30 April 1973 as he concluded his speech concerning Watergate.[7] Thereafter, it became a staple of virtually all major presidential speeches. Domke and Coe conclude that it wasn't that 'explicit language about God entered the presidency in 1981', but rather that it was 'with Reagan [that] explicit language about God became publicly embedded in the presidency – and, by extension, in US politics'.[8]

Reagan's religious rhetoric was not ubiquitous; his first inaugural, for example, wore its spirituality lightly. But it was widespread, and marked by confidence, moral certainty and sometimes open aggression, all delivered with a self-consciously Christian vocabulary. If Winston Churchill took the English language and sent it into battle for Britain in the 1940s, Reagan spiritualised the American political language in the 1980s and sent it out to reinvigorate American society and self-image.

MORAL REARMAMENT

The reinvigoration of American society was central to Reagan's mission, and he would have firmly countersigned Margaret Thatcher's conviction that underlying the economic ennui that was plaguing the UK (and the US) in the 1970s there lurked a profound spiritual problem. This belief was part of Reagan's mind from his earliest public statements, not least because it was part of the American mind. He had talked of America's unique destiny from his early years (it was, as noted, almost part of the Disciples of Christ's theology), and he subsequently adapted John Winthrop's famous phrase 'a city on a hill', adding the epithetic 'shining' to give it a quintessential Reagan lustre. The words 'blessed', 'promised land', 'divine plan' and 'providence' featured repeatedly in his speeches, and he often spoke of America as 'less of a place than an idea', that idea being 'God's gift of freedom to all mankind'.[9]

The opportunity, and the felt need, for such rhetoric had increased vastly from the mid-1960s as internationally, Vietnam gave the nation a military bloody nose and badly tarnished its image as the world's moral lighthouse, and domestically, clashes over civil rights, the rise of the permissive society, economic stagnation and the Watergate scandal disturbed national self-confidence. Disaffected groups emerged, the most influential coming to be known as the 'Religious Right', effected by a rapprochement between historically antagonistic Catholics and evangelicals. Many millions of Americans sought religious and cultural revival and, the star of Carter falling as rapidly as it had risen, Reagan was the man to deliver it.

The promise began while he was governor of California. Reagan remarked in an interview with *Christianity Today* in 1972 that 'there has been a wave of humanism and hedonism in this land', before going on to say that he was optimistic 'because I sense ... a great revolution against that ... a hunger ... for spiritual revival.'[10] He went on to make use of what Theodore Roosevelt called the bully pulpit of the White House, diagnosing the spiritual ills that ailed the nation and exhorting an appropriate response. He also liberally employed a remark Pope Pius XII had made in January 1946, first published in *Collier's Weekly* magazine, to the effect that 'God has placed an afflicted mankind ... into the hands of America'. Between leaving California in 1976 through to the end of his presidency, Reagan used it at least eleven times.[11] At times, he could go even further and intimate that to be truly American was to be Christian. Let us remember, he said on return from his one trip to Moscow in 1988, 'that being an American means remembering another loyalty, a loyalty as the hymn put it "to another country I have heard of, a place whose King is never seen and whose armies cannot be counted"'.[12]

None of this endeared him to his many secular critics, such as those who worked for the *New York Times*, which lambasted him for 'not worshipping in his church but in a Washington hotel' (where he had just delivered one such religiously charged speech) and said, 'You don't have to be a secular humanist to take offense at that display of what, in America, should be private piety.'[13] 'Private piety' was anathema to Reagan, however, as it became clear it was to a very large number of Americans.

THE RELIGIOUS RIGHT

As President, Reagan did not attend church regularly. This was explained in various ways – he didn't want to wreck the worship services of whichever church he attended, there were major security concerns after he survived an assassination attempt in 1981 – none of which was especially convincing (not least as they failed to deter subsequent Presidents). Either way, it was an odd decision, as it gave a hostage to fortune to his opponents, who used it to claim his religiosity was all for the cameras, and it vexed his conservative religious allies who, while wholly behind him, were far from wholly uncritical.[14]

Reagan vigorously courted this constituency, which was disaffected not only by the liberal turn in American cultural life but by the disappointment of Carter, who hid his Christian credentials tightly under a secular bushel. In the run-up to the 1980 election, Reagan spoke at the national convention of the Religious Roundtable, a group led by fifty-six prominent evangelical and fundamentalist religious leaders. The officially non-partisan nature of this group meant that they could not endorse any candidates. Recognising this, Reagan said, 'I know this is non-partisan, so you can't endorse me, but I want you to know that I endorse you.'[15] It struck the perfect note, as did his vow to appoint evangelicals in his administration according to their proportion in society. This was an all-but-impossible promise, one that Carter had made in a more non-committal way four years earlier and that remained, predictably, unfulfilled, and there was a touch of this kind of disappointment in Reagan's relationship with his core constituency with regard to a range of other issues, in particular school prayer and abortion.

Reagan was undoubtedly serious about wanting to return (the possibility of) public prayer to schools. The United States Supreme Court had ruled in *Engel v. Vitale*, in 1962, that voluntary recitation by New York public school students of a one-sentence non-denominational prayer composed by that state's board of regents violated the Establishment Clause of the First Amendment to the Constitution. The following year, in *Abington v. Schempp*, the court found that the voluntary recitation of the Lord's Prayer and reading of the Bible in public schools were also forbidden by the First Amendment.[16] This incensed millions of Americans and was one of the issues that galvanised the Religious Right in the 1970s. Reagan himself made repeated references to the issue,[17] asking rhetorically in a 1984 radio address, 'Can it really be true that the First Amendment can permit Nazis and Ku Klux Klansmen to march on public property, advocate the extermination of people of the Jewish faith and the subjugation of blacks, while the same amendment forbids our children from saying a prayer in school?'[18] In May 1982, he proposed to Congress a constitutional amendment to restore school prayer, to the effect that 'nothing in the Constitution shall be construed to prohibit individual or group prayer in public schools or other public institutions', adding also that 'no person shall be required by the United States or by any state to participate in prayer'.[19]

The amendment did not enjoy plain sailing, however, and when the debate returned in March the following year to the Senate, Reagan resubmitted it, declaring that 'the founders of our nation and the framers of the First Amendment did not intend to forbid public prayer … On the contrary, prayer has been part of our public assemblies since Benjamin Franklin's eloquent request that prayer be observed by the Constitutional Convention.'[20] Despite his personal commitment to the issue, however, and the huge public support for the bill – over 80 per cent according to *New York Times* polling – the amendment failed to carry and when the Democrats gained control of the Senate in 1986, the prospects of its success were finally lost.

If there is little doubt about Reagan's commitment to school prayer, there is less clarity about his attitude to abortion. When governor of California he had signed into legislation (this was before *Roe v. Wade* when abortion was still a state issue) the Therapeutic Abortion Act, an Act intended to reduce the number of 'back room' abortions but which resulted in many more abortions in total. This was only four months into his governorship and he later claimed that had he been more experienced he would not have signed it. One biographer, Lou Cannon, said that in his dealings with Congress Reagan gave only scant attention to this 'human life' file. By contrast, William P. Clark, a lead member of his staff in California and Washington, asserted that 'no issue was of greater importance to him than the dignity and sanctity of all human life',[21] and that Reagan personally made regular and significant pro-life noises.

In reality, Reagan's personal and rhetorical commitment to the issue, and indeed to the issues of personal morality that were gathering political significance at this time, is hard to doubt. He proclaimed a National Sanctity of Human Life Day in 1984 to coincide with the anniversary of *Roe v. Wade*, and two years later he stated in his State of the Union address that there is a 'wound in our national conscience. America will never be whole as long as the right to life granted by our Creator is denied to the unborn.' In a similar vein, he talked of a 'spiritual awakening' that was inextricably linked to this issue or those, like illegitimacy and promiscuity, that were marks of the nation's moral degeneration.

That noted, his attempts to reverse *Roe v. Wade* were even less successful than those on school prayer. The issue remained a juristic rather than a political one and hopes of returning it to state legislatures were as distant in 1989 as they had been in 1981.

Overall, while there is no doubting the closeness of the relationship between Reagan and the Religious Right, the marriage was more fractious than the honeymoon, as they tend to be. For all that he talked the talk, declaring 1983 the Year of the Bible and arguing that the Founding Fathers never intended the Wall of Separation to be 'a wall of hostility between government and the concept of religious belief itself',[22] many Religious Right leaders increasingly came to lament that Reagan had actually achieved little for them. Some, like Jerry Falwell, worked hard for him but got very little in return, their generic disappointment being spiced with personal bitterness. For others, it was more simply that the new day that had allegedly dawned in 1981 turned out to be as cloudy as the one that preceded it.

Some commentators subsequently claimed that Reagan and his administration's courting of the Religious Right was mere cynicism, and occasional quotations can be drawn to support this: 'We want to keep the Moral Majority types so close to us they can't move their arms,' remarked one anonymous Reagan administration official.[23] This is hard to sustain, however. For all his rhetorical genius, Reagan meant what he said. Rather, the problem seems to have been the problem itself, namely that what ailed America in Reagan's mind was a fundamentally cultural issue, not amenable to political, even presidential, action.

The ultimate result was a paradoxical one. The Reagan years enabled the Religious Right to grow in profile, membership and influence. But its goals lingered stubbornly on the horizon, fracturing the movement as some groups retained a chastened faith in the Republicans, some lost it altogether, and a few, like Pat Robertson, thought it best to strike out on their own presidential path.

No less worryingly, for them, the very profile and apparent influence of the movement boosted membership of liberal and secular groups almost as much as it did the Religious Right itself. The result was the intensifying of the culture wars, with which we are familiar today, although the extent to which blame for that can be laid at the door of Reagan himself is open to debate.

ECONOMIC POLICY

One of the reasons why the Religious Right lost faith in Reagan was that his administration made it clear that economic priorities trumped social and cultural ones in the opening years of his presidency (again, there is an echo with Thatcher's Conservatives here). In the words of Senate majority leader Howard Baker, in March 1981, as long as the economy of the nation was in turmoil, social issues would be put on the back burner.[24]

This, in itself, need not have alienated the Religious Right. Reagan's economic policy was wholly consonant with their cultural values, and his talk of hard work, honesty, success, affluence and above all freedom was itself deeply rooted in his Disciples of Christ upbringing. Reagan had left all traces of Franklin Roosevelt's New Deal far behind him, and saw the solution to the nation's economic woes in a smaller state, much lower taxes (especially at the top rate) and the market. The growth of material inequality and the emergence of a super-rich class were prices worth paying for this rescue and even, in the case of the latter, something to celebrate.

The reality, however, was that Reagan's economic policy was one step removed from his biblical faith. He was more wary about drawing a direct link between the two than was Margaret Thatcher. In an early speech on 'Losing freedom by instalments', from 1962, he explained the difference between proportionate and progressive taxation by means of the Bible:

There tithing is explained as the economic basis of our Judaic-Christian religions. The Lord says you shall contribute one-tenth and He says, 'If I prosper you ten times as much you will give ten times as much.' That is proportionate but look what happens today when you start computing Caesar's share. A man of average income suddenly prospered ten times as much would find his personal tax increased forty-three times.[25]

Such illustrations were a rarity in his mature political life, however, and although 'Reaganomics' was hardly in tension with his Christian faith, rooted ultimately in the same commitment to God-given freedom, it didn't quite animate his religious supporters as other more obviously 'moral' issues did.

COMMUNISM

For all that Reagan's religious commitments and rhetoric were in evidence in domestic concerns like abortion and school prayer, it was the threat of communism which brought out his most assured and muscular Christianity, a threat that dwarfed even the nation's economic problems.

Reagan had never, of course, had any sympathy for communism,[26] but it was during his time working for GE that he read *Witness*, the 1952 autobiography by Whittaker Chambers, a former communist and spy, whose powerful denunciations (combined with his own journey to Christianity) hardened Reagan's commitments. Chambers was clear on communism's 'evil', a word for which Reagan would become famous, and its complete incompatibility with Christianity – 'Communism is what happens when, in the name of Mind, men free themselves from God.'[27] The association became an impenetrably tight one in Reagan's own mind.

Reagan brought this fierce commitment to the White House but it intensified after he survived an assassination attempt in 1981 which sharpened his sense of providence and destiny. As far as he was concerned, détente was little more than acquiescence. Acutely aware of religious persecution in the USSR, he saw only cynicism or aggression in Soviet politics. Theologian Michael Northcott argues that 'the dispensationalist identification' – in which different peoples would finally be divided into wicked and true believers – 'of Russia as a key actor in the end times fuelled the Reagan administration's full-on engagement in the Cold War'.[28] This may well be true – some biographers have written that Reagan talked of Armageddon so often that he seemed to have an obsession with it – but it is probably also unnecessary. The moral simplicity of Reagan's worldview was sufficient. Communism was a religious issue.

He went on the verbal offensive; indeed, rarely has the phrase been so appropriate for a political leader. This was most famously illustrated in his so-called 'Evil Empire' speech, delivered to the National Association of Evangelicals in Orlando, Florida, on 8 March 1983.[29] In actual fact, this speech was rather more about domestic issues – abortion, illegitimacy, church–state separation and school prayer – than international ones. Nor was it wholly unreflective or un-self-critical. 'Our nation, too, has a legacy of evil with which it must deal,' he remarked. However, it was remembered for its fierce and uncompromising anti-communist rhetoric, and in particular for Reagan's entreaty to his audience to 'beware the temptation ... of blithely declaring [them]selves above it all and label[ling] both sides equally at fault' or 'ignor[ing] the facts of history and the aggressive impulses of an evil empire'. In reality, there was little danger that this particular audience was ever going to do that, but they might have favoured a 'nuclear freeze', or at least shown some nerves about Reagan's chosen policy of 'find[ing] peace through strength'.

Lukewarm support from large Christian constituencies was a fear that haunted the Reagan administration, in particular in its relations with the Vatican. Reagan had high hopes for this relationship, as the years of John XXIII and Paul VI, of the encyclical *Pacem in Terris* and the Vatican's repeated calls to end violence in Vietnam, gave way to the more stridently anti-communist views of the world's first Polish pope. Relations were good. Reagan appointed a personal envoy in his first term and John Paul II was delighted when he became the first President to extend diplomatic relations to the Vatican, a move long resisted by American Protestants. There was undoubtedly a consensus on communism, especially after the imposition of martial law in Poland in December 1981, a consensus that extended to Central American politics where 'the Reagan administration took every opportunity to encourage the Vatican's fears by projecting their own concerns that the Sandinistas were a hostile Marxist-Leninist force'.[30] It even extended to the subject of liberation theology, Republican advisors producing for

Reagan the 'Santa Fe document' during the 1980 campaign, which said that US foreign policy should begin to confront liberation theology.[31]

For all this consensus, however, the relationship was not the perfect alliance that Reagan would have liked. While John Paul II was hardly likely to suggest there was any moral equivalence between the US and the USSR, the equivocation that Reagan most feared, nor was he likely to unreservedly support Reagan's tactics for resolving the conflict. In late 1981, the Vatican sent both Leonid Brezhnev and Reagan the same letter asking them to receive a delegation from the Pontifical Academy of Science to present the findings of a study on nuclear war. Both agreed, though Reagan gave the delegation a somewhat frosty, twenty-minute stand-up reception when it arrived. When the academy subsequently produced a report that sharply criticised Reagan's Strategic Defence ('Star Wars') Initiative (SDI), it was buried following lobbying from Vice-President Bush and Reagan himself. This – and other disappointments, such as the pastoral letter published by American bishops which openly challenged the morality of a defence policy based on nuclear deterrence, and John Paul II's willingness to criticise the unbridled capitalism of the Reagan years[32] – proved a headache for the administration, which tended, incorrectly, to view Vatican actions solely through the prism of shared anti-communism.

Reagan's audience of evangelicals in Orlando were unlikely to be as critical, even if they did disapprove of his bellicose path to peace, but there were moments when he made his own job of persuasion more difficult, such as when he drifted from criticising the Soviet system to Soviet people:

> Yes, let us pray for the salvation of all of those who live in that totalitarian darkness – pray they will discover the joy of knowing God. But until they do, let us be aware that while they preach the supremacy of the state, declare its omnipotence over individual man, and predict its eventual domination of all peoples on the Earth, they are the focus of evil in the modern world.

Such a slip gave ammunition to his many critics, who were not slow in damning the speech as, in the words of the *New York Times*, 'sectarian...

dangerous… outrageous… simplistic… primitive.'[33] Indeed, domestic liberal criticism could be more severe than that which came from TASS, the official Soviet news agency.

While such presidential aggression was not wholly unprecedented – commentators have pointed out that Woodrow Wilson, Franklin Roosevelt and Harry Truman all used comparably strong language about the USSR – it was the combination of global moral certainty with domestic 'moral majority' politics, an evangelical audience and his openly theological worldview that infuriated his critics. For Reagan, it was a wholly natural and justifiable approach: God gave mankind freedom, and America was a precious reservoir of that divine gift, but the nation was in danger of abusing it at home and ignoring its abuse abroad, and it was the President's duty to shake his people from their moral torpor and reconnect them with their providential role. Others thought differently. 'The President should cease these celestial navigations,' opined *New Republic*. 'There is business on earth. He is not in the White House to save our souls, but to protect our bodies; not to do God's will, but the people's.'[34]

CONCLUSION

Ronald Reagan's Christian faith was sincere, deep rooted and straightforward. Always a prop to his politics, rarely a challenge, it fortified his personal optimism and his sense of personal and national destiny. God, freedom, providence and America were tightly woven in his mind and rarely divided in his rhetoric. As he said before the UN General Assembly, freedom was 'the universal right of all God's children'.

Despite some criticisms that his Christianity was a show or that it was distorted by his politics, the reality was that there was a neat, almost disturbing, complementarity between the two. And yet, in a strange way, Reagan's Christianity was not political so much as cultural. He sought a national moral and spiritual reinvigoration and in some ways he achieved it. But the moral and spiritual problems he identified as plaguing the nation from his earliest political days as a supporter of Barry Goldwater and then as governor of California were just as acute, if not more so, when he left office in 1989, precipitating a certain political disaffection among his closest supporters.

Reagan's Christianity was an authentic and serious affair, which catalysed a theo-political movement in the world's most powerful country. However, its greatest impact lay in its rhetorical power and the way in which it changed the dialogue around Christianity in public life, nationally and internationally.

NOTES

1. Stephen Vaughn, 'The Moral Inheritance of a President: Reagan and the Dixon Disciples of Christ', *Presidential Studies Quarterly*, vol. 25, no. 1, 1995, p. 111.

2. Quoted ibid., p. 110.

3. Quoted in Paul Kengor, *God and Ronald Reagan: A Spiritual Life* (New York: ReganBooks, 2005), pp. 116–17.

4. A sentiment echoed decades later when George W. Bush said in a debate for the Republican candidacy in 2000 that Christ was the philosopher he most admired.

5. David Domke and Kevin Coe, *The God Strategy: How Religion Became a Political Weapon in America* (New York: Oxford University Press, 2008), pp. 33–4. It has never since fallen below 90 per cent.

6. Interestingly, this pattern is not echoed in the location of presidential speeches. Domke and Coe calculated the percentage of speeches and visits made by Presidents to religiously significant places, institutions and people during their tenure. This rose steadily from the early 1960s, rather than jumping hugely in 1981 as religious rhetoric did, with the upward trend continuing thereafter. Interestingly Reagan, unlike Clinton for example, never once delivered a formal address in a church setting. One might argue, given his rhetorical vigour, he never needed to.

7. Domke and Coe, *The God Strategy*, p. 61.

8. Ibid., p. 35.

9. Kengor, *God and Ronald Reagan*, p. 95.

10. Quoted ibid., p. 125.

11. It then seemed to have fallen into abeyance until the 2016 Republican primaries when Senator Marco Rubio used it.

12. Quoted in Kengor, *God and Ronald Reagan*, p. 226.

13. Quoted ibid., p. 169.

14. Not least after he was forced to deny the continuing rumours that Nancy Reagan's (acknowledged) use of astrology influenced his policies.

15. Quoted in David John Marley, 'Ronald Reagan and the Splintering of the Christian Right', *Journal of Church and State*, vol. 48, no. 4, 2006, p. 853.

16. The First Amendment opens, 'Congress shall make no law respecting an establishment of religion.' Prior to these rulings, thirteen states had permitted the Lord's Prayer and twenty-six states had allowed Bible reading in their public schools.

17. For example in his 'Evil Empire' speech when he said, 'The Supreme Court opens its proceedings with a religious invocation. And the members of Congress open their sessions with a prayer. I just happen to believe the schoolchildren of the United States are entitled to the same privileges as Supreme Court justices and congressmen.'

18. Quoted in Kengor, *God and Ronald Reagan*, p. 176. Although I have no detailed knowledge of US law, I can't help but think that the answer to this question is actually no.

19. Lawrence J. McAndrews, '"Moral" Victories: Ronald Reagan and the Debate over School Prayer', *Religion and Education*, vol. 30, no. 1, 2003, p. 93.

20. Quoted ibid., p. 95.

21. Quoted in John Muggeridge, 'Ronald Reagan: An American Christian', *Human Life Review*, Summer 2004, pp. 72–3.

22. 'Remarks at the Annual Convention of the National Association of Evangelicals in Orlando, Florida', 8 March 1983, Ronald Reagan Presidential Library and Museum website, https://reaganlibrary.archives.gov/archives/speeches/1983/30883b.htm (accessed 19 January 2017).

23. Quoted in Marley, 'Ronald Reagan and the Splintering of the Christian Right', p. 851.

24. Ibid., p. 855.

25. Quoted in Kengor, *God and Ronald Reagan*, pp. 107–8.

26. He had testified in Washington about the communist presence in the film industry in the 1940s.

27. Whittaker Chambers, *Witness* (Chicago: Regnery, [1952] 1980), pp. 16–17.

28. Michael Northcott, *An Angel Directs the Storm: Apocalyptic Religion and American Empire* (London: I. B. Tauris, 2004), p. 66.

29. Reagan's slightly earlier speech to the House of Commons in June 1982 is also sometimes called the 'Evil Empire' speech, but although he did speak of the USSR as evil in this, the particular phrase 'evil empire' was not used.

30. Marie Gayte, 'The Vatican and the Reagan Administration: A Cold War Alliance?', *Catholic Historical Review*, vol. 97, no. 4, 2011, p. 728.

31. Ibid., p. 719.

32. John Paul wrote in his 1987 encyclical *Sollicitudo Rei Socialis*, for example, that 'each of the two blocs harbors in its own way a tendency towards imperialism, as it is usually called, or towards forms of neo-colonialism: an easy temptation to which they frequently succumb, as history, including recent history, teaches'.

33. Quoted in Kengor, *God and Ronald Reagan*, p. 249.

34. 'Reverend Reagan', *New Republic*, 4 April 1983.

VÁCLAV HAVEL
(1989–92, 1993–2003)

NATAN MLADIN

INTRODUCTION

Best known for his leadership role in the political miracle that was the bloodless 'Velvet Revolution' of 1989 in Czechoslovakia, Václav Havel continues to inspire and challenge, as a rare-breed politician whose influence derives from his wide recognition as a strong 'moral authority' and his conception of politics as 'morality in practice'. Mention responsibility as a guiding principle for political action and Havel's name is bound to come up as one of its staunchest defenders and ablest articulators.

If the rest of the politicians featured in this volume profess some kind of Christian faith and self-identify as Christians, however questionable their Christian credentials may be, Havel is a striking exception. Despite acknowledging 'an affinity for Christian sentiment'[1] and seeking to 'live in the spirit of Christian morality',[2] Havel never identified as a Christian.

This contribution is decidedly not an attempt to crowbar Havel into a religious identity he explicitly eschewed. Rather, it is an exploration of some of his core philosophical and religious ideas, his spiritual-but-non-religious outlook, and the way these may have shaped his political discourse and actions. The fertile ambivalence of his (metaphysical and ethical) convictions – something to be explored in depth below – reveals a deep affinity with Christian theism, while his conception of politics as 'morality in practice' chimes well with a Christian moral outlook. For that reason, he can be safely counted among the 'mighty' who looked up to the 'Almighty' on their political journey, even if, as mentioned, he conceived of neither 'might' nor the 'Almighty' in explicitly Christian terms.

BIOGRAPHY

Playwright, public intellectual, politician, statesman, Václav Havel is considered by many to be one of the most prominent political thinkers in the second half of the twentieth century. He was born in 1936 into an affluent family in Czechoslovakia. Before he turned twelve, the country fell into the hands of the Communist Party after the Soviets liberated it from the German occupation of 1939. It remained in the grip of communism and within the Soviet 'sphere of influence' from 1948 to 1989.

Havel first wanted to study film, then theatre, but was denied a university education by the communist government. He managed to secure theatre jobs with Prague's ABC Theatre, then the Theatre on the Balustrade, and to establish himself as an important literary voice by the time he was thirty, becoming one of the country's most notable playwrights. Havel wrote absurdist, deeply philosophical drama in the style of Samuel Beckett and Eugène Ionesco, tackling identity, language, moral duty, time and other similarly 'light' subjects, as they came to the fore in the experience of communism. His theatrical work was positively received at home, but performed particularly well abroad, earning him the reputation of a major dramatist rising in central Europe, and, with it, numerous prizes and accolades.

Never the aloof intellectual, Havel rose through the ranks to become one of the leaders in the dissident movement in Czechoslovakia. This reached a high point in the 1968 'Prague Spring' – a famous but short-lived period of reforms that was crushed by the Soviet invasion of Czechoslovakia in August of the same year. Under the leadership of Gustáv Husák, the regime banned all 'nonconformist' activity in an effort to 'normalise' public life – just one of the many communist euphemisms for a heavy-handed politics of repression. Havel continued to write despite the ban, contributing to the flourishing samizdat literary and intellectual culture.

The dissident movement took institutional shape in the founding of

Charter 77, a civic initiative led by the 'intellectual oppositionists'[3] that sought to defend human rights and basic liberties, and which provided a space for those wanting 'to think and live outside of the "normalised" box'.[4] As one of its leaders, Havel came to feel the iron fist of repression directly, and along with other leaders ended up in prison, where he spent almost four years in total, between 1979 and 1983. Incarcerated, he continued to write plays, albeit much more slowly, but his most important work of the period were his *Letters to Olga*. These were the weekly letters he was allowed to write to his wife, which became for him a true 'vehicle of survival' in prison. They provide an 'embarrassment of riches'[5] for the student of the soul, containing copiously introspective and wide-ranging reflections on the big questions of life, the foundations of belief and Havel's own spirituality.

He was released from prison on account of illness before serving his full term. After adjusting to civilian life, Havel continued to be actively involved with Charter 77, which grew and found its sharp edge in the 'Civic Forum'. This was the Prague-based organisation co-founded by Havel in 1989 that became the vehicle of the revolution, with Havel firmly in the driving seat. The forum managed the unthinkable: peaceful negotiations to end the communist regime in Czechoslovakia in what became known as the 'Velvet Revolution'. Thrust into the limelight, the former prisoner and vilified dissident Havel was unanimously elected by the country's Federal Assembly as President of his country on 29 December 1989.

From 1989 to 1992 he served as President of Czechoslovakia. After the peaceful split of the country he was elected President of the newly independent Czech Republic and served for two terms, from 1993 to 2003. He travelled the world over, giving speeches and lectures in various political and academic settings. He spoke unequivocally about good and evil, truth and lies; unashamedly defended politics as 'morality in practice' and as the 'art of the impossible'; and denounced ideology as a form of 'secularised religion'. He constantly pointed to a deeper spiritual dimension and a wider, transcendent horizon of meaning necessary to anchor ethics and responsible action. After a long illness, he died on 18 December 2011 in his cottage in northern Bohemia, leaving behind an important legacy and example for others to follow.

INTELLECTUAL INFLUENCES

Philosophically, Havel was indebted to the tradition of phenomenology and existentialism. The three strongest influences on his thinking were Martin Heidegger's existentialism, with his concept of 'Being', Emmanuel Levinas's ethics of responsibility, and Jan Patočka's phenomenology. Patočka was Havel's philosophical master, and his involvement with the Charter 77 dissident movement led to his martyr-like death as a result of harrowing police interrogations.[6]

Patočka's legacy was carried forward by the philosophical group humorously self-titled the Restored Platonic Academy of Kampademia, who met regularly at Havel's cottage in Hrádeček, a small village near the border with Poland. The members were mostly Catholic (Ivan M. Havel, Václav's brother, being the exception). An important source of inspiration for the Kampademians was the American New Science movement, developed originally at Berkeley and Princeton. New Science brought down artificial barriers between the social and natural sciences, tapping into religious thinking and mystical thought and paving the way for the New Age movement. The best known among the New Scientists was undoubtedly the scientist and philosopher of science Thomas Kühn, famous for his notion of 'paradigm shifts' in scientific fields.

The Kampademians had a playful approach and functioned as a type of spiritual-philosophical incubator. The literary historian Martin C. Putna of Charles University in Prague argues that Havel's *Letters to Olga*, and particularly the more philosophical of these, were addressed not only to Olga, his wife, but to the Kampademians as his philosophical companions.[7] In turn, they offered letter-length replies, but these have remained as yet unpublished. The *Letters* are therefore part of a dialogue of which we have only heard half. Even so, they bring into focus a Havel unafraid of the big, searching questions of life.

HAVEL'S SPIRITUALITY: 'BEING' AND THE 'ABSOLUTE HORIZON'

Behind and beyond the horizon of the visible world, of sense perception and mundane experience, lies ultimate reality. Havel refers to it as 'Being', usually with a capital B, a term commonly associated with G. W. F. Hegel and the existentialism of Martin Heidegger. He makes continual references to it throughout his writings without ever feeling the need to explain it in a systematic fashion. Intending the same reality, Havel speaks of a 'horizon of Being', an 'order of Being' or simply an 'absolute horizon' and 'realm of transcendence', which is, fundamentally, 'the source of meaning and hope'. What is important for Havel is that humanity acknowledges and is in a relationship to Being. Authentic existence, or what Havel calls 'living in truth', is reached only in the right relationship to Being or 'the order of Being'.

Havel's familiarity with this 'order of Being' comes from what he calls his 'existential metaexperiences', in which the veil of everyday is lifted to uncover a deeper horizon of meaning. Arguably Havel's most impactful experience of Being involved a shimmering tree which he contemplated from his prison cell in Heřmanice. Twice in his *Letters to Olga* he describes what sounds like a profound mystical experience, of being thrust into a 'moment of supreme bliss, of infinite joy' where he is filled with 'profound amazement at the sovereignty of Being ... the abyss of its mystery'. He is flooded with happiness and is overcome with a feeling of being in love 'though I don't know precisely for whom or what'.[8] It is worth noting that C. S. Lewis describes a similar phenomenon which he encapsulates in the notion of 'joy', while Charles Taylor, in *A Secular Age*, alludes to such experiences where a sense of transcendence pierces through the thick blanket of secularism.[9] This ecstatic experience points to a Being which Havel takes to be 'the essence of the existence of everything that exists; it is what joins everything that exists together, its order, and its memory, its source, its will and its aim'.[10]

A second memorable experience impressed upon Havel the moral nature of Being as revealed in the voice of his conscience. Havel did not report this as a vague awareness of moral obligation, but, strikingly, as a conversation. Poignantly, he mused:

> Who, then, is in fact conversing with me? Obviously someone I hold in high[er] regard ... higher, in some regards, than myself ... Someone who 'knows everything' (and is therefore omniscient), is everywhere (and therefore omnipresent) and 'remembers everything', someone who, though

infinitely understanding, is entirely incorruptible, who is for me, the highest and utterly unequivocal authority in all moral questions and who is thus Law itself; someone eternal, who through himself makes me eternal as well, so that I cannot imagine the arrival of a moment when everything will come to an end, thus terminating my dependence on him as well; someone to whom I relate entirely and for whom, ultimately, I would do everything. At the same time, this 'someone' addresses me directly and personally...[11]

WAS HAVEL A CHRISTIAN AFTER ALL?

This description is close, indeed almost identical, to a fully theistic conception of God. Havel's Being has personal attributes, possesses infinite memory and manifests as love ('is for me'). It seems to be a combination of Aquinas's understanding of God as 'pure being' with a more personalist, Kierkegaardian conception of God. But just as we prepare to connect this description and the Christian God, Havel pulls (us) back:

> But who is it? God? There are many subtle reasons why I'm reluctant to use that word; one factor here is a certain sense of shame (I don't know exactly for what, why and before whom), but the main thing, I suppose, is a fear that with this all too specific designation (or rather assertion) that 'God is', I would be projecting an experience that is entirely personal and vague (never mind how profound and urgent it may be), too single-mindedly 'outward', onto that problem-fraught screen called 'objective reality', and thus I would go too far beyond it.[12]

It seems that, regardless of the intensity and urgency of the experience, Havel displays a certain apophatic reluctance[13] even to try to find out who this Being really is. So Havel stops short of naming Being and remains content to question whether what he is experiencing is God or not. His most recent biographer, Michael Zantovsky, points out that, in fact, the source of his 'unmistakable spirituality' was something Havel struggled with throughout his life.[14] He was not a religious man, writes Zantovsky, but 'a man of faith'.[15]

Havel was aware that some interpreted his ideas within a religious framework, but he was never concerned to reject this. In analysing Havel's religious language, Daniel Brennan of Bond University, in Queensland, suggests he employed it simply because it helped him communicate a non-religious outlook and experience. Yet this explanation has a certain reductive feel to it and may obscure Havel's genuine openness to the possibility that what he was experiencing was in fact God, which would mean his moral outlook makes more sense in a religious rather than a non-religious framework. At any rate, his ambivalence only shows the nature and intensity of his life-long struggle in this area. And, since it was a struggle that lasted all his life, it goes without saying that to appropriate Havel for any particular religious tradition would be a serious mistake.[16]

When asked point blank, Havel always resisted a Christian self-identification. Among the reasons he could not, in good conscience, call himself a Christian was his realisation that he was missing 'the mystical experience of a genuine, personal revelation, that supremely important "last drop"'.[17] That would have meant, Havel reasoned, 'replacing an uncertain "something" with a completely unambiguous personal god, and fully, inwardly, [accepting] Christ as the Son of God, along with everything that that entails, including the liturgy'.[18] What he does say about Christianity is informed and generous. He acknowledges links between Catholicism, Continental philosophy and recent trends in the natural sciences. He speaks respectfully of Catholic doctrines, refusing to see them as just hollow metaphorical language: 'There are many other aspects to a faith in the Christian God, such as belief in the divinity of Christ, the Immaculate Conception of the Virgin Mary, etc. – and I take all that too seriously to pass off as belief various more or less figurative acceptances of those things.'[19]

Shortly after the revolution, in a speech during the historic visit of Pope John Paul II to Prague, Havel used the opportunity to return to his concept of Being as the ground of responsibility:

Your visit will remind us all of the genuine source of real human responsibility, the metaphysical source … of the absolute horizon to which we must refer, that mysterious memory of Being in which each of our acts is recorded and in which and through which they finally acquire their true value.[20]

Given the practical orientation of his own thought, after the Pope's visit Havel gently rebuked people of faith for losing the practical focus of religious devotion:

> The authentic Christianity of our deeds cannot be measured by the number of times we kiss the Pope's hand, but by our goodwill in peace to renew the relationship of man to man. If we are kind to one another, then the Pope will be satisfied. I know him and I know that he has little patience for kisses on the hand, especially those of a political nature.[21]

'LIVING IN TRUTH' AND LIVING RESPONSIBLY

We have established that Havel was not a Christian, but that nothing that he said was contrary to Christian teaching. Returning now to Havel's core beliefs, it's at this point that we may wonder what Being and the 'absolute horizon' have to do with 'life under the sun', with the here-and-now of everyday life and politics. Elusive, yet personal and active, Being provides the foundation for all ethical action in the world, the source of authentic humanity, and the anchor of responsibility. The two key notions for which Havel is famous bring this into practical focus: 'living in truth' and responsibility.

It is no exaggeration to say that 'living in truth' was the 'impetus behind his plays, the concern of his dissent, and [it is] foremost in his concerns as President.'[22] The consummate expression of Havel's notion of 'living in truth' is arguably his famous essay 'The Power of the Powerless', published in 1978. In it, Havel explains both the philosophical underpinnings but also the practical outworking of dissent and the 'principled challenge' of the 'post-totalitarian' system of 1970s socialism. The essay's famous example involves a greengrocer who puts up a sign that reads, 'Workers of the world, unite!' He may not believe in the tenets of socialism, but until he takes the sign down he is effectively accepting, confirming and reinforcing the lie, thereby participating in and fulfilling the 'system'.[23] But if he defiantly pulls it down, through this small act of 'living in truth' the greengrocer may in fact put into motion the wheels of change. Havel was a firm believer in what his most recent biographer calls 'the purifying and energizing role of an individual' whose small moral acts 'can gradually and indirectly, over time, gain in political significance'.[24] The human capacity to 'live in truth' is, Havel thought, the hidden power of the seemingly powerless.

This notion of 'living in truth' is closely tied in Havel's thought to his other famous ethical focus: responsibility. Living in truth means, quite simply, living responsibly. For Havel, authentic existence is tied up with responsibility, responsibility with freedom, and freedom with Being: 'To whom are we responsible? Being, of course, Being that is conscious to us via our conscience, Being that is infinite, omniscient, incorruptibly moral and seemingly personal. In acting responsibly we then make ourselves to be who it is we become.'[25]

Responsibility is first and foremost an orientation towards and a relationship with Being. This vertical responsibility then orders and imposes moral duties on all other horizontal relationships. The following section looks at how Havel seems to have translated his complex philosophical and moral thinking into political practice, on the domestic and international fronts.

POLITICS AS 'MORALITY IN PRACTICE': A VOICE IN THE WILDERNESS?

THE DOMESTIC FRONT

It is with the notions of 'living in truth' and responsibility that the high-minded philosophical rubber meets the concrete road of politics. Many examples could be given of what this looked like in practice for Havel, but for reasons of space we can only mention a few.

One incident during the animated winter days in the run up to the revolution stands out in particular. It provides a good illustration of Havel's understanding of politics as 'morality in practice'. It was at the time when nearly everyone supported him for the presidency, so the idea of a campaign was deemed unnecessary and scrapped accordingly. With all public attention focused on him, Havel made the suggestion that the country formally apologise for the expulsion of the Sudeten Germans, nearly three million in number, at the end of the Second World War.[26] Living in truth meant for Havel owning up to the past, accepting responsibility for wrongdoing – even in complicated historical circumstances – and saying simply 'we're sorry'. The idea was not well received, to put it mildly, and remained unpopular for a long time. In 2003, on a final state visit to Germany, Havel re-emphasised the need for full reconciliation between a reunified Germany and a post-communist Czech Republic and expressed his confidence that Czechs would continue to strive to come to terms with 'the terrible actions that we ourselves – even if in response to the terrible treatment of others – carried out'.[27]

He displayed a similar conciliatory attitude after taking up office in 1989. In his New Year's speech to the nation, shortly after he was elected President of democratic Czechoslovakia, he emphasised the abdication of personal responsibility that helped perpetuate the communist 'system' of lies. Using Christian vocabulary, he described this as 'a sin we committed against ourselves'[28] and called the nation to responsible action as the only true means of purifying and revitalising the country. To discourage scapegoating and the search for arch-villains, realising that the 'velvet was wearing thin', Havel led by personal example and made one of his 'glorious raids' to his former prison, looking to shake hands with both the warden who had treated him kindly and the one who had given him a hard time.[29] He only found the former one.

His ethics of responsibility also translated into a support for a majoritarian, rather than a proportional, vote system, which, Havel thought, would entail a relationship of responsibility between elected members of parliament and voters. His efforts were, however, fruitless. Havel was defeated on this front by former Communists who had regrouped under the name 'Renaissance' – a gross misnomer, no doubt.

Early in his presidency, his decision to cease the manufacturing of arms in the country – Czechoslovakia being the fourth largest manufacturer during communist days – sprung not only from humanitarian concerns but from Havel's strong ethics of responsibility and commitment to 'rebrand the country quickly as a responsible and morally aware member of the international community'.[30] It was an unpopular decision which put an end to the relative, but by then clearly precarious, prosperity the industry had brought to rural Slovakia. This was one of the controversies that paved the way for the eventual Czech–Slovak split, which Havel failed to prevent despite his best intentions and efforts.

He was re-elected twice, but his popularity diminished steadily through the years. A significant cause of this was the complicated and messy process of transferring previously nationalised property back to private owners. This was the time of 'the great bonfire of scruples' and of angry debates, with not a few taking advantage of loopholes in the patchy legislation and making dirty money through dubious schemes. Small banks folded and many participants in the voucher schemes for reclaiming property lost their investments. The whole country was morally wounded. It had 'lost its innocence'.[31] Havel could do little other than to remind the nation of the importance of moral values and responsible action but, by and large, the nation turned a deaf ear and began seeing him as 'a moralistic sorehead, badly out of touch and out of place'.[32]

Havel's relationship with Prime Minister Václav Klaus was somewhat uneven, given not only their differing personalities but also their respective political outlooks. Klaus was a comfortably conservative politician, a pragmatic technocrat pushing for wide-scale economic reforms. Havel largely approved of these and backed them. Where they differed sharply, however, was on the shape of Czech society. Working from his principle of responsibility, Havel wanted a politically engaged civil society, with various civic and advocacy groups and organisations making their voices heard in the public square. He consistently advocated care for the environment and was a strong supporter of human and minority rights. Klaus, on the other hand, saw these as dangerous 'leftisms' and was committed to an ideology-based politics which only allowed for two alternatives: the socialist way and the 'non-socialist', conservative, capitalist way.[33]

THE INTERNATIONAL FRONT

It was at the international level, however, that Havel arguably made his most significant contributions. To start with one of his more controversial stances, Havel expressed his ethics of responsibility in his support of the doctrine of humanitarian intervention.[34] This, he believed, emphasised shared responsibility in confronting and eradicating evil. He appealed to it in his decision to back and in certain cases to participate in the operations in Kuwait, Kosovo and Iraq. Fully aware of the dangers of the doctrine, he nonetheless emphasised the primacy of human beings over state inviolability: 'Defending human beings is a higher responsibility than respecting the inviolability of a state. One must, however, constantly and carefully scrutinize such humanistic arguments to determine that it is not just [a] pretty façade concealing far less respectable interests...'[35]

This attitude was not enough, however, to prevent the loss of his reputation as a 'saintly patron of non-violence'.[36] It may even explain, in part, why he never won the Nobel Peace Prize, for which he had been nominated more than once.

His ethics of responsibility grounded in the 'order of Being' also fuelled, much less controversially, his sustained efforts to fully integrate the Czech Republic into Europe, NATO and the wider international community, and thus share the 'responsibility for peace and justice'.[37] Through his diplomatic efforts, the Czech Republic finally acceded to NATO in 1999. In NATO, Havel saw a guarantor of peace and liberal democracy, while he, in turn, epitomised 'the fundamental unity of Central Europe with the rest of the West in terms of culture, philosophy and political thinking'.[38]

After the peaceful transition of power in 1989, 'living in truth' meant for Havel going to Munich and Berlin for his first foreign presidential trip. The two cities held particularly painful memories for Czechoslovakia. He saw the need to confront the dark legacy of the infamous Munich Agreement as the essential step towards taking his country back into Europe.[39] He pursued the dream of European integration for over ten years and in 2004, having ended his final presidential mandate a year earlier, he celebrated the Czech Republic's accession to the EU. Euro-enthusiasm fitted naturally with his life-long opposition to 'dividing lines and narrow nationalism' and his advocacy of perennial values and broad responsibility.[40]

He was not, however, uncritical of the EU. While admiring the achievements of the European project – with its European institutions, single market and by then the beginnings of a fiscal union – more than once he lamented the absence of 'a spiritual, moral or emotional dimension ... a charisma'[41] and universal values delineated by a clearly articulated ideal and European identity. In a speech delivered in the European Parliament on 11 November 2009, long after stepping down from office, Havel laid out the kind of future he envisioned for Europe, a future in which the Union would rediscover its 'soul', its spiritual foundation, moral horizon and values. Such a rediscovery would result, Havel hoped, in abandoning a profit-at-all-costs mentality, the idolatry of quantitative growth, a petty spirit of international one-upmanship, and the exploitation of natural resources without regard for environmental damage. But this would happen, Havel argued, only 'if something starts to change in the very soul of present-day Europeans'. This soul-change would include humility in light of scientific discoveries, long-term thinking and planning, but most importantly 'deference to the mystery of the universe and of being per se ... to renew a greater relationship with eternity and infinity, as was once the case in the initial phases of Europe-an development'.[42] Sadly, this was, and remains, the unheeded cry in the wilderness of bureaucracy, technicalities and purely economic and financial concerns.

CONCLUSION

To make Havel, who never identified with any religion in particular, into the Christian he never was, even an anonymous one,[43] would be a serious mistake. He came close to God, arguably in his experience, and certainly in his descriptions of those experiences, but never made the decisive step. Therefore, no less serious a mistake would be to play down, or worse, to deny the spiritual character of his struggles and thinking.

The argument of this chapter has been that Havel's understanding of 'Being' and his ethical vision chime well with, and are best accommodated within, the theological framework of the Christian faith. But, as the chapters of this volume make abundantly clear, professing a Christian faith does not automatically translate into a particular ideological orientation, let alone specify what political moves one will make. In the same way, no line can be drawn from Havel's beliefs about Being and his ethics to the particularities of his political career. In this he is no different from the rest of the politicians discussed in this volume, who self-identify as Christians. What their Christian faith, or in Havel's case his understanding of and respect toward the transcendent order of Being, arguably provides is a higher, nay, the highest, court of appeal where they can be held accountable.

NOTES

1. Václav Havel, *Letters to Olga*, trans. Paul Wilson (London: Faber and Faber, 1988), p. 269.
2. Edward E. Ericson, 'Living Responsibly: Václav Havel's View', *Religion & Liberty*, vol. 8, no. 5, 1998, available at Acton Institute website (http://www.acton.org/pub/religion-liberty/volume-8-number-5/living-responsibly-václav-havels-view) (accessed 20 January 2017).
3. Jeffrey C. Goldfarb, *Civility and Subversion: The Intellectual in Democratic Society* (Cambridge: Cambridge University Press, 1998), p. 85.
4. Daniel S. Danaher, *Reading Václav Havel* (Toronto: University of Toronto Press, 2015), p. 4.
5. Michael Zantovsky, *Havel: A Life* (London: Atlantic, 2014), p. 221.
6. Martin C. Putna, 'The Spirituality of Václav Havel in Its Czech and American Contexts: Between Unitarianism and New Age, T. G. Masaryk and Kampademia', *East European Politics and Societies*, vol. 24, no. 3, 2010, p. 361.
7. Ibid., p. 364.
8. Havel, *Letters to Olga*, p. 221.
9. Charles Taylor, *A Secular Age* (Cambridge, MA: Belknap Press, 2007), pp. 5, 19.
10. Havel, *Letters to Olga*, p. 359.
11. Ibid., pp. 345–6.
12. Ibid., p. 346.
13. Apophatic or negative theology is a method of theological reflection that begins from the recognition that all language ultimately fails with respect to God, and employs negative rather than positive descriptions of God (e.g. God is limitless; God is immaterial).
14. Zantovsky, *Havel*, p. 385.
15. Ibid., p. 385.
16. Ibid., p. 387.
17. Havel, *Letters to Olga*, p. 269.
18. Václav Havel, *Disturbing the Peace: A Conversation with Karel Hvížďala*, trans. Paul Wilson (New York: Vintage Books, 1991), p. 189.
19. Havel, *Letters to Olga*, p. 269.
20. Zantovsky, *Havel*, p. 385.
21. Václav Havel, *Projevy z let 1990–1992*, p. 173, as quoted in and translated by Martin C. Putna, 'The Spirituality of Václav Havel in Its Czech and American Contexts Between Unitarianism and New Age, T. G. Masaryk and Kampademia' in *East European Politics and Societies*, vol. 24, no. 3, Summer 2010, p. 371.
22. Daniel Brennan, 'An Appraisal of the Political Philosophy of Václav Havel', PhD thesis, Bond University, 2013, p. 48.
23. Václav Havel, 'The Power of the Powerless', in *Open Letters: Selected Prose 1965–1990*, ed. Paul Wilson (London: Faber and Faber, 1991), p. 136.
24. Havel, *Disturbing the Peace*, pp. 114–15.
25. Havel, *Letters to Olga*, p. 311.
26. 'Czechs' hidden revenge against Germans', BBC News website, 3 December 2002, http://news.bbc.co.uk/1/hi/world/europe/2536261.stm (accessed 20 January 2017).
27. 'Havel tries to repair rift with Germany', *Daily Telegraph*, 18 January 2003, http://www.telegraph.co.uk/news/worldnews/europe/czechrepublic/1419270/Havel-tries-to-repair-rift-with-Germany.html (accessed 20 January 2017).
28. Václav Havel, 'New Year's Address to the Nation', in *The Art of the Impossible: Politics as Morality in Practice – Speeches and Writings 1990–1996*, (New York: Alfred A. Knopf, 1997), pp. 4–5.
29. Zantovsky, *Havel*, p. 332.

30. Ibid., p. 405.
31. Ibid., p. 429.
32. Ibid., p. 430.
33. Ibid., p. 454.
34. Now known as 'responsibility to protect' (R2P) as a nod to Havel, its 'ideological father', alongside Madeleine Albright (born in Prague to Czech parents) as its 'ideological mother'.
35. Václav Havel, *To the Castle and Back*, quoted in Zantovsky, *Havel*, p. 435.
36. Zantovsky, *Havel*, p. 437.
37. Ibid., p. 434.
38. Ibid., p. 444.
39. Ibid., p. 336.
40. Ibid., p. 447.
41. Ibid., p. 448.
42 'Speech of Václav Havel, European Parliament, Brussels, November 11, 2009', http://www.vaclavhavel.cz/showtrans.php?cat=projevy&val=1290_aj_projevy.html&typ=HTML (accessed 20 January 2017).
43. The idea of an 'anonymous Christian' is associated with the German Catholic theologian Karl Rahner and is traditionally understood to describe people, particularly from remote areas of the world, who have never heard the Gospel but who, on account of the redemptive sacrifice of Christ, have accepted salvation without knowing it. The notion is much more complex than this explanation can begin to suggest, and remains controversial in theological circles.

BILL CLINTON (1993–2001)

SIMON PERFECT

In October 2016, Bill Clinton suddenly found himself at the centre of his wife's presidential campaign. Her opponent, Donald Trump, held a press conference with three women who had instigated sexual assault lawsuits against Clinton. All three claimed that Bill was a sexual predator, and that Hillary had ruthlessly hounded them to protect her husband's political position. Bill's sins, which he had prayed were dead and buried, had come back with a vengeance.[1]

Accounts of Bill Clinton's life are inevitably shaped by a tension between the public and the private – between a focus on his achievements as a politician and on his failings as a man. A core part of Clinton's self-image is that he is trapped between 'parallel lives' – an external life of energy, self-belief and religious striving, and an internal life of doubt, insecurity and moral failure.[2] He sees himself as a 'living paradox',[3] and indeed that is how many commentators view him. As Peter Edelman, a former member of his administration, puts it, 'Bill Clinton is a very, very complicated man.'[4] His religion, and how he has used or abused it, is at the centre of this struggle.

CHILDHOOD: WALKING TO CHURCH ALONE

Clinton's memoir, *My Life* (2004), is simultaneously a record of his politics, a cathartic confessional and an attempt to explain (to himself as much as to the public) the causes of his successes and failures. In it, he points to his childhood as having a defining influence over his life, including his religion.

He was born in Arkansas in 1946 to Virginia Dell and William Jefferson Blythe Jr, his father dying in a car accident a few months after Bill's birth.[5] In 1950, Virginia married Roger Clinton Sr and the family relocated to Hot Springs, Arkansas, a multiracial 'sin city' in a segregated South.[6] Virginia endured years of abuse from her alcoholic husband; at one point he even 'pulled a gun from behind his back and fired in Mother's direction'.[7] Roger's abuse forced Bill to become an adult prematurely, a father figure for his younger stepbrother. In the view of psychologist John Gartner, he was an archetypal hero-child and peacemaker, 'the child who strives to save his dysfunctional family'.[8]

This violent family background was an important influence on Clinton's burgeoning Christianity. He was raised a Southern Baptist but neither his mother nor stepfather were regular churchgoers.[9] Seeking solace from the turmoil at home, from the age of six he 'walked alone a mile or so to my church every Sunday. It wasn't something my parents did, but I somehow felt the need.'[10] In 1955, aged nine, Clinton responded to the altar call at the end of a Sunday service and 'professed my faith in Christ'. Looking back in 2004, he saw this as the culmination of an authentic born-again conversion.[11]

Throughout his teenage years, Clinton's religious fervour was clearly evident; some teachers thought he might become an evangelist.[12] Under the surface, however, lay anxieties and doubts: 'My faith was too weak to sustain a certain belief in God in the face of what I was witnessing.'[13] In his memoir, he describes developing a strong feeling in his childhood of leading 'parallel lives', a recurrent theme throughout his book's narrative. While his 'outside life' was filled with 'friends and fun, learning and doing', his 'internal life … was full of uncertainty, anger, and a dread of ever-looming violence'.[14]

The disjuncture caused him considerable unease. In his memoir, Clinton quotes from a high school essay: 'I am a living paradox – deeply religious, yet not as convinced of my exact beliefs as I ought to be … loving the truth but often times giving way to falsity'.[15] He felt shame that he was unable to live up to his idealised self-image. The adult Clinton includes the quote to portray himself as being, from a young age, on a quest of moral striving. He imagines himself as engaged in a heroic struggle 'to be a good man',[16] and hopes that by portraying himself as such the reader will forgive him his sins.

ARKANSAS YEARS

Although faith sustained him at home, when at university Clinton attended church infrequently.[17] In 1975, he married Hillary Rodham and they returned to Arkansas to launch his career as a Democratic politician. He became Arkansas's governor in 1978, but in 1980 lost the governorship to Frank D. White, a conservative Baptist.[18] The humiliating defeat taught him the need for caution in progressive politics.[19]

It was also a turning point in his religious life. After initial despondency at what he considered a personal failure, Clinton found solace by joining Immanuel Baptist Church in Little Rock. At the same time, Hillary's Methodism became more important to her; she gave lay sermons in various Methodist churches and read the Bible regularly.[20] Critics, however, were more cynical about this spiritual reawakening. Some suggested that Clinton's choice of Immanuel was a political ploy; the church was well known for broadcasting services and Clinton's participation in the choir made him clearly visible to the television cameras.[21] Whether true or not, certainly he attributed his 1980 defeat to his public image as a member of the progressive, educated elite.[22] He learned that emphasising religiosity signalled that he was a man of the people.[23] One biographer suggests it was the first of many times he would use church appearances for 'political opportunism'.[24]

Regardless, during the 1980s Clinton became more than a 'Sunday morning Christian'. He began his workday discussing a Bible passage with his secretary, and he received guidance from Immanuel's conservative pastor at the time, Worley Oscar Vaught, who had a major influence on Clinton's positions on abortion and capital punishment.[25]

Returning to the governorship in 1982, he held it for a decade. During the 1980s he became a leading figure among the New Democrats. This movement argued that their party needed to adopt a more centrist position to win power, combining the Democrats' traditional concern for social justice with calls for welfare reform, fiscal restraint and smaller government. It was an approach calculated to appeal beyond the Democrats' liberal base to the values of the blue-collar workers who had abandoned the party in recent decades.[26] It also suited Clinton's personal pragmatism and political flexibility, which, when he was President, critics would interpret as a lack of principles, accusing him of being a political chameleon driven by opportunism.[27]

In 1992, Clinton threw himself into the race for the White House. His rallying cry was the 'New Covenant', a way of describing his 'third way' politics in sacralised terms, in an attempt to make the Democratic Party appeal to religious voters. Beyond this, however, Clinton avoided making religion the core of his pitch. Whereas his fellow Democrat Jimmy Carter had made faith the defining feature of his public persona in the 1970s, Clinton adopted a more understated approach.[28] He talked freely about his faith in interviews, but also spoke broadly about failure, struggle and self-improvement – concepts that were intended to appeal to the sceptical Democratic left as much as the conservative Christian right.[29]

His cautious willingness to discuss faith in this way helped him to present a public religion that appealed to voters of all different shades of opinion. In stark contrast, the Republicans focused on their conservative core, emphasising that they were the defenders of traditional religious and moral values against the liberalising Democrats.[30] The broader approach proved more effective, and in 1993 the Clinton era began.

AN EXPERT ON FORGIVENESS

Clinton's faith is influenced by an unusually wide range of different Christian strands. He was exposed to Catholic social teaching at the Jesuit-run Georgetown University. One instructor there was even shocked to learn he wasn't Catholic, saying, 'I saw all the Jesuit traits in him.'[31] He is also fascinated with Pentecostalism and drawn to the intense emotionalism characteristic of Pentecostal worship. Almost every year between 1977 and 1992, he attended an annual summer camp of Pentecostals in Arkansas.[32]

In particular, Clinton identifies strongly with black churches, reflecting that his childhood Christianity was moulded by his rejection of Southern segregationism. He considers Martin Luther King Jr a spiritual hero and as a teenager would recite King's 'I Have a Dream' speech verbatim to his family. According to his political aide Paul Begala, Clinton would repeatedly quote a passage from Isaiah 58:12 like a mantra: 'And thou shalt be called the repairer of the breach'.[33] He aspired to be that repairer of the breach, bringing King's Dream to fruition.

In his political career, Clinton used his spiritual affinity with Pentecostalism to appeal to black voters. He made concerted efforts to appoint African Americans to his administration and was an advocate of affirmative action.[34] Congressman John Lewis, hero of the civil rights movement, describes a sense of 'ownership' among many African Americans towards Clinton;[35] the writer Toni Morrison even dubbed him the 'first black President'.[36]

These wide-ranging spiritual influences enabled Clinton to mould his religious rhetoric to suit the political context. But what are his beliefs? At the heart, there is a twin concern for social justice for the disempowered and for mercy for the individual sinner. He stated in his 1992 presidential campaign that he believed in 'the old-fashioned things like the constancy of sin, the possibility of forgiveness, the reality of redemption'.[37] Christianity, for him, is about second chances – a 'continuous coming back'.[38] In 1998, following the Monica Lewinsky scandal, he described himself as becoming an 'expert on forgiveness'. He was seeking public forgiveness, but needed to learn to forgive first in order to receive it.[39]

For Clinton, Jesus' key significance was that he revealed this possibility of redemption and was the great peacemaker. Clinton was more comfortable discussing Jesus' ethics and teachings than doctrinal matters in public – which political leader isn't? – but seems to have grown more confident in addressing the latter during his presidency. For example, in his 1994 Easter message he noted in general terms that Easter is 'a time to reflect on the blessings of rebirth';[40] but in 1999 he proclaimed that at Easter 'we celebrate Christ's victory over sin and death, and we rejoice in the new life that He won for us through His suffering, death, and rising from the dead'.[41] The former belongs on an Easter egg; the latter to a revivalist sermon.

Clinton's closest spiritual advisors attested to his Christian orthodoxy. Tony Campolo, one of the President's spiritual advisors after the Lewinsky scandal broke in 1998, commented that Clinton adheres to an evangelical theology and the doctrines of the Apostles' Creed, and 'believes the Bible to be an infallible message from God'.[42] Clinton's faith is indeed strongly Bible orientated. He freely quotes Scripture in personal conversation as well as in speeches, with Carol Willis, one of his leading advisors, even calling him 'a biblical scholar'.[43]

His precise attitudes to the Bible are a more complex issue. In 2004, Clinton stated that the Bible is 'completely true', but added that he was also sure that no one 'is smart enough to understand it completely'.[44] One of his favourite phrases is 'For now we see through a glass, darkly'.[45] He uses this to justify critical interpretation and doubt. He has also used it politically. When discussing his Israel–Palestine negotiations in a book in 2006, he emphasised that no one faith is 'fully revealed',[46] and therefore no one could claim a monopoly over truth. Like his politics, his religious rhetoric might shift depending on the context, moving between an emphasis on Christian truth and an emphasis on plurality.

Clinton has particular interest in and sympathy for the Psalms; indeed, he sees something of himself in King David. Jane Yoder, a friend of the Clintons, recalls discussing with him Michelangelo's statue of David in the Galleria dell'Accademia in Florence, and notes that he was 'profoundly affected' by it. During the Lewinsky scandal, Yoder wrote to Clinton reminding him of the statue: 'King David was not perfect ... Nevertheless, after a period of contrition ... David continued to serve his country.'[47] Clinton took solace in the idea that God will use fallen men for great deeds; and that through repentance, sinners can become righteous. David embodies Clinton's perception of himself as a man who strives for goodness, who stumbles along the way, but ultimately is deserving of praise for the effort.

WHITE HOUSE WARS: GAYS AND ABORTION

Clinton's presidency was a key period in American history, beginning after the Cold War and ending just before 9/11. Clinton saw this moment as a turning point for the world, and he saw himself as divinely called to be the 'repairer of the breach'.

In Washington, the Clintons became regular attendees at Foundry United

Methodist Church.[48] Bill sought regular spiritual guidance from various pastors, including Rex Horne Jr of Immanuel Baptist Church in Little Rock, who had weekly phone calls with the President.[49] He established a formal White House liaison with faith communities to discuss how to engage them in tackling social issues.[50] Yet he couldn't maintain links with all religious communities. Some were disinclined to work with him because of his well-known liberal stances on abortion and LGBT rights.

Gay rights became a central issue in the 1992 election, when Clinton promised to repeal the ban on LGBT people serving in the military.[51] The Republicans, presenting themselves as upholders of traditional values, accused him of having 'the most pro-lesbian and pro-gay ticket in history'.[52] At the start of his presidency, his plan was staunchly opposed by military chiefs and conservative politicians. Clinton reminded them that, in the Bible, 'homosexuality did not make the top-ten list of sins'.[53] Ultimately, he was forced to compromise, producing the 'Don't ask, don't tell' policy in 1993 which prevented military personnel from investigating service members' sexual orientations, but barred those who were openly gay from military service. In his memoir Clinton regrets his failure. He was accused by LGBT activists of betraying his principles.[54]

His signing into law of the Defense of Marriage Act (DOMA) in 1996 caused a similar response. This Act enabled individual states to refuse to recognise same-sex marriages performed in other states.[55] In later years (including during Hillary's 2016 election campaign), the Clintons would emphasise the other measures Bill took to improve gay rights (such as stopping discrimination against LGBT federal employees),[56] and would claim that he had signed DOMA out of fear that the Republicans would push through an outright federal ban on same-sex marriages. Critics have claimed, however, that no such ban was ever on the cards.[57] It is notable that, at the time, Clinton was personally opposed to same-sex marriage,[58] and his 1996 campaign used DOMA to shore up support among conservatives.[59] Tellingly, he makes no mention of DOMA in his memoir.

Abortion was also a key issue in the 1992 battle. On the fourth day of his presidency Clinton reversed the Reagan–Bush abortion and contraception policies, including the 'gag' rule, which barred abortion counselling at family planning clinics that received federal funds.[60] It was an unambiguous statement that Clintonism was a break with the past. After this, in 1993 Hillary was given charge of what Bill saw as his greatest task – the establishment of universal healthcare.[61] The final proposed package was huge, requiring every employer to provide health insurance for all employees, and all citizens to have insurance.[62] It would also mean that employers would have to contribute to the costs of abortions. Henry Hyde, a Catholic Republican congressman, saw this as a perverse attempt 'to make abortion a way of life and a way of death for everyone'.[63]

Inevitably 'Hillarycare' failed to pass Congress, one of Clinton's greatest regrets. But abortion continued to cause him problems. In 1996, Clinton vetoed a bill that would have banned partial-birth abortion, proposing instead a bill banning all late-term abortions except where the health of the mother was at risk. His proposed replacement, which he said would actually prevent more abortions than the original one, was an attempt to seize the moral high ground claimed by the Republicans over abortion, but it was rejected.[64]

Clinton's liberalism on these issues was influenced, and given justification, by his religious views. For example, his vision of Christianity as inherently supportive of the marginalised gave a theological framework for his instincts on gay rights. He told an LGBT magazine in 1996, 'Through prayer and Bible study I have learned that God's love is extended to all people.'[65] This was a defiant insistence that being a good Baptist and being supportive of LGBT rights were compatible. Privately, however, during his governorship he felt anxious about the Bible's teaching on these issues and sought advice from the pastor of Immanuel Baptist Church at the time, Worley Oscar Vaught, about abortion and capital punishment. Clinton claims Vaught assured him that the Bible only forbids murder, not all killing; and that it does not condemn abortion nor state that life begins at conception, but rather at the baby's first breath.[66] This satisfied Clinton's personal concerns, but more importantly gave him a biblical interpretation which he could use in public to defend his liberal beliefs.

Conservative Christian critics, however, considered this an example of his tendency to twist Scripture for immoral ends.[67] Throughout the presidency

the Southern Baptist Convention drew up resolutions against Immanuel
Baptist Church for failing to discipline Clinton for his policies.[68] The Convention leaders felt aggrieved at Clinton's perceived duplicity and betrayed
at the lack of influence they had in the White House. As Richard Land, a
leader of the Convention, put it, 'Bill Clinton could talk like a Southern
Baptist evangelist when he wanted to. But they hated what he was doing
with it … In the Clinton administration, they quit accepting our phone calls
after a while.'[69] Despite his public calls for unity, Clinton was only prepared
to work so far with people who challenged him. Eventually Clinton left the
Convention and in 2008 he and fellow Baptist Jimmy Carter launched the
New Baptist Covenant, which seeks to organise more liberally minded Baptist congregations.[70]

The administration's pushes on social issues and healthcare came at a heavy
electoral price in the 'Republican Revolution' in 1994, where the Republicans
seized control of Congress (the first time they had held the House for forty
years). Humiliated, Clinton responded by recalibrating his public philosophy. In his 1995 State of the Union address, his New Covenant rhetoric was
shifted to the right, and he pledged to do more to deport illegal immigrants
and cut taxes while slashing spending.[71] As one conservative analyst put it,
it was the 'most conservative State of the Union by a Democratic President
in history'.[72]

Welfare reform was a further battle. In 1992, Clinton pledged to reform
welfare (using the slogan 'Two years and you're off', denounced by a former
aide as 'bumper-sticker politics'[73]) but initially he was cautious about acting
on such rhetoric. However, in 1996 during the election campaign, he signed
the Republicans' major welfare reform programme, which among other
things ended the federal guarantee of aid to families with children who were
in need and set a lifetime limit on welfare receipt of five years.[74] Clinton
always claimed his faith inspired him to help the poor; now such claims
seemed pious platitudes. Critics on the left, as much as those on the right,
came to doubt the sincerity of his stated religious and moral principles. One
journalist denounced him as 'the ultimate political whore, a man who stands
for nothing'.[75]

Despite such criticisms, Clinton won again in 1996. He won large majorities among Jews, black Protestants and Catholics. But he lost the majority of the white Protestant vote, largely because of his positions on social issues.[76]

PURSUING FREEDOM

Clinton saw the promotion of religious freedom – 'perhaps the most precious of all American liberties'[77] – as being a critical part of his job.[78] He was strongly influenced by Stephen Carter's *The Culture of Disbelief*, which argues that there is a place for faith in public life, and warns against the church–state separation turning into a guarantee of public secularism.[79] In 2006, Clinton insisted that religious convictions 'can't be pulled on and off like a pair of boots'.[80] He feared that secularisation was unpicking the common bonds unifying society.

In 1993, he signed the Religious Freedom Restoration Act, which ensured that the federal government could only restrict individuals' religious freedom if it had a compelling reason. In 1995, concerned that secularism within public schools was prohibiting religious expression, he issued guidelines that clarified, for example, that students had the right to hold religious meetings on school property and say grace at lunchtime. He issued similar guidelines for federal workplaces in 1997.[81] These policies helped to counter some of the damage done to his relations with conservative Christians by his abortion policies.

Clinton also sought to advance the ability of faith-based organisations to provide public services. In 1996, 'Charitable Choice' was introduced. Previously, a faith-based organisation contracting with the government had to secularise, for example by removing religious symbols from the place of service provision. The new legislation ensured that government could no longer curtail the religious expression of faith-based providers in such ways.[82] The reforms represented a fundamental change to the church–state separation, driven both by Clinton's conviction about the power of local religious communities to transform society and by his determination to cut federal spending.

Most importantly, in 1998 he signed the International Religious Freedom Act, which enshrined the promotion of freedom of religion within US foreign policy and created the Office of Religious Freedom in the State Department, which produces annual reports on the state of religious freedom globally.[83] Clinton insisted that the expansion of religious freedom abroad was an essential step in promoting democracy and Western values, and ultimately American security.

FALL AND REDEMPTION

During his second term, Clinton had a number of successes. He ended a major budget impasse with the Republican-held Congress; as part of the budget compromise, healthcare insurance would be extended to five million children.[84] The economy continued to grow and by the end of his presidency, the federal budget showed a surplus.[85] But of course, it was the Lewinsky scandal and Clinton's fall from grace that dominated the term.

Scandals dogged the Clintons throughout the presidency – including the Whitewater controversy and the suicide (as concluded by a series of separate investigations) in 1993 of Deputy White House Counsel Vince Foster. Rumours spread linking Foster's death to the Clintons, just one in the long list of the 'Clinton body count'.[86] Though the Clintons were not found to have been involved in any wrongdoing in these matters, the ceaseless controversies made them convinced that there was, as Hillary put it, a 'vast right-wing conspiracy'[87] out to get them.[88]

Dodgy dealings were one thing; illicit sex was another. Bill's womanising was an open secret. In 1992, Gennifer Flowers claimed they had an affair (which he admitted to in 1998);[89] and in 1994, Paula Jones brought a sexual harassment lawsuit against him. During his deposition in that lawsuit in 1998, he was asked whether he had had sexual relations with a former White House intern, Monica Lewinsky. He denied it. But later that year, when facing a grand jury under Kenneth Starr (the independent counsel in charge of investigating Whitewater and other controversies), he admitted to the affair. He rejected Starr's accusation of lying in the Jones lawsuit, insisting that 'sexual relations' had been defined by the court in a particular way and that he thought oral sex was not covered. It was bizarre and desperate. In December 1998, the House of Representatives impeached him on grounds of perjury and obstruction of justice. The Senate ultimately voted to acquit him of both charges.[90]

In August 1998, Clinton gave an apology to the nation in which he admitted a 'critical lapse in judgement'. But his tone was partly defiant – his answers to the court were 'legally accurate' and, crucially, 'even Presidents have private lives'.[91] The statement was a declaration that the President's moral conduct is not a public matter. Inevitably he was attacked for his apparent lack of sincerity. Several weeks later, he raised the scandal again at the National Prayer Breakfast. This time religion was central to the matter. He used Psalm 51, written by King David after his adultery, as a basis for his speech.[92] He said he had sinned, repented and asked for God's forgiveness. He needed to have a 'willingness to give the very forgiveness I seek'. He prayed 'that God give me a clean heart, let me walk by faith and not sight'.[93]

Following the scandal, he underwent an extraordinary search for public forgiveness. He asked pastors J. Philip Wogaman, Tony Campolo and Gordon MacDonald to give him spiritual counselling.[94] They attested to Clinton's repentance and to his faith, yet even among them doubts remained – in an article on the topic, Campolo notes cautiously that religion can be used for political purposes.[95] Others insisted that Clinton had done nothing to demonstrate his sincerity. Around 200 theologians signed a declaration accusing him of abusing religious rhetoric in a self-exculpatory fashion, to evade rather than confront his responsibilities; and of cheapening repentance by thinking that it was enough to say sorry in a public performance of piety.[96] Jean Elshtain, a signatory, insisted that a President's ethics and moral behaviour are absolutely public issues, and that a leader of low moral character cannot be trusted.[97]

More than this, the sincerity of Clinton's faith was now questioned. Most damaging was the revelation of Clinton and Lewinsky's sexual exploits on Easter Sunday 1996, three days after he had given a speech recalling Jesus' resurrection.[98]

Clinton maintains that his contrition is sincere. In a 2004 interview, he stated frankly that he had acted as he did with Lewinsky 'just because I could'. He acknowledged, 'That's just about the most morally indefensible reason that anybody could have for doing anything.'[99] In his memoir, he says the scandal at last brought his 'parallel lives'[100] to the public eye, forcing him to confront the disjuncture between his idealistic, pious self-image and the flawed reality. Nevertheless, he insists that Starr's investigation was politically partisan and that Starr had tried everything to bring him down. Clinton's repentance was genuine enough, but he argues that the situation became a bigger deal than it should have done because of his enemies' machinations.[101]

Moreover, even in his second apology, it seems Clinton was trying to find theological justification to reduce the severity of his sin, suggesting that God might be able to bring 'good' out of the situation by turning him into living proof that 'God can change us and make us strong at the broken places'.[102] This was an aspiration to become a new King David: flawed, failed but striving for self-betterment.

FOREIGN POLICY: REPAIRING THE BREACH

With the Cold War over, the Clinton administration sought to articulate a new foreign affairs doctrine: 'democratic enlargement'. Clinton understood this to mean that America needed international stability in order to protect its economic interests, and that the proliferation of free trade and market democracies was essential for ensuring that stability. But enlargement did not mean that America was duty bound to promote democracy everywhere. It meant that policymakers should focus selectively on countries where the US had a 'geo-economic' interest.[103]

In practice, Clinton's foreign policy decisions were often determined by domestic pressures and democratic enlargement was criticised as being un-achievable. He led NATO in intervening militarily in Bosnia and Kosovo – in the latter without UN approval – but he slept while Rwandans mas-sacred each other. Critics like Republican senator John McCain accused him of lacking 'a conceptual framework', which explained why 'we keep getting ourselves involved in peripheral matters such as Northern Ireland and Haiti'.[104]

In 1992, Clinton claimed his childhood in a violent household had made him an instinctive peacemaker who had 'to work' to 'make conflict my friend, not my enemy', a noble image of self-sacrifice in the name of duty.[105] In his memoir, he presents his efforts in the Northern Ireland peace process and in the Israel–Palestine negotiations as being driven as much as by his sense of

America's, and his own, moral responsibility to the world as by US strategic self-interest. This feeling was rooted in his religious convictions, but was also shaped by his personal aspiration to heroism and greatness. In 1993, when Israeli Prime Minister Yitzhak Rabin and Yasser Arafat, then chairman of the Palestine Liberation Organization, shook hands on the White House lawn at the signing of the Oslo I Accord, Clinton placed himself between them for the cameras, arms outstretched, the perfect image of Priestly President. He notes paternalistically in his memoir that he welcomed 'the descendants of Isaac and Ishmael, both children of Abraham … and [urged] them to "go as peacemakers"'.[106] He nearly achieved a final settlement of the Israel–Palestine conflict, and its failure was another huge regret.

Following the Lewinsky scandal, Clinton's concern to be the global peacemaker became tied intimately to his personal life. In 1998, he made the remarkable claim that he had laboured in the Middle East because 'it was a part of my job as President, my mission as a Christian, and my personal journey of atonement'.[107] He sought to redeem his stained private life in the eyes of God and the people by achieving moral victories in his public life.

This linking of his private and public life was a way of seeking forgiveness from the American people. Some commentators, however, were horrified, with one arguing that the President was 'overpersonalizing the political'.[108] Moreover, there were real fears that this collapsing of the public into the private was not just rhetorical but dangerously practical. In 1998, when air strikes against suspected terrorist bases in Sudan and Afghanistan began three days after Clinton had testified before the grand jury about Lewinsky, he was accused of ordering the operation in order to distract the media from the scandal.[109] Similar criticism was raised that December, when Clinton ordered Iraqi military and chemical sites to be bombed at the same time as the House of Representatives was debating the President's impeachment (the bombing stopped a few hours after the impeachment vote).[110] Clinton was said to have committed flagrant war crimes to save his own neck.

'DOING GOD' AS CLINTON

In 2006, Clinton wrote that a President 'must make decisions with regard both to his or her own religious convictions and to the impact of those decisions on people of different faiths'.[111] This was a powerful rebuttal of what he saw as increasingly pervasive secularism. He deeply believed that religion should have a greater place in the public sphere and he helped to bring that about; but for his religious critics, this was too often overshadowed by his pro-choice policies.

Concerning his personal life, the Lewinsky scandal proved that America cared more about the President's personal morals and ethics than Clinton had supposed, but not as much as it cared about the economy. Ultimately, because of his economic and foreign policy successes (and because of the failures of his successors), he remains one of America's most popular Presidents.[112]

Part of this was because he came to understand how to turn his moral failures into political power. He recognised that the man who faces his demons and struggles on may be seen as being more virtuous than the man who is squeaky clean. As Michael Takiff puts it, 'We can't help loving Bill Clinton' because 'there are so few people so visibly, so extremely, so outrageously human. He is who we are.'[113]

NOTES

1. The women were Paula Jones, Kathleen Willey and Juanita Broaddrick. A fourth woman appearing on Trump's panel was Kathy Shelton, a victim of sexual assault whose accused perpetrator Hillary Clinton had defended in 1975. Trump held the press conference hours before a live television debate with Hillary. See Liam Stack, 'Donald Trump featured Paula Jones and 2 other women who accused Bill Clinton of sexual assault', *New York Times*, 9 October 2016, http://www.nytimes.com/2016/10/10/us/politics/bill-clinton-accusers. html?_r=0 (accessed 20 January 2017).

2. Bill Clinton, *My Life* (London: Hutchinson, 2004), p. 161.

3. Ibid., p. 70.

4. Quoted in Michael Takiff, *A Complicated Man: The Life of Bill Clinton as Told by Those Who Know Him* (New Haven, CT: Yale University Press, 2010), p. 434.

5. David L. Holmes, *The Faiths of the Postwar Presidents: From Truman to Obama* (Athens: University of Georgia Press, 2012), p. 216.

6. Clinton, *My Life*, p. 29.

7. Ibid., p. 32.

8. John D. Gartner, *In Search of Bill Clinton: A Psychological Biography* (New York: St Martin's Press, 2008), p. 109.

9. Clinton, *My Life*, p. 42.

10. David Gergen, Matthew Cooper and Donald Baer, 'Bill Clinton's hidden life', *US News and World Report*, 20 July 1992, http://www.usnews.com/news/national/articles/2008/05/16/bill-clintons-hidden-life (accessed 20 January 2017).

11. Clinton, *My Life*, p. 42.
12. Gary Scott Smith, *Religion in the Oval Office: The Religious Lives of American Presidents* (Oxford: Oxford University Press, 2015), p. 333.
13. Clinton, *My Life*, p. 59.
14. Ibid., p. 161.
15. Ibid., p. 70.
16. Ibid., p. 16.
17. James M. Penning, 'The Religion of Bill Clinton', in Mark J. Rozell and Gleaves Whitney (eds), *Religion and the American Presidency* (New York: Palgrave, 2007), pp. 196–8.
18. Holmes, *The Faiths of the Postwar Presidents*, p. 225.
19. Clinton, *My Life*, p. 314.
20. Scott Smith, *Religion in the Oval Office*, pp. 333–4.
21. Paul Kengor, *God and Hillary Clinton: A Spiritual Life* (New York: Harper, 2007), p. 64.
22. Clinton, *My Life*, p. 314.
23. Penning, 'The Religion of Bill Clinton', pp. 198–9.
24. Kengor, *God and Hillary Clinton*, p. 65.
25. Ibid., pp. 66–72.
26. Carl Bernstein, *A Woman in Charge: The Life of Hillary Rodham Clinton* (London: Arrow, 2008), pp. 258–9.
27. Scott Smith, *Religion in the Oval Office*, p. 347.
28. David Maraniss, 'Roots of Clinton's faith deep, varied', *Washington Post*, 29 June 1992, https://www.washingtonpost.com/archive/politics/1992/06/29/roots-of-clintons-faith-deep-varied/081f58ca-5974-4329-a675-0936011e96ac/ (accessed 20 January 2017).
29. Peter Steinfels, 'The 1992 campaign: religion in politics; Southern Baptist team of Democrats represents a new strain of the church', *New York Times*, 8 October 1992, http://www.nytimes.com/1992/10/08/us/1992-campaign-religion-politics-southern-baptist-team-democrats-represents-new.html (accessed 20 January 2017).
30. James E. Wood Jr, 'Religion and the US Presidential Election of 1992', *Journal of Church & State*, vol. 34, no. 4, 1992, p. 721.
31. Otto Heinz, quoted in David Maraniss, *First in His Class: A Biography of Bill Clinton* (New York: Simon and Schuster, 1995), p. 58.
32. Clinton, *My Life*, p. 262.
33. Quoted in Gartner, *In Search of Bill Clinton*, p. 124.
34. Scott Smith, *Religion in the Oval Office*, p. 340.
35. Quoted in Takiff, *A Complicated Man*, p. 378.
36. Toni Morrison, 'On the first black president', *New Yorker*, 5 October 1998, http://www.newyorker.com/magazine/1998/10/05/comment-6543 (accessed 20 January 2017).
37. Gergen et al., 'Bill Clinton's hidden life'.
38. Marvin N. Olasky, *The American Leadership Tradition: Moral Vision from Washington to Clinton* (New York: Free Press, 1999), p. 262.
39. David M. Bresnahan, 'Clinton's trouble in the pulpit', *WND*, 4 September 1998, http://www.wnd.com/1998/09/3320/#kZFoqqwms4bgoO5U.99 (accessed 20 January 2017).
40. William J. Clinton, 'Message on the observance of Easter, 1994', American Presidency Project website, http://www.presidency.ucsb.edu/ws/index.php?pid=49888&st=easter&st1= (accessed 20 January 2017).
41. William J. Clinton, 'Message on the observance of Easter, 1999', American Presidency Project website, http://www.presidency.ucsb.edu/ws/index.php?pid=57352&st=easter&st1= (accessed 20 January 2017).
42. Quoted in Kengor, *God and Hillary Clinton*, p. 173.

43. Quoted in Gartner, *In Search of Bill Clinton*, p. 123.

44. 'Bill Clinton's bully pulpit', Albert Mohler website, 2 September 2004, http://www.albert-mohler.com/2004/09/02/bill-clintons-bully-pulpit/ (accessed 20 January 2017).

45. 1 Corinthians 13:12. Clinton, *My Life*, p. 1001.

46. William J. Clinton, 'Introduction', in Madeleine Albright with Bill Woodward, *The Mighty and the Almighty: Reflections on America, God, and World Affairs*, 2nd ed. (New York: HarperCollins, 2007), p. xii.

47. Jane Warwick Yoder and Edwin M. Yoder Jr, 'The Clintons Up Close', *American Scholar*, Autumn 2012, https://theamericanscholar.org/the-clintons-up-close/ (accessed 20 January 2017).

48. Holmes, *The Faiths of the Postwar Presidents*, p. 233.

49. Scott Smith, *Religion in the Oval Office*, p. 338.

50. Clinton, *My Life*, p. 586.

51. J. Jennings Moss, 'Bill Clinton', *The Advocate*, 25 June 1996, available at https://web.archive.org/web/20050208184130/http://www.advocate.com/html/stories/824/824_clinton_710.asp (accessed 20 January 2017).

52. Patrick J. Buchanan, White House director of communications under Ronald Reagan, speaking at the Republican Party national convention in 1992. Buchanan was quoting and agreeing with a description of Clinton and Al Gore given at the Democratic Party national convention. See Jeffrey Schmalz, 'A delicate balance: the gay vote; gay rights and AIDS emerging as divisive issues in campaign', *New York Times*, 20 August 1992, http://www.nytimes.com/1992/08/20/news/delicate-balance-gay-vote-gay-rights-aids-emerging-divisive-issues-campaign.html (accessed 20 January 2017).

53. Taylor Branch, *The Clinton Tapes: A President's Secret Diary* (London: Pocket Books, 2010), p. 17.

54. Clinton, *My Life*, pp. 511–14.

55. The bill was introduced in response to *Baehr v. Miike* [1993], wherein the Supreme Court of Hawaii ruled that the state must show a compelling interest in prohibiting same-sex marriage. Republican politicians were concerned that, if same-sex marriage became legal in Hawaii, then other states would be compelled to recognise those marriages. DOMA was intended to protect against this possibility.

56. Moss, 'Bill Clinton'.

57. Steve Kornacki, 'Why Bill Clinton really signed DOMA', MSNBC website, 27 October 2015, http://www.msnbc.com/msnbc/why-bill-clinton-really-signed-doma (accessed 20 January 2017).

58. Moss, 'Bill Clinton'.

59. 'Ad touts Clinton's opposing gay marriage', *New York Times*, 15 October 1996, http://www.nytimes.com/1996/10/15/us/ad-touts-clinton-s-opposing-gay-marriage.html (accessed 20 January 2017).

60. Clinton, *My Life*, p. 509.

61. Takiff, *A Complicated Man*, p. 2.

62. Robert E. Moffit, 'A guide to the Clinton health plan', *Talking Points*, 19 November 1993, available at http://www.heritage.org/research/reports/1993/11/a-guide-to-the-clinton-health-plan#pgfId-929615 (accessed 20 January 2017).

63. Henry Hyde, 'The Clinton health plan covers abortion-on-demand', *Human Events*, 18 February 1994, available at http://www.catholicleague.org/the-clinton-health-plan-covers-abortion-on-demand/ (accessed 20 January 2017).

64. Clinton, *My Life*, p. 735.

65. Moss, 'Bill Clinton'.

66. Clinton, *My Life*, p. 381.

67. Wiley Drake, a controversial Southern Baptist pastor and implacable Clinton opponent, accuses him of lying – insisting that Vaught (who died in 1989) never accepted the idea that life begins at any stage other than conception. See Bresnahan, 'Clinton's trouble in the pulpit'.

68. Holmes, *The Faiths of the Postwar Presidents*, p. 235.

69. Interview with Richard Land, PBS website, 29 April 2004, http://www.pbs.org/wgbh/pages/frontline/shows/jesus/interviews/land.html (accessed 20 January 2017).

70. Emma Green, 'Jimmy Carter makes one final push to end racism', *The Atlantic*, 31 May 2016, http://www.theatlantic.com/politics/archive/2016/05/jimmy-carter-makes-one-final-push-to-end-racism/484859/ (accessed 20 January 2017).

71. '1995 State of the Union address', *Washington Post*, 24 January 1995, http://www.washingtonpost.com/wp-srv/politics/special/states/docs/sou95.htm (accessed 20 January 2017).

72. Quoted in Ann Devroy, 'Clinton calls for a centrist "social compact"', *Washington Post*, 25 January 1995, http://www.washingtonpost.com/wp-srv/politics/special/states/stories/sou012595.htm (accessed 20 January 2017).

73. Peter Edelman, 'The worst thing Bill Clinton has done', *The Atlantic*, March 1997, http://www.theatlantic.com/magazine/archive/1997/03/the-worst-thing-bill-clinton-has-done/376797/ (accessed 20 January 2017).

74. Ibid.

75. Jill Nelson, 'Apocalypse now', *The Nation*, 26 August 1996, available at https://www.thenation.com/article/august-22-1996-bill-clinton-ends-welfare-as-we-know-it/ (accessed 20 January 2017).

76. Scott Smith, *Religion in the Oval Office*, p. 344.

77. William J. Clinton, 'Remarks on signing the Religious Freedom Restoration Act of 1993', 16 November 1993, American Presidency Project website, http://www.presidency.ucsb.edu/ws/?pid=46124 (accessed 20 January 2017).

78. Clinton, *My Life*, p. 586.

79. Stephen L. Carter, *The Culture of Disbelief: How American Law and Politics Trivialize Religious Devotion* (New York: BasicBooks, 1993); Scott Smith, *Religion in the Oval Office*, p. 345.

80. Clinton, 'Introduction', in Albright with Woodward, *The Mighty and the Almighty*, p. xi.

81. Scott Smith, *Religion in the Oval Office*, pp. 348–9.

82. Ram A. Cnaan and Stephanie C. Boddie, 'Charitable Choice and Faith-Based Welfare: A Call for Social Work', *Social Work*, vol. 47, no. 3, 2002.

83. Scott Smith, *Religion in the Oval Office*, pp. 352–3.

84. Clinton, *My Life*, p. 798.

85. Kimberley Amadeo, 'President Bill Clinton's economic policies', *The Balance*, 16 November 2016, https://www.thebalance.com/president-bill-clinton-s-economic-policies-3305559 (accessed 20 January 2017).

86. Hannah Parry, 'Google buries "Clinton body count": search engine accused of hiding negative stories during Hillary's campaign', *Mail Online*, 23 August 2016, http://www.dailymail.co.uk/news/article-3754655/Google-buries-Clinton-body-count-Search-engine-accused-hiding-negative-stories-Hillary-s-campaign.html (accessed 20 January 2017).

87. Quoted in David Maraniss, 'First Lady launches counterattack', *Washington Post*, 28 January 1998, http://www.washingtonpost.com/wp-srv/politics/special/clinton/stories/hillary012898.htm (accessed 20 January 2017).

88. Many of the investigative reports behind the conspiracies were funded by conservative businessman Richard Scaife, who sought to bring down the administration through his

so-called 'Arkansas Project'. See Neil A. Lewis, 'Almost $2 million spent in magazine's anti-Clinton project, but on what?', *New York Times*, 15 April 1998, http://www.nytimes.com/1998/04/15/us/almost-2-million-spent-in-magazine-s-anti-clinton-project-but-on-what.html (accessed 20 January 2017).

89. Clinton, *My Life*, pp. 412–15. In 2016 Flowers claimed Clinton paid her $200 to have an abortion after she fell pregnant; see Kelly McLaughlin, 'Gennifer Flowers reveals a married Bill Clinton paid for her $200 abortion when she became pregnant just months into their 12-year affair', *Mail Online*, 14 October 2016, http://www.dailymail.co.uk/news/article-3838844/Gennifer-Flowers-says-married-Bill-Clinton-paid-200-ABORTION-pregnant-just-months-start-alleged-affair.html (accessed 20 January 2017).

90. Clinton, *My Life*, pp. 815–21, 845, 877–80, 889–90.

91. 'President Bill Clinton: "I misled people"', History Place website, http://www.historyplace.com/speeches/clinton.htm (accessed 20 January 2017).

92. Tony Campolo, 'Errant Evangelical? A Presidential Counselor in the Line of Fire', in E. J. Dionne Jr and John J. Dilulio Jr (eds), *What's God Got to Do with the American Experiment?* (Washington, DC: Brookings Institution Press, 2000), p. 107.

93. 'Transcript: Clinton speaks to prayer breakfast', CNN website, 11 September 1998, http://edition.cnn.com/ALLPOLITICS/stories/1998/09/11/transcripts/clinton.prayer.html (accessed 20 January 2017).

94. Penning, 'The Religion of Bill Clinton', p. 205.

95. Campolo, 'Errant Evangelical?', p. 111.

96. Jean Bethke Elshtain, 'The Clinton Scandal and the Culture of the Therapeutic', in E. J. Dionne Jr and John J. Dilulio Jr (eds), *What's God Got to Do with the American Experiment?* (Washington, DC: Brookings Institution Press, 2000), p. 101.

97. Ibid., pp. 101–2.

98. Kengor, *God and Hillary Clinton*, p. 166.

99. Tricia McDermott, 'Bill Clinton: his life', 60 Minutes website, 1 June 2004, http://www.cbsnews.com/news/bill-clinton-his-life/ (accessed 20 January 2017).

100. Clinton, *My Life*, p. 855.

101. McDermott, 'Bill Clinton'.

102. 'Transcript: Clinton speaks to prayer breakfast'.

103. Douglas Brinkley, 'Democratic Enlargement: The Clinton Doctrine', *Foreign Policy*, no. 106, 1997, pp. 116–18.

104. Quoted ibid., p. 124.

105. Gergen et al., 'Bill Clinton's hidden life'.

106. Clinton, *My Life*, pp. 572–3.

107. William J. Clinton, 'Remarks celebrating the 160th anniversary of the Metropolitan African Methodist Episcopal Church', 23 October 1998, American Presidency Project website, http://www.presidency.ucsb.edu/ws/?pid=55141 (accessed 20 January 2017).

108. Elshtain, 'The Clinton Scandal and the Culture of the Therapeutic', p. 104.

109. 'Flashback: Conservative lawmakers decried Clinton's attacks against Osama as "Wag the Dog"', *ThinkProgress*, 25 September 2006, https://thinkprogress.org/flashback-conservative-lawmakers-decried-clintons-attacks-against-osama-as-wag-the-dog-e1ca08cd43ad (accessed 20 January 2017).

110. The Clinton administration justified the Iraq bombings on the grounds that Saddam Hussein had failed to comply with the UN Special Commission concerning the destruction of weapons of mass destruction. See Elshtain, 'The Clinton Scandal and the Culture of the Therapeutic', p. 103; Christopher Hitchens, *No One Left to Lie To: The Triangulations of William Jefferson Clinton* (London: Verso, 1999), p. 98.

III. Clinton, 'Introduction', in Albright with Woodward, *The Mighty and the Almighty*, p. xi.

112. According to a Gallup poll, Clinton left office with a 66 per cent approval rating, one point higher than Ronald Reagan's. See Takiff, *A Complicated Man*, p. 4.

113. Michael Takiff, 'Bill Clinton, still the biggest dog in town', Huffington Post, 18 October 2010, http://www.huffingtonpost.com/michael-takiff/bill-clinton-still-the-bi_b_766820.html (accessed 20 January 2017).

NELSON MANDELA
(1994–99)

PAUL BICKLEY

INTRODUCTION

On 11 February 1990 Nelson Mandela walked through the gates of Victor Verster Prison, at liberty for the first time since 1962. His release, to paraphrase Churchill, was not the end, nor even the beginning of the end, but perhaps the end of a beginning. The next decade of his life would be dedicated to seeing the demise of apartheid and realising the vision of a reconciled, united, multi-racial and prosperous South Africa.

Some suggested his commitment to reconciliation and magnanimity towards his former enemies was almost Christ-like, and wondered if it was a product of Christian commitment. Mandela, however, was consistently and quite deliberately evasive about the nature of his personal beliefs. He was anxious to honour the Christian formation and education offered in South Africa's mission schools. He was occasionally drawn to expressing a Christian faith, albeit cautiously, in later life. But we know relatively little about what his beliefs were or their relative importance in his struggle, compared to other influences such as Marxism.

Mandela's reticence aside, religion cannot be ignored as either a personal or a sociological factor in the politics of the anti-apartheid movement. On the contrary, any honest attempt to understand Mandela must give attention to the religious aspects of his, and South Africa's, story. If Christianity was not a badge that Mandela wore comfortably, the question is: was it nevertheless a reality that shaped his politics? And what light can this shed on South Africa's theo-political present and future?

THE BOY AND THE MISSION

Rolihlahla Mandela was born on 18 July 1918 at Mvezo, in the rural, remote and relatively poor Transkei region. He was part of an aristocratic family. While Mandela's branch of the family was not wealthy – and became less so when his father was deposed from his chieftainship by a colonial magistrate – it was part of that society's elite.

Mandela's autobiography reports that two brothers from a different tribe lived in his village, George and Ben Mbekela: 'The brothers were an exception in Qunu [a village to which Mandela moved when he was baby]: they were educated and Christian.'[1] Evidently, these brothers exercised some influence. Mandela's mother became a Methodist, and Rolihlahla was baptised into the Methodist Church. The brothers also suggested that Mandela should begin attending school. It was at this small Methodist school that he was given the name Nelson.

When his father died in 1930, Mandela was sent to live with the Thembu regent Jongintaba Dalindyebo. Unlike Mandela's father, Jongintaba was a Christian and sent both Nelson and his own son Justice to board at the Methodist schools of Clarkebury (named after the Methodist theologian Adam Clarke) and Healdtown. Mandela went on to attend the University College of Fort Hare, a college with a Christian foundation that proved a clearing house for black African leaders.

Mandela did not graduate from Fort Hare as expected. He resigned from the student council as part of a protest over inadequate food. When he refused to alter his decision, he was expelled. He returned home only to flee an arranged marriage and, in 1941, he arrived in Johannesburg.

Mandela briefly worked as a mine security guard, then at the estate agency run by future ANC secretary general Walter Sisulu before being taken on at a Johannesburg law firm, where he began to encounter radical black leaders. After completing his first degree through a correspondence course, he began to study for a law degree. He also married for the first time in 1944, and at around the same time joined the ANC. Both the marriage and the studies became casualties of Mandela's political activism. By 1951 he was president of the ANC Youth League (which he had helped co-found) and in 1952 he became ANC deputy president.

At this stage in Mandela's journey, there are hints of an ongoing religious conscience. He reports, for instance, that he was put off the Communist Party by their antipathy to religion ('I was ... quite religious').[2] Involvement in the ANC would have been reasonably comfortable in comparison. It was by no means a secular movement, and some of its founders had been religious ministers. Leaders like Albert Luthuli and Oliver Tambo were devout practising Christians in a way that Mandela did not seem to be, but the tension between communism and Christianity would crop up later in his story.

APARTHEID

Though the rights of non-white South Africans had been restricted for centuries, the election of the Afrikaner-dominated National Party in 1948 saw existing segregation harden into 'apartheid'. This was a system of laws extending to all areas of life, intended to ensure that the different racial groups in South Africa developed separately. This ranged from setting up semi-autonomous 'Bantustans', which would be ethnically homogeneous, to outlawing marriage – and even sexual intercourse – between different racial groups.

Needless to say, what some claimed was a modest proposal for different ethnic groups to 'go their own way' (Hendrik Verwoerd, the architect of apartheid, said it could be thought of as a policy of good neighbourliness) in practice meant that black, 'coloured' (mixed-race) and Indian South Africans would be denuded of political and economic power. Although the ANC had been in existence and actively campaigning against segregation since 1912, the institution of formal apartheid forced a step change in its activities. New alliances were developed with the Communist Party and Indian campaigners. As yet, though, the ANC was committed to non-violent and passive resistance, not least because of the Christian commitments of leaders such as Luthuli.

The ANC Defiance Campaign of non-compliance with apartheid laws began on 26 June 1952. Conflict would escalate throughout the decade, and any hope for even medium-term success vanished with the Sharpeville massacre of 1960. Within a few weeks, a state of emergency was declared and the ANC was banned. Mandela went underground and launched Umkhonto we Sizwe (Spear of the Nation), an armed wing of the ANC.

Though the ANC itself remained officially committed to the principle of non-violence, it had effectively departed from its long-standing commitment to non-violent resistance, and this was the subject of some theological reflection in the movement – the principles of 'just war' were discussed, and Tambo (who once held the ambition of being ordained into the Anglican Church) would lead the ANC and MK in exile. Mandela would later justify the return to violence, saying that it had become clear that 'South Africa was a police state with a constitution that enshrined inequality and an army that responded to non-violence with force'.[3]

Mandela briefly left South Africa to build international support for the ANC, but also for military training in Algeria and Ethiopia. Returning in July 1962, he was soon arrested and imprisoned for leaving the country without a passport. A year later, on 11 July 1963, nineteen ANC leaders were arrested at a farm near the town of Rivonia. Ten of these, including Mandela, were tried on terrorism offences in the infamous Rivonia trial. Two were acquitted. The remaining eight were sentenced to life imprisonment and sent to Robben Island.

IMPRISONMENT

Mandela and the others on Robben Island were high profile enough to be spared the very worst that the South African prison system had to offer (along with the Red Cross, the liberal MP Helen Suzman was able to make regular visits and lobby for better conditions). In the early years they were cruelly treated, and were put to forced labour in a lime quarry. While it would be wrong to say that conditions for the prisoners were ever pleasant, the regime slowly relaxed, in large part because Mandela and his fellow prisoners refused to accept abuse as their lot.

Religion was very much part of life on Robben Island. Ministers were brought to the island to offer religious services to the (largely non-religious) prisoners. When services took place outdoors, however, even non-believing prisoners would make the most of the opportunity for a little fresh air. Mandela joked that there was a mass conversion to Islam because of the food the Muslim chaplain would bring to the island. On his own account, he was eager to participate. 'Though I am a Methodist, I would attend each different religious service.'[4]

Other accounts, however, suggest that Mandela was abandoning Christianity in favour of communism. Anthony Sampson, Mandela's official biographer, records that he was 'struck by ... the relentless logic of dialectical materialism, which he felt sweeping away the superstitions and inherited beliefs of his childhood, like "a powerful searchlight on a dark night, which enables the traveller to see all round, to detect danger spots and the way forward"', but that 'he experienced some pangs at abandoning the Christian beliefs that had fortified his childhood, such as the story of St Peter three times denying Christ'.[5] This is something of a conundrum, for we know that even towards the end of his imprisonment, when housed alone in Pollsmoor and Victor Verster prisons, he was meeting with chaplains, recording the subject of their talks on his day planner, for example: '19 AUGUST 1986: Rev Peter Storey on forgiveness ... 4 SEPTEMBER 1986: Father Michael Austin of Johannesburg. On how to live like Christ.'[6]

We return to the question of Mandela's Christianity and communism below, but two anecdotes around the Robben Island chaplaincy cast light on the impact of his long imprisonment, and perhaps provide some clues to the source of his generosity and magnanimity towards former enemies. Early on in Mandela's sentence, a minister was castigated by one of the inmates for offering a one-sided message of reconciliation: 'Finally, Eddie could take it no longer. "You're preaching reconciliation to the wrong people," he called out. "We've been seeking reconciliation for the last seventy-five years."'[7] Elsewhere in his autobiography, Mandela speaks of another minister, the 'crusty' André Scheffer of the Dutch Reformed Church, who came to the island to speak to the general (non-political) prisoners:

One Sunday, he wandered over to our section and we asked him why he didn't preach to us. 'You men think you are freedom fighters,' he said contemptuously. 'You must have been drunk on liquor or high on dagga [marijuana] when you were arrested. Freedom fighters, my foot!' But we challenged him to come to preach to us and, eventually, in the late 1960s, he responded ... As Reverend Scheffer became familiar with us, he became more sympathetic.[8]

When Scheffer preached on the Book of Exodus, he was told he was no longer acceptable. Mandela gave him a parting gift of a guava for his wife.[9]

In other words, rather than the abstract preaching of reconciliation, it was the fact of daily human contact with Afrikaners that was transformative on a deep level. Ahmed Kathrada, another of the Rivonia detainees, noted how 'ironically it is in jail that we have closest fraternisation between the opponents and supporters of apartheid'.[10]

WHAT IS PAST, IS PAST

In 1982, Mandela and three other prisoners were moved to Pollsmoor Prison on the mainland. Mandela suspected that this was both a response to growing international concern about his imprisonment and an attempt to fragment the anti-apartheid leadership network that had established itself on Robben Island.

Nonetheless, it's clear that the South African administration were looking for exits from the road to all-out civil war. In 1985, they offered Mandela early release if he would renounce violence. Mandela turned this offer down, saying he could not make that commitment while his people were not free. But, in spite of mounting violence, the stars were beginning to align for some form of rapprochement. International moral pressure, built by religious leaders like Father Trevor Huddleston, was beginning to have an effect. Opposition from churches in South Africa had become much stiffer. Sanctions were taking a psychological toll, even if their economic effects were marginal. Banks stopped 'rolling over' their loans to South Africa, forcing the government to borrow at higher rates. The retreat of communism also meant that fears around the place and involvement of the South African Communist Party in the anti-apartheid campaign could be allayed.

Mandela, sensing the moment, reached out to politicians in the ruling National Party with an offer of 'talks about talks', initially without consulting the formal leadership of the ANC. Though he didn't receive a direct answer, Minister of Justice Kobie Coetsee paid him an extended hospital visit while he was recuperating from tuberculosis. When he was discharged, Mandela was moved from Pollsmoor to Victor Verster Prison, where he was lodged relatively comfortably in a cottage, allowed to set his own routine, and even given a cook, Warrant Officer Swart, a former guard from Robben Island with whom he developed a close friendship. This cottage, though still a prison, became a base where Mandela could host meetings with fellow activists and government officials.

On 2 February 1990, the new President, F. W. de Klerk, opened the South African parliament with the announcement that the ban on the ANC – and a range of other anti-apartheid organisations – would be lifted and political prisoners would be released. Nine days later, Mandela himself was released.

Mandela's release was a moment of celebration, but the road to a democratic South Africa was still a winding – and bloody – one. Elections in 1994 saw the ANC under Mandela's leadership take 62 per cent of the vote, with the National Party on 20 per cent and the Inkatha Freedom Party on 10 per cent. Mandela became President, with Thabo Mbeki and de Klerk as his deputies. This was in many ways a triumph but it is often forgotten that somewhere around 10,000 South Africans died as a result of politically motivated violence in the transition period 1990–94 as different forces – including some within the South African government – sought to destabilise the negotiations. Mandela said, in Afrikaans, at his inauguration, '*Wat is verby, verby,*' or 'What is past, is past'. But he also knew that the past had to be dealt with before the rainbow nation could be built.

In 1996, the parliament adopted a new constitution, but the National Party withdrew from the Government of National Unity. That same year, the historic Truth and Reconciliation Commission (TRC) was launched. The TRC had a mandate to investigate violations of human rights from the Sharpeville massacre onwards. Amnesty could be granted on the basis of full disclosure.

Mandela asked two churchmen (Desmond Tutu and Alex Boraine) to chair the commission, but it was far from an exercise in fluffy idealism. Rather, the TRC provided a middle way between the unpalatable and deeply unpopular option of the general amnesty that the National Party wanted and the Nuremberg-style trials that the ANC would have liked to see. Effectively, the TRC exchanged the hope of justice in a minority of cases for the chance of an honest account of what happened in the majority.

But it was not only pragmatism. The TRC evidenced Mandela's sensitivity to the need for a process that was more than merely political. His own political journey had been one rooted in recognising the humanity of his political opponents, even his warders. He wanted people to know that it was possible to 'love the sinner, but hate the sin'. 'In prison, my anger towards whites decreased, but my hatred for the system grew. I wanted South Africa to see that I loved even my enemies while I hated the system that turned us against one another.'[11] Of course, the TRC could not do all this work, but it was an effort to ensure that all parties acknowledged wrongdoing – hoping, perhaps, that sunshine would provide some kind of disinfectant for the deep wounds that had been inflicted by both sides. As a process of justice, the TRC could only be thought to be partially successful at best. Its true purpose, however, was to set the tone for a united South Africa.

NO POWER ON THIS EARTH

Unlike almost any other politician in high office, Mandela's reputation grew over the duration of his presidency. In spite of all his protestations that South Africa's revolution had been achieved through a movement and in solidarity with others, he became quite literally a global icon. Whatever else he was, he was incredibly adept at symbolic politics – his patronage of the South African rugby team in the 1995 World Cup, for instance, demonstrated his ability to project himself as a national leader, not just the leader of his own community.

This may explain Mandela's reticence to come clean on his religious belief. As a figurehead for the anti-apartheid movement, he was a kind of eirenicon, gluing together Marxists, pan-Africanists, nationalists and liberals, the religious and non-religious. After 1994, he became the eirenicon for South Africa as a whole, bringing the nation together through the symbolic power of his own acts of reconciliation.

It follows that Mandela was far more comfortable when affirming religion as a social force than when addressing his own faith. In 2003, David Dimbleby conducted a series of reverential interviews with him. One series of questions captured the distinction nicely:

> Dimbleby: You were brought up by Methodists. Are you a Christian?
> Mandela: Well, you see, the relation between a man and his god is a private matter. But all that I can tell you, David, there is no power on earth that compares with religion. That's why I respect it. That's why I am saying to you, if the missionaries were not there, I would not have been here today. Because they are the people that gave us the most important weapon to lead: that of education.
> Dimbleby: You believe there is a God?
> Mandela: Well, I say that is a private matter between an individual and his God.[12]

Here we come full circle, to the mission schools which were so formative for Mandela. They were clearly part of the structure of British colonialism, but Mandela did not feel in the end that they were institutions of oppression. They provided indigenous elites and mission families with an education comparable to that received by whites, and indeed many alumni would go on to play a significant part in the anti-apartheid struggle. Anthony Sampson suggests that the networks were reminiscent of early Victorian British networks like the Clapham Sect. Hence Mandela's defence: 'Religious institutions built schools, equipped them, employed teachers and paid them salaries; therefore religion is in our blood. Without missionary institutions there would have been no Robert Mugabe, no Seretse Khama, no Oliver Tambo.'[13]

This, in many ways, is the territory which many politicians occupy. Questions of the truth and falsehood of this or that religious claim are elided. Religion is good when it does good. A similar thought can be found in the mouths and the pens of religious campaigners against apartheid, steeped in liberation theology and frequently burned by their ill-treatment at the hands of their own religious institutions: for them, what religious people said was less important than what they did. Conversely, the same was true of secular campaigners – what mattered most was that people were committed to a 'new order of justice', rather than ascribing to a particular creed.

That said, the question of what could enable such social good is likely to persist, particularly when it comes to Mandela. Did a lingering Christianity – or even something more substantial – play a part? Or had he set it aside?

In that section of his biography discussed above, Sampson is summarising a passage from Mandela's original manuscript of *Long Walk to Freedom*, written on Robben Island in 1976 and now available at the Nelson Mandela Centre of Memory website.[14] In it, Mandela reflects at some length on the implications of dialectical materialism on supernatural beliefs. He records that he embraced the former once he understood it, but that 'those of us' who had been brought up in religious homes would inevitably feel grieved when setting aside their beliefs (hence the St Peter reference). If this is a candid statement of his position, then it is one that pours cold water on any spiritual biography. On this reading, in spite of early opposition to communism, he eventually espoused it. He converted from Christianity to Marxism, hence materialism, hence atheism, but for whatever reason, he was unwilling to admit to this.

That is certainly a plausible story (after his death, for example, membership of the South African Communist Party came to light). But it is not the only plausible story. Another would see this as just one staging post on Mandela's intellectual and spiritual journey. It is hard to argue that the Mandela that emerged from Victor Verster Prison was a dialectical materialist, and his own autobiography records something of a conversion on economic questions during his presidency. It is quite possible – indeed probable – that over the subsequent fourteen years his religious beliefs changed again, even if he never got the point of being sufficiently confident of them that he could preach them.

We can never know for certain but Mandela's book *Conversations with Myself* records the following conversation with Ahmed Kathrada:

Kathrada: This is the way it's worded, page 62 [of the *Long Walk to Freedom* draft]: 'He felt some pangs at abandoning his Christian beliefs which had fortified his childhood, like St Peter three times denying Christ.' Now, is it correct wording to say you 'abandoned your Christian beliefs'?

Mandela: No, never.

Kathrada: It would be wrong, isn't it?

Mandela: I say it's absolutely untrue. I never abandoned my Christian beliefs.

Kathrada: OK.

Mandela: And I think it's proper, you know, it could do a lot of harm.

Kathrada: Exactly, ja.

Mandela: Ja, could do a lot of harm.[15]

This does not do much to clarify matters, but it does suggest that, in the many hours spent in reflection on Robben Island, Mandela's views may have continued to evolve. In 1985, the Reverend Dudley Moore wrote to the *Mail and Guardian*, a Johannesburg-based weekly newspaper, reporting that just a few days before Mandela had taken communion, and they had meditated together on Jesus in Gethsemane. Contra the manuscript above, Moore felt that Mandela might be influenced by Marx but was not a communist.[16] This mix of various commitments is perhaps the most plausible story. Indeed, in an aside in *Long Walk to Freedom*, Mandela suggests that 'Communism and Christianity, at least in Africa, were not mutually exclusive'.[17]

There is further corroboration. The theologian H. W. van der Merwe asked him outright if, like President Kenneth Kaunda of Zambia, Mandela was a Christian. He answered, 'Very definitely.'[18] A reference to an argument with two *Washington Post* journalists, who suggested that – unlike the non-violent Martin Luther King – Mandela could not be a Christian, indicates that they solicited a kind of confession:

I told them that I was a Christian and had always been a Christian. Even Christ, I said, when he was left with no alternative, used force to expel the moneylenders from the temple. He was not a man of violence, but had no choice but to use force against evil. I do not think I persuaded them.[19]

CONCLUSION

Similar references could be supplied, none of which are particularly helpful in opening up Mandela's religious psychology. It may be, in the end, there are no hidden depths to discover after all – he once spoke of himself as a 'mediocre man', and said that 'I'm one of those who possess scraps of superficial information on a variety of subjects'. Perhaps there is no great underlying philosophy to be mined, and Mandela was simply the product of various influences… family, tribe, school, movement and prison.

What is sure is that he left prison a very different man from the naïve firebrand of the 1960s. Far from overcoming resistance to apartheid, imprisonment resulted in a transformation that could help Mandela usher South Africa into the post-apartheid world. The spiritual and intellectual groundwork for South Africa's reconciliation seems to have been laid on Robben Island and in Pollsmoor and Victor Verster.

Anthony Sampson gives calls this groundwork 'forgiveness', and uses the word frequently. Whatever he felt towards the various representatives of the South African state that he encountered, Mandela himself notably does not describe his approach in those lofty terms.[20] Rather, he was unwilling to write off an opponent – even a persecutor – as finally an enemy. He was confident that he could always appeal to someone's sense of reason and justice, and that people's essential goodness was being overridden by the perverse politics of the time. 'All men', he said, 'even the most seemingly cold-blooded, have a core of decency, and … if their hearts are touched, they are capable of changing. Ultimately, Badenhorst [a Robben Island governor] was not evil; his inhumanity had been foisted upon him by an inhuman system.'[21]

If it was forgiveness, then it was of the 'show, don't tell' kind. It was practical, political and immanent – even necessary. And far from being the articulation of some abstract or theoretical value, it was something Mandela was able to live.

NOTES

1. Mandela, Nelson, *Long Walk To Freedom* (Abacus 40th Anniversary) (Little, Brown Book Group, Kindle Edition), Kindle locations 356–7.
2. Ibid., Kindle locations 1362–3.
3 Ibid., Kindle location 8591.
4. Ibid., Kindle locations 7476–7.
5. Anthony Sampson, *Mandela: The Authorised Biography*, rev. ed. (London: HarperPress, 2011), Kindle locations 1572–5.

6. Nelson Mandela, *Conversations with Myself* (London: Macmillan, 2010), Kindle locations 3354–5.

7. Mandela, *Long Walk to Freedom*, Kindle locations 7486–91.

8. Ibid., Kindle locations 7496–505.

9. In another account, it was not the minister's preaching but accepting a gift from Mandela that saw him dismissed from his position.

10. Sampson, *Mandela*, Kindle Locations 4826–7.

11. Mandela, *Long Walk to Freedom*, Kindle locations 9362–4.

12. 'Nelson Mandela, in his own words, BBC News', YouTube, 5 December 2013, https://www.youtube.com/watch?v=-dluDoyQltM (accessed 21 January 2017).

13. Nelson Mandela, speech to the Oxford Centre for Islamic Studies, 11 July 1997, quoted in Sampson, *Mandela*, Kindle location 586.

14. http://archive.nelsonmandela.org/home (accessed 21 January 2017).

15. Mandela, *Conversations with Myself*, Kindle locations 666–73.

16. 'The Nelson Mandela I know: by his minister', *Mail and Guardian*, 27 September 1985, http://mg.co.za/article/1985-09-27-the-nelson-mandela-i-know-by-his-minister (accessed 21 January 2017).

17. Mandela, *Long Walk to Freedom*, Kindle location 3208.

18. Sampson, *Mandela*, Kindle locations 6961–5.

19. Mandela, *Long Walk to Freedom*, Kindle locations 8586–94.

20. Martha Nussbaum notes the same, and reports an interview with Albie Sachs saying 'the language of forgiveness was utterly alien to the movement'. Martha C. Nussbaum, *Anger and Forgiveness: Resentment, Generosity, and Justice* (New York: Oxford University Press, 2016).

21. Mandela, *Long Walk to Freedom*, Kindle locations 7648–50.

JOHN HOWARD (1996–2007)

CLARE PURTILL

INTRODUCTION

Although Australia is a seemingly secular country, this has not been reflected in the people's choice of Prime Minister, with a disproportionate number of professed Christians having taken on the role over recent years. One such leader is John Howard, who followed Labor's Paul Keating and served as Prime Minister from 1996 until 2007, the second-longest term on record, after Sir Robert Menzies in the immediate post-war period.

Initial impressions would mark him out as a supremely successful politician. Howard came into office with a 45-seat majority, the second biggest in Australia's history. He was re-elected three times and stayed in power for over a decade. He titled his autobiography, the biggest-selling political memoir in Australian history, *Lazarus Rising*, the evocation of the story of Lazarus attesting to Howard's own recognition of the unlikelihood of his continued success. Described by *The Economist*'s columnist Bagehot as a 'man of common opinions and uncommon abilities', his uncommon abilities were matched by an uncommon temperament that 'allowed him to surmount defeat, criticism and ridicule to become a skilful, if prosaic, prime minister, never great but adequate'.[1] This adds to the notion that Howard was aware of his own shortcomings and endeavoured to project an image more suitable for a Prime Minister of Australia. Christianity was a key part of this.

Despite becoming an Anglican as an adult, Howard is most often associated with the religion of his childhood, Methodism. How far Methodism influenced his policies is debatable, but it proved to be pervasive in the public perception of him and was perhaps seen as more closely connected to his political identity than it was in reality. In Howard's decade in power, religion had a higher political profile than at any time since the 1950s Labor split, a process that resulted from internal conflict in the party and led to the establishment of the Democratic Labor Party, which had strong Catholic influences.[2] How far Howard was personally responsible for that raised profile is a matter for debate.

BACKGROUND

John Winston Howard, his name revealing his father's admiration for Winston Churchill, was born in 1939, the youngest of Mona and Lyall Howard's four sons. He grew up in the 1950s, a decade he describes as probably the most stable, secure and prosperous decade Australia had experienced in the twentieth century,[3] attending Earlwood Public School and winning admission to Canterbury Boys' High School, one of a limited number of selective state high schools in Sydney.

It was at Canterbury School that Howard developed a keen interest in politics, public affairs and debating. He excelled in 'off the cuff' speaking, which became a distinctive feature of his political career, less than 10 per cent of the speeches he gave as Prime Minister coming from prepared texts.[4] Both religion and politics seem to have played a significant part in his upbringing, with his parents encouraging engagement with both.[5]

The Howards were a Methodist family and attended their local church in Earlwood. Indeed, Howard's portrayal of himself as both a Christian and a politician cannot be understood separate from the context of Methodism. His Methodist faith was a large part of his life and he attended weekly until he left Earlwood in his late twenties. He described the influence of Christianity as 'strong and pervasive': 'The fundamentals of Christian belief and practice which I learned at Earlwood Methodist Church have stayed with me to this day, although I would not pretend to be other than an imperfect adherent to them.'[6]

Despite the prevalence in the public imagination of John Howard as a Methodist, this Methodism did not stay with him as an adult. In 1971, he

married an Anglican, Janette Parker, and from then on identified as an Anglican. Though he settled comfortably within that denomination, his personal
faith transcended denominational differences, a fact that may have opened
up opportunities for other denominations: for instance, his government was
the first federal coalition in which Catholics played a prominent role.[7] If
anything, he was seen as more inclined to Puritanism due to his serious
and dour disposition.[8] A non-denominational connection with Christianity
suited him, as it could adapt with him and serve his presentation of himself
in a way that a fixed denominational affiliation might not.

POLITICAL CAREER

As a member of the Young Liberals, Howard showed a strong interest in
politics from an early age. His first attempt to win a New South Wales state
seat in 1968 was unsuccessful but he persevered and was offered the chance to
run for a safe seat three years later. He failed to win the pre-selection but was
asked to work for the Prime Minister. Two years later, he was offered another
safe seat, Bennelong, and won. He climbed to leader of the opposition twice,
and finally won the 1996 election with a campaign framed as a referendum
on Paul Keating.

Howard was a socially conservative, economically liberal leader in a coalition government between the Liberal Party and the National Party, a coalition
that had existed in various forms since the 1920s. His coalition government
reflected Howard's public persona as a man of faith. Party and electoral politics specialist John Warhurst points out that, more than any other federal
government, the senior members of the Howard government were active in
being open about their religious credentials and belief and emphasising the
positive contribution of Christian values in their society.[9] Although it would
be an exaggeration to say that Howard effected a Christianisation of top-level
Australian politics to anything like the extent that Ronald Reagan had done
with US politics fifteen years earlier, his accession to highest office did appear
to signal a shift in Australian political discourse.

Howard was close with his American contemporary, President George W.
Bush. Indeed, he had been staying in a hotel with a view of the Pentagon
on 11 September 2001, and had suffered alongside Bush seeing a country

reeling after atrocious acts of a new kind of terrorism. This, and a similar worldview, bonded the pair and America continued to be Australia's major ally throughout Howard's time in office.

The similarity to, and difference from, American politics of the previous decade was further underlined by Howard's relationship with Australia's own 'Religious Right'. Attitudinally, this movement, in as much as it can be called a movement, was similar to its American counterpart, and it has been suggested that Howard used language, and references to the 'family' in particular, to denote a set of attitudes and values that Christian conservative voters would understand and appreciate.[10] He identified Judeo-Christian values as the 'greatest shaper, morally and ethically, of today's Australia'.[11] He presented the traditional family as being under attack. In the words of the (somewhat hostile) critic Marion Maddox, 'the sepia-toned traditional family, though making up the "mainstream", is imagined as embattled, its way of life jeopardised by single mothers, lesbians and untamed, fatherless children'.[12] The rationale for Howard's policies became more of an emotional drive, and there was a shift to values, particularly family values.[13]

There were important differences, however. Apart from the obvious one that any Australian Religious Right constituency was far smaller and therefore far less influential than its American counterpart, Australia has a compulsory voting system whereas America does not.[14] For this reason, making an emotional appeal to voters to turn up at an election is not an issue in Australia: there is less need for an Australian Prime Minister to court the constituency in the way that an American President must. Howard borrowed campaign strategies from the American Religious Right, supported by conservative religious activists and think tanks, but he did so to attract a wider, non-religious public.

Either way, it is not surprising that many people criticised him as the driving force behind a sinister political agenda that threatened those on the margins of society. Indeed, in his book on Howard and the conservative tradition, the academic Norman Abjorensen described him as the most destructive of all Australian conservative leaders, and suggested that Howard's ultimate service to conservativism was to 'reignite a class war that liberals and conservatives had insisted for more than a century did not exist'.[15] At times, he seemed to abandon his responsibility to minorities in the hope of winning over the group he perceived to be the majority.

METHODIST IMAGE

Almost all commentary on Howard links his politics to his Methodist up-bringing. The implication of this is that his social policy can be understood as 'a kind of default mechanism, ingrained in his childhood and never rethought'.[16] Harsh policies and an apparent disregard for marginalised communities did not help Howard's popularity in some quarters, and on the whole the Australian electorate does not like religious fanaticism, but the Methodists became the Uniting Church in 1977, so what could be safer than a religion that no longer exists? Howard's image may have benefited from handing over some of the responsibility for controversial policies to religious motivations.

It is noticeable that further investigation into his religious background does not evidence much foreshadowing of the more unpopular and definitive policies of his leadership. Indeed, the Methodist church of his early years was fairly socially progressive, and Howard and his peers were encouraged to befriend Aboriginal children in their area.[17] Howard himself, however, was not particularly socially progressive, and he could make light of the precise impact that his childhood faith had on him personally, once commenting that 'religion did play quite a role in my upbringing ... I still regard myself as having a strong Methodist deposit, I guess it's reflected in my attitude to some things like gambling. Though not drinking, I enjoy a drink.'[18]

The impact of his possible utilisation of the Methodist stereotype was no joke. Howard's identity seemed to come across in a way that worked to his political advantage to conceal the more divisive side effects of his social conservatism. By suggesting to the public that his policies were shaped by his Methodist childhood, they were confused and combined with the niceties of Methodism and as a result came across as less threatening.

This image of Howard utilising his youth to put himself across as endearing extends beyond his faith background. His repeated insistence that he wanted to be a parliamentarian from a young age also suggests an underlying earnest-ness.[19] Judith Brett, a professor of politics at La Trobe University, Melbourne, picked up on it as a distinctive feature of Howard's rhetorical style, and drew attention to the frequent references to his personal experiences, beliefs and feelings, suggesting that Howard used his own experience to legitimise his beliefs, rather than a more abstract system of cultural or social knowledge.[20]

There has been some suggestion that Howard's habit of fictionalising the narrative behind his policies extended beyond his portrayal of his own personal experiences. Some would go so far as to say Howard's political success was his skill in creating a new story about Australia's identity.[21] Whether or not this is true, Howard was certainly successful in establishing a rapport with his people. This was partly due to the ordinary image he portrayed, which brought him closer to the average Australian.[22]

This rapport with the Australian people should not be underestimated. He put the question of the role of faith in public life in terms the average Australian could understand: 'Those who would preference "Jingle Bells" but limit "Once in Royal David's City" at Christmas in schools, are doing a great disservice to the next generation,' he said.[23] While he may not have come across as devout, he was likeable and his Christianity became a part of this. Despite his use of us/them dichotomies, his rapport with mainstream Australia allowed him to communicate his experiences of faith and politics at their level. More often than not, the two were treated as separate entities.

MINORITIES AND LOST GENERATIONS

For all the Prime Minister's public faith, however, the major Christian churches became a consistent element of the opposition to the Howard government on some of the major issues of the decade.[24] Indeed, with a few notable exceptions, such as the Salvation Army's Major Brian Watters and Catholic Cardinal George Pell, and on issues such as euthanasia, abortion and same-sex marriage, he faced considerable ecclesiastical criticism.

This was particularly evident in the area of economic policy, but also included mandatory detention of refugees, infringement of Aboriginal rights and Australian military action. The government was fearful of institutions that presented a challenge to state power, and this included Christian churches. Howard moved to suggest they were speaking out of turn, offering guidance on moral issues that sounded partisan.

Howard's opposition to churches went further than criticism. In 1996, he urged rural churchgoers to withdraw financial support from their churches to punish them for backing the Aboriginal native title.[25] The Howard government seems to have had an easier relationship with newer evangelical churches than the more critical leaders of the mainstream churches. However, Howard did not readily welcome Christian advocacy in public life, and his attitudes to minorities, migration and the indigenous population all serve as examples of where his policies were in considerable tension with churches and the wider Christian community.

Howard's perspective on minority politics can perhaps be summed up in his line, 'I don't like hyphenated Australians, I just like Australians.'[26] A seemingly harmless comment, perhaps even a joke, it promoted a perception of otherness: us and them. The distinction between hyphenated and non-hyphenated Australians implies that those with a mixed sense of national identity are not Australians and, more worryingly, not liked by their political leader. Howard's time in office is particularly remembered as a period of hostility towards the indigenous population. This was fuelled by his decision to ignore the Australian Human Rights Commission's report on 'stolen children'[27] and his refusal to apologise for the stolen generations.[28] His approach was widely criticised, but his policies in this area were not clear cut.[29]

It is difficult to see how his uneasy relationship with the indigenous population relates to his faith, since his childhood church encouraged children to make friends with Aboriginals, as mentioned above, and took a careful approach to child removals.[30] When remembering his childhood, Howard remarked that the plight of indigenous Australians had yet to stir the national consciousness.[31] Perhaps he was unaware of his church's stance? We can infer that his childhood church's efforts made little impression on him in regard to this issue and there is no evidence to suggest his later Anglicanism did either.[32]

A similar approach is apparent elsewhere in his policies, particularly in his approach to human rights. His time in office saw the severe circumscribing of the Office for the Status of Women, the Affirmative Action Agency, the Human Rights and Equal Opportunities Commission, and the Race Discrimination Act.[33] His defensive strategy against groups he deemed excluded from mainstream society contributed to a culture of fear. His approach to minorities, including migrants, seems very distant from the Methodist stereotype of Howard in the public imagination and is hard to reconcile with the actual Methodism of his upbringing. Indeed, Howard's engagement with minorities went beyond migrants. As Marion Maddox acidly put it, his use of an us/mainstream model also excluded same-sex couples, mothers in the paid workforce, single parents, step-parents, stay-at-home fathers, feminists, Aboriginals, many mainstream churches, Muslims, other non-Christians, unions, ABC listeners and the tertiary-educated.[34]

For all that this may have appealed to a certain Christian constituency, it certainly vexed mainstream Christian opinion in Australia. In one study, the sociologist Hans Mol found that Australian churchgoers, while largely conservative, were largely at ease with racial minorities.[35] Howard's rhetoric about and politics concerning minorities may have been couched in his traditionally Christian image, but were hard to trace back to any serious Christian commitment or constituency.

CONCLUSION

The relationship between faith and politics was rather more evident in Howard's public image than it was in many of his policies. Howard was openly hostile to interjections from leaders of mainstream Christian churches. He was not anti-Christian, and maintained a consistent private faith, but he did not welcome church interference in politics, at least in any politics beyond a certain tightly drawn ring of moral issues. His explanation for this was that he saw churches as a partisan influence on moral issues. However, the far more likely reason for his reaction was that they presented him with a substantial threat and had the power to gather support for the opposition. In public life, Howard was clear in his designation of religion and politics as belonging to separate spheres.

With Howard, the image projected was of great importance. His faith was significant in that, indeed part of his rapport with mainstream Australians, and it helped him win elections. However, when it started to stand in the way of policies that might bring further victories he was happy to part ways with mainstream Christianity and even respond with hostility. Public perception mattered to Howard, as it does by definition to all politicians, and his faith was a part of that. Beyond that, his policies and approach to leadership sat quite loosely to his Christian faith.

NOTES

1. David Adams, John Howard: 'Never Great, Always Adequate' in Gwynneth Singleton (ed.), *The Howard Government: Australian Commonwealth Administration 1996–1998* (Sydney: University of NSW Press, 2000), p. 24.

2. John Warhurst, 'Religion and Politics in the Howard Decade', *Australian Journal of Political Science*, vol. 42, no. 1, 2007, 19–32, p. 19.

3. Howard, John, *Lazarus Rising* (Sydney: Harper Collins Publishers: 2013), p. 16.

4. Howard, p. 21.

5. Howard, p. 27.

6. Howard, p. 17.

7. Howard, p. 17.

8. Norman Abjorensen, *John Howard and the Conservative Tradition* (North Melbourne, VIC: Australian Scholarly Publishing, 2008).

9. Warhurst, p. 23.

10. Marion Maddox, *God under Howard: The Rise of the Religious Right in Australian Politics* (Crows Nest, NSW: Allen and Unwin, 2005), p. 39.

11. Quoted in Rob Ward, 'Christianity is the greatest shaper of Australia, says John Howard', *Eternity*, 6 May 2016, https://www.eternitynews.com.au/opinion/christianity-is-the-greatest-shaper-of-australia-says-john-howard (accessed 21 January 2017).

12. Maddox, *God under Howard*, p. 81.

13. Abjorensen, *John Howard and the Conservative Tradition*, p. 73.

14. Marion Maddox, 'God under Gillard: Religion and politics in Australia'; http://www.abc.net.au/religion/articles/2011/11/10/3360973.htm (accessed 24 February 2017).

15. Norman Abjorensen, *John Howard and the Conservative Tradition* (Victoria: Australian Scholarly Publishing Pty Ltd, 2008), p. 170.

16. Maddox, *God under Howard*, p. 2.

17. Ibid., pp. 7–8.

18. Howard, *Lazarus Rising*, p. 3.

19. Abjorensen, *John Howard and the Conservative Tradition*, p. 57.

20. Maddox, *God under Howard*, p. 19.

21. Robert Garran, *True Believer: John Howard, George Bush and the American Alliance* (Crows Nest, NSW: Allen and Unwin, 2004), p. 7.

22. Abjorensen, *John Howard and the Conservative Tradition*, p. 113.

23. Rob Ward, '"Christianity is the greatest shaper of Australia", says John Howard', 6 May 2016, https://www.eternitynews.com.au/opinion/christianity-is-the-greatest-shaper-of-australia-says-john-howard/ (accessed 24 February 2017).

24. Warhurst, p. 26.

25. Warhurst, p. 28.

26. Carol Johnson, 'John Howard's "Values" and Australian Identity', *Australian Journal of Political Science*, 2007, vol. 42. no. 2, 195–209, p. 202.

27. *Bringing Them Home: National Inquiry into the Separation of Aboriginal and Torres Strait Islander Children from Their Families* (Commonwealth of Australia, 1997), available at http://

www.humanrights.gov.au/sites/default/files/content/pdf/social_justice/bringing_them_
home_report.pdf (accessed 21 January 2017).

28. Frank Brennan, 'The history of apologies Down Under', *Thinking Faith*, 21 February 2008,
http://www.thinkingfaith.org/articles/20080221_1.htm (accessed 21 January 2017).

29. For example, his encouragement of private ownership of public housing was supported
by some prominent Aboriginal figures, although criticised by others as an assimilationist
attempt. Johnson, p. 203.

30. Maddox, *God under Howard*, pp. 8, 12.

31. Howard, p. 16.

32. It seems that Howard's policies here were increasingly out of step with the Australian public.
In 2000, cities across Australia demonstrated their support for Aboriginal reconciliation by
joining in with bridge walks, showing widespread resistance to one of the key policy stances
taken by Howard in his time in office.

33. Maddox, *God under Howard*, p. 5.

34. Ibid., p. 78.

35. Ibid., p. 140.

TONY BLAIR (1997–2007)

ANDREW CONNELL

INTRODUCTION

Tony Blair became leader of the British Labour Party in 1994, and served as Prime Minister of the United Kingdom from 1997 to 2007. He won three successive general elections and became the longest-serving Labour Prime Minister in British history. However, for nearly a decade after 2007 his reputation lay very low, tainted by accusations of authoritarianism and of an excessive fondness for neo-liberalism, and by a long and messy war following his decision to join the American invasion of Iraq in 2003. The purpose of this chapter is not to attempt to confirm or reappraise that reputation, but to explore the relationship of Blair's Christian faith to his politics at home and abroad.

In the public mind, Blair was probably more closely associated with Christianity than any Prime Minister since Gladstone. It was easy for cartoonists and satirists to draw on this association: every fortnight for ten years, he was lampooned in the satirical magazine *Private Eye* as the embarrassingly earnest and enthusiastic 'Vicar of St Albion's'. In one way this is strange and perhaps unfair, not only because Blair's faith placed him among the great majority of post-war British Prime Ministers,[1] but because for most of his political career he played down his religious beliefs. He did not hide them but with very few exceptions he did little to draw attention to them.

This was a conscious decision which was, once Blair became leader of the opposition and then Prime Minister, strongly reinforced by the guidance of his press secretary, Alastair Campbell. Campbell firmly believed that British politicians who referred overtly to their personal faith were laying themselves open to wilful misrepresentation, and charges of sanctimony, from their opponents. When, at Easter 1996, Blair gave an extended interview about his faith to the *Sunday Telegraph* newspaper (see below), Campbell was furious: hostile commentators accused Blair of using religion for political ends and of trying to co-opt God for the Labour Party. Blair accepted Campbell's verdict and for many years afterwards very seldom discussed his faith directly in public.[2] As he would say in a speech delivered the year after his resignation, in Britain a politician's admission of his or her faith opened up a range of unhelpful suppositions – that he or she was 'weird' and prone to make decisions on a basis of 'the promptings of an inscrutable deity' rather than reason, was seeking to impose faith on others, was pretending to be better than other people, and was seeking to 'bestow a divine legitimacy' on his or her politics.[3] He did from time to time, as for example in his Millennium Speech in 1999, talk about the value of religion in more general terms,[4] but even these references could be suspect. For example, in 2000 he accepted an invitation to deliver a speech at Tübingen University in the presence of the distinguished Catholic theologian Hans Küng: Campbell recorded in his diary his concern that the speech would be seen as 'eccentric' and noted that 'on the plane [to Germany] we worked on the speech and I was trying to get the religion out and more politics in'.[5] At the beginning of the Iraq War, when Blair wanted to end a television address with the words 'God bless you', he gave way to the protests of his advisors and instead concluded with a simple 'thank you'.[6]

Nonetheless, when in 2003 Campbell famously told a journalist visiting 10 Downing Street that 'we don't do God',[7] he was referring to presentation rather than content. This chapter argues that Blair's politics were situated within a moral framework which was intimately connected to his religion. In his memoirs, written after he left office, Blair would say that 'I have always been more interested in religion than politics'.[8] Even in matters such as the Iraq War, which was opposed by many Christians, including Pope John Paul II and other church leaders, Blair's faith underpinned his whole political mission.

BLAIR'S FAMILY AND EARLY LIFE

Tony Blair was born in Edinburgh in 1953. Soon after his birth the family moved to Adelaide where his father, Leo, a lawyer, took up a university post. In 1959, the Blairs returned to the UK and settled in Durham, where Leo combined lecturing at the university with practice as a barrister from chambers in Newcastle. Blair, like his elder brother, attended a preparatory school with connections to Durham Cathedral, and then boarded at Fettes, the Edinburgh public school. In 1972, he went up to St John's College, Oxford, to read law, and on graduation in 1975 moved to London where he followed his father to the Bar. There he met Cherie Booth, one of the cleverest young lawyers of her generation. They married in 1980 and settled in north London, where they began a family. Booth came from a working-class Liverpool family, as staunch in its Labour politics as it was in its Roman Catholicism. She was a committed member of both party and Church. By the time that he met her, Blair, too, was an active Labour Party member and a convinced Christian, although at that time an Anglican. He would remain, formally, an Anglican until 2007, but for most of his life after his marriage the family would worship together in Roman Catholic churches. While he was Prime Minister there were from time to time speculations that he had secretly converted, but his formal reception into the Church in 2007 showed that these had been unfounded.

Blair appears to have held back from becoming a Roman Catholic until after he had resigned as Prime Minister for reasons of domestic politics. These included the Prime Minister's role in appointing Church of England bishops, which was then less of a formality than it has since become and in which Blair took an active interest,[9] and, perhaps more importantly, the wish not to appear to favour one side above another in the ongoing peace negotiations in Northern Ireland. One might still ask why Blair did not convert in the years between his marriage and his becoming Prime Minister in 1997, or at least leader of the opposition in 1994. The simplest answer may be that as a self-described 'ecumenical Christian' he did not see any particular need to: he was in practice able to participate quite fully in worship alongside his family. But whatever the reason for these later developments, the basic pattern of Blair's religion had, like his politics, crystallised as a result of a wider awakening of social and political consciousness while he was at Oxford.

THE EMERGENCE OF BLAIR'S FAITH

When Tony Blair was growing up, his family were not regular church-goers. The conventional religious practices associated with his schools seem to have meant little to him: as a teenager he was not confirmed, as many of his contemporaries would have been. But although Leo Blair had been a non-believer, Blair's mother, Hazel, to whom he was close, was 'religious though not church-going'.[10] She taught her son, as a child, to pray, and has been credited with laying the foundations not only of his religious faith, but of his social conscience.[11]

It was at Oxford that Blair encountered probably the most important single influence on his spiritual and political development. Peter Thomson, seventeen years Blair's senior, was an Australian Anglican priest who had come to St John's as a mature student. A (small-c) charismatic figure, he soon gathered around him an informal group of students, of whom Blair was one. Much has been written about Thomson's influence on Blair, but Blair, writing after Thomson's death in 2010, simply said, 'He shaped my life, gave it meaning and purpose; and set its course.'[12] Specifically, it was as a member of Thomson's coterie that Blair began to think seriously about ethics, politics and religion, including Christianity. After conversations with Thomson and with his college chaplain, at the end of his second year he was, rather quietly, confirmed into the Church of England in the college chapel. If Hazel Blair had laid a foundation for faith in her son, it was under Thomson's influence that a definite religious commitment came to be formed.

THOMSON, MACMURRAY AND BLAIR'S DOCTRINE OF COMMUNITY

Thomson transmitted to his disciple the strong social element which characterised his own Christianity and, importantly, introduced him to the thought of the Scottish philosopher John Macmurray. Macmurray had been a significant figure in British philosophy earlier in the century, but by the

1970s had become rather unfashionable. He was a Christian, albeit one disillusioned with institutional religion,[13] and the basis of his political philosophy is summed up in the title of his last major work, published in 1961, *Persons in Relation*.

For Macmurray, people could realise their humanity and their human potential only through relationships with others. Put in this way, this is not a particularly distinctive position: it is to be found, for example, in a great deal of early twentieth-century British progressive political thought. In fact, Macmurray's thinking was a good deal more complex than this rather simplistic summary would suggest, and some commentators have argued that Blair did not properly understand it.[14] But what matters in this context[15] is that Blair believed that he had derived from Macmurray a basic message about human interdependence and, thus, the importance of community – a belief that 'people owed obligations to each other and were social beings, not just out for themselves'.[16]

This is not specifically a Christian, or even a religious, position, but for Blair it was inextricably entwined with his Christian faith. He made this clear in one of his most complete public statements of his religious beliefs, an article published in the (Conservative-supporting) *Sunday Telegraph* newspaper on Easter Day, 1996.[17] Blair was still then leader of the opposition, but he knew that a general election would be called within a year and the article has to be seen as part of his positioning himself as a potential Prime Minister. However, the enormous care that he took over this article also indicates the importance he attached to his faith.[18]

In the article, Blair took care to pre-empt any possible charges of sectarianism, either religious or political. He declared himself to be an 'ecumenical Christian' who found many sectarian debates 'baffling', and was similarly careful to deny any suggestion that Christians should necessarily vote Labour. But he himself rejected the self-interested and isolationist tendencies which, he claimed, characterised much of modern Conservatism. Christianity, he argued, was a social faith, bringing the believer into relationship not only with God but, necessarily, with the outside world. The Christian could not, therefore, detach himself or herself from his or her surroundings: Christian faith imposed a duty and a responsibility to act, and unless one accepted the responsibilities as well as the benefits of membership of a community, all would suffer.

This, then, is the doctrine of community which Blair had held since his undergraduate days, presented as an integral part of Christianity. For Blair the connection between individual duty, the greater good and the interests of community was one of the things that the Church celebrated in the Eucharist. It is a doctrine which Blair would apply in domestic politics in the UK, first to critique the then Conservative government and then, after 1997, to underpin his own government's approach, especially in the fields of social policy and criminal justice. It would also, a little later, come to be applied to foreign policy, at first successfully but in the end disastrously.

COMMUNITY AND RESPONSIBILITY IN DOMESTIC POLITICS

In a commentary that appeared alongside Blair's *Sunday Telegraph* article, Matthew d'Ancona, the journalist who had worked closely with Blair on the piece, suggested that Blair was seeking 'to associate a vote for Labour with moral responsibility rather than revolution, ethical decency rather than ideological radicalism ... he is colonising ethical terrain foolishly surrendered by the Conservative Party'.[19] D'Ancona was a Conservative journalist, making his point in a Conservative paper, but the remark pointed to an important truth.

Undoubtedly, Blair, and those around him, believed that Labour had too often been associated, in the minds of many voters, with an attachment to an impersonal and statist model of public services, a weak approach to crime and disorder, and a tendency to see individuals' (mis)behaviour in terms of social and economic factors rather than personal moral responsibility. If Labour were to avoid losing a fifth successive general election, they argued, the party would have to regain the moral trust of the electorate. For Blair, this was not merely a matter of electoral calculation. As d'Ancona wrote, 'In the Christian notions of fellowship, neighbourliness, and duty ... Blair... found an idiom natural to him.'[20]

This idiom suffuses Blair's first major speech as Prime Minister, delivered on a south London council estate in June 1997.[21] In it he set out his stall for the new government, outlining a number of initiatives which were, he argued, necessary both to ensure Britain's prosperity in a changing world and to address the social divisions that had opened up since the Conservatives came to power in 1979. Crucially, they had to be underpinned by a new – or restored – moral order:

> The next decade will be defined by a simple idea: 'we are all in this to- gether'. It will be about how to recreate the bonds of civic society and community in a way compatible with the far more individualistic nature of modern economic, social and cultural life.

The cost of economic and social failure had been paid by all levels of society; a new social bargain could appeal to enlightened self-interest. But the bargain had to have a strong moral dimension which rejected both uncritical liberalism and self-centred libertarianism:

> We should reject the rootless morality whose symptom is a false choice between bleeding hearts and couldn't-care-less, when what we need is one grounded in the core of British values, the sense of fairness and a balance between rights and duties. The basis of this modern civic society is an ethic of mutual responsibility or duty.

Blair went on to set out in some detail what this might mean in practice in fields such as the economy, education, employment, welfare, and law and order. But throughout, he emphasised the centrality of duty, responsibility, and reciprocity:

> To reverse the slide towards a divided nation, we also need to tap a wider ethic of responsibility. The making of one nation is not just a job for gov- ernment. It is a task for everyone, a responsibility that applies as much at the top of society as at the bottom.

There was no explicit mention of Christianity in this speech, but it is safe to say that it was an attempt to work out, in domestic policy, the principles of community which Blair believed he had derived from Macmurray, through Thomson, as an undergraduate.

THE INTERNATIONAL COMMUNITY

Before Blair became Labour leader, he had shown no particular interest in foreign policy. Although he did have an interest in the world outside the UK, originating in part perhaps from the international group of friends that he had made in Thomson's circle, his front-bench jobs had all been in domestic fields.[22] However, once he became Prime Minister, he could not avoid turning his attention to the international stage and in April 1999, in a speech in Chicago,[23] he set out the application of the principle of community beyond the nation-state. The immediate context for the speech was the crisis in Kosovo, and NATO's intervention in defence of the Kosovar Albanians against Serbian attacks. Blair was determined that the example of Rwanda, where genocidal massacres had taken place earlier in the decade in the face of Western and especially American unwillingness to intervene, should not be repeated. Once again, the United States was reluctant to get involved, and Blair's speech was part of a concerted effort to bring the Americans on side.

In the speech Blair set out five criteria which might justify a breach of the principle that sovereign states should not intervene in each other's internal affairs.[24] More broadly, the title of the speech – 'Doctrine of the International Community', a title apparently only decided at a late stage[25] – makes clear the connection between this new doctrine in international affairs and the principles which were, for Blair, so closely related to his Christian faith. Blair argued that in a globalised world, states could not but be interdependent:

> We are all internationalists now, whether we like it or not. We cannot refuse to participate in global markets if we want to prosper. We cannot ignore new political ideas in other countries if we want to innovate. We cannot turn our backs on conflicts and the violation of human rights within other countries if we want still to be secure.

States, like individuals, were intimately and unavoidably connected with each other; the wellbeing of one was dependent on the wellbeing of all. The doctrine of community which applied domestically, therefore, had to be applied internationally as well: 'Just as within domestic politics, the notion of community – the belief that partnership and co-operation are essential to advance self-interest – is coming into its own; so it needs to find its own international echo.'

Perhaps here Blair emphasised self-interest where Macmurray would have emphasised development of one's higher capacity, but the common point is that people, and states, need to exist in community for their own sake as much as for the sake of others. Furthermore, this was more than a doctrine of mere enlightened self-interest. Blair had spoken at the beginning of the speech of the 'unspeakable' and 'evil' events unfolding in Kosovo, and had declared that the intervention there was 'a just war, based not on any territorial ambitions but on values'. Those who had the power to prevent evil had a duty to act to do so – a point hammered home towards the end of the speech when Blair said that 'just as with the parable of the individuals and the talents, so those nations which have the power have the responsibility'.

This was the only explicitly Christian reference in the speech, and one may ask how far we can identify Blair's doctrine of community, national or international, as Christian. As Lance Price, a member of Blair's Downing Street team, pointed out, it was perfectly possible to be horrified by events such as those in Kosovo without being a person of faith. Similarly, a belief in human interdependence does not depend on a faith perspective. An answer may be found in Blair's own discussion, in his memoirs, of the relationship between faith and politics in general. 'The frame within which you see the world', he wrote,

> is different if religion comes first. Religion starts with values that are born of a view of humankind. Politics starts with an examination of society and the best means of changing it ... Of course politics is about values; and religion is often about changing society. But you start from a different place.[26]

The starting point is different but the destination may be the same, and Price would conclude that in the case of Kosovo – and, we might suggest, later in Sierra Leone and in Iraq – a good deal of Blair's moral motivation for action came from his Christian faith.[27] Others close to Blair would agree that his religion underpinned these aspects of his foreign policy. John Burton, his friend and constituency agent, and a fellow committed Christian, said that Blair 'believed that if it was possible to do something about injustice, then you should do it – which is why it's very simple to explain the idea of Blair the Warrior. It was part of Tony living out his faith.'[28]

RESPONSIBILITY AND ACTION

If community was one strand of Blair's politico-religious ethic, then, as Burton's observation and Blair's own reference in Chicago to the parable of the talents remind us, responsibility was the other. For example, we may cite his expression of the principle, again in biblical terms, in his 1995 Labour Party conference speech: 'I am my brother's keeper, I will not walk by on the other side',[29] and his references to duty in his 1996 *Sunday Telegraph* article: 'For a politician, this ... means that you see the need for change around you and you accept your duty to do something. Christian belief means you cannot detach yourself from the world around you.'

This sense of responsibility informed Blair's domestic politics, but it also shaped his foreign policy. Bishop Graham Dow, who had known Blair since he had been college chaplain at St John's when Blair was an undergraduate, saw Blair's decision to join the American attack on Iraq in these terms. In relieving Iraq of a murderous dictator, Blair saw himself, Dow believed, as putting into practice his obligations as his brother's keeper.[30] And responsibility meant not only a responsibility to act, but a responsibility – ultimately to God – for those actions.

This was certainly a responsibility that Blair took seriously. Again, the Iraq War provides an example. The journalist Peter Stothard, who spent a month shadowing Blair at the height of the fighting in March and April 2003, observed the 'momentary blankness' in his eyes as he contemplated his own responsibility for shedding blood. While Blair had said that he was 'ready "to meet my maker" and answer for "those who have died or been horribly maimed as a result of my decisions"', he was also aware that there were many others, including other Christians, who believed that 'the last judgement will be against him'.[31]

This last point, which applies particularly to the Iraq war (the military actions in Kosovo and Sierra Leone were widely, if not universally, seen as successful humanitarian interventions, not least by many of the Kosovars and Sierra Leoneans themselves), draws attention to a curious aspect of Blair's ethic of community and responsibility. On the one hand, it is a social ethic, denying that lives can be lived in isolation; but on the other, it gave rise to demands that were intensely individual in their focus and, certainly in Blair's international policy, could lead to the adoption of a distinctly isolated position. In the case of the Iraq War, it led Blair the Christian to put his faith into action in a way that attracted the opposition of eminent church leaders including Pope John Paul II and the then Archbishop of Canterbury.[32] Clare Short, the international development secretary who opposed the Iraq war but remained in office for a while after it had begun, would ask how a real Christian could ignore the views of the chief leaders of Christianity to pursue a course which was in her judgement based on deception.[33]

BLAIR, ROBINSON CRUSOE AND PONTIUS PILATE

Short's question highlights the ambiguities present in Blair's relationship with religious authority. As we have seen, Blair saw himself as someone without a strong denominational identity, but in practice his Christian life was lived in comparatively hierarchical and structured contexts. This is true, to some extent, of the Anglo-Catholicism that he embraced as a young man, and to a much greater extent of the Roman Catholicism to which he converted in 2007. However, he consistently reserved for himself the right to make up his own mind about things that mattered to him. As a politician, he adopted positions on many issues, especially those relating to aspects of human sexuality and abortion, that were opposed to those of the Roman Catholic hierarchy. In aspects of his own religious observance, he paid little heed to denominational discipline. He certainly received communion in the Roman Catholic Church while still officially an Anglican, although when this was brought to the attention of the then Archbishop of Westminster, Cardinal Basil Hume, the cardinal instructed him to cease doing so.[34] Blair accepted the instruction, albeit reluctantly.

Plainly Blair had an extremely strong trust in his own moral judgement, once his mind was made up. George Carey, Archbishop of Canterbury during the first half of Blair's time in Downing Street, described him as a Robinson Crusoe figure in terms of his faith, alone on an island without other Christians around to nourish him. This may have been a reference to Blair's immediate entourage in Downing Street,[35] but the image encapsulates something which comes through quite strongly in accounts of how Blair sought to put his faith into action. This is a sense that he saw making moral decisions – and it seems that for him very many decisions in public and private life were moral ones – as essentially a matter between himself and God.

This does not mean that he took such decisions lightly: the passage from Stothard cited above suggests that he took them extremely seriously and recognised the possibility that others starting from his position might have decided differently. Rather, it is the sense of an overwhelming personal responsibility before God which could not be evaded or passed onto others; a direct individual responsibility which might be thought to have more in common with old-fashioned evangelicalism than with the sacramental and catholic tradition which Blair inhabited.

From this position, the views of others, whether political advisors or Church authorities, might be heard, but they should never be allowed to prescribe the answers. Again, the Easter 1996 *Sunday Telegraph* article illuminates the point. Seasonably, the article included a reflection on aspects of the Passion story, in which Blair considered the moral ambiguities of some of the key characters involved: in particular of Pilate, whom he described as 'so nearly a good man'. Blair was acutely conscious of the temptation for any politician to do what was expedient rather than what was right; the intriguing thing about Pilate was

the degree to which he tried to do the good thing rather than the bad … It is possible to view Pilate as the archetypal politician, caught on the horns of an age-old political dilemma … the struggle between what is right and what is expedient … Do you apply a utilitarian test or what is absolute?

Pilate's fault, Blair suggested, lay in his choosing to follow the advice of those around him rather than his own conscience. 'One can imagine him', he wrote, 'agonising, seeing that Jesus had done nothing wrong, and wishing to release him. Just as easily … one can imagine Pilate's advisers telling him of the risks, warning him not to cause a riot or inflame Jewish opinion. It is a timeless parable of political life.'[36]

Matthew d'Ancona reflected in 2005 on the significance of Blair's reading of Pilate for his actions in Iraq. It would, he suggested, have been easy and expedient for Blair to have committed the UK to a symbolic token support for the American action against Saddam Hussein. But Blair believed that he was doing a morally right thing in overthrowing Saddam, even if the cost of doing so was high.[37] We may see this approach, too, in some areas of domestic policy. For example, in his memoirs he explained how he had come to believe that conventional, judicially based sanctions had little effect against organised crime and extreme anti-social behaviour. Instead, what was required were 'draconian powers that can be wielded administratively and with instant effect. Hence the anti-social behaviour laws, DNA database, "proceeds of crime" legislation, anti-terror laws and so on.'[38] Claims that those accused of crimes had been denied their rights by these measures had, Blair argued, to be balanced against the 'lives lost or buried by criminality unchecked. They are victims and the criminality could be stopped; but not by conventional means. So choose; but don't delude yourself that this is not a choice.'[39]

This is not quite an assertion that the end justifies the means – an assertion which traditional Christian teaching firmly opposes. But one may ask whether Blair sometimes saw the high cost of a course of action as confirmation that it was the right one; whether, at times, his determination not to follow the easy and expedient course may have affected his judgement of what was right or wrong.

CONCLUSION

It would be wrong to think of Blair's faith as having simply mandated or commanded his actions as Labour leader and Prime Minister. He is said, for example, to have been appalled at George W. Bush's claim in 2005 that God had told him to 'go and end the tyranny in Iraq'.[40] Much of what he did, at home and overseas, might have been done by others who did not necessarily share his faith. One cannot but recall that one of the world's most prominent and uncompromising 'New Atheists' during the decade of Blair's premiership, Christopher Hitchens, was also one of the most vocal supporters of the Iraq invasion.

Moreover, the former defence minister Peter Kilfoyle believed that Blair's decision to go to war in 2003 could be explained not with reference to Blair's faith but entirely in terms of his desire to remain close to the USA. Clare Short believed that Blair's couching of his foreign policy in moral terms was an attempt to move away from the association with spin and focus groups that had characterised his first term to construct the image of a conviction politician.[41] But the evidence from those closer to Blair, and from even such a brief analysis of Blair's earlier speeches and writing as this chapter has been able to present, suggests otherwise.

Blair saw asking moral questions – and by extension seeking to apply his faith – as a way to navigate an uncertain and messy political and strategic landscape. Asking such questions did not, he argued, 'inexorably lead to a [particular] solution, but it establishe[d] a framework which could do so'.[42] Here, as elsewhere in Blair's career, it is possible to imagine other leaders doing similar things for different reasons. But to understand why *he* chose to act in the way that he did, his faith, and the moral framework which he derived from it, is crucial.

NOTES

1. Andrew S. Crines and Kevin Theakston, '"Doing God" in Number 10: British Prime Ministers, Religion, and Political Rhetoric', *Politics and Religion*, vol. 8, no. 1, 2015, p. 156.
2. John Burton and Eileen McCabe, *We Don't Do God: Blair's Religious Belief and Its Consequences* (London: Continuum, 2009), pp. 62–3.
3. Tony Blair, 'Faith and Globalisation', speech delivered at Westminster Cathedral, 3 April 2008, available at http://www.tonyblairoffice.org/speeches/entry/tony-blair-faith-and-globalisation-lecture (accessed 23 January 2017).
4. Burton and McCabe, *We Don't Do God*, p. 94.
5. Alastair Campbell, *The Alastair Campbell Diaries, Vol. 3: Power and Responsibility 1999–2001* (London: Hutchinson, 2011), pp. 355–7.
6. Anthony Seldon, *Blair*, 2nd ed. (London: Free Press, 2005), p. 520.
7. Ibid., p. 518.
8. Tony Blair, *A Journey* (London: Hutchinson, 2010), p. 690.
9. Seldon, *Blair*, p. 524.

10. Ibid., p. 18.

11. Ibid., p. 22.

12. Blair, *A Journey*, pp. 78–9.

13. In 1934 Macmurray described himself as a 'Christian outside the Churches' and in 1959 he became a Quaker. See Vincent Geoghegan, *Socialism and Religion: Roads to Common Wealth* (Abingdon: Routledge, 2011), pp. 16, 187.

14. See for example Geoghegan, *Socialism and Religion*, p. 15; Sarah Hale, 'Professor Macmurray and Mr Blair: The Strange Case of the Communitarian Guru That Never Was', *Political Quarterly*, vol. 73, no. 2, 2002, pp. 191–7.

15. See for example Christian Roudaut, Françoise Daucé, Alexis Delahousse and Emmanuel Saint-Martin, *Ces croyants qui nous gouvernent* (Paris: Payot, 2006), p. 40.

16. Blair, *A Journey*, p. 79.

17. Tony Blair, 'Why I am a Christian', *Sunday Telegraph*, 7 April 1996.

18. Seldon, *Blair*, p. 518.

19. Matthew d'Ancona, 'The Tory faith of Tony Blair', *Sunday Telegraph*, 7 April 1996.

20. Ibid.

21. Tony Blair, 'The Will to Win', speech given at the Aylesbury Estate, London, 2 June 1997, available at https://web.archive.org/web/20070626045507/http://archive.cabinetoffice.gov.uk/seu/newsa52f.html?id=400 (accessed 23 January 2017).

22. Blair had been a member of the shadow Treasury and Trade and Industry teams. He then became successively shadow energy secretary, shadow employment secretary and shadow home secretary. Seldon, *Blair*, pp. 97–107, 149–50.

23. Tony Blair, 'Doctrine of the International Community', speech to the Economic Club of Chicago, 24 April 1999, available at http://webarchive.nationalarchives.gov.uk/+/www.number10.gov.uk/Page1297 (accessed 23 January 2017).

24. These owed much to the input of Professor Lawrence Freedman. See Peter Lee, *Blair's Just War: Iraq and the Illusion of Morality* (Basingstoke: Palgrave Macmillan, 2012), p. 17.

25. Seldon, *Blair*, p. 398.

26. Blair, *A Journey*, p. 79.

27. Roudaut et al., *Ces croyants qui nous gouvernent*, p. 219.

28. Burton and McCabe, *We Don't Do God*, p. 133.

29. Tony Blair, leader's speech, Brighton 1995, available at http://www.britishpoliticalspeech.org/speech-archive.htm?speech=201 (accessed 23 January 2017).

30. Roudaut et al., *Ces croyants qui nous gouvernent*, p. 222.

31. Peter Stothard, *30 Days: A Month at the Heart of Blair's War* (London: HarperCollins, 2003), p. 189.

32. Seldon, *Blair*, pp. 522, 525; Roudaut et al., *Ces croyants qui nous gouvernent*, pp. 221–2.

33. Roudaut et al., *Ces croyants qui nous gouvernent*, p. 223.

34. The details of this are disputed. Anthony Seldon (*Blair*, p. 521), like most other commentators, suggests that Blair was a fairly regular communicant until this point. John Burton, on the other hand, stated that on the many occasions when he had attended Mass with the Blairs, he had never seen Blair take communion. Fr John Caden, the Roman Catholic parish priest in Sedgefield, said that Blair had told him that the incident which gave rise to Hume's rebuke was an isolated one when Blair had, spontaneously, decided to communicate with the rest of his family on the occasion of his daughter's first communion (Burton and McCabe, *We Don't Do God*, pp. 210–11).

35. Seldon, *Blair*, p. 520.

36. Blair, 'Why I am a Christian'.

37. Roudaut et al., *Ces croyants qui nous gouvernent*, p. 221.
38. Blair, *A Journey*, p. 644.
39. Ibid.
40. Burton and McCabe, *We Don't Do God*, p. 147.
41. Roudaut et al., *Ces croyants qui nous gouvernent*, p. 223.
42. Blair, *A Journey*, p. 229.

MARY MCALEESE
(1997–2011)

ELIZABETH OLDFIELD

INTRODUCTION

Mary McAleese was President of Ireland from 1997 to 2011. The Republic of Ireland, at least in previous generations, has been one of the places where openness about religious faith is less of a barrier to high office than elsewhere. Presidents have not all been Catholic, however, and the current incumbent describes himself as 'spiritual but not religious'. Irish Presidents are very much global leaders in the sense of visibility, directly elected by the people. However, while providing the public face of Ireland to the world, the role is largely ceremonial, with executive functions resting instead with the Taoiseach. Despite the less policy-focused nature of the role, McAleese's very public expressions of faith, her mediation between different faith communities and her at times fractious relationship with the Catholic Church make her a valuable addition to this volume.

BIOGRAPHY

Mary McAleese was born Mary Leneghan on 27 June 1951. Her mother, Claire, had been an apprentice hairdresser before marrying her father, Paddy, who worked as a bar manager. Both were Catholics. The family lived for the majority of Mary's childhood in Ardoyne, a working-class and predominantly Catholic and nationalist area of Belfast, though most of the various houses they lived in were in mixed Catholic and Protestant areas. McAleese recalls having friends from both traditions, and regularly encountering Protestants at school debating competitions.

The area was marked by sectarian tensions and the Leneghan family experienced this at close quarters. It was not an unusual occurrence for Catholic homes to be burned; school pupils threw bricks at each other, and Mary's brother John, who was profoundly deaf, was beaten up. On two separate occasions, their own house was attacked, once by a mob smashing windows, and once, while the family were all absent, riddled by machine gun fire.

During one incident, Catholics engaged in a street battle with security forces came into the house looking for bottles that they could throw 'to defend themselves'. Mary went to take bottles to them, but Paddy Leneghan stopped her, saying, 'I didn't rear a rabble.' Despite the violent backdrop to her childhood, McAleese says her parents' faith and example meant the Leneghan children 'all become peacemakers, very staunch peacemakers, every one of us'.[1]

Mary studied law at Queen's University Belfast, and was called to the Northern Irish Bar in 1974. She did not practise for long, moving on to a successful academic legal career that began with her appointment in 1975 to the Reid Professorship at Trinity College Dublin, which had previously been held by Mary Robinson. In 1976, she married Martin McAleese, an accountant and later dentist. Between 1979 and 1981, she was a television reporter for RTÉ, Ireland's national public service broadcaster, interrupting her tenure at Trinity. McAleese worked for RTÉ part-time for four further years following a return to the Reid Professorship, juggling her academic and media roles.

In 1987, McAleese made her first foray into party politics, standing as the Fianna Fáil candidate in the Dublin South-East constituency. She was heavily defeated, saying at the time, 'I'm done with politics … I was talked into it.'[2] Shortly afterwards, the couple returned to Belfast for Mary to take up a post at her alma mater, Queen's University. She was made the first female pro-vice-chancellor of Queen's in 1994.

During this period McAleese became heavily involved with the Northern Ireland peace process through the Redemptorist Peace Ministry, based at Clonard Monastery in Belfast. She took part in secret meetings with other key players, who 'while not directly involved in the dialogue taking place between John Hume and Gerry Adams ... were briefed regularly so they could help garner further support'.[3] Father Alex Reid, a primary facilitator of the talks, said McAleese was 'central to the efforts of the Redemptorist Peace Ministry in taking the gun out of politics ... her endorsement, support and enthusiasm for the Hume–Adams dialogue ... meant that those who had opposed it began to agree with it as the way forward.'[4]

McAleese's involvement with the process continued until the presidential election campaign began in 1997. On her election she was the first person from Northern Ireland to be made President of Ireland, and the second woman, following Mary Robinson. In 2004, she was re-elected for a second term.[5]

PERSONAL FAITH

What is missing from the short biography above is the centrality of McAleese's devout Catholicism, perhaps the defining fact of her life. She was born into a Catholic family and baptised a Catholic in the pre-Vatican II era, which, she says, means she lived 'in a Catholic cocoon'.[6] She was educated by nuns in both primary and secondary school, and one of the houses she grew up in backed onto a monastery. The children had a key to the gardens, and the young Mary went to Mass every day and used to creep in to sit in the silent church at other times. She says she 'still loves quiet contemplative spaces, choral music and Latin Mass',[7] continues to pray and meditate daily and has sought to bring her children up in the faith.[8]

Perhaps the biggest influence on McAleese, outside personal connections, was Daniel O'Connell, the early Irish nationalist leader often known as the Liberator. He was a lawyer who campaigned for Catholic emancipation and sat as an MP in Westminster. McAleese describes him as the 'first great civil libertarian and democrat', and he was a committed Christian. McAleese says her belief in the 'power of persuasion and prayer to change the human heart' is inspired directly by O'Connell. Indeed, her and her husband's devotion was such that their honeymoon was spent on a pilgrimage to O'Connell's house to dedicate their lives to these values. The timing was important. Two close friends died in a terrorist attack on the day of the wedding and the decision to reject anger, violence and bitterness was aided by O'Connell's legacy.

The context for the reception of strong religious views from public figures in Ireland is a complex one. Although 84 per cent of people described themselves as Catholic in the 2011 census, only a small drop from the previous census, this disguises a wider hostility towards the Church, seen particularly since the sex abuse scandals that have emerged over the last two decades. A poll conducted in 2011 showed 47 per cent of adults had unfavourable attitudes to the Church, compared to 24 per cent favourable (the rest were neither).[9] While more than 80 per cent of the population attended weekly Mass in the 1980s, the figure is now about one in three.

This perhaps helps explain why McAleese has experienced criticism for her Catholicism, even in such a seemingly religious country. At various points she has expressed traditional views on subjects such as abortion and contraception, most notably publicly supporting the 1983 pro-life constitutional amendment. Although she has not expressed a position on abortion in a long time, and in 2016 publicly criticised the ban on contraception,[10] during the election campaign she was certainly perceived as, and criticised for being, conservative on these subjects.

Her time at RTÉ was also not a peaceful one, especially around religious and political issues. She drew criticism for taking part in the Catholic bishops' delegation to the New Ireland Forum in 1984. This was convened by the then government to explore ways of bringing the two parts of Ireland closer together. After repeatedly coming to blows with management, she left after being suspended by the National Union of Journalists for apparently holding two jobs at once. McAleese herself characterised this suspension as a symptom of the 'anti-Catholic' and anti-nationalist prejudice she observed at the station, this being many years before the level of trust in the Church had fallen to the level it is now. Whether or not that was the reason for her suspension, McAleese has certainly been repeatedly perceived by some as 'an extreme nationalist, an extreme Catholic ... spouting traditional Catholic nonsense', particularly around the 1986 divorce referendum, which she opposed.[11]

CONFLICTS WITH THE CHURCH

Criticism of her faith has not simply been from the secular side, however.

Many have seen her religious perspective as a paradox, at once committed and devout, but also critical and unorthodox.

Even before the period at RTÉ, McAleese would not fit neatly into an ideological box. She had been centrally involved in the Campaign for Homosexual Law Reform from the mid-1970s, publicly advocating gay marriage forty years ahead of the referendum that legalised it. She was a key voice in favour in that 2015 campaign, causing some to raise eyebrows at the constitutional appropriateness of a President who had stepped down only four years earlier being quite so outspoken. Whatever the political ramifications, her consistent support of gay rights and same-sex marriage flew in the face of traditional Church teaching. She baldly said 'I believe my church is egregiously wrong' on the issue.[12] On women priests she has been equally outspoken, happily writing in the British Catholic publication *The Tablet* and elsewhere against the 'sexist cant' of the Church's teaching on women.

This refusal to accept some fairly central Church teaching has led to an uncomfortable, sometimes painful relationship with her Church. She has come close to leaving repeatedly. Pope John Paul II's position on women caused a real discomfort – she calls it 'cod-ology dressed up as theology'.[13] At that stage, baulking at the idea of instructing her young children in what the Church taught on women, McAleese wondered whether she was out of communion with the church, as communion requires 'submission to the magisterium'. She wrote to the Pope outlining her worries on this and the fact that she couldn't in good faith pass on the position. She got a response from his office saying 'essentially, don't worry, it was okay to disagree'.[14] She needed to accept that this was the Church's position but she didn't have to agree with it. Since then she has been happy that 'conscientious dissent is perfectly acceptable'.[15]

She is not sure that this has always been fully understood about Catholic teaching by the wider world, or indeed by Catholics themselves: 'In actual fact *Dignitatis Humanae* [the Second Vatican Council's Declaration on Religious Freedom] is very big on freedom of conscience, speech and dissent; it's a shame that this plank of Catholic thought is often overlooked.'[16]

Summing up her turbulent journey with the Church, she quotes the eighth-century Irish poem *Donal Oge*, which ends:

> You have taken the east from me; you have taken the west from me,
>   You have taken what is before me and what is behind me;
>   You have taken the moon, you have taken the sun from me,
>   And my fear is great that you have taken God from me!

The Church didn't 'take God' from her but she clearly thinks it has come close. She has, she says, been close to 'despair', and has had a 'deep sense of betrayal'.[17] However, she remains a communicant, and her post-presidential career has been notable for Catholic involvement – she is undertaking a PhD in canon law in Rome and has recently completed a six-month stint at St Mary's University, Twickenham, a Catholic university to the west of London. She says she has stayed within the Church 'because of people around who truly lived the faith'.[18] In 2015, she gave an interview to the *Irish Catholic* newspaper in which she restated her commitment:

> The Catholic Church is woven into me and I relate to it and, for all its messiness, it calls me home … I see myself as a member of the Church trying my best to be a member of that Church, trying to live the faith that I inherited and grew up with and have decided to remain with.[19]

FAITH AND POLITICS

Untangling how Mary McAleese's faith impacted her political outlook is easier than for several other leaders in this volume. Unusually among global political leaders, she is very frank about how strongly her faith has informed her public life. She says she 'wasn't going to make it difficult for myself by pretending I'm not a Christian'. As President, she regularly and publicly praised the work of missionaries in the developing world, and in fact saw the presidency as more about faith than politics. She describes herself as 'not a particularly political person, or at least not party political'. She had been briefly a member of the SDLP as well as Fianna Fáil, but 'is no better at being bound by the "party magisterium"' than she is by the church's.[20]

Rather, she says, the presidency 'gave my faith the greatest chance of my life'. She calls the presidency a 'pastoral role', a statement and intent that is rather less alarming than it might sound elsewhere due to the constitutional particularities of the Irish presidency. The fact that the role doesn't require or permit the development of policies allowed McAleese to hold her faith more straightforwardly and publicly than some other global leaders. There was no need for her expressions of faith as President to come into conflict with government policy, because she was speaking in the main in very general terms.

Instead, Christianity was the inspiration driving the theme of her presidency. In her inauguration speech she said, 'Presidents, under the Irish Constitution, don't have policies. But ... a President can have a theme. The theme of my presidency ... is "Building Bridges".'[21] 'Building Bridges' was not just a nice phrase. For McAleese, it was the 'gospel in action', a fourteen-year experiment in what it really looks like to follow the commandment to 'love one another'.[22] A child who had grown up among the worst of sectarian violence, she came to the presidency with the desire to paint a picture of what Ireland was and could be: 'At our core we are a sharing people. Selfishness has never been our creed. Commitment to the welfare of each other has fired generations of voluntary organisations ... it has made us a country of refuge for the hurt and disposed of other troubled places.'[23]

Interestingly, she called for better understanding across difference, an end to tribalism, and healing of sectarian hurts using explicitly Christian language:

> I know the distrusts go deep and the challenge is awesome. Across this island ... there are people of such greatness of heart that I know, with their help, it can be done. I invite them to work in partnership with me to dedicate ourselves to the gift of the Child of Bethlehem, whose 2,000th birthday we will soon celebrate – the gift of an island where difference is celebrated with joyful curiosity and generous respect.[24]

She closed her inauguration speech by asking 'those of faith, whatever that faith may be, to pray for me'.[25]

Within weeks, the new President had demonstrated how seriously she took this mission of building bridges by taking communion at the (Protestant) Christ Church Cathedral, Dublin. Seamus Heaney wrote of this event that 'it wasn't politics but theology that provided a test of strength for one of the earliest arches of the President's bridge'.[26] This essentially theological issue provoked a very strong public reaction, which provides a clue to how closely religion and politics are sometimes bound together in Ireland.

Not just attending, but taking communion in a Protestant church was a very public statement for Protestants, many of whom were suspicious of this nationalist, Catholic leader. With one action McAleese shattered the expectations that her agenda was nothing more than platitudes. Drew Nelson, now grand secretary of the Grand Orange Lodge of Ireland, called it 'a public act of solidarity.'[27]

However, alongside positive and supportive reactions from Protestants, it drew sharp and public criticism from several leaders in the Catholic Church, including the then Archbishop of Dublin, Desmond Connell, who called it 'a sham' and the taking of communion by Catholics in Protestant churches 'a deception'.[28] The action reinforced for many her reputation for being 'arrogant and independent where Church authority was concerned'.[29]

The Archbishop's comments were taken by some in the media and consequently many Protestants to imply that Protestant communion itself was a sham, although it's clear in context he meant that McAleese's action indicated that full communion with the Church of Ireland existed when it did not. The resulting furore caused further senior figures to intervene. The US ambassador to Ireland, who was from one of America's leading Catholic families at the time, felt prompted to repeatedly take communion at Christ Church Cathedral, presumably as a show of solidarity with Protestants. Archbishop Connell later apologised, blaming the editing of his remarks for the offence caused.

BRIDGING DIVERSITY

Once settled into the role, the President set about an energetic project of bringing diverse groups together. Her explicit intentions were to reach out to people estranged in all directions and to focus on fleshing out the language of reconciliation, repeatedly speaking about and demonstrating consensus, forgiveness, generosity and communal hospitality. She wanted to construct 'new relationships built on mutual respect and understanding'.[30]

McAleese used the President's residence, Áras an Uachtaráin, as a base for hospitality to a wide range of groups and communities, including those perceived by some to be on the margins of Irish society. Northern loyalist communities, usually working class and committed to the most hard-line form of nationalism, had traditionally been beyond the reach of cross-community and ecumenical efforts. The President both visited them in their schools and community buildings, and invited them into her home. One visitor recalls buses full of loyalists and republicans being escorted to Áras an Uachtaráin by blue-lit police outriders: 'It was the first time that republicans and loyalists were together that the sirens sounded and no one ran'.[31]

Those of a secularist bent might have worried about a President so open about her faith, calling her political role 'the gospel in action'. McAleese is clear that by speaking of her faith motivation for the Presidency, she didn't mean that it was about evangelism or proselytising. In fact, she says, she is nervous of Christian public engagement that is 'driven by the desire to convert'. For her human dignity demands 'you accept people for what they are'.[32]

There were, of course, missteps. The most obvious controversy was her comparison in 2005 of the treatment of northern Catholics by Protestants to that of the Jews under Nazi Germany. She apologised swiftly and in heartfelt fashion, saying, 'I did not intend to inflict on one side of the community the entire burden of responsibility, or blame ... it is shared blame. Sectarianism is a shared problem'.[33]

CONCLUSION

Despite these occasional missteps, the supposed hard-line nationalist northern Catholic, who was expected by some to be a divisive force, is now admired by many for her 'unsentimental devotion to peace'.[34] She would describe this as coming directly from her faith tradition. The non-executive role of the presidency allowed her to remain above the fray of party politics and the policy coalface, and thus to build a new set of relationships across difference. Ultimately, Mary McAleese managed to win over many of those who disagreed with her, whether secular liberals or hard-line Protestant loyalists, all the while speaking openly about 'my faith in Christ' and crediting that for 'the sense that every single person is a child of God, it is that which infuses me, gives me the outlook I have on the world'.[35]

NOTES

1. Patsy McGarry, *First Citizen: Mary McAleese and the Irish Presidency* (Dublin: O'Brien Press, 2008), p. 68.

2. Justine McCarthy, *Mary McAleese: The Outsider* (Dublin: Blackwater Press, 1999), p. 86.

3. McGarry, *First Citizen*, p. 132.

4. Quoted ibid, p. 142.

5. In order to stand for President of Ireland, candidates must be a citizen of Ireland. A series of laws, most notably the Irish Nationality and Citizenship Act of 1956, grants citizenship to those born in Northern Ireland under identical conditions as to those born in the Republic of Ireland. This has been controversial at points, as international law sees it as an attempt to extend citizenship beyond the state's jurisdiction. The 1998 Good Friday Agreement continues to recognise that 'Irish citizenship is the birthright of those born in Northern Ireland' (the spirit behind the 1956 Act), but it makes clear that individual acceptance is voluntary. In practice the 1956 Act continues to extend citizenship automatically.

6. Mary McAleese, interview with Elizabeth Oldfield, 8 June 2016, St Mary's University, Twickenham.

7. Ibid.

8. McGarry, *First Citizen*, pp. 127–8.

9. *Attitudes towards the Catholic Church: An Amárach Report for the Iona Institute*, October 2011, available at http://www.ionainstitute.ie/wp-content/uploads/2014/11/Attitudes-to-Church-poll.pdf (accessed 23 January 2017).

10. In September 2016 she signed the 'Wijngaards statement'; see Patsy McGarry, 'Mary McAleese challenges Catholic ban on contraception', *Irish Times*, 19 September 2016, http://www.irishtimes.com/news/social-affairs/religion-and-beliefs/mary-mcaleese-challenges-catholic-ban-on-contraception-1.2796130 (accessed 23 January 2017).

11. McGarry, *First Citizen*, p. 183, quoting Eoghan Harris, a journalist at RTÉ at the time.

12. Mary McAleese, interview with Elizabeth Oldfield, 8 June 2016, St Mary's University, Twickenham.

13. Ibid.

14. Ibid.

15. Ibid.

16. Ibid.

17. Ibid.

18. Ibid.

19. Martin O'Brien and Greg Daly, 'Opposition to the Church is not reflective of my faith – McAleese', *Irish Catholic*, 12 November 2015, http://www.irishcatholic.ie/article/opposition-church-not-reflective-my-faith-%E2%80%93-mcaleese (accessed 23 January 2017).

20. Mary McAleese, interview with Elizabeth Oldfield, 8 June 2016, St Mary's University, Twickenham.

21. Mary McAleese, inauguration speech, Dublin Castle, 11 November 1997, reprinted in *Building Bridges: Selected Speeches and Statements* (Dublin: History Press, 2011).

22. Mary McAleese, interview with Elizabeth Oldfield, 8 June 2016, St Mary's University, Twickenham.

23. McAleese, inauguration speech, Dublin Castle, 11 November 1997.

24. Ibid.

25. Ibid.

26. Seamus Heaney, 'Foreword', in Mary McAleese, *Building Bridges: Selected Speeches and Statements* (Dublin: History Press, 2011), p. 12.

27. McGarry, *First Citizen*, p. 226.
28. Ibid., pp. 200–201.
29. Ibid., p. 198.
30. Mary McAleese, interview with Elizabeth Oldfield, 8 June 2016, St Mary's University, Twickenham.
31. McGarry, *First Citizen*, p. 25.
32. Mary McAleese, interview with Elizabeth Oldfield, 8 June 2016, St Mary's University, Twickenham.
33. McGarry, *First Citizen*, p. 259.
34. Heaney, 'Foreword', p. 13.
35. Martin O'Brien, 'There's something about Mary…', *Irish Catholic*, 12 November 2015, http://irishcatholic.ie/article/there%E2%80%99s-something-about-mary (accessed 23 January 2017).

VIKTOR ORBÁN
(1998–2002, 2010–)

JOSEPH EWING

INTRODUCTION

Public audiences outside of Hungary are, on the whole, not well acquainted with Viktor Orbán, three-time and current Prime Minister. What little is known of him tends to revolve around his noticeable attempts to centralise power in Hungary and his loud opposition to the ideology of the European Union. Even less widely acknowledged are Orbán's invocations of faith. Orbán has frequently cited Christianity in declaration of some of his central policy positions, making it an integral part of his political platform. In and of itself this is not unique to Hungary. However, the way that Orbán invokes Christianity bears analysis. Orbán's references to 'Christian Hungary' and 'Christian Europe' play into a national narrative that has resonated in Hungary for many (perhaps hundreds of) years: one in which the Hungarian and European communities are under threat, and in which religion 'could suggest the salvation of both'.[1]

WHO IS VIKTOR ORBÁN?

Orbán was born in 1963 in Alcsútdoboz, a small village in a then Soviet-controlled Hungary. The first twenty-six years of his life were lived under communist rule, during which he studied as a lawyer in Budapest, including a brief visit to Oxford University to study political philosophy. Orbán briefly played professional football, and has continued to express his love of football through government funding of the game.[2]

In 1988, a then relatively unknown, aspiring politician and recent co-founder of the Alliance of Young Democrats (or Fidesz), Orbán shot to political fame. That year, a memorial service was held for previously unhonoured martyrs of the 1956 Hungarian Uprising – a temporarily successful but ultimately short-lived and blood-stained attempt to resist communist rule. At this service, while communism still reigned in Hungary (albeit waning), the young Orbán gave a speech calling for an end to the communist government and the withdrawal of Soviet troops. The speech was a well-received surprise,[3] and his demands became a reality (owing to a variety of factors, of course, rather than just his speech) just months later.

Since then, Orbán has been an ever-present player in Hungarian politics. He won his first parliamentary seat in 1990, regained it in 1994 and then, in 1998, ten years after his impassioned political debut, he became the 'youngest democratic Prime Minister in Hungarian history'.[4] Since post-communist elections began, the Fidesz party have won power three times – in 1998, 2010 and 2014 – each time as the big brother in a centre-right coalition (partnering with the Christian Democrat People's Party in 2010 and 2014), and each time with Orbán at the helm. All the while, Orbán has developed for himself a reputation for strength and ruthlessness.[5] According to most of what has been written or said about Orbán's personal character, he is at the least determined and competitive, and at the most aggressive and power hungry.[6]

WHAT DOES ORBÁN BELIEVE?

Orbán did not have a religious upbringing, and when he entered politics he did so without religious affiliation. Indeed, at the start of his political career, not only did Orbán not hold religious beliefs himself, but he was openly derisive of politicians from the Christian Democratic People's Party (KDNP) – now his coalition partners.[7] Some time in 1993 or 1994, however, Orbán is purported to have been brought to the Christian faith by his wife, and now identifies himself as a committed Protestant believer. Little more than this is known of the private dimension of Orbán's faith; rather it is to his public persona that we are largely confined, for understanding and interpreting his engagement with Christianity. That is, we must ask what faith (if any) he reveals through his politics.

Orbán 'does God' by doing Christian nationalism. His politics is fundamentally nationalistic, focusing on the promotion and protection of Hungary's national identity and interests. Crucially, a part of the national identity he espouses on Hungary's behalf is Christianity. The first step to understanding this, and its significance, is to note how Orbán defines Christianity, and to what ends he invokes it.

HOW ORBÁN DEFINES CHRISTIANITY

From Orbán's own words on the subject, it is clear that by 'Christianity' he has in mind, first and foremost, the concept of Christian *culture* (both general and ambiguous at first sight) as opposed to religious Christianity. 'Christianity is not only a religion, but is also a culture on which we have built a whole civilisation. This is not a choice, but a fact.'[8] When Orbán refers to Christianity he does so primarily in support of a particular socio-political position, namely a politically right-wing and socially conservative vision of society. At one level, he references Christianity in advocacy of conservative stances on social issues, such as on the family: 'There are many of us in Europe that adhere to the Christian concept of the family. We are not saying that other forms of co-habitation are not possible; however, we have to say that in Christian Europe the family is the union between a man and a woman.'[9]

On their own, such exhortations – of views held historically by most sincerely religious Christians – do not reveal the extent to which Orbán's view of Christianity tends towards the cultural and political, rather than the religious. In other instances, however, Orbán's characterisation of Christianity in primarily political – rather than religious – terms is more readily visible. In expressing concerns about immigration from the Middle East (a theme to which we will return), Orbán made the following bald association between Christianity and a right-of-centre politics:

> According to available surveys, the large majority of immigrants will be left-wing voters. This factor upsets the entire system of European party-politics that developed from Christian foundations ... We must clearly

understand that the person who has come from Islam will not vote for a Christian-based party – we wouldn't do this either in the opposite case – but will gravitate toward the left wing, because there it will at least not be necessary to come to terms with the Christian foundations.[10]

This characterisation of right-wing politics as the natural derivative of 'Christian foundations', and of left-wing politics as at odds with the idea of 'a Christian-based party', is a marker for what Orbán means when he says 'Christianity'. Even taking into account the evidence (scant as it is) of Orbán's own personal religiosity, we have good reason to think that when he mentions 'Christianity' in his political discourse, he is invoking a particular view of society (socially conservative, politically right wing) more than a particular religious way of life. Christian Democratic parties across Europe have traditionally occupied the right or centre-right of the political spectrum, and it is the vision of society that traditionally accompanies this political position to which Orbán seems to be referring when he talks of 'Christian Hungary'.

There is, however, another layer of significance to 'Christianity' in Hungarian political discourse, beyond its association with a particular socio-political positioning. This can be seen by considering the ends to which Orbán invokes Christianity in his politics.

HOW ORBÁN USES CHRISTIANITY

Orbán invokes 'cultural Christianity' in two major contexts: in opposition to the European Union and in opposition to (non-Christian) immigrants from the Middle East. In both cases he casts Hungary, and indeed Europe, as Christian, and then portrays this identity as under threat:[11] from the EU, depicted as a transnational monster of liberalism and multiculturalism, undermining national identities and forsaking Europe's proud Christian (right-wing, conservative) heritage; and from Middle Eastern immigrants, portrayed as untrustworthy, non-Christian diluters of Hungary's and Europe's Christian way of life. Orbán declares on the one hand that 'there is no road back from multicultural Europe to either Christian Europe or to the world of national cultures'[12] and on the other that Hungarians 'do not want to see

among us significant minorities that possess different cultural characteristics
and backgrounds than us. We would like to preserve Hungary as Hungary.'[13]

In an interview with the German newspaper *Die Welt*, Orbán told the
paper it was '"simple mathematics" that Muslims will overtake Christians as
they place greater emphasis on "family, children [and] community cohesion",
things that Christians no longer seem to value'.[14] This is one of the clearest
examples of the narrative Orbán is painting: of Christian Hungary under
threat, and of himself and his government as defenders of the threatened
Christian way of life.

It is noteworthy that such rhetoric is not (or at least not always) echoed by
the Hungarian churches themselves. The General Convent of the Hungarian
Reformed Church, for example, claimed in a statement on the European
migration crisis that 'we are convinced that the European Union is not only
an association of economic interests, but a manifestation of spiritual, political and moral values, which are rooted in the Judeo-Christian culture'.
Accordingly, the statement went on:

> We ask the European Union and the responsible decision-makers to deter-
> mine immigration and refugee policies beside the aspects of solidarity and
> active love, based solely on these European values rather than economic
> expediency or fear and prejudice. Our conviction is that if we fail to do
> this, immigrants will not respect our values either.[15]

Even those churches that sound more sympathetic towards Orbán's often aggressive stance do so in less aggressive tones. Thus, the Hungarian Reformed
Church diocese of Csongrád County, which borders Serbia, formally stated
in 2015 that 'We are thankful to God that our country has a government now
which regards the protection of our country and people as a task given by
God ... while it promotes and practices brotherly love toward those arriving
in our homeland'.[16]

Church opinions notwithstanding, Orbán's sustained anti-EU and an-
ti-immigrant rhetoric, whose centre of gravity is a defence of the Christian
way of life of Hungary (and Europe), has resonated deeply with the voting
population, winning an Orbán-led coalition over two thirds of parliamentary

seats (a 'supermajority') in the last two general elections.[17] There is more than sympathy with centre-right politics lying behind the resonance of Christian nationalism in Hungary.

To understand what this is, we must step back and take note of the context into which Orbán is speaking, the context of religion in Hungary. In particular, we must look backwards to a narrative of religious nationalism that has both a recent and a long history in Hungary, which sets the scene for Orbán's words.

A NATIONAL NARRATIVE: THREAT TO NATION, AND RELIGION AS SAVIOUR

For most of the first half of the twentieth century the vast majority of Hungarians identified as religious, the Roman Catholic Church and the Reformed (Calvinist) Church between them accounting for approximately 85 per cent of the population.[18] During communism, church attendance and membership waned (or rather, was suffocated),[19] but from 1981 restrictions on religious freedom were relaxed, and eventually communism fell altogether, leading to a 'religious revival'[20] in Hungary, with increases in reported church attendance, prayer, beliefs about God and other religious beliefs, and 'a steady increase in religiosity from 1978 [to 1993]'.[21] More recently, religious identification in Hungary has dropped, and, according to a 2012 Eurobarometer poll, 58 per cent of Hungarians identify as Catholic, and only 7 per cent as Protestant and 6 per cent as 'other Christian' (with 21 per cent as agnostic but only 1 per cent as atheist).[22]

Fear over the security of Hungary's national identity is deep seated. Two connected historical examples bring this out: a long-standing insecurity about ethnic, cultural and religious invasion, with a subsequent need for resistance, reaching back to the 14th–17th-century conflict with the Ottoman Empire; and fears during the inter-war period (1918–39) of a pan-European 'Judeo-Bolshevism' that threatened to undermine the integrity of nation states, as well as to capitalise on the demise of Hungary after its devastation post-war and after the Treaty of Versailles.[23]

Pertinently, in both cases, both the nature of the threat and the resistance to it were defined in relation to Christianity. It was the Christian identity of

Hungary and Europe that the Ottomans and later the Soviet government threatened, and it was Christianity that offered the rallying point of national self-identification. In the first instance, resistance against the Ottoman empire was and is understood and spoken of in religious terms, as a definitive contest between Christianity and – for the Magyars (ethnic Hungarians) – an invading Islam. As Orbán has put it, 'I have to say that when it comes to living together with Muslim communities, we are the only ones who have experience because we had the possibility to go through that experience for 150 years.'[24]

The combination of religion and nationalism put down roots during the Ottoman conflict. Later, in the inter-war period, when fears of threat to national survival led many to seek answers as to what it was to be (and remain) Hungarian, explicit connections began to be made between Christianity, national identity and national survival.[25] The search led many thinkers to reflect on the Catholic Church's historical role in resisting the former Ottoman oppression, and so inspired them to rally around Hungarian Christianity as the means of national survival.[26] This resulted in the crystallisation of the concept of 'Christian Hungary'. One author summarises the connection between inter-war period and the legacy of the Ottoman conflict succinctly:

> The campaign waged by the [Catholic] church and the Habsburg state in the seventeenth century to defend Hungary from the Muslim Turks took on a new and suggestive power in a society struggling to make sense of revolution and national collapse. This historic mission to serve as a bulwark of Western Christendom against the advances of the infidel inspired Hungary's political elite in their counter-revolutionary zeal. Where once Hungary had battled against the Turks, it would now stand against the new enemies of Christian Europe – the Bolsheviks.[27]

It is quite possible that a similar process is taking place in modern times in Hungary; that the identity of the national enemy is shifting, not this time from the Ottomans to the Bolsheviks, but from the Bolsheviks to immigrants from the Middle East and the EU. Before we turn in full to this possibility, it is worth noting the extraordinary appeal of the concept of

Christian Hungary. The idea of Christian Hungary as a rallying point of identification against the perceived threat to national identity found its roots strongly in the church in the inter-war period,[28] and it was powerful enough to provide common ground for Catholics, Protestants and even secular nationalists, who 'all called themselves Christian nationalists in these years'.[29]

REPEATING THE NATIONAL NARRATIVE

That Orbán is 'combining national identity with religion'[30] is clear to see. More than this, however, his particular brand of Christian nationalism echoes the historic Hungarian national narrative of threat to national identity (perceived or actual), and emphasis on the concept of 'Christian Hungary' as a means of avoiding national degradation. His rhetoric, channelled as it is towards a (supposedly) encroaching EU and (supposedly) invading immigrants, makes direct parallels between Hungary's current political situation and historical revolutionary milestones: 'True to our oath, in 1848 we did not let Vienna dictate to us, just as we did not let Moscow dictate to us in either 1956 or 1990. And we will not let anybody dictate to us now either, from Brussels or anywhere else.'[31]

Coupling this revolutionary fervour with the aforementioned references to the Christian identity of Hungary and even Europe, Orbán offers Christianity as a means of national identification, in a time when the nation's identity is, he perceives, under threat. It is essentially a contemporary iteration of the long-standing, powerful national narrative born under the oppression of the Ottoman empire and cultivated in the shameful aftermath of defeat in World War I. In Orbán's narrative, 'post-[communist] national regeneration [is] part of a broader transnational struggle to reassert Christian values against a powerful pan-European foe described as [social liberalism, embodied in the EU, and multiculturalism, embodied by refugees]'.[32] Applying the words of one historian to modern-day Hungary, 'in a time of political instability and revolutionary fear, religion helps to define the threat to both nation and European civilization. In turn, it could suggest the salvation of both.'[33]

PROSELYTISM OR PRAGMATISM?

The way in which Christianity figures in Orbán's politics – providing a focal point for a national (and international) identity under threat – is a distinct question from whether Orbán's use of Christian nationalism is personally sincere or politically cynical. Orbán's Christian nationalism may be merely political; it may be religious. What little we know of his personal faith leaves us lacking a definitive answer.

One possibility is that Orbán is genuinely concerned about a conglomeration of national and international factors, which seem together to pose a threat to Hungary as he and others know it: the apparent failure (at least partial) of the great promised Western liberalism to revive Hungary and other neighbouring eastern and central European countries post-communism;[34] genuine concerns about the handling of the refugee crisis (concerns which are held far beyond Hungary, even by the key proponents of accepting and resettling refugees[35]); sincere anxieties about the effect on known culture of mass migration of people with different viewpoints;[36] the apparent failure of free market economics after the 2008 crash;[37] and widely held concerns about the direction and future of the European Union, and of nation states within it (Brexit being the most recent evidence that Orbán is not alone in criticising the EU). Orbán's Christian nationalist invocations may well be a sincere response to a very real feeling of political, cultural and even religious insecurity.

The alternative possibility is that Orbán is first and foremost a pragmatist, and that his use of Christianity is a matter of convenience more than of conscience. There is certainly evidence of ideological pragmatism throughout Orbán's political career. In 1994, in response to his party's failure to gain a significant number of parliamentary seats, Orbán directed an ideological shift away from the centre-left of the political spectrum (where Fidesz had sought to offer a credible left-wing alternative to communism) towards the centre-right (to a platform of conservative Christian nationalism). A shift in a party's ideological position is not unthinkable (take the UK's Labour Party in 1997), but for many this dramatic left-to-right swing was a sign of Orbán's willingness to prioritise holding political power over maintaining a particular principled ideology. More recent shifts by Fidesz further towards the right, in order to block the only real challenging party, the extreme-right Jobbik – in particular, adopting hard-line immigration policies – further suggest the prominence of pragmatism over principle in Orbán's politics.[38] And this is not even to mention a persistent centralisation of power by Orbán's government – including a legal, but controversial, rewriting of the constitution – which exudes cynicism.[39]

If Orbán is as politically ambitious and ideologically flexible as these examples suggest, his use of Christianity in politics may fall under the same umbrella. Certainly, his transition from heckling Christian members of parliament (the derision of KDNP members, mentioned above) to advocating the defence of Christendom fits a narrative of expediency over principle. On this reading, Orbán has identified the resonance of the Christian nationalist narrative with the Hungarian population, and is exploiting it for his own political gain. In these terms one author summarised Orbán's politics as 'a crude nationalism wrapped up in the pieties of Christianity purely for the purpose of gaining political power and then, having achieved it, of securing his own political dominance'.[40] Perhaps, like the secular reformists in the inter-war period who donned the mantle of Christian Nationalists,[41] Orbán's Christian nationalism is little more than nationalism, plain and simple.[42]

Compelling as this interpretation is, we have seen it is not the only plausible explanation of Orbán's actions; and it is not so self-evidently true as to rule out other possibilities entirely. To dislodge just one loose tile, if it is true that 'Orbán's gravitation to Christianity in 1993/94 … coincided with the transformation of Fidesz from an anarcho-liberal party, to the country's main conservative force', then we might understand the sudden and dramatic political shift (which otherwise strikes as insincere) as reflective of a genuine conversion to the Christian faith, a sincere change in worldview, from which we should expect a dramatic difference in words and actions.[43] Ultimately, we cannot easily avoid the difficulties in discerning the motivations behind Orbán's Christian nationalism. As in Jesus' parable of the weeds (Matthew 13:24–30), it is not always possible to discern, in the moment, whether a plant is weed or wheat.

CONCLUSION

Even with some doubt cast over the presence of religious sincerity in his motivations, we are left in little such doubt about the way in which Orbán 'does God', about his Christian nationalism. Orbán offers to defend and promote

Hungary's (even Europe's) identity and interests, and it is to Christianity that he points as the focus. That is to say, Christianity figures in Orbán's politics as a glove on the hand of nationalism, which Orbán is placing firmly on the shoulder of the Hungarian nation.

NOTES

1. Paul Hanebrink, 'Transnational Culture War: Christianity, Nation, and the Judeo-Bolshevik Myth in Hungary, 1890–1920', *Journal of Modern History*, vol. 80, no. 1, 2008, p. 59.
2. E. S. Balogh, 'Viktor Orbán on football', *Hungarian Spectrum*, 4 August 2013, http://hungarianspectrum.org/2013/08/04/viktor-orban-on-football (accessed 30 January 2017).
3. Paul Lendvai, *Hungary: Between Democracy and Authoritarianism* (London: Hurst, 2012).
4. Ibid., pp. 86–7.
5. Ibid., p. 97.
6. Many actually view Orbán's strong approach to politics as verging on the undemocratic, but even those who are more supportive of Orbán, who offer a more sympathetic interpretation of his politics, observe that he is 'all in all a kind of human bulldozer in politics' (John O'Sullivan, 'Introduction', in John O'Sullivan and Kálmán Pócza (eds), *The Second Term of Viktor Orbán: Beyond Prejudice and Enthusiasm* (London: Social Affairs Unit, 2015)).
7. Christopher Adam, 'Hungary's Orbán family and religion', *Hungarian Free Press*, 15 April 2016, http://hungarianfreepress.com/2016/04/15/hungarys-orban-family-and-religion (accessed 30 January 2017).
8. 'Orbán Viktor's speech at the Europe Forum conference', Website of the Hungarian Government, 8 May 2014, http://2010-2014.kormany.hu/en/prime-minister-s-office/the-prime-ministers-speeches/orban-viktor-s-speech-at-the-europe-forum-conference (accessed 30 January 2017).
9. Ibid.
10. 'Notable Quotes: Prime Minister Viktor Orbán', *Orange Files*, https://theorangefiles.hu/notable-quotes-prime-minister-viktor-orban-by-subject (accessed 30 January 2017)]. Bold added.
11. I do not here use 'casts' or 'portrays' pejoratively, to imply that Orbán is being deliberately misleading. Although there is evidence for this evaluative claim, I am here merely describing the narrative Orbán employs to form his political platform.
12. 'Notable Quotes: Prime Minister Viktor Orbán'.
13. Ibid.
14. Nick Hallett, 'Orban: Eventually there will be more Muslims than Christians in Europe', *Breitbart*, 17 September 2015, http://www.breitbart.com/london/2015/09/17/orban-eventually-will-muslims-christians-europe (accessed 30 January 2017).
15. 'Statement of the General Convent on the European Migration Crisis', Reformatus.hu website, 13 November 2015, http://www.reformatus.hu/mutat/11604 (accessed 30 January 2017).
16. Krisztina Than, 'Hungarian Church thanks God, government for fending off migrants', Reuters, 2 October 2015, http://www.reuters.com/article/us-europe-migrants-hungary-church-idUSKCN0RW0YK20151002 (Accessed 30 January 2017).
17. One could argue Orbán's popular majorities are artificial, for he has pursued a campaign of centralising power which undemocratically disadvantages opposition. Certainly his more authoritarian policies must be considered, but the argument does not hold water for two

reasons: first, it does not apply to his first supermajority in 2010, before which no centralising policies had been implemented; second, although Orbán has indeed leant towards the centralisation of power quite dramatically, and almost certainly wrongly in many cases, he has not (yet, at least) centralised power so far as to make opposition impossible and victories obviously assured. Opposition exists, many protest against him, and authoritarian measures have been repealed (O'Sullivan, 'Introduction'). We must not underestimate the problem – pretending Orbán is not acting unduly in many ways – but we must not overestimate it by the same count.

18. Paul Froese, 'Hungary for Religion: A Supply-Side Interpretation of the Hungarian Religious Revival', *Journal for the Scientific Study of Religion*, vol. 40, no. 2, 2001, p. 252.

19. Ibid., pp. 253–5.

20. Ibid., p. 257.

21. Ibid., p. 259.

22. Discrimination in the EU 2012, Special Eurobarometer 393, November 2012, https://web.archive.org/web/20121202023700/http://ec.europa.eu/public_opinion/archives/ebs/ebs_393_en.pdf (accessed 30 January 2017).

23. Bolshevism was a form of communist government which flourished briefly following the end of World War I. Its membership in Hungary was predominantly of Jewish origin. The Treaty of Versailles saw Hungary lose two thirds of its territory and one third of the ethnic Hungarian population to other territories. (Leslie Laszlo, review of Paul A. Hanebrink, *In Defense of Christian Hungary: Religion, Nationalism, and Antisemitism, 1890–1944, Catholic Historical Review*, vol. 93, no. 3, 2007, p. 697).

24. Quoted in Robert Mackey, 'Hungarian leader rebuked for saying Muslim migrants must be blocked "to keep Europe Christian"', *New York Times*, 3 September 2015, http://www.nytimes.com/2015/09/04/world/europe/hungarian-leader-rebuked-for-saying-muslim-migrants-must-be-blocked-to-keep-europe-christian.html (accessed 30 January 2017).

25. Hanebrink, 'Transnational Culture War', p. 59. Paul Hanebrink also details the development of the concept of 'Christian Hungary', both within and outside the church, in *In Defense of Christian Hungary: Religion, Nationalism, and Antisemitism, 1890–1944* (Ithaca, NY: Cornell University Press, 2006).

26. Hanebrink, 'Transnational Culture War', pp. 59–79.

27. Ibid., p. 79.

28. 'For years before the war, [Bishop] Prohászka, together with other prominent religious and lay figures in the Hungarian Catholic Church, had argued that an alien Jewish morality – one that knew no national boundaries – was slowly destroying the nation' (ibid., p. 57). See also Hanebrink, *In Defense of Christian Hungary*.

29. Hanebrink, 'Transnational Culture War', p. 59.

30. George Soros and Gregor Peter Schmitz, '"The EU is on the verge of collapse" – an interview', *New York Review of Books*, 11 February 2016, http://www.nybooks.com/articles/2016/02/11/europe-verge-collapse-interview (accessed 30 January 2017).

31. Speech during annual commemoration of 1848 revolution against Habsburg rule, 15 March 2011. See 'Notable Quotes: Prime Minister Viktor Orbán'.

32. Hanebrink, 'Transnational Culture War', p. 58.

33. Ibid., p. 59.

34. Peter Pomerantsev and Anton Shekhovtsov, 'Rolling back freedom', *Prospect*, March 2016, p. 29.

35. See Donald Tusk, 'By being tough on migration Europe can also be humane', *The Guardian*, 22 April 2016, https://www.theguardian.com/commentisfree/2016/apr/22/europe-migration-crisis-abandoned-values (accessed 30 January 2017); 'Point taken, Mr Orban',

The Economist, 26 September 2015, http://www.economist.com/news/europe/21667956-
europes-migration-hardliners-have-some-reasonable-concerns-point-taken-mr-orban (accessed 30 January 2017), on how, despite his objectionable style and methods, Orbán makes
some valid points about the handling of the migration crisis, which many others share.

36. The discussions leading up to the UK's recent popular vote to leave the European Union
have caused many to take somewhat more seriously the concerns of a large number of
people, across Europe, about the effects of immigration.

37. O'Sullivan, 'Introduction'.

38. See for example Vanessa Gera and Alex Kuli, 'Hungary's anti-migrant steps show Orbán's
right-wing shift', CNSNews.com, 15 October 2015, http://www.cnsnews.com/news/arti-
cle/hungarys-anti-migrant-steps-show-orbans-right-wing-shift; Miklós Haraszti, 'Behind
Viktor Orbán's war on refugees in Hungary', *WorldPost*, 8 September 2015, http://www.
huffingtonpost.com/miklos-haraszti/viktor-orban-hungary-refugees_b_8100906.html;
Amy Brouillette, 'The autocrat inside the EU', *Foreign Policy*, 21 August 2014, http://for-
eignpolicy.com/2014/08/21/the-autocrat-inside-the-eu (all accessed 30 January 2017).

39. 'Big, bad Visegrad', *The Economist*, 30 January 2016, http://www.economist.com/
news/europe/21689629-migration-crisis-has-given-unsettling-new-direction-old-alli-
ance-big-bad-visegrad (accessed 30 January 2017).

40. Lendvai, *Hungary*, p. 114.

41. Hanebrink, 'Transnational Culture War', pp. 59–80.

42. Karl Barth once chastised a communist-era leader of the Reformed Church in Hungary for
conflating his own political ideology with Christianity (Froese, 'Hungary for Religion', p.
253); it is not outlandish to suggest that a similar charge could be levelled at Orbán.

43. C. Adam, 'Hungary's Orbán family and religion', *Hungarian Free Press*, 15 April 2016. Available at: http://hungarianfreepress.com/2016/04/15/hungarys-orban-family-and-religion/
(accessed online 22 February 2017).

VLADIMIR PUTIN
(2000–2008, 2012–)

BEN RYAN

BIOGRAPHY

Few major world leaders have been able to cultivate quite as enigmatic or obscure a public persona as Vladimir Putin. Beyond a series of basic facts, any detail on Putin's life, opinions and even career specifics is subject to a significant degree of deliberate obscurity, mythologising and heavily partisan interpretation. Biographies rely heavily on interviews with enemies or close allies, and officially sanctioned and carefully released information.[1] Putin's own pronouncements are very deliberate; there seems to be a consensus that he rarely uses words without a careful consideration of the effect he is creating. The closest thing to a Putin autobiography, *First Person* (*Ot pervogo litsa*),[2] typifies this. It is not an autobiography but a selection of carefully prepared interviews on particular topics with a trusted selection of Russian journalists.

It is a persona that perhaps deliberately fascinates and terrifies a Western audience, a picture alien to anything that anyone in the West would want to portray. Putin cultivates the image of a hard man. Much is made of his childhood scrapping in his block with the local gangs, getting into martial arts (a hobby he still maintains), the KGB man, and latterly the strong man who is prepared to stand up to those who would weaken Russia, whether internal (the oligarchs, Chechens) or external (NATO).

For all that, certain details of his life are clear. He was born in St Petersburg (then Leningrad) in October 1952 to Vladimir and Maria. His father was a Soviet patriot who had been severely wounded in the siege of Leningrad, his mother also having lived through the whole siege. The story Putin has told is that soon after his birth he was baptised as a baby, his mother apparently being a committed Christian, which, if true, although not unheard of, would nonetheless have been rather bold at a time when religion was banned.

Rated as a good but not outstanding student, Putin's great love as a teenager was martial arts, particularly judo and a Soviet martial art known as sambo. He was apparently a real talent, winning trophies and training relentlessly. He went to university to study law and developed a desire to join the KGB. He accomplished that aim after graduating at a time when future premier Yuri Andropov was the head of the KGB, a man whom Putin by all accounts still holds in high regard. Despite the conspiracy theorists, Putin appears not to have been an especially prominent agent. He spent some years working in Moscow before he was sent to East Germany to work in counter-intelligence in Dresden, his only experience outside Russia. In his own words, he worked in political intelligence, collecting information on parties and politicians. He denies the more exotic stories, such as that he obtained documentation on the design of the Eurofighter or that he ran Hans Modrow, a prominent East German politician.[3] He met his future wife Lyudmila (an air hostess) in 1980 and married her in 1982 or 1983.[4]

Putin and his family saw the end of communism first hand in Germany, but witnessed the effects of *perestroika* and *glasnost* at home only from a distance. His sense of abandonment when the Soviet system failed to support his office as the Berlin Wall came down was said to be acute. The great sell-off of state assets under the early years of the Yeltsin administration completed the effect – and perhaps goes some way to explaining the obsession with recreating a strong Russia and Russian zone of influence.

Putin returned to Russia and after finishing a second law degree went to work for Anatoly Sobchak in St Petersburg – a man who would go on to become a key patron and ally.[5] Some believe he was assigned the role by the KGB to keep an eye on the dangerous Sobchak.[6] Others report that though Putin retained his KGB reserve role, he was not assigned to watch Sobchak but was recommended by an ally and performed no intelligence role.[7] Whatever the truth, there is little doubt Putin soon proved a valuable asset to Sobchak and went through a series of increasingly significant roles through the early 1990s, gaining a reputation as a fixer without ever really proving himself in any election.[8]

If the story of how Putin came to work for Sobchak is somewhat shrouded in mystery, how he became part of Boris Yeltsin's inner circle and his eventual successor as President of the Russian Federation is even more curious. In 1996, after Sobchak had lost power in St Petersburg, Putin left for Moscow and got his break in the central government via another ally, Pavel Borodin. Even Putin in talking about Borodin finding him an appointment in Moscow claims, 'I don't know why.'[9] From there he rapidly went through a number of increasingly prominent positions in the infamously volatile Yeltsin presidency, including serving as head of the FSB (the successor to the KGB) and as Prime Minister. So it was that with Yeltsin's health failing Putin was named as the preferred successor.

Having become President, Putin has successfully held the position since 2000 with only a four-year interlude from 2008 to 2012, when Dmitri Medvedev[10] held the reins until Putin was eligible again (Putin served that time as Prime Minister). In his time as President Putin has had some notable successes. For all that opinion polls (and indeed some election polls) have had their authenticity questioned,[11] there seems little doubt that Putin has a significant support base and a remarkably high level of popularity for a man who has been in office as long as he has. His economic record, at least until the last few years, has been notably successful, helped of course by Russia's enormous mineral wealth.

The political power of the oligarchs has been largely curtailed. Among the group that successfully managed to strip away huge portions of previously state-owned industry for a fraction of their real value, several have been effectively exiled, imprisoned or forced to sell up large parts of their gains back to the state or else to other oligarchs better in favour with Putin. If Russian business continues to be dominated by a small sect of oligarchs, they at least have learned the hard way to keep themselves out of the political sphere.

In foreign policy terms, Russia's increased confidence was obvious long before the recent Ukraine crisis. Whether it was military action in Georgia or the critical role played by Putin in the 2013 dispute over the possibility of international action in Syria, Russia has been prepared to appear increasingly prominent in recent years. The decision to annex Crimea is only the latest in a string of efforts to shore up the Russian sphere of influence and stand up to the perceived encroachment of NATO and the EU.

Putin inspires a great deal of fear in the West.[12] The combination of aggressive nationalism, increased military confidence, domestic repression, human rights questions and, of course, the continued nuclear capacity is a dangerous cocktail. That notwithstanding, Putin has been a remarkably successful President and today sits as one of the most powerful world leaders.

PUTIN'S FAITH AND POLITICS

PERSONAL FAITH

Putin has been keen to present himself as a man of serious personal faith. This is a trend that has seemed to become more pronounced throughout his time in office. Cynics suggest that the increasingly confident assertion of faith is part of a broader trend of seeking a nationalist agenda as economic performance has declined. However, even relatively early in his presidency Putin had spoken at times about his faith and had already formed an apparently close bond with certain members of the clergy in the early 2000s, when his popularity was at its peak.

In early meetings with then US President George W. Bush, Putin certainly stressed his personal faith, showing off the small aluminium cross that he wore round his neck and making much of his Christian commitment. Bush was by all accounts impressed, relating an account of the meetings in his book *Decision Points*.[13] Bush, of course, is famous for his own evangelical faith and it is entirely possible that Putin emphasised this precisely to win a friend in the US President. However, the story of this little baptismal cross is one which Putin has highlighted on several occasions and figures prominently in a passage from the biography written by Chris Hutchins and Alexander Korobko.[14]

The story goes that this baptismal cross was given to Putin by his Christian mother when she had him secretly baptised in the early 1950s and it has apparently been an object of great sentimental value to him ever since. Putin did not wear it while he was an active KGB officer, but he reports that 'in 1993 when I worked on the Leningrad City Council,* I went to Israel as part of an official delegation. Mama gave me my baptismal cross to get it blessed at the Lord's Tomb. I did as she said and then put the cross around my neck. I have never taken it off since.'[15]

The tale takes on a mythical element, however, in an account of a fire at the Putin family dacha. According to the story, the property burned down in the mid-1990s, destroying many of the family's key possessions including a good portion of their money. However, the cross survived the fire and was presented back to Putin by one of the firemen. If the account seems extraordinary it is nonetheless one which has been repeated often. It bears, in fact, a close resemblance to an ancient Russian religious myth in which an icon of St Nicholas was said to be impervious to flame.[16] Whether or not that connotation is deliberate and the tale of Putin's cross is a mythical construct, it is striking that this story is one that forms part of the official narrative on Putin's faith. Putin certainly wishes to portray a strong personal faith that is exemplified in these stories.

There is some reason to believe that this goes beyond cynical self-image. For many years Putin has certainly had a close relationship with Archimandrite Tikhon, the father superior of Sretensky Monastery. So close, in fact, is this relationship that there are those who would paint Tikhon as an éminence grise. Certainly Tikhon, a former film student with a reputation as a spiritual healer, seems to have served for some years as confessor to Putin. One biographer speculates that Tikhon probably knows more about Putin's life than anyone else.[17] He is also a priest with some rather remarkable political views, having publicly criticised democracy as a force that weakens a country and its spiritual basis, spoken out in favour of censorship as a necessary instrument and worked as a well-known public media figure. He has certainly seemed to profit from the relationship with Putin and other prominent political figures, securing a string of new offices and promotions in recent years. However, he himself has always been keen to be clear that Putin

---

* Though Leningrad had been renamed St Petersburg in 1991, Putin, a native of the city, continued to use the previous name for some time.

is very much his own man, and certainly for all the closeness in their relationship Putin has stopped short (at least so far) of fully endorsing Tikhon's
model of church–state relations. They did, however, work closely together
in 2007 in the process of reunifying the Russian Orthodox Church and the
Russian Orthodox Church outside Russia (ROCOR), and speculation over
the extent of their influence on one another has continued for years.[18]

Tikhon has reported in the past that Putin prays daily in a small chapel
next to the presidential office. Putin's mother and ex-wife were both certainly
religious and the claim that Putin prays regularly is not implausible. As an
overall picture of Putin's personal faith then, while recognising the usual
problems when it comes to unpicking truth from myth and managed public
image, we can at the very least see that Putin wants to give the appearance of
a man with a committed personal faith.

POLITICS AND FAITH IN THE SERVICE OF THE STATE

The debate about the relationship between the Orthodox Church and political power is nothing new. Indeed it goes all the way back beyond the Great
Schism in 1054 and even to the working out of Christianity's relationship with
power with Constantine, the first Christian emperor of the Roman Empire.
The Russian state, and its predecessors in the Tsarist empire, Muscovy and the
Grand Duchy of Kiev, adopted a trajectory of religion and power that did not
follow that of Catholic or Protestant Europe. The Orthodox Church, even
more than the established churches of western Europe, was fully part of the
structure of the government. Indeed, it was this intimate relationship with the
ruling system of the state that prevented the Orthodox Church in Russia (as
opposed to other European churches) from acting as a critical or independent
voice, and which explained in part the Bolshevik revolution.

Under communism, the Church was a threat to the state as a body closely
associated with power structures, a rival ideology capable of inspiring the
affection and support of a large proportion of the Russian population. Putin,
however, is on record as seeing that attitude as a mistake on the part of
the USSR. The Church, for Putin, has a significant and powerful value in
forging a strong Russian state. Under Putin, the Church and nationalism are
increasingly closely united. The Church serves a powerful role in supporting

Putin's true political ideology – his identity as a *gosudarstvennik* or 'statist'.[19] The 'Russian Idea' as described by Putin in his so-called Millennium Message, delivered in 1999 and still seen as the core of his political model, includes patriotism, collectivism, solidarity and *derzhavnost'* (destiny to be a great power). Religion, even were Putin not religious himself, has a very clear and obvious instrumental value in meeting those goals.

This instrumental use of the Church has been seen on a number of occasions both internally and, increasingly, externally. Internally, Putin has done much to encourage and support the growth of the Orthodox Church and to restrain the proselytising activities of other religious bodies (Jehovah's Witnesses and Pentecostal groups have found it very difficult to be registered as official belief groups in Russia; indeed they are portrayed as a security threat to the Russian state).[20] Under Putin's watch, icons and church bells that were sold or smuggled out of Russia under communism have been restored[21] and churches have been built or rebuilt (particularly the vast Cathedral of Christ the Saviour in Moscow[22]), with oligarchs and local businesses strongly encouraged (even allegedly coerced[23]) into funding the work.

It can also be seen in education, where Orthodox culture is now part of the school curriculum, and even, increasingly, in direct control of popular media. Putin's government is heavily suspected of fixing the results of the 2008 poll for the 'greatest Russian' in favour of Alexander Nevsky, a warrior who resisted foreign invaders as Prince of Novgorod, Grand Prince of Kiev and Grand Prince of Vladimir and was later proclaimed an Orthodox saint. Independent polls revealed that this result was probably fraudulent. That, of course, in some ways makes the result more interesting as an example of whom the Russian government want people to value – a figure of both nationalist pride and religious prestige.

Externally, this instrumental relationship has been gaining in importance too. As mentioned above, Putin played a role in the reunification of the Russian Orthodox Church and ROCOR, in the process creating an effective foreign policy tool.[24] As Putin has looked to reinforce a sense of ethnic and linguistic Russianness even beyond the federation's borders, the Church has been a valuable part of that process. A quotation from Patriarch Kirill[25] is illustrative of this point:

The Patriarch is the custodian of the internal unity of the Church and, together with his brothers in the episcopate, guardian of the purity of the faith ... The Patriarch is the defender of the canonical borders of the church. This ministry takes on special significance in that situation that arose after the formation of independent states on the territory of 'historic Russia'. While respecting their sovereignty and caring for their well-being, the Patriarch is called, at the same time, to be concerned with the maintaining and strengthening of spiritual ties between people living in these countries for the sake of preserving the system of values which the one Orthodox civilization of Holy Russia reveals to the world.[26]

Certainly this sense of the 'canonical borders' that exceed the current federation borders has been employed rhetorically on several occasions – particularly in relation to Russian operations in Ukraine and the annexation of Crimea. Explicit note was made of the special status of Crimea in the history of Russian Orthodoxy – as the site where Grand Prince Vladimir adopted Orthodoxy and was baptised. Putin noted, 'His spiritual feat of adopting Orthodoxy predetermined the overall basis of the culture, civilisation and human values that unite the peoples of Russia, Ukraine and Belarus.'[27] This narrative of unifying the Russian peoples defined by language and religion has been a growing trend in which the Moscow patriarch and President mutually reinforce one another. The Church has become mobilised as part of the defence of this policy and the state more broadly – creating a concept of 'spiritual security'. In official Church documents, spiritual security is now the official missional activity of the Orthodox Church in Russia, propping up a bold ideological vision for the role of the Church in society and politics.[28]

With that, of course, comes a sense that other religious groups undermine the security of the state. How to manage the other faiths in Russia has become a new political problem. Under communism, all religions were equally illegal; under Putin, a more difficult relationship has had to be worked out. Russia's Muslim population is considerable, if difficult to calculate accurately, with numbers ranging in different surveys anywhere between 5 and 10 per cent of the overall population.[29] That population, of course, is especially prevalent in the southern part of the country and in Chechnya.

Chechens present a particular problem as a secessionist nationalist group with strong ties to Islamic extremist groups including Al-Qaeda and Islamic State. Similar conflicts now exist across Russia's North Caucasus regions. A Caucasus Emirate was established in 2007, though its leaders have mostly now transferred their allegiance to Islamic State.[30] Putin's response (and indeed Yeltsin's) to these threats has been with strong military action. There have been two Chechen wars, one, under Yeltsin, from 1994 to 1996 and one, under Putin, from 1999 to 2000. In both cases the Russian military was able to reassert control only after heavy fighting and the deaths of thousands of soldiers and civilians. In 2000, Putin declared that his 'historical mission … consisted of resolving the situation in the Northern Caucasus'.[31] This is quite an ambition, and one that would seem only to have got harder since then, and might provide a particularly difficult test for Putin's instrumental use of the Church.

CONCLUSION

Overall, the Orthodox Church and Putin have a rather unusual symbiotic relationship. Putin has allowed the Church to return to prominence and has supported it in a way unheard of since the Revolution. The Church has, in turn, provided some of the intellectual and cultural backing for Putin's statist vision for Russia and the wider Russian sphere of influence.

There is an open question which is seemingly impossible to answer: to what extent was Putin inspired by the resources provided by Orthodoxy in his statist model, or does his model simply use the resources provided where it can find them? Certainly Putin has seemed to use the Church more and more in an instrumental way to support his actions at home and abroad – and it is notable that he has chosen to do so. No other Russian leader since the Tsars has felt the need or desire to do so. Even Yeltsin, who also professed a nominal Christianity and a desire to rewrite some of the weaknesses of the disintegrating USSR, made little effort to involve the Church in that. Nor, to any great extent, have many of Putin's political rivals. This is very much a Putin concern – and with that in mind it is too simplistic to assume that all this faith material is only instrumental. There seems to be some legitimate sense of interaction between Orthodox thought and faith and Putin's politics and political model.

Certainly some of Putin's opponents seem to see things that way. When Pussy Riot, the feminist punk anarchist group, staged one of their performances in protest against Putin, the government and the establishment, it is notable that the site for their provocative gesture was inside a Moscow cathedral. It is difficult to think of another secular European leader for whom the most symbolic locus for an attack would be a cathedral – and that if nothing else is a notable example of the close symbiotic relationship between the President, his politics and his faith.

NOTES

1. Fiona Hill and Clifford G. Gaddy note that 'it is remarkable – almost hard to believe – that for 15 years there has not been a single substantive biography published in Russian, by a Russian, of President Putin' (Hill and Gaddy, *Mr Putin: Operative in the Kremlin*, rev. ed. (Washington, DC: Brookings Institution Press, 2015), p. 6).

2. Vladimir Putin, Nataliya Gevorkyan, Natalya Timakova and Andrei Kolesnikov, *First Person: An Astonishingly Frank Self-Portrait by Russia's President* (New York: PublicAffairs, 2000).

3. Ibid., pp. 72–3.

4. Accounts disagree, but this is not uncommon with Soviet marriages, which were often badly recorded.

5. Sobchak became a legislator in the last few years of the USSR and then mayor of St Petersburg in 1990. An authoritarian and a pragmatist, he finally lost the role after an electoral defeat in 1996. He was regarded as one of Russia's most significant politicians, a sometime ally and sometime threat to Boris Yeltsin. He became one of Putin's great allies as his former protégé sought the presidency until he died in suspicious circumstances of a heart attack in 2000.

6. This is the version recorded in Chris Hutchins with Alexander Korobko, *Putin* (Leicester: Matador, 2012).

7. This is the version included in Hill and Gaddy, *Mr Putin*, and the one that Putin himself has always claimed – see for example Putin et al., *First Person*, pp. 88–9.

8. Quite the reverse: Putin ran Sobchak's failed re-election campaign in 1996.

9. Putin et al., *First Person*, p. 125.

10. Medvedev was a long-standing Putin ally who had worked with him in Sobchak's office in St Petersburg.

11. See Hill and Gaddy, *Mr Putin*, pp. 230–32.

12. Roger Boyes, the diplomatic editor of *The Times*, typifies this, with a string of articles over the past few years warning of a return to Cold War politics, nuclear threat and the risk of a major war.

13. George W. Bush, *Decision Points* (New York: Crown, 2010), p. 96.

14. Hutchins and Korobko, *Putin*, pp. 126–8.

15. Putin et al., *First Person*, p. 12.

16. See W. F. Ryan, *Bathhouse at Midnight: An Historical Survey of Magic and Divination in Russia* (University Park: Pennsylvania State University Press, 1999).

17. Hutchins and Korobko, *Putin*, p. 241.

18. See for example Sophia Kishkovsky, 'Russians see Orthodox Church and state come closer', *New York Times*, 1 November 2012, http://www.nytimes.com/2012/11/01/world/europe/russians-see-orthodox-church-and-state-come-closer.html (accessed 23 January 2017).

19. Hill and Gaddy, *Putin*, p. 39.

20. Inna Naletova, 'Religion, the State and Civil Society', *Perspective*, vol. 12, no. 3, 2002, p. 2.

21. Hill and Gaddy, *Putin*, p. 67.

22. Originally a nineteenth-century cathedral destroyed by Stalin, it was rebuilt at considerable cost and reconsecrated in 2000.

23. Wealthy businessmen, including non-Christians, have consistently been encouraged to spend money on religious buildings (Hill and Gaddy, *Putin*, p. 103). However, in the case of the cathedral, there were allegations of serious pressure from government (both local and national) on local businesses to contribute towards the funding or face threats from tax officials.

24. D. R. Jackson, 'Canonical Territory and National Security: Patriarch, President and Proselytism in the Russian Federation', p. 4. Available at http://www.academia.edu/905364/Canonical_territory_and_national_security_Patriarch_President_and_Proselytism_in_the_Russian_Federation (accessed 23 January 2017).

25. Patriarch Kirill, whose secular name is Vladimir Mikhailovich Gundyaev, became the Patriarch of Moscow and All Rus' and Primate of the Russian Orthodox Church in February 2009.

26 Quoted in 'New Russian Patriarch Kirill I pledges to keep church unified' in ENI, 2 February 2009.

27 Address by President of the Russian Federation, 18 March 2014, The Kremlin, Moscow, http://en.special.kremlin.ru/events/president/news/20603

28. Jackson, 'Canonical Territory and National Security', pp. 5–8.

29. Michael Lipka, 'Sochi Olympics shine spotlight on Russia's Muslim population', Pew Research Center website, 7 February 2014, http://www.pewresearch.org/fact-tank/2014/02/07/sochi-olympics-shine-spotlight-on-russias-muslim-population (accessed 23 January 2017).

30. Regis Gente, 'Is this the end of the Caucasus Emirate?', openDemocracy, 29 June 2015, https://www.opendemocracy.net/regis-gente/is-this-end-of-caucasus-emirate (accessed 23 January 2017).

31. Putin et al., *First Person*, p. 139.

GEORGE W. BUSH (2001–09)

HANNAH MALCOLM

B orn to an Episcopalian father and a Presbyterian mother in 1946, George Walker Bush was baptised as an infant into the Episcopal Church. Thirty-one years later he married a Methodist and, after a long struggle with alcohol, joined a non-denominational community Bible study group, met Billy Graham, went teetotal and began to describe himself as 'born again'. This personal conversion experience would go on to play a central role in the way he presented himself and his administration, both to the American public and on the international stage. While the jury is still out on the degree to which Bush's Christian faith was subject to political calculation, it undoubtedly manifested itself in a kind of missional zeal that shaped both his national and his foreign policy – a zeal that he made no effort to disguise. Bush's presidential inaugural address in 2001 pledged America to a particular goal: 'When we see that wounded traveller on the road to Jericho, we will not pass to the other side.'[1] Bush certainly endeavoured to uphold this over the eight years that followed.

Bush's autobiographies locate much of the origin of his political ambition and fervour for faith in the years prior to running for President. Though his critics are swift to point to Bush's 'frat boy' reputation at Yale and his not quite successful attempt to break into the Texas oil business, Bush highlights a 'work hard, play hard' mentality and a deep love of the study of history that shaped his political thought. Of a college class on the Soviet Union, he reflected, 'The class was an introduction to the struggle between tyranny and freedom, a battle that has held my attention for the rest of my life.'[2] And, while visiting his parents in China, his observations on the results of the revolution there 'deepened [his] conviction that freedom – economic, political and religious – is the only fair and productive way of governing a society'.[3]

His commitment to the ideological notion of American freedom was joined by (and frequently merged with) a belief in divine providence and the personal power of faith to change lives, emerging after attending an evangelical Bible study group and a meeting with Billy Graham in the summer before he turned forty. Commenting on his recovery from alcohol abuse, Bush wrote, 'Faith showed me a way out. I knew I could count on the grace of God to help me change.'[4]

And change he did. Now a teetotaller and committed evangelical, Bush soon after moved to Washington to help run his father's campaign for presidency, and, in 1987, took over the job of liaison to the Religious Right. He had begun to learn the language of conservative American religion, which would later characterise his campaign for presidency. Bush ran successfully for governor of Texas in 1994, and became the first to be elected for two consecutive four-year terms, a popularity helped by large tax cuts and funding for drug and alcohol abuse education. His second term saw the increased promotion of faith-based community organisations and the introduction of 'Jesus Day' (10 June 2000), on which he 'urge[d] all Texans to answer the call to serve those in need'.[5] His first autobiography, *A Charge to Keep*, named after the hymn by Charles Wesley, was released near the end of his time as governor and during his presidential campaign. It outlines his measure of America's moral failings and what his presidency would seek to address. 'I worried about my country, about an increasing drift that I felt threatened America's promise of opportunity for all at home and America's place as the keeper of freedom in the world.'[6]

He would address these two issues, he assured his voters, with God's blessing. His presidential campaign began by assembling leading pastors to lay on hands and pray for him, telling them that he had been 'called' to seek higher office.[7] He was not only assured of his own mission, but assured of who would guide it to completion. When asked in the Republican Party primary debates of 1999 who his favourite political philosopher was, he responded

'Christ', because 'he changed my heart'.[8] Critics saw this as the ultimate 'God strategy' move – a direct appeal to the American evangelical voter. Bush denies such assertions, even claiming the opposite: 'I was sceptical of politicians who touted religion as a way to get votes ... it was not the role of government to promote any religion. I hadn't done that as governor of Texas, and I certainly didn't intend to do it as president.'[9]

Whether or not a 'Jesus Day' could be argued to promote any particular religion, Bush's words certainly connected with a particular religious audience, who identified with his personal expression of faith and appreciated this apparent moment of vulnerability. He won the controversially close presidential election in 2000.

A NEW KIND OF PRESIDENT?

Bush's 2001 inaugural address began his presidency as he meant to go on – affirming his leadership over a country blessed by God. His aim for a 'single nation of justice and opportunity' was possible because 'we are guided by a power larger than ourselves who creates us equal in His image'.[10] While he was certainly not the first or last President to appeal to a higher power in an inaugural address, Bush arguably presented his presidency as having a particularly evangelical stripe – down to his transformation of the White House into a 'teetotal, non-smoking, non-cussing affair' where cabinet meetings opened with prayer.[11] This was a *public* personal faith; in his account of Bush's religious life, Stephen Mansfield notes that 'Americans have had opportunity to know more about the president's conversion, prayer life, what Bible he reads, what devotional he uses, and who his spiritual influences are than they have ever known of any other president'.[12]

God followed Bush everywhere he went. Bush reportedly bonded with Vladimir Putin over a cross the Russian President wore, and his 'special relationship' with Tony Blair was described by one *New York Times* columnist as having used God as 'a kind of fraternity handshake'.[13] In particular, Bush continued to make regular references to his own redemption narrative and personal transformation. At the National Prayer Breakfast of 2008, he affirmed, 'I believe in the power of prayer because I have felt it in my own life.'[14]

THE FAITH-BASED INITIATIVE

Bush's conversion from wayward alcohol abuser to born-again teetotaller also appears to have heavily influenced his Faith-Based Initiative programme, a scheme designed to increase the share of federal social welfare resources for religious groups, and to protect and revitalise the religious identity of these groups.[15] Here was Bush's 'compassionate conservatism' at work – a *modus operandi* he promised in his inaugural address ('Compassion is the work of a nation, not just a government. And some needs and hurts are so deep they will only respond to a mentor's touch or a pastor's prayer')[16] and again emphasised at his first National Prayer Breakfast as President: 'We want to encourage the inspired, to help the helper ... my administration will put the federal government squarely on the side of America's armies of compassion.'[17]

These 'armies of compassion' had one particular weapon to offer: the ability to 'change hearts'. Bush having reduced the solutions of government social projects and economic growth to 'materialism' in his earlier autobiographical manifesto,[18] the Faith-Based Initiative was to 'help all in their work to change hearts while keeping a commitment to pluralism', and his administration would 'look first to faith-based programmes and community groups, which have proven their power to change and save lives'.[19]

The 'compassionate conservatism' of Bush's Faith-Based Initiative has provoked considerable discussion as to the religious basis on which it might rest. Lew Daly, author of *God's Economy: Faith-Based Initiatives and the Caring State*, points to the Dutch Calvinist theory of sphere sovereignty and the Catholic principle of subsidiarity, whereby the state is limited and the church extended – as Abraham Kuyper saw it, family, church, charities and confessional schools were the 'natural community' acting as intermediary structures between individual and state.[20] This is certainly reflected in remarks made at Bush's second inaugural address:

> Self-government relies, in the end, on the governing of the self. That edifice of character is built in families, supported by communities with standards, and sustained in our national life by the truths of Sinai, the Sermon on the Mount, the words of the Koran, and the varied faiths of our people.[21]

Or, as he wrote elsewhere, 'the government … can encourage people and communities to help themselves and one another. The truest kind of compassion is to help citizens build better lives of their own.'[22] Bush the 'self-help Methodist'[23] was implementing his plan to 'close the gap of hope'[24] on American soil.

A NATION AT WAR

Bush's second autobiography presents this social agenda as having been dramatically forced to the back burner after the attacks of September 2001: 'The focus of my presidency, which I had expected to be domestic policy, was now war … September 11 redefined sacrifice. It redefined duty. And it redefined my job. The story of that week is the key to understanding my presidency.'[25]

Certainly, the horrific events of 11 September would have forced in a new era of American international relations, no matter how the government had responded. It is, however, interesting to note that Bush had already expressed a desire for America to take up its place as 'the keeper of freedom in the world':[26] 'My vision of compassionate conservatism also requires America to assert its leadership in the world. We are the world's only remaining superpower, and we must use our power in a strong but compassionate way to help keep the peace and encourage the spread of freedom.'[27]

His 'armies of compassion' were, to his mind, already globally committed, not just nationally so. There was no doubt as to how America would respond, nor how Bush wished to highlight the *moral* obligation in its response:

> I … wanted the [address to the nation] to convey my sense of moral outrage. The deliberate murder of innocent people is an act of pure evil. Above all, I wanted to express comfort and resolve – comfort that we would recover from this blow, and resolve that we would bring the terrorists to justice.[28]

No longer just a 'self-help Methodist', Bush the 'Messianic Calvinist'[29] took on a new calling as God's instrument in the war on terror, charged with bringing the gift of freedom to the world. His address to the nation put the words of the psalmist ('I will fear no evil, for You are with me') against the 'evil' the nation had witnessed,[30] and, with the words 'blessed are those who mourn, for they will be comforted' he announced that Friday 14 September would be a national day of prayer and remembrance.[31] Stephen Mansfield notes that 'what followed [9/11] was a freer rein for religion in American society. Bush seemed to embody it. He prayed publicly and spoke of faith, divine destiny, and the nation's religious heritage more than he ever had.'[32] Bush's approval ratings shot to 90 per cent, and troops were sent into Afghanistan. One year after 9/11, the National Security Strategy was released, promising that America would exploit its military and economic power to encourage 'free and open' societies.[33] In 2003, upon the invasion of Iraq, the United States embarked on its first aggressive or pre-emptive (as opposed to defensive) military campaign in history.[34]

THE AMERICAN RELIGIOUS DOCTRINE: EVIL, FREEDOM AND PROVIDENCE

These statements of resolve and national unity in the face of threat were not simply meant as a form of comfort. Bush considered them to be a vital prong in his attack on the perpetrators of 9/11. This 'freedom agenda' aimed to 'advance liberty and hope as an alternative to the enemy's ideology of repression and fear'.[35] Bush was marking out the line between 'good' and 'evil', and, in 2002, he named the latter: North Korea, Iran and Iraq.[36] Reagan's 'evil empire' had a rhetorical successor – the 'axis of evil'. Bush would frequently return to the ideals of 'freedom' and 'hope' as the 'good' America had to offer over and against the 'evil' of its enemies. For example, on the first anniversary of 9/11 he said, 'This ideal of America is the hope of all mankind ... that hope still lights our way. And the light shines in the darkness. And the darkness will not overcome it.'[37]

In the aftermath of 9/11, Bush developed quite a habit of reassigning scripture or Christian writings in his political addresses. The successful invasion of Iraq in May 2003 was marked with the command in Isaiah 49 for the captives to 'be free';[38] his State of the Union address in that year affirmed that there is 'power, power, wonder working power in the goodness and idealism and faith of the American people';[39] and the National Prayer Breakfast of 2008 gave thanks for 'our liberty and the universal desire for freedom that

He has written in every human heart'.[40] In the latter quote, 'God' is replaced with 'freedom', giving it divine status, and the replacement of 'the blood of the lamb' with 'the American people' in the former gives the United States a messianic role, whether the world was asking to be redeemed by it or not.

Such a task could only be taken on by a nation with a great deal of self-assurance. Bush possessed this in abundance. As a *New York Times* article in 2003 observed, 'perhaps the most important effect of Mr Bush's religion is that, for better or worse, it imports a profound self-confidence once he has decided on a course of action'.[41] Bush affirmed this confidence as the power of providence in his own life long before 9/11. In his first autobiography, he declared, 'I could not be governor if I did not believe in a divine plan that supersedes all human plans ... my faith frees me ... frees me to try to do the right thing, even though it may not poll well.'[42]

This personal confidence was quickly extended to the American people as a whole. At the National Prayer Breakfast of 2002 Bush asserted that 'faith gives the assurance that our lives and our history have a moral design ... as a nation, we know that the ruthless will not inherit the earth.'[43] In 2003, it went still further when he compared America's 'cause in the world' to 'providence':

> We can be confident in America's cause in the world ... we can also be confident in the ways of providence, even when they are far from our understanding. Events aren't moved by blind change and chance. Behind all of life and all of history, there's a dedication and purpose, set by the hand of a just and faithful God.[44]

In fact, even when 'the road of providence is uneven and unpredictable' the American people 'know where it leads. It leads to freedom.'[45] Perhaps there is, crudely, a sense of 'passing the buck' onto God here – after all, if it is divine will, Bush is hardly to blame. But, more importantly, the language of providence in association with American military intervention does the job of sanctifying policy and presenting the President as a kind of conduit for divine will. While this is, in part, simply a reflection of a pattern in post-Reagan American politics towards invoking God's approval of one's office,[46]

Rogers Smith points out that George Bush was ahead of the presidential curve in expressing religious or moral sentiments in relation to *particular policies*, rather than general divine backing.[47] Though this increased after 9/11, the groundwork for it is evident early on. 'The world seeks America's leadership, looks for leadership from a country whose values are freedom and justice and equality ... our greatest export is freedom, and we have a moral obligation to champion it throughout the world.'[48] His enemies responded by calling him a 'modern day crusader'.[49]

Bush attempted to distance himself from the idea that 'freedom' was a uniquely 'American' or 'Christian' gift ('freedom is a universal gift from Almighty God ... freedom is not an American value; it is a universal value')[50] and put in considerable effort to present a multi-faith position of tolerance. He was the first President to expand the standard homages to churches and synagogues to include mosques, and repeatedly emphasised that the 'noble' faith of Islam was not the same as 'those whose actions defile that faith'[51] – upon meeting Recep Tayyip Erdoğan of Turkey, Bush told him they would make 'great partners' because they both 'believe in the Almighty'. He also made a point of drawing attention to this at National Prayer Breakfasts, in line with the 'great American tradition of religious tolerance'.[52] However, the rhetoric of 'good' and 'evil' was already closely tied to 'America' and 'America's enemies'. The idea that Al-Qaeda's evil behaviour did not actually make America 'good' was too rhetorically complicated to render into a sound bite. Observations such as those made on Eid al-Fitr 2001 ('People of many faiths are united in our commitments ... to build a more peaceful world'[53]) were lost alongside calls to war ('We are in a conflict between good and evil, and America will call evil by its name ... we will lead the world in opposing it'[54]).

THE CONSERVATIVE BATTLES FOR SANCTITY

Although it is difficult to find areas of Bush's political life which were not touched by religious sentiment or appeals to Christian moral frameworks, debates over the sanctity of life and marriage are some of the more (in)famous. Opposed to same-sex marriage, he called in his 2004 re-election campaign for an amendment to the US Constitution which would ban such marriages but allow for same-sex civil unions on a state level. However, he also drew criticism from certain evangelical corners for not stating his position strongly enough, or not using 'anti-gay' language. His 2004 State of the Union address made clear that 'the same moral tradition that defines marriage also teaches that each individual has dignity and value in God's sight',[55] a rather more eloquent version of his statement in the leaked Doug Wead tapes that he 'would not kick gays because [he was] a sinner'.[56]

Moral statements came rather more easily on the topic of sanctity of life, most clearly reflected in his firm veto of stem cell research. His language on the issue was clear: it was a 'violation' of 'our morals' and a 'destruction' of 'human life', and it crossed the 'ethical' and 'moral' line of the 'sanctity of human life'.[57] With regard to abortion, while Bush's autobiography is careful to present a 'personal' perspective ('The abortion issue is difficult, sensitive, and personal. My faith and conscience led me to conclude that human life is sacred'),[58] his first day in office was marked by the 'Mexico City Policy', preventing non-governmental organisations from using government funds for abortion procedures or promotion. He also successfully passed the Born-Alive Infants Protection Act (2002) and the Partial Birth Abortion Ban (2003), a position that emerged from his conviction that 'even the most vulnerable member of the human family is a child of God'.[59] In his words, he was acting to protect a 'culture of life', a phrase coined by Pope John Paul II and adopted by the Republican Party's official platform in 2004.

BUSH'S GOD STRATEGY

How much was all this 'God talk' a convincing political agenda, and how much can we truly know of the faith behind the phraseology? Given his place in a line of Presidents beginning with Reagan who have heavily invoked God, faith and providence for America in their political rhetoric,[60] it seems naïve to suggest that Bush's use of faith in his political agenda was not also deliberate and calculated. His faith language is, in part at least, simply the language required of the President of the United States. And it was successful – during the 2004 presidential campaign, Focus on the Family founder James Dobson (whose organisation had a reach of 200 million people worldwide at the time) broke with his previously non-partisan position to back Bush.[61] This does not, however, mean that his faith was not also 'genuine'. As Doug Wead put it in a PBS interview in 2004, 'There's no question that the President's faith is real, that it's authentic ... and there's no question that it's calculated.'

This does, to a certain degree, apply to all public figures in the distinction between their personal life and character and the public perception of them. But why is religious belief so significant in an American President? Randall Balmer's history of presidential faith, *God in the White House*, raises an interesting proposition:

> Perhaps it's inevitable that in the United States, which has no religious establishment, we look to the president as a kind of moral figurehead, the sum total of our projections about the supposed goodness and honor and moral superiority of America ... we expect the president to be the vicarious embodiment of the myths we have constructed about the United States of America.[62]

For George W. Bush, as for Presidents before him, the role of American leader was a kind of religious vocation, a calling, even a sacred duty. For Bush, however, this calling also came with a clear mission – whether dealing with social breakdown at home or terrorism overseas, people needed to be free. And they needed to be free to find God.

NOTES

1. George W. Bush, inaugural address, 20 January 2001, Miller Center website, http://miller-center.org/president/gwbush/speeches/speech-3645 (accessed 23 January 2017).
2. George W. Bush, *Decision Points* (New York: Broadway, 2011), p. 15.
3. Ibid., p. 23.
4. Ibid., p. 2.
5. The 'Jesus Day' memorandum, 10 June 2000: see www-tc.pbs.org/wgbh/pages/frontline/shows/jesus/art/pop_jesusday.jpg (accessed 24 January 2017).
6. George W. Bush, *A Charge to Keep* (New York: William Morrow, 1999), p. 224.
7. Bush, *Decision Points*, p. 36.
8. Ibid., p. 70.
9. Ibid., p. 71.
10. George W. Bush, inaugural address, 20 January 2001.
11. Stephen Mansfield, *The Faith of George W. Bush* (New York: Jeremy P. Tarcher/Penguin, 2004), p. 118.
12. Ibid., p. xiv.
13. Bill Keller, 'God and George W. Bush', *New York Times*, 17 May 2003, http://www.nytimes.com/2003/05/17/opinion/god-and-george-w-bush.html (accessed 24 January 2017).

14. 'President Bush attends National Prayer Breakfast', White House website, 7 February 2008, http://georgewbush-whitehouse.archives.gov/news/releases/2008/02/20080207-1.html (accessed 24 January 2017).

15. Lew Daly, 'European Dream: The Political Theology of George W. Bush's Faith-Based Initiative', *Theoria: A Journal of Social and Political Theory*, no. 115, 2008, p. 33.

16. George W. Bush, inaugural address, 20 January 2001.

17. George W. Bush, 'Remarks at National Prayer Breakfast', 1 February 2001, http://www.gpo.gov/fdsys/pkg/PPP-2001-book1/html/PPP-2001-book1-doc-pg42.htm (accessed 24 January 2017).

18. Bush, *A Charge to Keep*, p. 11.

19. George W. Bush, 'Remarks on signing executive orders with respect to faith-based and community initiatives', 29 January 2001, http://www.gpo.gov/fdsys/pkg/PPP-2001-book1/pdf/PPP-2001-book1-doc-pg26.pdf (accessed 24 January 2017).

20. Daly, 'European Dream', p. 40.

21. George W. Bush, second inaugural address, 20 January 2005, Miller Center website, http://millercenter.org/president/gwbush/speeches/second-inaugural-address1 (accessed 24 January 2017).

22. 'Fact sheet: compassionate conservatism', White House website, 30 April 2002, http://georgewbush-whitehouse.archives.gov/news/releases/2002/04/20020430.html (accessed 24 January 2017).

23. Jim Wallis, 'Dangerous Religion: George W. Bush's Theology of Empire', *Mississippi Review*, vol. 32, 2004, p. 62.

24. Bush, *A Charge to Keep*, p. 232.

25. Bush, *Decision Points*, pp. 139–51.

26. See above, p. 142.

27. Bush, *A Charge to Keep*, p. 236.

28. Bush, *Decision Points*, p. 137.

29. Wallis, 'Dangerous Religion', https://sojo.net/magazine/september-october-2003/dangerous-religion (accessed 7 March 2017).

30. George W. Bush, 'Address to the nation on the terrorist attacks', 11 September 2001, American Presidency Project website, http://www.presidency.ucsb.edu/ws/?pid=58057 (accessed 24 January 2017).

31. 'National day of prayer and remembrance for the victims of the terrorist attacks on September 11, 2001', White House website, 13 September 2001, http://georgewbush-whitehouse.archives.gov/news/releases/2001/09/20010913-7.html (accessed 24 January 2017).

32. Mansfield, *The Faith of George W. Bush*, p. 173.

33. 'Chronology: the evolution of the Bush doctrine', PBS website, http://www.pbs.org/wgbh/pages/frontline/shows/iraq/etc/cron.html (accessed 24 January 2017).

34. Randall Balmer, *God in the White House: A History* (New York: HarperOne, 2009), p. 167.

35. Bush, *Decision Points*, p. 397.

36. 'President delivers State of the Union address', White House website, 29 January 2002, http://georgewbush-whitehouse.archives.gov/news/releases/2002/01/20020129-11.html (accessed 24 January 2017).

37. 'President's remarks to the nation', White House website, 11 September 2002, https://georgewbush-whitehouse.archives.gov/news/releases/2002/09/20020911-3.html (accessed 24 January 2017).

38. 'President Bush announces major combat operations in Iraq have ended', White House website, 1 May 2003, https://georgewbush-whitehouse.archives.gov/news/releases/2003/05/20030501-15.html (accessed 24 January 2017).

39. George W. Bush, State of the Union address, 28 January 2003, Miller Center website, http://millercenter.org/president/gwbush/speeches/speech-4541 (accessed 24 January 2017).

40. 'Remarks at the National Prayer Breakfast', 7 February 2008, http://www.gpo.gov/fdsys/pkg/PPP-2008-book1/html/PPP-2008-book1-doc-pg155-2.htm (accessed 24 January 2017).

41. Keller, 'God and George W. Bush', http://www.nytimes.com/2003/05/17/opinion/god-and-george-w-bush.html

42. Bush, *A Charge to Keep*, p. 6.

43. 'Remarks at the National Prayer Breakfast', 7 February 2002, http://www.gpo.gov/fdsys/pkg/PPP-2002-book1/html/PPP-2002-book1-doc-pg187.htm (accessed 24 January 2017).

44. 'Remarks at the National Prayer Breakfast', 6 February 2003, http://www.gpo.gov/fdsys/pkg/PPP-2003-book1/html/PPP-2003-book1-doc-pg130.htm (accessed 24 January 2017).

45. George W. Bush, State of the Union address, 2 February 2005, Miller Center website, http://millercenter.org/president/gwbush/speeches/speech-4464 (accessed 24 January 2017).

46. David Domke and Kevin Coe, *The God Strategy: How Religion Became a Political Weapon in America*, rev. ed. (New York: Oxford University Press, 2010) outlines the 'profound change' that took place in American political rhetoric with the election of Reagan in 1980. Through an analysis of rhetorical devices in presidential public communication, it presents a convincing case for an era of 'calculated, deliberate, and partisan use of faith' (p. 7), which has 'transform[ed] the role of religion in American politics' (p. 8). This is not limited to *direct* invocations of God, but also includes religious language used in a political context – e.g. in 1981, the use of 'mission' in presidential addresses more than tripled, and 'crusade' more than quadrupled (p. 42).

47. Rogers M. Smith, 'Religious Rhetoric and the Ethics of Public Discourse: The Case of George W. Bush', *Political Theory*, vol. 36, no. 2, 2008, pp. 281–3.

48. Bush, *A Charge to Keep*, p. 240.

49. Madeleine Albright with Bill Woodward, *The Mighty and the Almighty: Reflections on America, God, and World Affairs* (HarperCollins, 2006), p. 157.

50. Bush, *Decision Points*, p. 397.

51. 'President's remarks to the nation', 11 September 2002; State of the Union address, 31 January 2006, Miller Center website, http://millercenter.org/president/gwbush/speeches/speech-4461 (accessed 24 January 2017).

52. 'Remarks at the National Prayer Breakfast', 5 February 2004, https://www.gpo.gov/fdsys/pkg/WCPD-2004-02-09/html/WCPD-2004-02-09-Pg195.htm (accessed 24 January 2017). See also remarks at NPB 2001 & 2002.

53. 'Remarks on the celebration of Eid al-Fitr and an exchange with reporters', 17 December 2001, http://www.gpo.gov/fdsys/pkg/PPP-2001-book2/pdf/PPP-2001-book2-doc-pg1524.pdf (accessed 24 January 2017).

54. 'Commencement address at the United States Military Academy in West Point, New York', 1 June 2002, http://www.gpo.gov/fdsys/pkg/PPP-2002-book1/pdf/PPP-2002-book1-doc-pg917.pdf (accessed 24 January 2017).

55. George W. Bush, State of the Union address, 20 January 2004, Miller Center website, http://millercenter.org/president/gwbush/speeches/speech-4542 (accessed 24 January 2017).

56. Wead, a political advisor to both Presidents Bush, recorded at least nine hours of telephone conversations with George W. Bush between 1997 and 2000, without his knowledge. Excerpts were then published at the start of Bush's second term in office. See David Kirkpatrick, 'In secretly taped conversations, glimpses of the future President', *New York Times*, 20 February 2005, http://www.nytimes.com/2005/02/20/politics/

in-secretly-taped-conversations-glimpses-of-the-future-president.html (accessed 24 January 2017).

57. 'President Bush discusses stem cell veto and executive order', White House website, 20 June 2007, http://georgewbush-whitehouse.archives.gov/news/releases/2007/06/20070620-8. html (accessed 24 January 2017).

58. Bush, *Decision Points*, p. 112.

59. 'President Bush speaks to March for Life rally participants', White House website, 22 January 2008, http://georgewbush-whitehouse.archives.gov/news/releases/2008/01/20080122. html (accessed 24 January 2017).

60. See Domke and Coe, *The God Strategy* for in-depth analysis of this pattern, and Nicole Janz's study of American 'civil religion' and Bush, *And No One Will Keep That Light from Shining: Civil Religion after September 11 in Speeches of George W. Bush* (Münster: LIT, 2010).

61. Domke and Coe, *The God Strategy*, pp. 6–7.

62. Balmer, *God in the White House*, p. 163.

ANGELA MERKEL (2005–)

NICK SPENCER

INTRODUCTION

When she first came to power in 2005, Angela Merkel was often called Germany's Margaret Thatcher. The two leaders, it seemed, had much in common. Not only were they both prominent women in the largely male political world, but both had trained as scientists, both were conservatives, and both had risen to the top of their (male-dominated) parties primarily through intelligence and hard work rather than connections and networks.

In some ways, however, Tony Blair makes for a better comparison figure for the German Chancellor than does Margaret Thatcher. Whereas Thatcher was an ideologue who set out her views with force and clarity and then sought to show the public why they were right, Merkel, like (at least the early) Blair, has always been more attentive to public opinion. Merkel's is not a politics of Martin Luther's apocryphal 'Here I stand, I can do no other' but rather one that prefers to 'measure the mood on the streets and govern by it'.[1]

Again like Blair, Merkel has done much to reform her party, taking it to-wards the political centre ground (in her case from the right) by, for example, accelerating a nuclear phase-out, backing a minimum wage and abolishing army conscription. Finally, again like Blair (and unlike Thatcher), Angela Merkel is a serious Christian believer whose faith, although much speculated about, is thoroughly private and difficult to discern with any confidence or in any detail.

UPBRINGING

Angela Merkel was born in 1954 in Hamburg, in West Germany. Her father, Horst Kasner, was a Lutheran pastor and theologian, and her mother, Herlind, an English and Latin teacher. When Angela was six weeks old, the family made the unusual move east to the German Democratic Republic (GDR), just as thousands were travelling west, her father having been asked to head up an evangelical congregation in Berlin-Brandenburg. Three years later, they settled fifty miles further north-east in Templin, where her father ran a theological seminary, and lived in a house with a church-run centre for people with mental and physical disabilities.

The GDR severely restricted the speech and movement of its citizens, in particular those whose origins, like Merkel's family, lay in the West, and constantly scrutinised the activities of those deemed in any way suspect. Horst Kasner was not given to question the state's socialist government, whose political creed was close to his own, and he was critical of West Germany and ideas of reunification. Nevertheless, his family was still under surveillance, the Stasi infiltrating his congregation as it did every aspect of life in the GDR. Subsequent biographers and commentators have surmised that Angela Merkel's strong sense of privacy was inculcated by this upbringing, although others have noted that it was precisely 'by remaining deliberately open in the certainty that everything was being monitored, [that] the church became the one sphere of East German life where alternative viewpoints could be expressed'.[2]

Merkel was a member of the GDR's official Free German Youth movement, a voluntary association in theory although one without which academic or social progress was very difficult. She was, it appears, a reluctant member, however, and she eschewed the movement's *Jugendweihe* or secular 'Coming of Age' ceremony, preferring instead to be confirmed. She went on to study physics at the University of Leipzig, allegedly because 'the truth couldn't be distorted so easily' there as it was everywhere else in the communist state,[3] and then earned a doctorate in quantum chemistry at the German Academy of Sciences at Berlin, around which time she married Ulrich Merkel, another physicist. The marriage lasted only five years but she retained his name even after she married Joachim Sauer in 1998.

By her own account, Merkel was heavily influenced by her father, although this was in the realm of 'clarity of argument' and 'logical rigour' rather than politics.[4] Although no dissident, Merkel decisively rejected her father's socialism. He, she has said, was captivated by the idea of 'socialism with a human face', and was also inspired by liberation theology, but in the end Merkel's own experience and assessment of East German socialism eradicated any early political sympathies she may have inherited.

Following the fall of the Berlin Wall in 1989, Merkel joined Democratic Awakening, an East German party with links to the Lutheran Church, and served briefly as its spokeswoman before it merged with what was effectively its West German counterpart, the Christian Democratic Union (CDU), in October 1990. She was promptly elected to the Bundestag for the electoral district of Stralsund–Nordvorpommern–Rügen in northern Germany, an area that she still represents today. The following month she was appointed as federal minister for women and youth by Chancellor Helmut Kohl, who recognised her talent but also wanted a Protestant woman from the East with a science background to help make his cabinet, comprised disproportionately of Roman Catholic men trained as lawyers, more representative.

Three years later, Merkel was promoted to minister for the environment and nuclear safety and when the CDU was voted out in 1998 she became secretary-general of the party. Merkel was still seen as Kohl's protégée but when, the following year, he admitted taking illegal campaign donations, she surprised everyone by publicly criticising him and urging the party to move on. The battered party elected her as leader in 2000 and, although it was Edmund Stoiber, leader of the CDU's Bavarian sister party the Christian Social Union, who ended up challenging the incumbent Gerhard Schröder for the chancellorship in 2001, she became leader of the opposition when he lost and then, in 2005, Chancellor of a coalition Cabinet after an extremely tight and indecisive election.

FAITH AND UNITY

Angela Merkel is not an ideologue. Her political movements are slow, thoughtful, sometimes hesitant and prone to changes. She is politically flexible, not averse to shifting her party's policies, even to the extent of adopting

those of her SPD opposition. Her tone is moderate and neither naturally antagonistic nor confrontational. She is not given to big visions, grand
speeches or confessional moments. Personally modest and anything but vain,
she is essentially private, with a loyal staff and a very low-profile husband
compounding the sense that even now, after more than a decade in power,
most Germans still don't really know much about their Chancellor. This is
also the sense one gets of her Christian faith.

This is undoubtedly real, for all its privacy. Merkel 'was more intensely
affected by her family home and the Christian faith than she was by her
study of physics and scientific thinking', according to her biographer Volker
Resing.[5] 'I am a member of the evangelical church. I believe in God and
religion is also my constant companion, and has been for the whole of my
life,' she said in a videoblog interview with a theology student in 2012.[6] The
Bible is the book that has most influenced her life, she told students at Trinity College, Dublin, in 2014.[7] When sworn in as Chancellor, she chose to say
the optional, if traditional, phrase 'So help me God' as part of the ceremony.

Inevitably critics claim this is mere political make-up, stock phrases
tailored to appeal to an electorate, many – perhaps a majority – of whom
are reassured by their Chancellor's *moderate* faith. As always, this cannot be
gainsaid, and there is a good argument that Merkel has a particular need
to appeal to the more traditional, Catholic elements in her party who are
disaffected with her more centrist politics; she needs, in effect, to appeal to
the C in the CDU. That recognised, the comparison with Thatcher, who
foregrounded her Christian faith as she made a pitch for power in the later
1970s, and Blair, who made something of his Christian faith (until told not
to) as he did the same in the mid-1990s, is instructive. If Merkel has been
intent on playing the faith card for narrow or cynical political purposes, she
has not done so either very frequently or very well. However sincere her faith
is – and judgement on questions like that often says more of the judge than
the political leader being judged – it is largely private.

Assessing its impact on her politics is, therefore, challenging. 'We as Christians should above all not be afraid of standing up for our beliefs,' she said
in a videoblog interview in 2012. Personally, those beliefs provide her with a
'framework for my life that I consider very important'. That may well mean

her personal life, although Merkel is the least confessional of politicians so it is difficult to say with any confidence. In 2011, Merkel asked religious leaders to pray for European politicians struggling to overcome the Eurozone debt crisis.[8] This is about as personal as Merkel gets – and one might point out that given that she was speaking at the International Meeting of Prayer for Peace, organised by the Roman Catholic lay movement Sant'Egidio, it was hardly very personal or very surprising. Nevertheless, it is worth noting that Merkel accepted the invitation to speak there in the first place and that she said what she did about prayer in the context of an issue as incomprehensible and apparently intractable as the Eurozone crisis – worth noting if only because of the comical hysteria there is in some sections of the British media when a political leader admits that they themselves believe in prayer.

The broader sentiments surrounding her comments on prayer were perhaps more indicative of the framework her Christian faith provides for her. Merkel said that although the debt crisis is repeatedly explained in technical terms, the truth is that it is 'forcing us to live differently, namely to live sustainably, not constantly consuming at the expense of future generations'. In the light of that, she said, 'I ask you to help us with your prayers and your conference here to simply make it clear that Europe is a rich continent and we should be able to avoid also consuming the wealth of future generations.' This is Christian faith as a moral framework that nudges and orientates the politics that goes on within it: Christianity as 'moral compass' in Gordon Brown's sense, although not, of course, one that points in the same political direction. Whereas in Brown's case his 'Christian moral compass' led him to walk across the treacherous fiscal road, taking government resources with him in the process, Merkel's orients her towards responsibility to the future.

Margaret Thatcher always insisted that it was entirely possible and right to find Christians across the political spectrum, but there was little doubt in which direction she felt the Bible and Christianity pointing, and she was not afraid to wade into divisive waters. Merkel, we have seen, seeks to foster unity politically, and the same applies to her engagement with Christianity in public life. Two examples will illustrate this.

Having won the 2013 election, Merkel knew she would be in power during the 500th anniversary of the (start of the) Reformation. This is unlikely to be an uncomplicatedly good (or bad) anniversary anywhere in Europe, but it stands to be particularly contentious in Germany, which suffered more than any other country in the ensuing wars of religion and remains divided, if nothing like as bitterly, along confessional lines. As a result German plans for the anniversary have been tense – the idea of a 'Luther Jubilee', such as that to which the Evangelical Church has invited Catholics – being deeply problematic. In the context of this, Merkel made a rare visit to the Evangelical Church's annual synod in a Baltic resort near Lübeck and urged Germany's Protestant and Roman Catholic churches to stress their common beliefs. 'Especially in a very secular world, we should always stress what is common in the Christian religion,' she said.[9]

Second is the issue of gay marriage. A number of members of Merkel's Christian Democrats called on the German parliament in August 2012 to grant gay couples the same tax benefits as married heterosexuals. This was a minority position in a party that was generally opposed to the move, and the sense was that those who made the call did so because of Merkel's recognised willingness to break some traditional tenets of her party.[10] The following year, Germany's supreme court pronounced that gay couples were indeed entitled to the same tax benefits, a decision that further threatened a rift within the party (at the time only three months before the election). This was an opportunity for a clear and decisive signal on the part of the leader. Typically, Merkel did not make one. Keen to avoid a split between the party's social liberal and more conservative constituents, she did not come down on one side or the other in public.[11] This, of course, was of a piece with Merkel's generally responsive and conciliatory style but simultaneously with her insistence that religion, or deep-felt religious issues, whether half a millennium old or thoroughly contemporary, should not prove divisive and destabilising. Once again, whether this is deemed sensible, principled, pragmatic or cynical is likely to depend on who is making the judgement.

GERMANY, ISLAM AND CHRISTIANITY

Overall, Merkel's Christianity seems real, personal, private and, typically, oriented towards unity and accord, a framework that is held in place by genuine personal convictions but remains generous enough to encompass and accommodate those who do not necessarily share those underpinning convictions. This could serve well as an example of the CDU's politics as a whole, which sees the Christian ethic, and in particular the Christian understanding and valuing of humanity made in the image of God, as its foundation for politics. This Christian understanding and valuing instinctively feels like a sufficiently broad, and therefore uncontroversial, political belief but it has been drawn into one of Germany's most contentious current debates, namely the role of Islam in the country.

Germany, like many other European countries, has experienced historically very high levels of immigration over recent years. Almost 400,000 permanent migrants arrived in 2012, a figure that was dwarfed three years later when an estimated million arrived. Many of these did so on account of Merkel's uncharacteristically bold move of promising a welcome to those who were fleeing the civil war in Syria. This was not a popular decision and her approval rating dropped more than 20 points. She was unrepentant. 'If we now have to start apologising for showing a friendly face in response to emergency situations,' she said, 'then that's not my country.'[12]

A large proportion of immigrants into Germany have been Muslim, the majority coming from Turkey, and this has provoked widespread resentment and protests coalescing, in 2014, into the movement known as PEGIDA (*Patriotische Europäer gegen die Islamisierung des Abendlandes*, or Patriotic Europeans against the Islamisation of the West). Marked by xenophobia and even neo-Nazism, PEGIDA has drawn on Christian (or Judeo-Christian) language and sentiment in its weekly marches in Dresden, while calling for stricter rules of immigration, integration and the protection of Germany's historic (Christian) culture. Moreover, it is not simply a populist or grassroots movement, finding echoes (albeit far more measured ones) in some mainstream political discourse. Thus, Volker Kauder, leader of Merkel's CDU party within parliament, told the German newspaper *Passauer Neue Presse* in 2012 that Islam was 'not part of our tradition and identity in Germany and so does not belong in Germany', while being careful to add that 'Muslims do belong in Germany. As state citizens, of course, they enjoy their full rights.'[13]

This is treacherous ground, as the very fact that Kauder's intervention was reported under the headline 'Merkel ally says Islam does not belong in Germany' shows. Any politician, like Merkel, who believes that Christianity offers a serious ethical framework for politics (or who is prepared to recognise the obvious and irrefutable fact that Christianity has been pivotal in shaping German society and culture) but who doesn't want to give any support, encouragement or opportunity to PEGIDA faces a perilous balancing act.

Merkel has stated that Muslims are under obligation to obey the constitution, and not sharia law, if they want to live in Germany: 'The values represented by Islam must correspond with our constitution.'[14] She has also paid tribute to freedom of speech at a ceremony for the Danish cartoonist Kurt Westergaard, whose image of the Prophet Muhammad with a bomb in his turban proved immensely controversial. The Chancellor analogised the Westergaard controversy with the lack of freedom she endured when growing up in East Germany[15] and had her photo taken next to Westergaard. This was 'a huge risk', the conservative *Frankfurter Allgemeine Zeitung* claimed, and although the image didn't turn out quite as provocative as some predicted, it certainly did provoke: Aiman Mazyek, of the Central Council of Muslims in Germany, said that 'Merkel is honouring the cartoonist who in our view trampled on our prophet and trampled on all Muslims'. On a more emollient note, Merkel has reacted vigorously to the anti-Islamic sentiments of PEGIDA by saying clearly that 'Islam belongs to Germany' and that 'attacks on mosques will be prosecuted rigorously, because we won't be divided by those using Islamist terrorism to cast suspicion on all Muslims in Germany'.[16]

In the light of this, it is noteworthy that Merkel has not been silent about Christianity in Germany – surely a temptation given the divisive atmosphere generated by Islamic extremism and its Islamophobic reaction. Some years before PEGIDA emerged, but long into the time when anti-Islamic sentiment was widespread in Germany, Merkel sought to emphasise Christianity's centrality and significance in German culture and life. In 2010, talking at the Ecumenical Church Congress in Munich, she spoke of Christianity as the main foundation of the country's values system.[17] Vatican Radio's German service highlighted her comments, in particular those that were not in the prepared text (and which got almost no coverage elsewhere):

Our society lives on premises that it cannot create by itself. Without a doubt, one of these very important premises is Christianity. Christianity has shaped our country ... I'm not saying we could not have arrived where we are in any other way, but here in Germany it's very clear that we came to our values system through Christianity. That means we know that freedom does not mean freedom from something, but it means freedom given by God through His Creation to commit oneself to help others and stand up for causes. This may be the most important source of social cohesion.

This is a sophisticated argument, associated (in Germany; it has also been made elsewhere) with the legal philosopher Ernst-Wolfgang Böckenförde, who argued in 1967 that 'the liberal secular state lives on premises that it cannot itself guarantee',[18] and debated subsequently by Jürgen Habermas and Joseph Ratzinger, shortly before the latter became Pope Benedict.[19] Altogether, this was a brief, rare, seemingly unscripted but revealing philosophical excursion from the German Chancellor.

Philosophically sophisticated as it may be, it is still a sensitive argument given the context of German politics, so it is instructive to note that later the same year, addressing her party, Merkel made the point that Germany suffered not from 'too much Islam' but 'too little Christianity'.[20] 'We have too few discussions about the Christian view of mankind,' she said, and we need more public discussion 'about the values that guide us (and) about our Judeo-Christian tradition'. Multiculturalism, she said, had failed, and it was only through a confident reclaiming of this Judeo-Christian tradition that that 'we will also be able to bring about cohesion in our society'.

Such sentiments, it should be noted, are common among CDU politicians, especially when speaking to their party, but Merkel's willingness to engage in this debate in this way, combined with her clever positive spin on the presenting issue – not too much Islam but too little Christianity – nonetheless mark her out as a leader. After all, such sentiments would be impossible in France and improbable in the UK.

CONCLUSION

For all her high profile, Angela Merkel is neither particularly prophetic nor confessional as a politician. She manages, firmly, adroitly, patiently, persistently, and even though she does not set out to inspire with big visions, she has earned considerable admiration among her electorate and won three election victories.

The same principles that govern her political life shape her theo-political life. Admittedly, a chancellorship that has largely been dominated by the Eurozone debt crisis has not exactly lent itself to the kind of ideological politics of a Margaret Thatcher or Gordon Brown, or the more confessional politics of a George W. Bush or Kevin Rudd. Nevertheless, Merkel's Christian faith is real and sincere, seemingly a genuine motivation, providing a framework that anchors and orients her politics, without ever risking being divisive or antagonistic. Willing to articulate her own faith, and to recognise the formative influence of Christianity not only on German society and culture, but also on the very foundations of liberal democracy, Merkel is an interesting counterpoint to every recent British Prime Minister.

NOTES

1. Sara Miller Llana, 'The mind of Angela Merkel', *Christian Science Monitor*, 20 September 2013, http://www.csmonitor.com/World/Europe/2013/0920/The-mind-of-Angela-Merkel (accessed 24 January 2017).

2. Alan Crawford and Tony Czuczka, *Angela Merkel: A Chancellorship Forged in Crisis* (Chichester: Bloomberg Press, 2013), p. 30.

3. Quoted ibid., p. 27.

4. Ibid., p. 28.

5. 'Merkel: I believe in God, religion is my companion', *The Local*, 6 November 2012, http://www.thelocal.de/20121106/45993 (accessed 24 January 2017).

6. Ibid.

7. '6 things we learned about Angela Merkel from her Q&A with Trinity Students', TheJournal. ie, 7 March 2014, http://www.thejournal.ie/angela-merkel-trinity-philsoc-1350436-Mar2014 (accessed 24 January 2017).

8. Tom Heneghan, 'Merkel asks religious leaders for prayers to help get through eurozone crisis', Reuters, 13 September 2011, http://blogs.reuters.com/faithworld/2011/09/13/merkel-asks-religious-leaders-for-prayers-to-help-get-through-eurozone-crisis (accessed 24 January 2017).

9. Tom Heneghan, 'Merkel urges German churches to agree on Luther fest', Reuters, 5 November 2012, http://uk.reuters.com/article/2012/11/05/us-germany-reformation-merkel-idUS-BRE8A41C620121105 (accessed 24 January 2017).

10. Madeline Chambers, 'Merkel's CDU breaks taboo with call for gay couple tax equality', Reuters, 8 August 2012, http://in.reuters.com/article/2012/08/08/germany-gays-idINL6E-8J84BS20120808 (accessed 24 January 2017).

11. Madeline Chambers, 'German court backs gay couples' tax rights in setback to

Merkel', Reuters, 6 June 2013, http://www.reuters.com/article/2013/06/06/germany-court-gay-idUSL5N0EI1MN20130606 (accessed 24 January 2017).

12. Quoted in Nancy Gibbs, 'The choice', *Time*, December 2015, http://time.com/time-person-of-the-year-2015-angela-merkel-choice (accessed 24 January 2017).

13. Madeline Chambers, 'Merkel ally says Islam does not belong in Germany', Reuters, 19 April 2012, http://blogs.reuters.com/faithworld/2012/04/19/merkel-ally-says-islam-does-not-belong-in-germany (accessed 24 January 2017).

14. Stephen Brown, 'Constitution, not sharia, is supreme law in Germany – Merkel', Reuters, 7 October 2010, http://blogs.reuters.com/faithworld/2010/10/07/constitution-not-sharia-is-supreme-law-in-germany-merkel (accessed 24 January 2017).

15. 'German chancellor Merkel honours Mohammad cartoonist at press award', Reuters, 9 September 2010, http://blogs.reuters.com/faithworld/2010/09/09/german-chancellor-merkel-honours-mohammad-cartoonist-at-press-award (accessed 24 January 2017).

16. Stephen Brown, 'Angela Merkel vows to protect Germany's Jews and Muslims from extremism', Reuters, 15 January 2015, http://blogs.reuters.com/faithworld/2015/01/15/angela-merkel-vows-to-protect-germanys-jews-and-muslims-from-extremism (accessed 24 January 2017).

17. Tom Heneghan, 'Merkel cites Christian roots as Berlin resumes Muslim dialogue', Reuters, 17 May 2010, http://blogs.reuters.com/faithworld/2010/05/17/merkel-cites-christian-roots-as-berlin-resumes-muslim-dialogue (accessed 24 January 2017).

18. The full relevant quotation is: 'The liberal secular state lives on premises that it cannot itself guarantee. On the one hand, it can subsist only if the freedom it concedes to its citizens is regulated from within, inside the moral substance of individuals and of a homogeneous society. On the other hand, it is not able to guarantee these forces of inner regulation by itself without renouncing its liberalism.' See Ernst-Wolfgang Böckenförde, 'Die Entstehung des Staates als Vorgang der Säkularisation', in *Säkularisation und Utopie: Ebracher Studien – Ernst Forsthoff zum 65. Geburtstag* (Stuttgart: Kohlhammer, 1967), quoted in Reinhart Hutter, *Dust Bound for Heaven: Explorations in the Theology of Thomas Aquinas* (Grand Rapids, MI: Wm. B. Eerdmans, 2012), p. 104.

19. See Jürgen Habermas and Joseph Ratzinger, *The Dialectics of Secularization: on Reason and Religion* (San Francisco: Ignatius Press, 2006), p. 21.

20. Tom Heneghan, 'Merkel: Germany doesn't have "too much Islam" but "too little Christianity"', Reuters, 15 November 2010, http://blogs.reuters.com/faithworld/2010/11/15/merkel-germany-doesnt-have-too-much-islam-but-too-little-christianity (accessed 24 January 2017).

ELLEN JOHNSON SIRLEAF (2006–)

MADDY FRY

INTRODUCTION

Ellen Johnson Sirleaf was the first woman to become an elected head of state in Africa. After studies in the USA and a marriage that produced four children, she moved to Kenya to forge a successful career in banking. She became politically active in Liberia in the 1980s during the autocratic regime of General Samuel Doe, who was notorious for imprisoning his opponents. Sirleaf endured time in jail for being a dissident but eventually went on to work for the United Nations after her release. She made a bid for the Liberian presidency and won in 2005. She and fellow peace activists Leymah Gbowee and Tawakkul Karman were jointly awarded the Nobel Peace Prize in 2011.

BIOGRAPHY

As one of the most powerful women in the world, Ellen Johnson Sirleaf's life has been a mixture of privilege and struggle. She was born in 1938 of mixed Liberian and German descent. Her father, Jahmale Carney Johnson, was a lawyer and the first indigenous Liberian to occupy a seat in the country's national legislature. Her mother, Martha, was descended from a mixture of German and Kru ancestry (a group from the centre of the country) but as a child was put into foster care with a prominent American-Liberian family. She went on to work as a teacher and preacher.

Ellen was brought up in the Liberian capital, Monrovia, where she was educated at the College of West Africa, a Methodist secondary school that counted many of Liberia's former leaders among its alumni. In 1961, she travelled to America with her husband, where she gained an associate degree in accounting from Wisconsin's Madison Business College. She was to return to the US in 1970 after her divorce, where she went on to gain a Master of Public Administration degree from Harvard.

Sirleaf's relocation to America in the 1960s had initially been prompted by her husband James's decision to take up a scholarship offer to study agriculture at the University of Wisconsin-Madison. Back in Liberia, she had been a housewife and full-time mother to their four sons, but in the USA she started to harbour career aspirations of her own. This reportedly aroused considerable jealousy in her husband, which led to the relationship becoming increasingly abusive. The couple eventually divorced.

It wasn't until 1972 that Sirleaf returned to Liberia. She worked as the assistant to the government's then finance minister before occupying the post herself in 1979. As the country's political situation became increasingly turbulent, so did Sirleaf's career: the execution of President William Tolbert in 1980 caused her to flee to Kenya for fear of assassination at the hands of a coup led by General Samuel Doe. While in exile in Nairobi she directed the multinational firm Citibank between 1983 and 1985. Her attempt to return to Liberia resulted in a jail sentence after she was accused of criticising the regime. She managed to avoid serving the full term and escaped back to America, where she returned to banking before joining the United Nations Development Programme Regional Bureau for Africa, a body aimed at reducing poverty and inequality levels in developing countries.

At this point, a comfortable life in America seemed the most appealing and logical option. Yet in 1997 Sirleaf went back to her homeland and made a bid for the presidency. She lost to Charles Taylor, the leader who became notorious for his brutal involvement in the civil war in Sierra Leone. Taylor's disastrous rule caused civil war to escalate in Liberia for a second time (the first war lasted from 1989 to 1997), leaving thousands of the country's civilians dead or displaced. His eventual removal by a group of African armies allowed Sirleaf to stand again in 2005. This time she overwhelmingly beat her rival, George Weah, winning nearly 60 per cent of the vote. She was the first woman in history to occupy the position of an elected head of state in an African country.

None of this is to suggest her track record has been flawless. Critics have accused her of nepotism, mixed results on tackling corruption, and a massive error of judgement in initially lending her support to Taylor (a position she has since recanted). Yet Sirleaf has also been praised for overseeing ten years of relative peace and stability in Liberia, with her role in opposing the country's legacy of dictators having won her considerable respect abroad.[1]

RELIGION

When asked in an interview in 2009 where she drew her strength from during the years of struggle against the regime of Samuel Doe, Sirleaf cited not only her faith in herself but her faith in God.[2] There is much to suggest that her religious beliefs have played a significant role in her ascendancy on the Liberian, and indeed global, political stage.

Educated at a Methodist school during her teenage years, Sirleaf's faith background in some ways goes against the grain within west Africa, an area of the continent largely associated with Pentecostal and Charismatic movements. Yet at the same time, as Dr David Harris, an expert in African studies at the University of Bradford, points out, 'all leaders of Liberia have been Christian, often Baptist or Methodist, and a President would be expected to be a pious Christian'.[3] One can sense, however, that Sirleaf's convictions go deeper than merely a genuflection to the established political culture of Liberia. Although she was raised a Presbyterian at home, Methodism's understated emphasis on graft and diligence bears its influence on the dedication in her autobiography (ironically, the somewhat self-servingly titled *This Child Will Be Great*): 'In memory of my mother, Martha Cecelia Johnson, who instilled in us the value of hard work, honesty, and humility.'[4] In a 2008 speech she gave to the United Methodist General Conference in Texas, she also drew on Methodism's history of concern for social justice, insisting that the church was needed in getting the government to 'improve health and education' and 'give people hope'.[5]

Furthermore, despite the strong Christian strain within the country's political culture, leaders often, according to Harris, give themselves a position in the 'traditional religious hierarchy', based on the indigenous pre-Christian religious practices many in the country still adhere to. In Harris's words, these include 'Poro and Sande secret societies' – single-gender groups that promote the social, political and sexual interests of their members – that are 'still influential at a local level'. Many people in Liberia believe that ancestral spirits play a role in the affairs of humans, in ways that can be understood by priests and diviners. In their darkest form, these pre-Christian beliefs incorporate practices such as those of the 'heart men', contracted to kill others and supply their organs to clients in the belief that eating them will enhance a person's power. Yet Harris claims Sirleaf is evidently 'one exception' to this rule, in that she has defined herself only as a Christian.[6]

This can be traced back to Sirleaf's devout religious upbringing. Her mother, like many women in Liberia, had been forced to endure her husband's polygamous tendencies, but she sought solace from it in faith. Sirleaf's memoir describes her family as 'deeply religious'.[7] She talks of how Martha Johnson even became an 'itinerant minister in the Presbyterian Church, traveling through the countryside to preach the Word of God', claiming that it was 'rare in those days for a woman to serve as a travelling preacher, but my mother did'. The young Ellen and her siblings would sometimes go with her, walking or canoeing for miles to towns and villages. The work often involved singing hymns and giving recitations in front of crowds of worshippers. Sirleaf cites these experiences as her first exposure to public speaking, giving her a determination to excel at it.[8]

Her mother's resilience was also evident in her refusal to allow her daughter to wallow in self-pity over how she was teased for having fairer skin than her classmates. In Sirleaf's words, her mother would simply tell her to 'stop wasting time and energy regretting things that could not be helped'.[9] This also laid the foundations for Sirleaf's endurance during her incarceration under the rule of General Doe. In her prison cell after being given a ten-year sentence by a military tribunal as a punishment for opposing his rule, she would console herself with the passage from Psalm 46:10 often quoted by her mother: 'Be still and know that I am God.'[10]

An incident that involved her abduction by Doe's soldiers after she found them surrounding her house almost resulted in her execution at their hands. She survived by a fluke, as a senior officer ordered the men to take her to a prison camp instead of bringing her in front of Doe – which, as a known dissident, would have resulted in her being shot on sight. She claims she was able to appeal to the common humanity of the soldiers, and she was made to undergo a regime of imprisonment and forced labour. She recounts it calmly, stating that she felt as long as 'God kept me from the hands of killers, I could survive the discomfort and even pain of prison'.[11]

By the time her career as a political agitator took off Sirleaf had embraced her husband James' more cosmopolitan Methodist faith, in contrast to the rustic Presbyterianism of her childhood. Methodism was strongly associated with the debonair mixed-race Liberians in Monrovia, many of whom were of European or American descent. Sirleaf's exposure to it began as an adolescent, when she had been educated at one of Liberia's oldest and most prestigious European-style schools – an experience that provided her with an education far better than that which many of her peers would have received. She described it as a refuge from the tensions of home life, where the students were spirited – including her husband, whom she met in her final year – and the teachers enthusiastic and motivated. However, she acknowledges it sprang from an elitist system. As a Methodist institution that only the 'privileged and well-connected could attend', the teenage Ellen gained a place only through her father's influential position in the government.[12]

This was in sync with the way Methodism was viewed across Liberia in general, which contrasted strongly with its European roots in frugality, integrity and concern for the poor. In his recent collection of interviews with Liberian expats in New York, Jonathan Steinberg records how from the late nineteenth century, Methodists in Liberia were associated strongly with attempts by Americo-Liberians, the ethnic group descended from freed slaves that dominated politics within the country until the 1980s,[13] to assert their difference, as well as dominance, over the indigenous population. One of them recounted how some among them were 'unable to set themselves apart from the locals in skin colour or physical type' and so would attempt to underscore their difference in other ways. As well as their regal dress sense and fondness for erecting manors and palaces similar to those in the American

South, their religious circles were 'similarly closed and inaccessible to the native Africans'. They were 'ardent Baptists and Methodists', constructing 'simple churches in the new land' and spending all their free time 'singing pious hymns and listening to topical sermons'.[14]

Steinberg's own assessment is even more scathing: 'The notion that Americo-Liberians are not of Liberia, but simply settled there to milk it, runs deep in Liberian consciousness.'[15] This evokes a Liberian Methodism out of touch with the cultural and religious sensibilities of the vast majority of the country's population – something that Sirleaf's words and gestures have mostly seemed to strive against.

Yet despite her church's association with advantage and elitism, as well as her eventual break with her husband, Sirleaf has continued to define herself as a devout believer in the ideals at the core of Methodism, in line with John Wesley's exhortation to 'feed the hungry, clothe the naked, and help the stranger, the widow and the fatherless'. This is evident not only in her heartfelt concern for the inequalities and divisions existing in Liberian society, but in her unashamed conviction that her desire to eradicate them is sanctioned from above.

CHRISTIANITY AND
THE SIRLEAF PRESIDENCY

Sirleaf's autobiography is peppered with references to the guiding hand of the Christian God. Her inaugural speech after being voted in as President began with an exaltation of praise to God and a request for those present to take a moment to pray for all those who perished during the civil war.[16] She describes Liberians as an innately 'forgiving people' and 'God-fearing'.[17] She states her belief throughout the book that she was determined to act on her presidential duties with 'God's help and guidance', and talks of wanting to do right by him according to 'His messages'.[18] She builds on this by linking God's plan for the country with her own, seeking to bring peace and prosperity to Liberia 'with God's blessings', and by saying that she believed her mother's prayer every night had been for God to lead her to do what was right – 'by Him, by my people, and by my land'.[19]

Her vision for the country is, therefore, a profoundly religious one. The above statements seem to imply that she feels the leading hand of God everywhere and that her actions are sanctioned by Him, so long as she feels they are done in His name and under His tutelage. She gave voice to this feeling most during the Ebola crisis, when during an interview in 2014 with Christian Broadcasting Network (CBN) News she insisted that the churches had an important role to play in providing calm and stability during the epidemic. 'When you meet circumstances that you don't understand and that you don't control … you can turn somewhere, where do you turn? You have to turn to your faith, you have to turn to God and that's a Liberian experience that's deep rooted,' she said.[20]

Yet her ambitions for the country have been no small challenge, largely because, to quote Liberia scholar Robtel Neajai Pailey, in a naked contradiction of its Christian foundations, Liberia's recent history has been one of 'intolerance, war-mongering and structural violence'.[21] These contradictions will probably continue to define the national psyche. In 2012, a campaign spearheaded by Liberian clergy members tried to have the country defined in the constitution as a Christian nation. The campaign was controversial, partly because, despite the influence of Christianity as a central pillar of the country's foundation in 1847 by freed slaves, memories of tense relations between Christians and Muslims, even though they have become more amicable in recent years, are still fresh in many people's minds.[22] Yet Sirleaf has not been afraid to place herself firmly within the Christian tradition, and to allow it to play a significant, and many would argue positive, role in her strategy for the country.

WHAT HAS SIRLEAF'S FAITH MEANT FOR HER PRESIDENCY IN PRACTICE?

It is important to take into account the fact that Sirleaf's vision for Liberia, amid all its piety, has been faced with accusations of hypocrisy and inconsistency. The Liberian Truth and Reconciliation Commission, a body set up with the aim of investigating the crimes of the civil war years, accused her of secretly channelling funds into the military activities that sparked the first wave of civil unrest.[23] The final report from the commission went so far as to recommend that Sirleaf, along with fifty other people, be banned from holding public office for thirty years for lending assistance to different militant groups within the country.[24] Although the report's findings were condemned by a plethora of NGOs and foreign governments, the allegations lingered. Coupled with the criticism over her decision to elevate her own sons to exalted positions within her government,[25] even ordinary Liberians who had voted for her felt she deserved to be punished.

Yet, by the same token, her acknowledgement of the commission of her ideological failure in supporting Charles Taylor's early campaigns was followed by an apology and an admission that it was an error of judgement, and it was notable that she chose to go before the commission and confess rather than be summoned.[26] Furthermore, despite the long shadow cast by the civil war, it hasn't managed to eclipse the respect Sirleaf has been accorded at home and abroad for her work in promoting reconciliation efforts between different religious groups in Liberia, as well her championing of women's rights. In a 2010 speech to a conference of female Baptist missionaries in Liberia's Montserrado County, she praised the evangelising efforts of those present, but also lauded their role in helping women 'grow to their full potential', in order to 'impact the world around them' and 'recognise their value'. She described religion and spirituality as being 'the cornerstone of hope, faith and love for all peoples and races', with faith being the 'basis of strength and resolve for Liberians' during the civil war. She also claimed the main way to justice and development is through 'prayer, witness and service'.[27] Drawing heavily upon St Paul's letter to the Galatians, she implored those present when planning for the future to work towards 'the fruit of the Spirit: love, joy, peace, patience, kindness, goodness, faithfulness, gentleness and self-control', and to encourage the next generation of leaders to 'grow in the faith and actively share the love of Christ in their communities'.[28]

It is clear that in Sirleaf's vision, conflict resolution and social justice are intrinsically linked with religious faith, with her beliefs informing her stated conviction that religious tolerance and gender equality are essential for the future of Liberia. For all its controversies, this is demonstrated in her presidential record. One of the women who organised the first peer review of Sirleaf's presidency was Leymah Gbowee, an activist noted for her work in inspiring many women in Liberia to campaign for an end to the country's violent hostilities. Despite the disagreements the two would have over the years, Gbowee claimed Sirleaf had 'done things no one else could have'[29] in improving the lives of the country's women. They were jointly awarded the Nobel Peace Prize in 2011.

Such actions were a further break with the country's past not just for the central role played by women, but also for the ecumenical nature of the movement for peace. As David Harris acknowledges, it was an example of modern inter-faith efforts at peacemaking amid Liberia's historically tense relationship between its different religious factions. This was clearly an intention of Sirleaf's from the first days of her presidency, as in her inaugural speech she made clear her aim of 'settling differences' between all ethnic and religious groups in Liberia, but also her readiness to 'forcefully, swiftly and decisively' respond to any 'lawlessness' or 'destabilising actions that could return us to conflict'.[30] Despite the Nobel committee lauding her for the non-violent nature of her previous actions, her belief in the need for tolerance and unity clearly extends to using violent methods to maintain it if the need arises.

Ultimately, one can view the outworking of Sirleaf's Christianity as being one with its own explicitly multi-faith and women-focused character – a rupture within the male-dominated interpretations of religious and political interactions in Liberia, which at their core were often violent and egotistical, and, in the case of Charles Taylor, used to bolster his supposed messianic traits and thereby lend legitimacy to his bid for the presidency. As Robtel Neajai Pailey describes it, 'The ecumenical religious solidarity of the women is sharply contrasted with the divisive religious posturing by the men.'[31] For as long as Sirleaf is President, this strand of her thinking will likely continue to be a defining feature of political life in Liberia.

Ellen Johnson Sirleaf, for all her faults, undoubtedly holds a faith that is profoundly sincere, one that she has not imposed on the political system in the way Charles Taylor did – which is to say she has not used Christianity as a vehicle to promote the idea that the position of the Liberian presidency is reserved for her alone. Instead, her professed focus on social justice, particularly gender equality, carries with it a Methodism-flavoured Christian influence in its concern for those in Liberian society who have suffered greatly as a result of past injustices. Sirleaf's aims have not always resulted in success, yet any attempt to use religion for overtly nationalistic and prophetic ends has been absent from her track record. If nothing else, this is a deviation from the norm in Liberian politics. It will be a significant feature of her legacy.

NOTES

1. Adekeye Adebajo (ed.), *Africa's Peacemakers: Nobel Peace Laureates of African Descent*, (London: Zed, 2014), p. 283.
2. 'Liberia President says she's driven by her faith', NPR website, 9 April 2009, http://www.npr.org/templates/story/story.php?storyId=102903666 (accessed 24 January 2017)
3. Interview with Dr David Harris, 5 February 2015.
4. Ellen Johnson Sirleaf, *This Child Will Be Great: Memoir of a Remarkable Life by Africa's First Woman President* (New York: Harper, 2009), p. 17.
5. Linda Bloom and Kathy L. Gilbert, 'Liberia President Sirleaf addresses United Methodists', United Methodist Church website, 29 April 2008, http://www.umc.org/news-and-media/liberia-president-sirleaf-addresses-united-methodists (accessed 24 January 2017).
6. Interview with Dr David Harris, 5 February 2015.
7. Sirleaf, *This Child Will Be Great*, pp. 129–30.
8. Ibid., p. 18.
9. Ibid., p. 27.
10. Ibid., p. 130.
11. Ibid., pp. 130–50.
12. Ibid., p. 27.
13. Jonny Steinberg, 'A Truth Commission Goes Abroad: Liberian Transitional Justice in New York', *African Affairs*, vol. 110, no. 438, 2011, p. 41.
14. Jonny Steinberg, *Little Liberia: An African Odyssey in New York City* (London: Vintage, 2012), p. 37.
15. Steinberg, 'A Truth Commission Goes Abroad', p. 41.
16. Sirleaf, *This Child Will Be Great*, p. 317.
17. Ibid., p. 334.
18. Ibid., pp. 258, 270, 272.
19. Ibid., pp. 272, 286.
20. George Thomas, 'God help us! Liberian leaders lead prayer charge', CBN News website, 13 October 2014, http://www.cbn.com/cbnnews/world/2014/October/God-Help-Us-Liberian-Leaders-Lead-Prayer-Charge (accessed 24 January 2017).
21. Robtel Neajai Pailey, '"Pray the Devil Back to Hell" and the making of Leymah Gbowee, Nobel laureate', *African Arguments*, 16 December 2011, http://africanarguments.org/2011/12/16/in-praise-of-leymah-gbowee-and-pray-the-devil-back-to-hell-by-robtel-neajai-pailey (accessed 24 January 2017).
22. George Stewart, 'Liberia: getting back to the founding faith', *Christianity Today*, June 2012, http://www.christianitytoday.com/ct/2012/june/founding-faith.html (accessed 24 January 2017).
23. Steinberg, 'A Truth Commission Goes Abroad', p. 42.
24. Jonny Steinberg, 'Liberia's Experiment with Transitional Justice', *African Affairs*, vol. 109, no. 434, 2010, pp. 137, 141–2.
25. Adebajo, *Africa's Peacemakers*, p. 287.

26. Ibid., p. 141.
27. 'Keynote address by HE President Ellen Johnson Sirleaf to Baptist Women Missionary Unions of Africa Conference, Baptist Youth Camp, Schiefflin Highway, Montserrado County, Liberia, Monday, November 15, 2010', p. 3. Available at http://www.emansion. gov.lr/doc/20101115President_keynote_address_Baptist_Women_Unions_FINAL.pdf (accessed 24 January 2017).
28. Ibid., p. 4.
29. Leymah Gbowee, *Mighty Be Our Powers: How Sisterhood, Prayer, and Sex Changed a Nation at War – A Memoir* (New York: Beast, 2011), p. 218.
30. Sirleaf, *This Child Will Be Great*, pp. 332–3.
31. Pailey, '"Pray the Devil Back to Hell" and the making of Leymah Gbowee, Nobel laureate'.

GORDON BROWN (2007–10)

PAUL BICKLEY

INTRODUCTION

It's ironic that an era of Labour politics defined by Alastair Campbell's phrase 'We don't do God' produced three consecutive religious leaders. Following John Smith, Tony Blair offers an obvious example, but he in turn was followed as Prime Minister by a politician to whom religious descriptions seemed to cling. Gordon Brown was a 'son of the manse', carrying a powerful 'Presbyterian heritage', with a 'Calvinist background' that left him with a strong 'moral compass'.

Brown himself, however, gave contradictory impressions about his faith. On the one hand, unlike Blair at least in his pre-prime ministerial days, he was largely circumspect about his personal religious views. Although he was/ is a member of the Church of Scotland, he usually refused any deeper discussion. Private and reserved by temperament, Brown was always unlikely to wear his faith – or indeed lack thereof – on his sleeve. On the other hand, he frequently riffed on this theological hinterland when seeking to unpack his own political vision and approach. He was clear on the importance of public faith, and worked closely with faith-inspired campaign groups on issues dear to his heart, such as the cancellation of debt in the developing world. Brown consciously made extensive use of biblical material in speeches, particularly those delivered to faith audiences. Perhaps more tellingly, scripture often found its way into off-the-cuff remarks.

It is possible to make two mistakes when exploring the connections

between Brown's faith and his politics. The first is to assume that these connections – often made by Brown himself – were pure cant, a fact betrayed
by his harsh treatment of political opponents. The second is to accept them
without some kind of critical appraisal, ignoring the ways in which Brown
was clearly uncomfortable with strong personal expressions of faith. Either
way, further investigation is invited. When it comes to Gordon Brown, it is
not only legitimate but important to take account of his faith when trying to
understand his legacy as a politician.

EARLY LIFE AND POLITICAL CAREER

Born in Giffnock near Glasgow in 1951, at the age of three Gordon Brown
moved to Kirkcaldy where his father, John Brown, had become the minister
of St Brycedale Kirk, a congregation of the Presbyterian Church of Scotland.
His upbringing was not one where politics and religion were kept neatly
apart – rather, they were seamlessly intertwined. Brown's political consciousness developed early enough for him to be found campaigning against Alec
Douglas-Home in the Kinross & West Perthshire by-election at the tender
age of twelve. He joined the Labour Party in 1969.

Brown's life in the manse has often been the source of ridicule, but there
is no reason to doubt that his upbringing was an important influence and
the source of his sympathy with what he later called 'social Christianity'.
We do not know to what extent the young Brown experienced a deeply felt
personal faith, but it was certainly an upbringing that sensitised him to the
life of ordinary working people in the context of Christian responsibility to
the needy. Living in a manse, he related, 'you find out very quickly about
life and death and the meaning of poverty, justice and unemployment'.[1] His
early life marked him with a connection to communities in need, a sense of
the importance of gainful employment and the waste of unemployment (the
subject of his highly regarded maiden speech in the House of Commons in
1983), and a Presbyterian-flavoured egalitarianism.

After a three-year term as an unusually young rector of the University of
Edinburgh (at which he was accepted to study at the age of sixteen), Brown
served his political apprenticeship in a Scottish Labour Party that was simultaneously full of talent but mired in internecine conflict between Bennite,

old-right and Tribunite (democratic socialist) factions (Brown was essentially a Tribunite). Tom Bower – not a friendly biographer – notes, tellingly, that before he was selected as a parliamentary candidate the party 'wanted evidence of more than a commitment to the community and worship of the Bible, Burns and Keir Hardie'.[2] Brown obliged, becoming chair of Scottish Labour's Devolution Committee and leading the Labour campaign in support of a Scottish Assembly. By taking on what his contemporaries called a 'poisoned chalice' (the party was divided on the issue), he developed a national profile before even being elected to Parliament.

At this formative stage of Brown's early career, his religious beliefs are more or less hidden from view. What we know of his intellectual interests indicate his wholehearted absorption in the world of Scottish Labour and left-wing politics. His PhD thesis focused on the Scottish Labour Party between 1918 and 1929. In his PhD, and a subsequent book, he took special interest in James Maxton, the fiercely socialist leader of the Independent Labour Party. And in an introductory essay to *The Red Paper on Scotland*, a collection that he edited at the age of twenty-four, he revealed an admiration for Marxist thinkers Paulo Freire, Antonio Gramsci and E. P. Thompson. If his faith was important at points, at other times it is either absent or undocumented. At this stage in his career, the Scottish Labour Party was Brown's church, its ideology was his theology and its success was his salvation.

Bower speculates that Brown's rugby injuries at school, which resulted in partial loss of sight, multiple operations and an extended and lonely convalescence, were accompanied by a loss of personal faith: 'Neither in public nor in private would he ever express thanks to God or refer to Christianity as an influence, guide or support for his life.' This is too speculative. What seems clearer is that politics and Brown's political conscience and career – including several abortive attempts to be selected as a parliamentary candidate – took priority over almost everything else in his life. In the late 1970s, a relationship with Princess Margareta of Romania ended, in spite of mutual affection and to mutual regret. Brown's inattentiveness was allegedly to blame, and this was down to his relentless focus on politics.

At this time, in combination with his Labour activities, Brown was working as a lecturer in politics at the Glasgow College of Technology and at the Workers' Educational Association. In 1979, he had his first opportunity to fight a seat (unsuccessfully on that occasion), and from 1980 to 1983 he worked for Scottish Television. In the general election of 1983, he was finally elected as the member of Parliament for Dunfermline East, but arrived in Westminster with the wider party in disarray.

REFOUNDING LABOUR

In the next decade, Brown was increasingly engaged in attempts to reconstruct Labour's electoral viability after the population at large had decisively rejected the socialist alternative. Even in 1983, there was a strong sense that the country needed a moderate social democratic option. Brown's views on core political questions – the role of the state, the nature of the economy and the place of civil society – were changing substantially.

Meanwhile, the party as a whole still needed a framework within which it could offer a serious ethical critique of individualism without resorting to wholesale renationalisation, nuclear disarmament and whatever other resolutions it had adopted during its annual conference. During the Labour leadership elections in 1983, *The Guardian* was prompted to observe that the ideal leadership/deputy ticket would be Tawney/Tawney, referring to the famous Christian socialist R. H. Tawney.

Brown supported Neil Kinnock's leadership bid in 1983, and under his leadership served as shadow chief secretary to the Treasury and shadow secretary of state for trade. After Kinnock's unexpected defeat in the 1992 general election, Brown was encouraged to stand for the Labour leadership, but refused. Under Kinnock's successor, John Smith, Christian socialism experienced something of a revival in the party. Over half of the Labour front bench were members of the Christian Socialist Movement (CSM), a 'socialist society' affiliated to the Labour Party. It is not clear if Gordon Brown ever was a member, but Tony Blair had joined Smith as part of the group in 1991.[3]

In 1993, a group of Christian Labour politicians and activists published *Reclaiming the Ground*, a collection of essays including Smith's Tawney Lecture of that year (the annual lecture of the CSM), in which he claimed that Christianity can be allied to democratic socialism and said that the 'Church has always focused on the moral purpose of political action'.[4] The collection didn't include a contribution from Gordon Brown, although it is worth noting that Smith's lecture bears strong affinities with lines of argument later pursued energetically by Brown – for example, a rereading of Adam Smith drawing greater attention to his argument for the moral embeddedness of markets. A strong mutual influence could and should be inferred.

It is important to recognise what was and what wasn't happening at this stage. Front-bench Labour MPs weren't scouring the pages of the New Testament for economic and social policy. In the period after Smith's death, and in the early years of the New Labour administration, policy was organised under the mantra of fairness and equality of opportunity. But ethical and Christian socialism often provided the beat of the drum. Labour's critique of government policy wasn't just that it didn't work, but that it had fallen short on the level of morality, community and the common good.

It's fair to say that Brown was less inclined than Blair to philosophise in speeches or in print. But you can still detect a religious sensibility in his egalitarianism – the way that fairness became his mantra – and his frustration at deep-rooted privilege and disadvantage. 'My vision of a fair Britain means not just taking on entrenched interests that hold people back, and pursuing a modern social policy that offers pathways out of poverty, but a new economic policy – a new economic egalitarianism.'[5] The Scottish political commentator Gerry Hassan detects a sense of 'mission and purpose to Brown' at this stage,[6] rooted in Puritan self-discipline and shaped by a Protestant work ethic – a sense of the goodness and salvation of work. Hassan notes that his speeches were filled with talk of 'making work pay' and building a 'revived work ethic'. Later, Brown became much more explicit in his faith engagement – not least through the use of the Bible in speechmaking, but perhaps here we can detect the influence if not of personal faith then certainly of a culture shaped by a particular kind of Protestantism.

BROWN'S BIBLE

From around the turn of the millennium onwards, Brown, who as Chancellor of the Exchequer already had significant power, was beginning to exercise a broader leadership both domestically and internationally. As his appetite for leadership grew so did the need to give the general public a greater sense of who he was. He would increasingly allude to his upbringing, and particularly to the influence of his father and his career as a minister in the Church of Scotland. Alongside this biographical trope, Brown increasingly began to use the Bible in his speechmaking. We will confine ourselves to three examples of the ways in which Brown did this, though we could refer to many more.

THE GOOD, THE WICKED AND THE LAZY: THE PARABLE OF THE TALENTS

First, with regard to his conviction of the redemptive power of work, Brown would frequently allude to the Parable of the Talents (Matthew 25:14–30, paralleled in Luke 19:12–27). Thus, in his speech at the Labour Party conference in 2007 he said: 'My father was a minister of the church, and his favourite story was the Parable of the Talents because he believed – and I do too – that each and every one of us has a talent and each and every one of us should be able to use that talent.'[7] This text was here being deployed to support the idea of equality of opportunity. In other speeches, such as at the previous year's party conference, Brown connected the idea of talents more with the idea of duty (those with 'talents' have a duty to exercise them). For Brown the parable offered a paradigm of individuals who use their human gifts and those who do not, finding the latter wicked or lazy. In other words: those that can work should work.

Of course, these passages don't really mean these things. Historically a talent was a unit of weight, then later a unit of coinage, and only in the Middle Ages developed the popular meaning of an ability or aptitude. The metaphorical talents are most likely the privileges and duties of the covenant people of God, and the 'wickedness and laziness' of the servants is the failure of God's people to fulfil their obligations. In the parable, Jesus is offering a prophetic critique of Israel, not a general admonition to 'make the most of what you got'.[8]

That said, Brown's use of this text is surprising and fascinating. Naturally, the reference had a purpose, probably one of enhancing Brown's prudent and austere public image and fending off any critique that would see him as a 'soft touch' when it came to unemployment. Yet the fact that this text was used in this way says something about Brown's background and the ways in which his conscience was shaped.

UNTYING THE YOKE: ISAIAH AND BROWN
ON INTERNATIONAL DEVELOPMENT

In January 2000, Gordon Brown delivered the Gilbert Murray Memorial Lecture. As with a number of speeches in the period either side of the millennium, Brown used Isaiah 58:6 in defence of policies seeking to 'establish a new virtuous circle of debt relief, poverty reduction and economic development':

> [So ours is a] call to action as new as the debt crisis, but it is as old as the call of Isaiah to 'undo the heavy burdens and let the oppressed go free' ... But the quest for prosperity round the world is the greatest challenge and greatest moral imperative of our times.[9]

For Brown, Isaiah 58 was, first and foremost, indicative of an 'ancient dream' – a moral world of those who 'believe in something bigger than themselves'. Participants in this 'one moral universe' – people of 'conscience', 'idealism' and 'conviction and faith' – are to eschew self-interest and seek to help the weak.

Isaiah's call is binding not because it is in any sense revelatory but because it is representative of a prior moral sense; Brown was often cautious not to seem exclusive or sectarian in his use of scripture. Tellingly, just a few lines prior to the quote above, Brown had referenced the deist Tom Paine (who wrote in *The Age of Reason* that the Bible and the Testament are 'impositions upon the world ... fabulous inventions, dishonourable to the wisdom and power of the Almighty'): 'We have it in our power to begin the world anew.'

Again, there was a certain interpretive naivety in Brown's use of this and similar texts (such as Amos 5:24,[10] which Brown would often use in similar contexts). In the Pope Paul VI CAFOD Memorial Lecture of December 2004, Brown referenced Isaiah 57:10 in tandem with Isaiah 40:31. His rhetorical goal was to stiffen political resolve in the face of lack of progress towards the Millennium Development Goals:

> Let us hear the words of Isaiah: 'Though you were wearied by the length of your way, you did not say it was hopeless – you found new life in your

strength.' And let us answer with Isaiah also as our motto for 2005: that we shall indeed 'renew our strength, rise up with wings as eagles, walk and not faint, run and not be weary'.[11]

Brown appears unaware that in Isaiah 57 the prophet relates Yahweh's judgment to Israel. The 'wearying way' of the text is not anything to do with loosening the chains of the oppressed but Israel's persistence in idolatry. Brown (hopefully) unwittingly uses these verses not only out of but against their own literary context.

We should not, of course, be too hard on Brown; he was not, after all, speaking as a biblical scholar. But these examples do reveal some of the tensions that emerge from political uses of the Bible. Interpretive mistakes usually stem from the desire to draw general humanistic lessons from tradition-specific verses. The rhetorical power of the text is retained, but careful exploration of their meaning in their canonical and historical contexts would only hinder the speechmaking objective.

WALKING BY ON THE OTHER SIDE:
THE PARABLE OF THE GOOD SAMARITAN

Of all of Brown's uses of scripture his most frequent was the deployment of the Parable of the Good Samaritan. Brown's speech to the Church of Scotland General Assembly in May 2008 was laden with biblical references. Unlike other instances, he does not tend to 'declare' the citation, but weaves it into the speech through the theme of neighbourhood in a globalised world:

Today, to ask that simple searching question: 'Who is my neighbour?' is also to ask: how can we – facing as we do now such a range of urgent challenges: threats to the global environment; the rise – and evident fragility – of the global economy; a crisis in feeding the world's people; gross injustices between the richest and the poorest nations; and threats of nuclear proliferation, international terrorism, and new pandemics; how can we discover right across the world common ground on which to act?[12]

Brown moves on to conclude his speech along the same lines, suggesting

that, since we share the same globe and the same moral universe, neighbourhood is universal: 'We are not moral strangers to each other.'

Yet again, there are some missteps in Brown's interpretation, but his use of
the text is once more revealing. It later proved to be his oratorical mainstay
for justifying government action to tackle the global economic crisis, often
juxtaposed with the 'do nothing' approaches of other political actors. The
interpretive emphasis here has changed from the nature of neighbourliness
to that of walking by on the other side:

> We are prepared to spend money to help the unemployed; we are not
> going to walk by on the other side, we are going to help them. However,
> when it comes to the Conservatives' main proposal for spending money,
> let us be absolutely clear that we are spending money to help the unem-
> ployed whereas the Conservatives' first priority is an inheritance tax cut for
> the 3,000 top estates in the country.[13]

Rhetorically, Brown seeks to bracket his political opponents with the priest
and the Levite, who won't dirty their hands in an effort to assist those strick-
en by circumstance. In this way, the citation is far more 'political', in the
sense of being used to back specific ideological positions. It is interesting also
that this reference is – unlike many others – unscripted. These verses helped
form Brown's early political conscience, and at key moments at times of
national crisis he would reach for these ideas and this language.

CONCLUSION

After a bright start, Brown's prime ministerial career ended in the messy
aftermath of the 2010 general election. Since that time, however, he has
continued to be an actor on the national political stage with notable interventions in the Scottish independence referendum. His career has in many
ways come full circle.

During his premiership and since, Brown's use of the 'son of the manse'
narrative has attracted some derision. Many feel it to be too calculated and
insincere, and would note – just as we have above – that Brown was far more
circumspect about his faith than some of his contemporaries.

Brown's unease was not imagined. Even his public comments on his father's faith indicate a degree of distance from the subject: in his 2006 Labour Party conference speech, Brown observed: 'My father was a minister of the church. His motive was not theological zeal but compassion ... Most of all my parents taught me that each of us should live by a moral compass.' Elsewhere, Brown has contrasted his father's 'social Christianity', expressed as the desire to treat everyone equally, with 'fundamentalism'. Theologian Doug Gay finds Brown to be one among a generation of high-profile Scottish Protestants who would display a residual loyalty to the Kirk as a source of identity, but who show very little sign of having ever been emotionally, spiritually or intellectually captured by the Christian gospel: Brown is the 'quintessential, modernist, demythologized, liberal, *kultur*-Presbyterian.'[14]

Such an account would interpret all evidence of the influence of the Church and the Bible on Brown's political thinking and language as cant and cynical invention. However, this analysis is too abstract – and cynical – focusing on his public discomfort and assuming disbelief rather than reserve. Brown really did grow up in a manse under the tutelage of parents with a profound faith. From that start, he dedicated his life not to discipleship but to the success of the Labour Party, first in Scotland and then across the UK, and also latterly to humanitarian political interventions, both national and international. In other words, he is a complicated and multi-faceted politician, but one for whom his formative faith is a not insignificant aspect of his thinking.

In a speech delivered at Lambeth Palace in 2011, we are given a direct window onto Brown's thinking about the relationship between faith and politics. This extended reflection contains no big surprises – Christians, says Brown, must avoid the sin of commission (attempting to assert a theocracy) but also the sin of omission (failing to recognise the public dimensions of their faith). The speech revisits many of the arguments and ideas familiar from Brown's earlier career. What is surprising is that it has a significant emotional charge. Brown begins with recollection of his infant daughter's baptism just days before her death:

Our first child, our only daughter, was born prematurely three days after Christmas in 2001. Over the next ten days when my wife and I held her

tiny hand or held her close to us, the heartbeat monitor registered a quick-
ening heart-beat. She knew that people who loved her were there: that she
was surrounded by love.

But in an incubator in intensive care, she did not grow or flourish.
Within a few days we had sensed ourselves what we were subsequently told
by doctors: that she was too fragile, too frail to survive.

On the last Sunday night, knowing she was likely to die that night or
the next day, we asked our minister if she would come to the hospital after
her evening church service to baptize Jennifer. As I held her in my arms
– her beautiful face unaffected, untouched by the scale of the tragedy that
had befallen her – Sarah and I took our vows as parents to do everything to
'bring her up in the nurture and the admonition of the Lord'.

The baptism was not, for us, just a comfort and not just a ritual: it was
a recognition that every single life, even the shortest life, has a purpose and
that every single person is irreplaceable.[15]

At different points in his career, Brown's faith has surfaced and then receded
from view. It's hard to draw a direct link between this or that policy and his
faith, but his remarks at Lambeth in 2011 should serve to remind us that his
political consciousness was formed by faith as well as by the traditions of the
Scottish Labour Party.

NOTES

1. Tom Bower, *Gordon Brown, Prime Minister* (London: HarperPerennial, 2007), p. 2.

2. Ibid., p. 25.

3   Andrew Bradstock, 'History of our movement', Christians on the Left website, 1 November
    2013, http://www.christiansontheleft.org.uk/history_of_our_movement (accessed 25 Janu-
    ary 2017).

4. John Smith, 'Reclaiming the Ground', R. H. Tawney Memorial Lecture, 20 March 1993,
    http://www.johnsmithmemorialtrust.org/media/63970/Reclaiming-the-Ground.pdf   (ac-
    cessed 25 January 2017).

5. Gordon Brown, 'The Politics of Potential: A New Agenda for Labour', in David Miliband
    (ed.), *Reinventing the Left* (Cambridge: Polity Press, 1994), pp. 113–22.

6. Gerry Hassan, 'Labour's Journey from Socialism to Social Democracy: A Case Study of
    Gordon Brown's Political Thought', in Gerry Hassan (ed.), *The Scottish Labour Party: His-
    tory, Institutions and Ideas* (Edinburgh: Edinburgh University Press, 2004).

7. Gordon Brown, speech to Labour Party conference, 24 September, 2007. See 'Gordon
    Brown's speech in full', BBC News website, 24 September 2007, http://news.bbc.co.uk/1/

hi/uk_politics/7010664.stm (accessed 25 January 2017). Other key instances of this citation are his party conference speech in 2006 and his speech to the Church of Scotland General Assembly in 2008.

8. See, for instance, N. T. Wright, *Jesus and the Victory of God* (London: SPCK, 1996), p. 635.

9. Gordon Brown, Gilbert Murray Memorial Lecture, 11 January 2000.

10. 'Let judgment run down as waters, and righteousness as a mighty stream.'

11. Gordon Brown, Pope Paul VI CAFOD Memorial Lecture, 8 December 2004. Transcript available at http://www.indcatholicnews.com/news.php?viewStory=12160 (accessed 25 January 2017).

12. Gordon Brown, speech before the Church of Scotland General Assembly, 17 May, 2008. Transcript available at http://www.britishpoliticalspeech.org/speech-archive.htm?-speech=335 (accessed 25 January 2017).

13. Gordon Brown, Hansard, HC Deb, 18 March 2009, vol. 489, col. 902.

14. Doug Gay, 'Faith in, with and under Gordon Brown: A Scottish Presbyterian/Calvinist Reflection', *International Journal of Public Theology*, vol. 1, nos. 3–4, 2007, pp. 318–19.

15. Gordon Brown, 'Faith in Politics?', lecture given at Lambeth Palace, 16 February 2011. Transcript available at http://rowanwilliams.archbishopofcanterbury.org/articles.php?903/faith-in-politics-lecture-by-gordon-brown (accessed 25 January 2017).

KEVIN RUDD (2007–10)

ANDREW CONNELL

INTRODUCTION

Kevin Rudd's career as a political leader was relatively brief. Having entered the Australian House of Representatives in 1998, he became leader of the Australian Labor Party (ALP) and of the federal opposition in December 2006. After the ALP decisively defeated John Howard's Liberal–National coalition government at the December 2007 general election, Rudd became Prime Minister. His government ratified the Kyoto climate change accord and largely avoided recession after the global financial crisis, while his Apology to the Stolen Generations, delivered in Parliament in February 2008, was hugely important in recognising the mistreatment of indigenous Australians. However, his credibility was damaged by the failure of key policy proposals and increasing questions about his leadership style, and in June 2010 his deputy Julia Gillard successfully challenged him for the party leadership and, thus, the prime ministership. After the August 2010 general election Rudd became foreign minister in Gillard's minority government until early 2012. In June 2013, he became Prime Minister again after challenging Gillard for the party leadership, but the ALP lost that autumn's general election to the coalition. Rudd promptly resigned from Parliament and is now (2017) president of the Asia Society Policy Institute, a New York-based international affairs 'think-do tank'.[1]

Rudd is a controversial figure. Although in his early years as ALP leader and Prime Minister opinion polls gave him consistently and unprecedentedly high personal approval ratings, his record of achievement in government was mixed, and his role in the internal wranglings of the ALP alienated many members of the party's parliamentary caucus. On Rudd's return to power in 2013, Scott Stephens, the Australian Broadcasting Corporation's (ABC) online religion and ethics editor, wrote of his 'tendency to bend certain moral causes [including Christianity] into the service of his own political vanity', and of his 'penchant for high-moral rhetoric and his failure to attend to the ... no less morally significant mechanics of patient governing'.[2] There were undoubtedly domestic policy failures, most notably over an unsuccessful proposal for a carbon emissions trading scheme, which led directly to Rudd's resignation in 2010. But Rudd's personal style also played its part. Even a generally sympathetic commentator could write of his 'nasty side' as Prime Minister and concede that while stories of his 'bad temper, profane language, and overweening pride' might have been exaggerated by his opponents for political reasons, they nonetheless could not all be baseless.[3]

This chapter suggests that Rudd is remarkable less for his record during in his three years in power than for how he achieved office. Between 2004 and 2007, Rudd very successfully 'did God' in electoral politics, and did so from a left-of-centre political position. He was overt about the influence of his faith on his politics, thereby becoming respected as a politician of principle and winning a general election. It is this achievement, perhaps a counter-intuitive one in a relatively secular Western democracy, which we discuss here.

RUDD'S EARLY CAREER AND SPIRITUAL FORMATION

Rudd was born in 1957 in Nambour, Queensland, and was brought up in his mother's Roman Catholic faith. He has described this faith as essentially practical, characterised by 'a deep, deep Catholic view that if you saw someone in distress ... you had to do something about it'.[4] After his father's death in 1968, Rudd spent two years boarding at a Roman Catholic school before returning home.[5] Throughout this time he continued to attend Mass but 'there was no particular sense of personal faith'.[6] On leaving school, he spent a year working in Brisbane and Sydney while deciding on a university course, and during this year concluded that he was indeed a Christian. This was the result of reading and reflection on the Christian church's claims about the existence of God and the life of Christ, rather than of any discrete conversion or revelation: the proofs upon which it was based were 'no more remarkable than were available to people who have reflected on these things over the centuries; no more persuasive or unpersuasive depending on who is reflecting on them'.[7] He began to worship with the Uniting Church (the then-recent union of Methodists, Presbyterians and Congregationalists in Australia) and continued to do so as an undergraduate at the Australian National University (ANU), Canberra.[8] There, at a Christian meeting, he met Thérèse Rein, his future wife and an Anglican.[9] In 1981, shortly after Rudd had graduated with a first-class degree in Asian studies, they married in St John's Anglican Church, Reid, where they would subsequently worship when in Canberra. Rudd is now often described as an Anglican although it appears that he has never formally left the Roman Catholic Church.[10]

After graduation Rudd became a diplomat, serving in Sweden and in China. In both countries he maintained his church involvement and in China even became a lay preacher.[11] He also joined the ALP, a party which represented to him wider horizons than had been available in the Country (now National) Party stronghold of Nambour. In 1988, he secured a secondment from the Foreign Service to become chief of staff to Wayne Goss, the Queensland ALP leader and, from 1989, state premier. In 1991, still on secondment, he became director-general of the Office of the Cabinet in Queensland, but resigned from the public service in 1995 to seek a parliamentary career of his own. In 1998, he became federal MP for Griffith, in suburban Brisbane.

Rudd's spiritual formation indicates four elements that help us understand how he 'did God' as a politician. First, for Rudd Christian belief demanded a practical response. Just as he characterised his mother's Catholicism as requiring the believer to respond to distress and need, so he argued that to be a person of faith 'causes you to reflect properly on how the resources of the earth should equitably be used'.[12] While faith did not mandate a particular political position, it did require the believer to engage with practical questions on a morally informed basis.

Second, Rudd emphasised that his Christianity was a matter of 'faith and reason', based on conclusions that he drew after considering long-established arguments.[13] This implies that other people might reasonably draw different conclusions from considering the same arguments. For Rudd, faith-based propositions must be subjected to the same process of reasoned debate as any others. Specifically, in politics 'the key thing in a system such as ours is to have those propositions tested properly, through reason, in the secular forum of the Parliament'.[14] Rudd would, on occasion, ground arguments specifically in Christian teaching: for example, a parliamentary speech in 2005 on industrial relations was larded with references to Catholic social teaching.[15] But that speech was directed against a Roman Catholic government minister. When addressing more diverse audiences, Rudd expected faith-based arguments to be taken seriously but did not claim that they had any particular authority in themselves.

Third, Rudd's Christianity was not sectarian.[16] Traditionally the Liberal Party, associated with an Anglo-Scots establishment, had been largely Protestant, while Roman Catholics, including those of Irish descent, were more likely to be found in the ALP.[17] Recently this has changed, and there are now numerous conservative Catholic Liberals, including Rudd's (second) successor as Prime Minister, Tony Abbott. But Rudd could, when appealing to broadly Christian audiences, use references and discourses that might be either closely focused on a particular tradition or deliberately broad and inclusive (drawing attention, for example, to the Presbyterian contribution to Christian socialism in the UK and in Australia).[18] Combined with his emphasis on a reasoned and reflective faith, then, this reassuringly post-sectarian Christianity[19] helped present him as an inclusive and unthreatening kind of Christian. But it was – and this is the fourth element – rooted in mainstream Australian Christianity. Rudd's faith journey encompassed Roman Catholicism, Anglicanism and the Uniting Church – denominations that between them still accounted, by 2011, for over 75 per cent of Australian Christians.[20] This is significant because when the coalition parties began to court Christian opinion in Australia in the early 2000s it was to the newer evangelical and Pentecostal churches that they principally looked. Although Rudd would seek, with some success, to win support for the ALP from members of these denominations, his grounding was in the traditional churches, all of which had in different ways emphasised the social as well as the personal message of Christianity.

Rudd was initially reluctant to speak about his faith in public, although his maiden speech in Parliament argued strongly for the centrality of values to politics.[21] In 2000, when asked what he thought of the invocation of theological positions in public debate, his reply was brief and blunt: 'It makes me vomit.'[22] However, by 2004 he would have developed a stronger stomach.

THE CHALLENGE OF THE 'RELIGIOUS RIGHT'

Christianity had never been absent from post-war Australian politics: Paul Keating (1991–96), for example, was a believing Catholic and Bob Hawke (1983–91), though an agnostic, was raised and shaped by a Congregationalist minister father and a devout mother.[23] That recognised, under John Howard religion in Australian public and political life became, as noted elsewhere in this volume, increasingly de-privatised.[24] Church-based organisations became more engaged in delivering public services, school chaplaincies received public funding, and government ministers acquired new confidence in speaking about their beliefs.[25]

Paradoxically, at the same time relationships between the mainstream churches and the federal government became 'strained to breaking point'.[26] The coalition approved when churches took over provision of social services; it did not approve when, as they frequently did, they criticised neo-liberal social and economic policies, or Australia's intervention in Iraq. Government ministers increasingly accused church leaders of speaking out of turn on matters in which they lacked expertise, and courted the emergent evangelical and Pentecostal churches, which espoused individualist aspirations and traditionalist family values.[27] Ideologically and electorally, the coalition was identifying Christianity with its own politics. In 2004, an electoral deal with the small Family First party, which had deep roots in Pentecostalism, helped the coalition win at least four marginal seats in that year's federal election and gave Family First itself a seat in the Senate.[28] Many observers interpreted all this as evidence of the rise of a Religious Right in Australia.[29]

For Rudd, now shadow foreign minister, this 'Americanisation of political Christianity' in Australia placed a 'moral responsibility' on Christians of the left to re-emphasise the place of faith in their own tradition.[30] This became the project that would define him politically after 2004. A month after the election, he declared on television that he would not accept any assertion that 'God has somehow become some wholly owned subsidiary of political conservatism in this country'.[31] In 2005, he established a working group on values and ethics within the ALP parliamentary caucus, sending out a clear signal that the ALP was asserting the importance of values within politics. He began to use the language of the Religious Right to frame arguments from the left, arguing for example that 'family values' must include the family's ability to feed, care for and educate its children.[32] Similarly, he contended that the coalition's 'Workchoices' legislation, which pursued labour market flexibility by allowing national employment standards to be replaced by local agreements, undermined the family as an institution by eroding workers' rights to statutory holidays and overtime payments.

Most notably, Rudd began to speak much more explicitly about religion. Already an able communicator, he now turned his skills to the presentation of his faith and its political consequences.

'FAITH IN POLITICS'

The most accessible and developed articulation of Rudd's views on the relationship between Christianity and politics is his essay 'Faith in Politics', published in the magazine *The Monthly* in October 2006. Although in its timing the essay sat firmly within Rudd's campaign to loosen ties between the coalition and the Christian right, it nonetheless expressed themes developed over a sustained period.[33] Overcoming his earlier reluctance, Rudd had already referred explicitly to faith positions in a number of parliamentary speeches. He had discussed his faith on television in October 2004 and again in May 2005, and also in a lecture delivered in October 2005 and partly broadcast on national radio the following January.[34] That lecture contributed significantly to the essay, which had 'a huge resonance' and was the catalyst for a public debate about faith in politics.[35]

The essay examined the relationship between faith and politics in the modern world. Rudd began by considering the work of Dietrich Bonhoeffer – a man of 'faith' and 'reason', and 'without doubt, the man I admire

most in the history of the twentieth century'.[36] Bonhoeffer, he argued, had
exemplified prophetic Christianity in politics. Rejecting the 'two kingdoms'
doctrine by which religion concerned itself with the inner person and the
state reigned supreme in public affairs, he had insisted that the church
engage fully in public life. The principle underpinning this engagement,
Rudd argued, was that the church should always take the side of 'the marginalised, the vulnerable and the oppressed'. This principle, derived from Old
Testament prophetic literature and the Gospel accounts of Jesus, would not
in itself answer specific social, economic or security questions, but it would
help shape answers. In all these fields, 'the function of the church ... is to
speak directly to the state: to give power to the powerless, voice to those who
have none, and to point to the great silences in our national discourse where
otherwise there are no natural advocates'.

Rudd then turned to five possible models of individual Christian engagement in politics. The first of these was the claim that Christian voters should
'vote for me because I'm Christian'. This Rudd described as being about as
intelligent as claiming political support on the basis of common support of
a football team. A second claim was summarised as 'Vote for me because I'm
Christian, and because I have a defined set of views on a narrowly defined
set of questions concerning sexual morality.' This reflected an inadequately
narrow concept of Christian morality. A third position added to the previous
two the tag of 'family values' – an overused, and abused, term which invariably left 'to one side the ability of working families to survive financially'. The
fourth model, claiming that 'religion should keep out of politics', added to
the previous three a 'political fusillade against anyone who dares suggest that
Christianity might have something concrete to say about the broader political,
economic and social questions'. Finally, Rudd's favoured model of engagement, building on Christ's teaching that his followers would be judged by
their response to those in need, emphasised the social imperatives of the
Gospel. Inevitably, the social Gospel would become political, because politics was collective action: it required Christians to debate problems 'within
an informed Christian ethical framework'. Public policy could not be left to
'practical' politicians: Christians had a right and a duty to be engaged. In a
secular polity, Christian perspectives had to be weighed alongside arguments

grounded in other traditions, but they should not be excluded from the public square.

Rudd presented these arguments in general terms but their application to contemporary Australian politics was obvious. He then specifically accused the Howard government of hypocrisy and of habitual untruthfulness. Bonhoeffer's principle that the Church should be a voice of truth, he argued, inevitably entailed looking 'beyond the sound-and-light show of day-to-day political "debate"' to identify 'the real underlying fault lines in the polity'. Values mattered; and there was a clear distinction between those of social democracy and neo-liberalism. Unfettered liberal capitalism would destroy any institution that stood in the way of economic individualism – and here again Rudd singled out the effect of Workchoices on family life. The churches' criticisms of the government, he argued, were a prophetic exposition of the truth that lay behind the government's rhetoric. Rudd called for Australia to be guided, nationally and internationally, by the values of 'decency, fairness and compassion', which were 'still etched deep in [its] national soul'. 'Bonhoeffer's vision of Christianity and politics', he concluded, 'was for a just world delivered by social action, driven by personal faith.' As such, it provided 'an eloquent corrective' to those who sought to co-opt Christianity for the political right.

'DOING GOD' RUDD-STYLE: THE 2007 FEDERAL ELECTION, AND AFTER

We have seen that Rudd's faith was oriented towards practical action; that it drew on reasoned reflection and expected its claims to be tested by reasoned argument; and that it was rooted within traditional Australian Christianity. Rudd believed that politics should be based on values, and he turned some of the right's own language against itself. All these elements are clearly expressed in his Bonhoeffer essay. Although Rudd would claim that it was 'addressed very much to people out there in the Australian community who are Christians', this statement was preceded by the observation that according to census data up to 75 per cent of the population believed in God: so 'Christians' here seemed to be broadly defined, and the widespread interest which the essay aroused perhaps reflects this.[37]

Rudd's biographer suggests that no Australian politician of the left had ever appealed so directly to Christian voters; the essay signalled that in Rudd's ALP they could find a 'congenial home'.[38] Another commentator contrasted Rudd's widely appealing 'mature, non-threatening' political Christianity with that offered by 'the fundamentalist zealots of the New South Wales Liberal Party'.[39] Within the ALP, even non-believers recognised the electoral value of Rudd's approach as a way of outflanking the coalition's conservative Christianity.[40] It established Rudd in the public mind as a person of 'integrity' and a principled politician.[41] Perhaps counter-intuitively, 'Australians liked the idea that here was someone who wasn't afraid to be different. A politician who could use terms like "morality" without blushing seemed to be a rare treat in the political scene.'[42]

It is an exaggeration to say that Rudd won the 2007 election by 'doing God'. At least two respectable histories of the 2007 ALP campaign barely mention Rudd's religion.[43] One scholar argues that 'having "ticked the faith box" [early in the campaign], Labor focused on secular electoral themes and events' thereafter.[44] But Rudd did assemble a broad base of electoral support, which the political analyst and former senator John Black described as looking 'a little like a 1970s [ALP] rally held in a Queensland rural church hall … with high-school educated, skilled and unskilled blue-collar workers sitting side by side with the evangelical and activist religion'.[45] In this, the religious element was important, although not sufficient.

Although Rudd's roots were in mainstream Christianity, he did not neglect the evangelical vote. During the campaign, alongside John Howard, he addressed the 'Make it Count' forum organised by the Australian Christian Lobby, a rather conservative pressure group, although unlike Howard's his address focused largely on social and economic issues and did not seek to appeal to a particular religious position.[46] Perhaps more importantly, Rudd looked – and was – socially conservative. He emphasised values-driven politics, and his values were those of traditional rural Queensland. By combining the promise of dynamic change with 'personal social conservatism[,] … social-justice principles based upon Christian socialism', attacks on neo-liberalism, and a religious appeal which was nonetheless attuned to the requirements of a diverse secular polity, Rudd assembled a formidable and balanced body of support.[47] As Black put it, 'While the blue collar workers provided the grunt with the national swing, the religious activists provided the leverage and the key seats' – and many of those religious activists were Pentecostals and evangelicals.[48] But while, in 2007, Rudd successfully appealed to Christian voters from those backgrounds, he did not adopt the values of the Religious Right. Instead, he demonstrated that a politician of the left could use the language of faith in a way that could appeal to voters in a pluralistic Anglophone democracy.[49]

It might be argued that Rudd's success was short lived. He was Prime Minister for less than three years and while some observers see some of what his government did – for example, in response to the global financial crisis, on climate change and in some areas of social and welfare policy – as being to his credit, in other areas he is seen as having failed or, perhaps worse, as having failed to live up to the moral principles which he espoused. An example of the latter criticism relates to asylum policy, where Rudd has been accused of having shifted his rhetoric to deterrence (and the evils of people-smuggling) rather than an understanding of the needs of asylum seekers.[50] Nor can Rudd be said to have turned the coalition of support that he assembled in 2007 into a lasting power base for the ALP. Under Julia Gillard – incidentally a declared atheist – Labor did retain power, albeit as a minority government, but the overall impact of religion in that federal election of 2010 was slight.[51] After Rudd's brief return to office, the party was soundly defeated by the coalition in 2013. Tony Abbott, a conservative Catholic, became Prime Minister, and Family First again won a Senate seat.

Nonetheless, Rudd's achievement in 2007 was a notable one. His faith had contributed to his electoral success, as voters saw him as a man of principle and integrity. Many lower-income Christians, of all denominations but especially Protestants, who would not normally have voted Labor were persuaded to do so.[52] But Rudd had insisted that while Christian arguments had a place in the public square, they carried no special authority there: they had to be weighed alongside other perspectives. He had been equally adamant that a Christian politician should not expect to gain the support of Christian voters merely on the basis of a common faith. Christianity could not alone constitute a platform or an electoral appeal, although it could inform both. Christian politicians could not, therefore, expect their faith to trump voters' judgements on their records or wider positions. In 2010, and in 2013, Rudd's own faith did not save him from public perceptions that he was an unsuccessful party leader and Prime Minister. Paradoxically, then, his fall from electoral favour after 2007 was entirely in the spirit of the political Christianity which he espoused.

NOTES

1. Kevin Rudd's personal website, http://kevinrudd.com/biography (accessed 25 January 2017).

2. Scott Stephens, 'The resurrection of Kevin Rudd: What will he do with his second lease on political life?', ABC website, 27 June 2013, http://www.abc.net.au/religion/articles/2013/06/27/3790786.htm (accessed 25 January 2017). In the same article Stephens nonetheless conceded that 'there was a kind of moral intelligibility about what Rudd was trying to do, even if the intention and execution were severely compromised', and suggested that it was 'the inability of many in the electorate to discern a set of guiding moral principles that proved terminal to the leadership of Julia Gillard'.

3. Roy Williams, *In God They Trust?: The Religious Beliefs of Australia's Prime Ministers, 1901–2013* (Australia: Bible Society, 2013). Williams does argue, however, that 'on every major count, Rudd has been defended by people who should command respect – colleagues, political opponents, journalists, speech-writers, staffers'. It is also notable that Rudd's ultimately unsuccessful campaign for nomination for the post of UN secretary-general in 2016 divided opinion. Although some politicians and commentators questioned his personal fitness for the post, many others, including political opponents, considered him to be suitably qualified for it.

4. 'Kevin Rudd: The God Factor', *Compass*, ABC TV, 8 May 2005. Transcript available at http://www.abc.net.au/compass/s1362997.htm (accessed 25 January 2017).

5. This should not be misunderstood as implying affluence. Rudd's father was a share farmer and although the family were not poor their circumstances were modest. When, after his death, his widow and children had to leave the farm, they went through a period of some hardship. Rudd's mother would retrain as a nurse, but meanwhile Rudd's period at boarding school, where his fees were paid charitably, was a way of relieving the financial burden on the rest of the family.

6. Quoted in Robert Macklin, *Kevin Rudd: The Biography* (Camberwell, VIC: Viking, 2008), p. 47. This biography was written with Rudd's cooperation.

7. Ibid.

8. Williams, *In God They Trust?*

9. David Marr, 'Power Trip: The Political Journey of Kevin Rudd', *Quarterly Essay*, vol. 38, 2010, pp. 26, 27. Marr's essay is largely critical of Rudd but it does provide a useful summary of factual and biographical detail, as well as of selected responses to Rudd's politics.

10. See for example John Warhurst, 'Religion and the 2010 Election: Elephants in the Room', in Marian Simms and John Wanna (eds), *Julia 2010: The Caretaker Election* (Canberra: ANU EPress), pp. 303–11; 'Fast facts: Kevin Rudd', Australia's Prime Ministers website, http://primeministers.naa.gov.au/primeministers/rudd/fast-facts.aspx (accessed 25 January 2017).

11. Williams, *In God They Trust?*

12. Quoted in Macklin, *Kevin Rudd*, p. 150.

13. Quoted ibid., p. 47.

14. Quoted ibid., p. 151. Rudd has consistently expressed support for the separation of Church and state in Australia's constitution, and for the largely secular nature of the country's institutions. His statements 'I am a Jeffersonian separatist' (Marr, 'Power Trip', p. 63) and 'We are proud of the fact in Australia we have a secular, pluralist, polity. That's as it should be, I'm a strong defender of that, and will always be such a defender' (*The Religion Report*, ABC Radio National, 4 October 2006) are typical of this.

15. Commonwealth of Australia, Parliamentary Debates. House of Representatives, 14 March 2005, pp. 98–102.

16. Macklin, *Kevin Rudd*, p. 47.

17. John Warhurst, 'The religious beliefs of Australia's Prime Ministers', *Eureka Street*, 11 November 2010, http://www.eurekastreet.com.au/article.aspx?aeid=24159#.VWiIzoajhWs (accessed 25 January 2017).

18. 'Kevin Rudd: The God Factor'.

19. Mungo MacCallum, 'Australian Story: Kevin Rudd and the Lucky Country', *Quarterly Essay*, vol. 36, 2009, p. 40.

20. 'Reflecting a nation: stories from the 2011 census, 2012–2013', Australian Bureau of Statistics website, 21 June 2012, http://www.abs.gov.au/ausstats/abs@.nsf/Lookup/2071.0main+features902012-2013 (accessed 25 January 2017).

21. Commonwealth of Australia, Parliamentary Debates, House of Representatives, 11 November 1998, pp. 162–5.

22. Quoted in Marion Maddox, *For God and Country: Religious Dynamics in Australian Federal Politics* (Canberra: Department of the Parliamentary Library, 2001), p. 141.

23. I am grateful to Roy Williams for clarifying this issue, and more broadly for his extremely helpful *In God They Trust?*.

24. Todd Donovan, 'The Irrelevance and (New) Relevance of Religion in Australian Elections', *Australian Journal of Political Science*, vol. 49, no. 4, 2014, p. 628.

25. A. Crabb (2009) 'Invoking Religion in Australian Politics', *Australian Journal of Political Science*, vol. 44, no. 2, pp. 259–79.

26. Warhurst 2007, p. 27.

27. Ibid., p. 29.

28. 'Kevin Rudd: The God Factor'.

29. Rodney Smith, 'How Would Jesus Vote? The Churches and the Election of the Rudd Government', *Australian Journal of Political Science*, vol. 44, no. 4, 2009, pp. 613–37.

30. Macklin, *Kevin Rudd*, p. 150.

31. Marr, 'Power Trip', p. 60.

32. Ibid., p. 62.

33. Macklin, *Kevin Rudd*, p. 145; MacCallum, 'Australian Story', p. 4.

34. 'What Our Leaders Believe', *Compass*, ABC TV, 3 October 2004. Transcript available at http://www.abc.net.au/compass/s1201238.htm (accessed 25 January 2017); 'Kevin Rudd: The God factor'; 'Church and State: Politicians Speak Out', *The Spirit of Things*, ABC Radio National, 29 January 2006. Transcript and audio download available at http://www.abc.net.au/radionational/programs/spiritofthings/church-and-state-politicians-speak-out/3306624 (accessed 25 January 2017).

35. Macklin, *Kevin Rudd*, p. 145.

36. Rudd, 'Faith in Politics'. All quotations in this and the two following paragraphs are from this source unless otherwise indicated. Rudd seems first to have encountered Bonhoeffer

through reading his *Letters and Papers from Prison* as an undergraduate: see Macklin, *Kevin Rudd*, p. 147.

37. 'Kevin Rudd: Bonhoeffer and "the Political Orchestration of Organised Christianity"', *The Religion Report*, ABC Radio National, 4 October 2006. Transcript available at http://www.abc.net.au/radionational/programs/religionreport/kevin-rudd-bonhoeffer-and-the-political/3350160#transcript (accessed 25 January 2017).

38. Macklin, *Kevin Rudd*, p. 144.

39. MacCallum, 'Australian Story', p. 40.

40. Nicholas Stuart, *Rudd's Way: November 2007–June 2010* (Melbourne: Scribe, 2010), p. 253.

41. MacCallum, 'Australian Story', p. 4; Stuart, *Rudd's Way*, p. 253.

42. Stuart, *Rudd's Way*, p. 253.

43. Christine Jackman, *Inside Kevin07: The People, the Plan, the Prize* (Melbourne: Melbourne University Press, 2008); Peter Hartcher, *To the Bitter End: The Dramatic Story behind the Fall of John Howard and the Rise of Kevin Rudd* (Crows Nest, NSW: Allen and Unwin, 2009).

44. Smith, 'How Would Jesus Vote?', p. 619.

45. Australian Development Strategies, *Profile of the 2007 Australian Election* (Brisbane: Australian Development Strategies, 2008).

46. Smith, 'How Would Jesus Vote?', p. 618.

47. Warhurst, 'Religion and the 2010 Election', p. 303.

48. Australian Development Strategies, *Profile of the 2007 Australian Election*.

49. Smith, 'How Would Jesus Vote?'.

50. Williams, *In God They Trust?*

51. Warhurst, 'Religion and the 2010 Election', p. 308.

52. Williams, *In God They Trust?*

NICOLAS SARKOZY
(2007–12)

BEN RYAN

INTRODUCTION

Nicolas Sarkozy is a man of uneasy contradictions. He is a social conservative who has spent his political career calling for 'rupture' from the old ways France has done things. This rupture is proposed for education, for politics and for religion. If his political programme defies the easy tag of social conservatism, his personal life seems to thoroughly reject it. A man known as 'President Bling-Bling' with a taste for expensive suits, he is twice divorced and had at least one public extra-marital affair.

When it comes to religion, Sarkozy is, perhaps unsurprisingly therefore, a somewhat difficult case study. His own personal piety is, by his own admission, rather 'episodic'.[1] Yet what is astonishing is the degree to which he has been prepared to embrace and talk about religion and challenge the prevailing model of secularism (*laïcité*) in a political climate in which doing so is rare, even to the point of being considered anti-French (or at least anti-republican). His efforts in this area have provoked accusations of populism and of using religion for political purposes. These accusations, however, seem unfair. For all his many contradictions and complexities, Sarkozy's commitment to finding a new religious settlement for France seems sincere, long held and defiant despite remaining resolutely unpopular. His own personal religious conviction may be ambiguous, but his commitment to 'positive *laïcité*' is not.

BIOGRAPHY

THE BEGINNINGS

Sarkozy's father was born Pál Sárközy de Nagy-Bócsa (or, in Hungarian, nagybócsai Sárközy Pál). He was a minor Hungarian aristocrat who fled his homeland to escape the communists in 1945. He joined the French Foreign Legion, changed his first name to a more French-sounding Paul and moved to Paris. There he met Andrée Mallah, a law student who was the daughter of a Greek Sephardic Jew, Aaron Mallah, who had settled in Paris, converted to Catholicism, changed his name to Bénédict and become a prominent doctor.

The couple had three sons, of whom Nicolas Paul Stéphane Sárközy de Nagy-Bócsa was the second (he would soon drop 'de Nagy-Bócsa' and the accents). His father left when Nicolas was four, and Andrée moved in with her father. Though he had converted to Catholicism, the depth of Bénédict Mallah's faith is unclear. What is less in doubt is Mallah's deep-felt support for French republican values and Charles de Gaulle. This would mark Sarkozy profoundly. In a number of interviews and conversations Sarkozy has recalled the importance of his grandfather in his upbringing and in shaping his outlook and politics.[2] Together they went to lay a flower at the funeral of de Gaulle in 1970.

Growing up there were few signs Sarkozy was heading for the highest office in the land. Famously self-conscious over his height (he stands 5 feet 4 inches) and, as a teenager, his weight, he was awkward at school and an unexceptional student. In one of his rare teenage interactions with his father, Sarkozy was told that 'with the name you carry and with the results you obtain you will never succeed in France'.[3]

With an average academic record, and lacking a degree from one of the *grandes écoles*, the elite universities that dominate French politics, Sarkozy took a different route into politics. In a passage in *Testimony* he explains:

> My political journey was a lot harder than people have often said and even than I have admitted. A lot of political leaders have found their vocation by working in a ministerial cabinet right after graduating from ENA [the

pronouncements, while leading a complicated and extravagant personal life and pushing through radical political reforms. To this the critics add the observations that both men come from non-French minor aristocratic families and that both are short. The comparisons are rarely designed to be positive. Alain Duhamel, the political commentator, devoted a whole book to the theme which included the observation that both men were iconoclastic, morally conservative and politically reformist – with Sarkozy a 21st-century vision of Napoleon or 'Bonaparte in a suit'.[12] In Sarkozy's case, his break with the past included taking on some of the most sacred aspects of the French state, notably *laïcité* (see below), the economy and the labour market. His presidency was marked by policies that had far from universal support, but which he managed to force past France's notoriously powerful unions nonetheless.

The global economic crash hurt Sarkozy's reforms. Having come to power with promises of a new confident France more involved in global capitalism and the free market, the last years saw the consequences of global capitalism writ large. In the 2012 election, his economic record could not save him. He had promised a rupture, but most of his policies fell short of creating the radical change he had pledged.

The disappointment of that failure hurt his 2012 campaign. So too did an effort to court the far right and prevent votes being siphoned off by the National Front by resorting to ever-tougher language on immigration and Islam. Finally, his personal life, both in his marriages and in his well-publicised enjoyment of 'bling-bling', grated on many. Always a divisive politician, he was unable to secure enough voters to hold off the challenge of François Hollande.

SARKOZY AND RELIGION

When it comes to considering Sarkozy's record on religion there is an important distinction to be made between his personal faith and his attitude towards religion as a political or public issue. On the latter point we can further sub-divide the key aspects between Sarkozy's attempt to introduce a new settlement on *laïcité*, the extent to which his approach to religion was simply a populist political move, and finally his contentious relationship with Islam.

Sarkozy was raised a Catholic. Along with his brothers he was baptised and confirmed within the Church. Describing his own faith in his 2004 book *La République, les religions, l'espérance* ('The Republic, Religions, Hope'), Sarkozy described himself as belonging 'to the Catholic religion, the Catholic tradition, the Catholic confession', but then went on to concede that his religious practice was 'episodic'.[13] In the same book he discusses how he enjoys taking his children to Mass, particularly during religious festivals.[14] Elsewhere he discusses how he has appreciated time in monasteries and the importance in bad times of prayer.[15] In an interesting passage he mentions how important he thinks saints are as an example to inspire people before, in a moment of introspection, conceding that 'alas I find myself a long way from such faith'.[16]

Sarkozy's critics would no doubt agree heartily with that conclusion. His lifestyle is seemingly some way from what might be expected of a committed Catholic and his private life has been subject to some very public criticism. His first marriage, to Marie-Dominique Culioli, with whom he had two sons, ended acrimoniously. For some years while still married to Marie-Dominique he was living with Cécilia Ciganer, who left her own husband to be with Sarkozy.

Cécilia and Sarkozy went on to marry, but this marriage also ended in a messy public fashion. Both had affairs, and Cécilia's unhappiness soon after Sarkozy became President led to her awkwardly abandoning her husband at a number of very public diplomatic meetings. Soon after they divorced, Sarkozy announced his engagement to the pop star Carla Bruni. The French are famously forgiving of the personal lives of their politicians – Mitterrand had kept a whole secret second family throughout his presidency. Nonetheless, Sarkozy's personal behaviour, combined with a very open love of some of the finer things in life, has led to a certain degree of incredulity.

However justified the criticism of his personal faith may be, Sarkozy certainly does believe that religion has an immensely important societal role to play, to the extent that he was prepared to take on and challenge *laïcité*, one of the great French republican principles, to a far greater extent than any other major French politician for decades.

UNE LAÏCITÉ POSITIVE

Sarkozy has consistently advocated a new approach to the French model of secularism. In this respect, as with so much else in Sarkozy's vision, France requires a 'rupture' from the way it has done things in the past. When it comes to *laïcité*, as Sarkozy himself recognises, this is to take on one of the great taboos of modern France. This taboo, for Sarkozy, has negative consequences for French society as a whole.

For example, in *La République, les religions, l'espérance* Sarkozy noted the unfortunate lack of dialogue between spiritual and temporal leaders, concluding with the explicit wish that religion shouldn't be '*un sujet tabou*'.[17] He also suggested that in recent years 'we have overestimated the importance of sociological questions, while the religious dimension, the spiritual question has been very much underestimated'.[18] That book, though broadly very positive about the role of religion, was not naïve. It saw religion as being central to France in the twenty-first century as the basis for hope, but also as a major challenge.[19]

Some of the areas Sarkozy identified for change are the need for a discussion on affirmative action, collecting proper statistical evidence on the underlying issues afflicting different ethnic and religious communities, the need for good public bodies like the CFCM, and letting schools teach religion to combat xenophobia.[20] On other occasions, he challenged the fact that the French state doesn't recognise diplomas from Catholic universities, the value of theology degrees or the religious character of charitable agencies.[21]

These are all practical measures, which vary in how controversial they are within the French public debate. Sarkozy's vision of positive *laïcité* also has a more theoretical element. In both his book on religion (itself just by its existence an astonishing gesture in a country where secularism is a republican value and religion is usually limited to the personal sphere) and in other speeches, Sarkozy has advocated a new approach to religion that takes account of it as important for morality, for the transmission of values and in establishing the roots of the nation.

In particular, Sarkozy has been keen to talk about religion as being crucial to forming good citizens – not least in creating a sense of hope. A good example of this is the frankly astonishing speech he delivered at the Lateran

Palace in Rome on 20 December 2007. The speech was to mark his induction as an honorary canon of the Basilica of St John Lateran, a traditional honour presented to the French head of state and one that usually passes without comment. Sarkozy's speech instead created a national stir as he called for positive *laïcité* and noted the 'suffering' that the *laïcité* law had caused for many Catholics. Perhaps more interestingly, he noted that 'a person who believes is a person who hopes, and it's in the interests of the republic that there be many women and men who nourish hope'. That is also a consistent theme of his book on religion, for example in arguing that Islam and other religions had a key role in providing hope in the *banlieues*, where spiritual hope was preferable to violence and drugs.[22] Religion has, for Sarkozy, a civilising role in society.

This ties into a broader sense in which religion is important in creating values. The single line in Sarkozy's Lateran speech that really caused outrage in the French press was the one that claimed that 'in the transmission of values and in learning the difference between right and wrong, the school-teacher will never be able to replace the priest or the pastor'. Coverage of that remark was not favourable, and polling showed that 73 per cent of the French population disagreed with it.[23] Sarkozy would subsequently claim that he didn't mean that religious morality was superior, though it is difficult to escape that sense when in the same speech he also said that 'secular morality always runs the risk of becoming exhausted, or transforming itself into fanaticism, when it is not supported by a hope which addresses the human aspiration for infinity'.

A final aspect of this attempt at busting the religious taboo is Sarkozy's insistence on religion as the root of France. In *La République, les religions, l'espérance* he notes that 'our roots are Christian', though he goes on in the same chapter to give significant space to other religions in defining France in the present and future.[24] Again the Lateran speech is more striking, in that it notes not only that Christianity is in the roots of France but that *laïcité* needs to recognise that and stop negating the religious aspect of French identity as it has done in the past, on the basis that 'a nation which ignores the ethical, spiritual and religious inheritance of its history commits a crime against its own culture ... To take away those roots means to lose meaning, to weaken the cement of national identity and to further fray social relationships.'

All of this paints a picture of a political figure prepared to challenge French political orthodoxy on *laïcité*. It would appear as if this is a particular preoccupation of Sarkozy's that significantly marks him out from other mainstream French political figures. There are plenty of critics, however, who dismiss this stance as being nothing but populist politics being used to draw the fangs of the National Front.

A POPULIST MOVE?

With respect to religion Sarkozy is not short of critics who dismiss his moves as populism dressed up as piety. Jean Baubérot, the prominent French historian and sociologist of religion and secularism, condemned Sarkozy as conducting 'a neo-clerical effort to relink religion and politics and for the instrumentalisation of religion by politicians'.[25] On another occasion, he would link Sarkozy's stance on religion to efforts to pacify the extreme right, and particularly the National Front.[26] The prominent French Christian Democrat politician François Bayrou likewise criticised Sarkozy's Lateran speech on the grounds that 'it makes the religious question partisan. And it works! He made the Lateran speech not out of conviction, but for the political mobilisation of Catholic power.'[27]

There was more. Sarkozy delivered a remarkable speech in Riyadh in 2008, in which he praised 'the transcendent God who is in the thoughts and the hearts of every person' and described Islam as 'one of the greatest and most beautiful civilisations the world has known'.[28] The reaction back in France was, to say the least, mixed. François Hollande, then the leader of the Socialist Party, accused Sarkozy of using religion to sell nuclear energy to Muslim countries.[29]

Are these accusations fair? It is of course difficult to know the full inner workings of someone's mind, and were they true it is hardly likely that Sarkozy would admit as much. It is worth noting, though, that, if he were to adopt a 'populist' move, challenging *laïcité* is a poor choice, given that to do so is singularly unpopular. According to a poll by the Institut Français d'Opinion Publique (IFOP) in 2015, 46 per cent of French adults believe *laïcité* is the most important republican principle (ahead of universal suffrage at 36 per cent and freedom of association at 8 per cent). Nearly three quarters, 71 per cent, put it in the top two republican principles.[30] The importance of *laïcité* is taken as a given in French politics across the political spectrum. The data from the IFOP survey bear that out with no real difference between left- and right-wing voters in the proportion ranking it as the top republican value. Admittedly, there is a definitional issue here, concerning the true meaning of *laïcité*. After all, Sarkozy himself is in favour of *laïcité* and views it as important. However, what is not in doubt is that *laïcité* is a thoroughly supported part of Frenchness and any strategy which could be perceived as challenging that is, accordingly, one fraught with risk.

It's also fair to say that if Sarkozy were simply keen to court religious votes he was not afraid to risk conflict with such voters either. His relationship with the Islamic French population is complex, but generally perceived as being strained, despite the Riyadh speech. He also provoked a major conflict with the Catholic Church over his treatment of the Roma community. Sarkozy made the decision to deport Roma from France back to the Balkans, using fairly draconian methods. This led to prominent condemnations from Pope Benedict XVI, the French bishops and the Christian Democrat party, who had been among Sarkozy's parliamentary allies. *Le Monde* went so far as to run the headline 'Nicolas Sarkozy et les Catholiques, le divorce?'[31]

For these reasons, it seems unfair (in this if not in other policy areas) to criticise Sarkozy for populism. There is little populist ground to be won by picking at the consensus on *laïcité*, and the consistency of Sarkozy's interventions, including his book and speeches and his record at the interior ministry, suggest that this is a genuine interest and ongoing concern for him.

THE MUSLIM QUESTION

A final much-discussed aspect of Sarkozy's stance on religion is his relationship with Islam. This is often portrayed as one of mutual suspicion and intolerance. As interior minister and as President, Sarkozy was responsible for hard policies and harder rhetoric on immigration, with a perception

that Muslims bore the brunt. An interesting example of this was the controversy over the 2005 riots and Sarkozy's use of the term *racaille* to describe
the rioters. *Racaille* is commonly translated as 'scum' in English, but in
French it comes with a stronger sense of sub-humanness. The term is not,
in itself, necessarily racial or targeted inherently at any religious community. However, in the context of a riot that was broadly perceived as being
at least in part a racialised protest by an increasingly marginalised north
African (and therefore largely Muslim) community, the use of the term
became part of a narrative about Sarkozy's attitude towards the community
as a whole.

Another example was when in 2009 Sarkozy called for a 100-day 'Grand
Debate on National Identity'. Meetings were held in 350 town halls across
France and a dedicated website was launched to facilitate this debate, which
came to focus very largely on immigration. The debate came at a time of
growing strength for the National Front, while the wounds of the 2005 riots
festered and research showed that Muslim neighbourhoods remained among
the worst for unemployment.

Sarkozy's own election as President had been in part tied to a programme
of being tough on immigration. In 2009, he opposed the Islamic face veil,
and in September 2010 officially banned 'concealment of the face in public
space'. Though the ban also officially covers balaclavas, masks and helmets,
there is little doubt who was in the political mind, and certainly Muslims
felt that this was a targeted policy against their religious freedom. It certainly
seems a poor fit with Sarkozy's stated support for positive *laïcité*.

Yet Sarkozy's record is not all negative from a Muslim perspective. He was
instrumental in the establishment of the CFCM and he is immensely proud
of that achievement, which receives significant space in both *Testimony* and
La République, les religions, l'espérance. In the latter he describes that body as
'*un atout précieux*' (a precious asset) for the country.[32] He also notes the failure of any other interior minister to have managed to bring in such a body.[33]
He also appointed the first north African woman to a French ministerial
post, Rachida Dati, who had been raised as a Muslim. This was part of a
concerted effort on Sarkozy's part to diversify politics and challenge some of
the preconceptions of French society.

Do these achievements outweigh the other policies? Perhaps not, but they do illustrate at least a slightly more nuanced picture of Sarkozy's attitude towards Islam and public life than is usually presented. It would seem a fair criticism, though, to say that Sarkozy's positive *laïcité* seems a more positive story for Christians than it does for Muslims.

CONCLUSION

There is a risk, in studies of this kind, to look to put political leaders on pedestals and show how important and significant their faith has been in cultivating behaviour and policies. Nicolas Sarkozy is many things, but he has never claimed to be an especially pious Catholic. Indeed, he is admirably honest in his books on what he is. He is a Catholic, and feels that that is important, but the extent of his faith and practice comes and goes. In his more introspective moments he suggests he wants to be a better Catholic and live a life more in keeping with the saints, but is honest enough to concede that he often falls short of that ideal. An amusing story that illustrates that is provided by the journalist Patrice de Beer:

> This is a leader who, after all, announced that he would retire for a few days in a monastery to meditate after his election, and then chose instead to go on a luxury cruise aboard a yacht belonging to a billion-aire friend; and who has been nicknamed 'President Bling-Bling' for his glitzy style. Is Nicolas Sarkozy the man to teach the French anew about God?[34]

But if Sarkozy's personal piety is some way short of Catholic ideals, what is sincere and absolutely not in doubt is that Sarkozy believes in rupture. He believes the French state and society would benefit from some significant changes and breaks with the past in terms of how it does economics and society. This is certainly true of religion. Sarkozy values religion as something he believes is useful for French society in providing hope and moral forma-tion. He believes in a more American vision of positive *laïcité* than the more familiar French consensus.

NOTES

1. Nicolas Sarkozy, *La République, les religions, l'espérance* (Paris: Cerf, 2004), p. 155.
2. A good account (at present only available in French) of Sarkozy's childhood and his grandfather's influence is provided in the early chapters of the Sarkozy biography written by Catherine Nay, *Un pouvoir nommé désir* (Paris: Grasset et Fasquelle, 2007).
3. Dennis Abrams, *Modern World Leaders: Nicolas Sarkozy* (New York: Chelsea House, 2009), p. 33. If Paul Sarkozy's comments seem harsh, it is worth noting that the struggles of French immigrants other than a few exceptional cases to reach the top are well documented.
4. Nicolas Sarkozy, *Testimony: France in the Twenty-First Century* (New York: Pantheon, 2007), translated from the French by Philip H. Gordon (New York: Harper Perennial, 2007), p. 3.
5. An interesting long account is given in Adam Gornik, 'The human bomb: the Sarkozy regime begins', *New Yorker*, 27 August 2007.
6. A number of articles and videos focusing on these events appeared around the 2007 presidential contest. Many of the videos are still available online.
7. Nicolas Sarkozy, *Libre* (Paris: Fixot, 2001).
8. This was the presidential election that shocked France when the Socialist candidate, Lionel Jospin, failed to make the final run-off, beaten by notorious hard-right politician Jean-Marie Le Pen.
9. Nicolas Sarkozy, *Testimony: France in the Twenty-First Century* (New York: Pantheon, 2007), p. 22.
10. Ibid., p. 26.
11. Ibid., p. 29.
12. Alain Duhamel, *La Marche consulaire* (Paris: Plon, 2008).
13. Sarkozy, *La République, les religions, l'espérance*, p. 155.
14. Ibid., p. 156.
15. Ibid., p. 39.
16. Ibid., p. 41.
17. Ibid., p. 30.
18. Ibid., p. 13.
19. Ibid., p. 15.
20. Ibid.
21. Nicolas Sarkozy, speech delivered at Lateran Palace, Rome, 20 December 2007.
22. Sarkozy, *La République, les religions, l'espérance*, p. 18.
23. Tracy McNicoll, 'Sarkozy ignites church and state debate', *Newsweek*, 9 February 2008, http://europe.newsweek.com/sarkozy-ignites-church-and-state-debate-93651 (accessed 26 January 2017).
24. Sarkozy, *La République, les religions, l'espérance*, p. 135.
25. In an article in the newspaper *Libération* in December 2007, an accusation he would later repeat in Jean Baubérot, 'The Evolution of Secularism in France: Between Two Civil Religions', in Linell E. Cady and Elizabeth Shakman Hurd (eds), *Comparative Secularisms in a Global Age* (Basingstoke: Palgrave Macmillan, 2010).
26. See Jean Baubérot, 'Le président Nicolas Sarkozy et la laïcité', Huffington Post (France), 11 February 2012, http://www.huffingtonpost.fr/jean-bauberot/sarkozy-laicite_b_1267613.html (accessed 26 January 2017). The National Front (FN, Front National) is a French political party of the extreme right. It first came to major prominence under the leadership of Jean-Marie Le Pen, who shocked everyone when he made it to the second round of the presidential ballot in 2002, beating the Socialist candidate in the process. The party has continued to grow in strength and prominence, now under the leadership of Le Pen's daughter Marine.

27. 'Nicolas Sarkozy, le pape François, la laïcité et la religion catholique', *Le Figaro*, 21 March 2016.

28. Nicolas Sarkozy, speech delivered in Riyadh, 14 January 2008.

29. McNicoll, 'Sarkozy ignites church and state debate'.

30. 'Les Français et la laïcité', IFOP, February 2015, http://www.ifop.com/media/poll/2929-1-study_file.pdf (accessed 26 January 2017).

31 'Nicolas Sarkozy et les catholiques, le divorce?', *Le Monde*, 24 August 2010.

32. Sarkozy, *La République, les religions, l'espérance*, p. 9.

33. Ibid., p. 58.

34. Patrice de Beer, 'Sarkozy and God', openDemocracy, 6 February 2008, https://www.open-democracy.net/article/sarkozy_and_god (accessed 26 January 2017).

LEE MYUNG-BAK (2008–13)

HENRY VAN OOSTEROM

INTRODUCTION

Unlike many of the figures in this collection, Lee Myung-bak is not a household name.[1] An understated (if impactful) President of an east Asian nation that generally receives far less international media attention than its immediate neighbours of China, Russia and North Korea, one could be forgiven for not knowing who Lee is, still less that he is a devout Presbyterian whose religiosity played a central role in his politics. More broadly, it may not even be known that Korea had, and continues to have, one of the most convoluted relationships with Christianity of any Asian territory. Therefore, before delving into the role that faith played in Lee's controversial presidency, it is worth taking a step back and giving a brief account of the vibrant and violent history of Christianity in Korea.

A BRIEF HISTORY OF KOREAN CHRISTIANITY

Christianity (specifically Catholicism) officially arrived in Korea in 1784. Years earlier, a group of Korean Confucian scholars become intrigued by a curious text entitled *The True Doctrine of the Lord of Heaven*, a work written in Chinese by an Italian Jesuit missionary named Matteo Ricci, operating at the imperial court of China in the sixteenth century. They sent an associate, Yi Sung-hun, to Peking to find out more about this peculiar Western philosophy. Yi returned to Korea in 1784, not only armed with numerous Christian texts, but baptised himself, and with the new moniker 'Peter' – prophetic, as Yi would turn out to be the rock upon which the Korean Church was founded.[2]

The inchoate Catholic Church subsequently spread rapidly across Korea over the following decades. The particular salvific emphasis of Christianity found fertile ground in the minds of a nation historically bullied by more powerful surrounding neighbours. Its growth was also aided by the fact that key Christian notions overlapped conceptually with native Confucian and Buddhist equivalents that had been well entrenched in Korean society for centuries. Deeply pervasive Korean cosmological principles of *yin–yang*, male–female, dark–light, old–young meant people could readily comprehend a certain dualistic framework of Christianity: heaven–hell, righteous–evil, flesh–spirit, this world–the world to come.[3] Further, Confucian teaching places a strong moral emphasis on 'right behaviour' in a society, which missionaries were able to reframe in the context of Jesus' teachings about socially minded selflessness. Interestingly, certain Korean Buddhist schools had, since the sixteenth century, emphasised prophecies of the Mireuk, an eschatological figure who would descend from heaven and usher in a new age free from suffering.[4] In short, Korea had the pre-existing intellectual and spiritual soil which enabled Christianity to take root, cultivated subsequently by a steady flow of Western missionaries.

The rapid and zealous expansion of an alien religion was met by the ruling powers with alarm. The government, profoundly suspicious of this radical foreign philosophy, engaged in enthusiastic persecution of both Korean Christians and visiting foreign missionaries until the 1880s, which heralded the end of Korea's historical isolationism and its subsequent engagement with Western nations. In 1884, Protestantism arrived where Catholicism had led, chiefly thanks to Horace Allen, an American missionary-physician who had spent time teaching Presbyterianism in China. While in Korea, Allen tended to an injured prince following an attempted coup in Seoul, and as a result won Christianity a grudging toleration among the authorities. With its message celebrating the suffering poor, Christianity continued to spread with remarkable speed among the significant proportion of the population who occupied the lowest strata in a feudal society. By the early twentieth century, such was the established presence of both Catholic and Protestant Christianity on the peninsula that Pyongyang became known as the 'Jerusalem of the East'.[5]

The annexation of the Korean peninsula by imperial Japan in 1910 marked the beginning of a socially and politically tumultuous period for Korea. The Japanese administered the country harshly: state-wide secret surveillance was implemented, Korean landowners were dispossessed, active suppression of 'inferior' Korean culture and language occurred and wholesale censorship was introduced to curb dissent.[6] After liberation in 1945, the Allied victors established two zones of administrative control, the Soviets attending to the northern half and the Western Allies the southern. Thus, guided by the communist and capitalist ideologies of their respective caretakers, the Democratic People's Republic of Korea ('North Korea') and the Republic of Korea ('South Korea') were formally founded in 1948. Just two years later, the peninsula found itself the site of arguably the most brutal proxy war in modern history (the Korean War, between the Chinese-supported North and the South, backed by a US-led UN coalition, claimed around three million lives in three years;[7] to put that perspective, a roughly comparable number died in the Vietnam War over two decades). Even after the war, violent military dictatorships governed in the South from 1961 until 1988, while the North remains under totalitarian rule to this day.

Ironically, however, it has been this very suffering of the Korean people over the last century that has allowed the Church there to flourish. During the period of Japanese occupation, churches became the primary platforms for conversations about democracy and freedom from despised colonisers. Catholic and Protestant ministers invoked biblical stories of David and Goliath, and the Jewish captivities in Egypt and Babylon, to stir up dissent among Korean congregations,[8] which invited furious Japanese recriminations and the systematic execution of numerous Christian ringleaders. Church leaders were instrumental in organising the famous Independence Movement of March 1919, which saw pro-democracy, anti-Japanese protests spring up all over the peninsula. Decades later, under the military dictatorship of General Park Chung-hee (1961–79) in South Korea, it was Christian leaders who were at the forefront of protests against the regime's abysmal human rights record, condemning the 'non-democratic dictatorship', with many subsequently imprisoned for 'instigating rebellion'.[9]

A similar story emerged during the dictatorial reign of the unelected General Chun Doo-hwan (1979–88). In protest at the state's use of torture in prison, leading church pastors issued the 'Statement on Social Injustice', condemning the government's violence against its citizens and quoting Amos 5:24: 'Let judgement run down as waters and righteousness as a mighty stream.'[10] Thanks to its history of courageous dissent, Korean Christianity thus came to be associated with a proud sense of Korean nationalism, a conceptual connection that continues to this day: to be a Christian is to be part of a noble tradition of struggle for national autonomy, democracy, human rights, religious freedom and the cessation of foreign interference.

Like the Korean peninsula itself – divided as it is today between the miraculous success story of the flourishing South and the sluggish dystopia of the North – so the present-day fate of Christianity is deeply dichotomous. In South Korea, Christianity's social, cultural and political importance can hardly be overstated. From having zero adherents at the time of its introduction in the late eighteenth century, Christianity is now the faith of 30 per cent of South Koreans, and dominates among the educated and powerful social classes. Single churches can have memberships in the hundreds of thousands. Seoul contains all but one of the eleven largest Protestant congregations in the world; Christian rallies in the city's Yoido Plaza routinely draw crowds of more than a million.[11] Christian faith has played a deeply influential role in the lives of many of South Korea's leading figures, including Lee Myung-bak, and has thus impacted much of contemporary national politics.

By contrast, North Korea has topped the list of the worst countries for Christian persecution for sixteen consecutive years[12] despite the country's constitution theoretically guaranteeing freedom of religion.[13] Since the inception of the totalitarian Leninist-Marxist state, Christianity has been suppressed and actively persecuted wherever it has been encountered; it is the religion of the traditional Korean *yangban* landowning classes, as well as of the despised Americans. It is also viewed by the authorities as ideologically threatening, diverting citizens' attention away from that which they should truly venerate: the state, and its quasi-divine ruling Kim dynasty. Estimates currently place 50,000–70,000 Christians in the North's network of gulags as a direct result of their religion.[14]

LEE MYUNG-BAK'S EARLY LIFE
AND PRE-POLITICAL CAREER

Even his most vocal critics accord Lee Myung-bak, tenth President of the Republic of Korea, a grudging respect. His extraordinary rags-to-riches rise to becoming the youngest ever CEO of global conglomerate Hyundai, mayor of Seoul and eventual President originated in truly inauspicious circumstances. In a highly Confucian society in which social hierarchy, order of birth and ancestry influence all of one's professional prospects, Lee's journey from malnourished middle-born child of a decidedly unprivileged family to democratically elected leader of the world's eleventh wealthiest nation is a genuinely exceptional one.

Born in 1941 in Osaka, Japan, Lee returned with his family to their native Korea when he was four, following liberation of the country in 1945. Even this journey was fraught with difficulty, as the overloaded ferry carrying Lee's family sank in the Sea of Japan. The family settled in the port city of Pohang, on Korea's south-east coast, surviving on Lee's father's meagre salary as a farm manager until the advent of the Korean War in 1950, which shattered all stability on the peninsula. The family fled further south in the face of the approaching communist forces. Unfortunately, the shockwaves of the conflict reached even the most rural parts of the country, and Lee lost both a brother and a sister when American planes mistakenly bombed their village.

The years that followed were marked by perpetual poverty. Lee recalls this late childhood and early teen era as one unending search to find sufficient food. For weeks at a time, the whole family was forced to survive off rice lees, the dregs left over from the brewing process, meaning Lee passed his junior school years in a constant state of gnawing hunger and slight inebriation.[15] In his memoirs, Lee remembers the two driving forces that kept him going during this period. The first was a fighter's spirit, born out of the necessity of survival; by the fifth grade, Lee was selling homemade matches of woodchips and sulphur to raise money so the family could eat, determined 'never to let poverty smother [them]'.[16] His second source of solace was the resolute Christian faith that surrounded him, emanating particularly from his mother. 'Were it not for my mother's unwavering Christian faith, I'm certain that our family would have succumbed to poverty and its hardships,'[17] Lee said, referring to the fact that it was his mother's trust in divine benevolence that gave her the strength to carry on working and raising children in the face of near destitution. The family day would begin at 4 a.m. with a prayer circle, subsequently imbuing the future President with a Protestant faith and worldview that would pervade his entire career. Indeed, Lee once claimed that the greatest blessing he ever received was 'coming to know the love of God', thanks to the way his mother had raised him.[18]

While a student at Korea University, Lee was a ringleader of massive anti-government student demonstrations in 1964, which eventually led to his detention for several years as an enemy of the state. As noted, the Church had historically been at the heart of pro-democracy, anti-authoritarian protest in Korea, and in placing himself at the helm of his own rallies, Lee revealed the way in which the historic ideals of the Korean Church had already made a profound impression on him.

Upon graduating in 1965, Lee applied to Hyundai, then a small construction company of around ninety employees. Ambitious, outspoken and extremely hardworking, Lee rose through the ranks of the rapidly growing company at astonishing speed. By 1971, he had been made a director, and set about transforming Hyundai from a medium-sized construction company into a vast conglomerate, a global operator with innumerable subsidiaries involved in virtually all conceivable areas of heavy industry.

Lee's approach to business was aggressive and untiring. He doggedly pursued and won vast construction contracts in the emerging markets of the Middle East, and in 1977, aged only thirty-five, he was promoted to company president. The professional ruthlessness and stubbornness he evinced in this period earned him the nickname 'the Bulldozer', a nickname that would be resurrected in his later political career, characterised as it was by unwillingness to compromise or shift opinions.

His relentless work ethic, which saw him rise at 5 a.m. every day, eventually caught up with him, and in November 1977 he suffered a collapse and was diagnosed with hepatitis B. During the lowest ebbs of his battle with the condition, Lee prayed intensively, pleading with God for more time to fulfil his professional ambitions,[19] and over the next two years he recovered completely, despite disobeying all medical advice to immediately stop working. He saw the hand of God as having intervened, and came to understand this as divine endorsement of his political and professional dreams to come.

In 1988, Lee was finally promoted to chairman and CEO of Hyundai, the highest possible position. The Bulldozer continued his bold and headstrong business strategy, daring to visit and attempt to open contract negotiations in both the Soviet Union and China, at the time stalwart allies of their communist counterparts in North Korea, and thus widely understood as no-go areas for the great capitalist *chaebols* (powerful South Korean conglomerates such as Hyundai, Samsung and LG). Having taken Hyundai to this tantalising new frontier and the brink of truly global expansion for the company, Lee decided his corporate journey had reached its fitting end, stepped down and set his eyes instead on political prizes.

POLITICAL CAREER

SEOUL

In March 1992, Lee became a member of the National Assembly as part of the Democratic Liberal Party. His rise to this position was accomplished with relative ease. He was already known throughout the country for the extraordinary success story he had made of Hyundai, and in a newly minted capitalist country undergoing meteoric economic expansion (as South Korea had been since the 1960s), Lee's demonstrable business acumen marked him out as politician material.

After spending a successful two years (1996–98) as the member of the parliament for the Jongno-gu constituency in central Seoul, Lee decided to take a sabbatical from politics and took up a position as visiting fellow in business management at George Washington University in Washington, DC. His ultimate political ambitions remained undimmed, however, and upon his return to Korea in 2002, he decided to run for mayor of Seoul, partly driven by a sense of wanting to repay the city that had dragged him from the countryside backwaters, educated him and given him his life-changing opportunity in the form of Hyundai.[20]

Lee won the election by an impressive margin (9.3 per cent) on a manifesto promising significant investment in urban regeneration and a focus on environmental issues. While in office, he was responsible for constructing the beautiful and immensely popular Cheonggyecheon – a wide recreational creek which runs through the heart of Seoul for seven miles, now one of the country's premier tourist attractions. He opened up various extensive green spaces throughout the city (such as Seoul Forest and Seoul Plaza) and overhauled its antiquated public transport system. It is no exaggeration to say that the eco-friendly, attractive, clockwork-efficient Seoul of today is a product of Lee's time as mayor between 2002 and 2006.

There are hints of Lee's Christian convictions underpinning his particularly 'green' agenda: eco-theology has historically had significant traction with large numbers of South Korean Christians, and in 2003, Tonghap Presbyterians (of which Lee is one) adopted a new confession of faith which emphasised God's role as creator and the destruction of creation as the ultimate expression of sin.[21] Commentators have attributed this enthusiastic engagement with environmental issues to the fact that South Korea was an agrarian society as recently as sixty years ago and is underpinned by Confucianism, a philosophy that explores in depth the relationship between humans and nature[22] (pioneering environmental policies would later feature prominently in Lee's 2008 presidential manifesto, further proof of his sincere commitment to ecological progress[23]). The people of Seoul appreciated Lee's forward-looking policies as mayor; during his tenure, Seoul's national and international image was acknowledged to have been revitalised, and this laid the groundwork for his successful bid to become the nation's President in 2008.

THE PRESIDENT AND NORTH KOREA

Lee's presidential administration (2008–13) at the head of the Saenuri Party (the later manifestation of his original Democratic Liberal Party), perhaps inevitably, divides opinion significantly more than the legacy of his previous office: it is harder, after all, to be a President than to be a mayor. Widely credited for his role in bringing South Korea to the global fore (for example, by hosting the 2010 G20 summit) and steering the country through the global recession of 2008, Lee was equally criticised for his national macroeconomic policy (known as 'MBnomics', taken from 'Myung-bak') and his conservative unwillingness to address issues of social inequality in Korean society. What cannot be doubted, however, is the decisive role that Lee's strong Christian faith had to play in the politics of his presidency.

The scope of this chapter does not allow us to touch on all the key aspects of the 'LMB' administration which were affected by Lee's Protestant heritage and faith, including his notably pro-American outlook, his frosty relationship with Japan, his inclusive educational views and his progressive environmental attitude. Instead, I shall focus on three facets of the LMB government where the President's religious background played a demonstratively influential role: his policy towards North Korea, the accusations of both nepotistic abuses of power and outright corruption that dogged Lee, and the worsening of interreligious relations in South Korea during his tenure.

How to handle the seemingly intractable thorn in the side that is North Korea is always an aspect of a South Korean President's administration that is scrutinised with particular interest internationally. For South Koreans themselves, the relationship between the two Koreas is less politically significant than it once was; the economic and social gulf between the two countries is now astronomic (the GDP of the South is roughly *110 times* that of the North). Nevertheless, governments and companies the world over tend to take the stability of the relationship seriously. The North is an unpredictable nuclear weapons state with the fourth largest standing army in the world, and thus its bellicose sabre-rattling and occasional threats to 'turn Seoul into a sea of flames'[24] tend to have real ramifications for the confidence of South Korean, and wider east Asian, markets.

There was therefore understandable international alarm when the Lee administration, upon taking power in 2008, dramatically reversed official policy regarding the North, a decision made in no small measure due to Lee's personal religious convictions. For the decade before Lee came to power, 1997–2008, the successive left-wing governments of the South had adopted a conciliatory approach to the North known as the Sunshine Policy.[25] The central premise of the Sunshine Policy was that unilateral aid and political concessions, rather than threats and strong-arming, would eventually cause the isolated North to open up and adopt economic and social reforms of its own accord, much as China and Vietnam had done in the 1970s and 1980s, paving the way for societal transformation, naturalisation into the international community and, ultimately, the reunification of the two Koreas. These left-wing governments refused to participate in UN resolutions on North Korean human rights issues,[26] fearing that chastising would prompt anger from the North, and going so far as proactively blocking a North Korean human rights archive and the provision of support to NGOs working on the issue.[27]

In notable contrast, the Lee administration explicitly tied all humanitarian aid and material assistance to the North with the requirement for a tangible improvement in the human rights situation.[28] During Lee's leadership, the government voted for (and often co-sponsored) UN resolutions criticising the human rights record of the North.[29] Lee also took the bold political step of asking Chinese premier Hu Jintao to stop repatriating North Korean refugees who escaped into his country (a process known as *refoulement*), for they would certainly face imprisonment, torture and often death.[30]

This uncompromising stance by Lee's government is well anchored in religious precedent. Conservative Christian politicians and Christian NGOs have long been at the forefront of efforts to publicly confront the North's human rights violations, and to bring tangible change to the plight of people there. In essence, by vocally bringing the human rights issue to the forefront of all dealings with the North, the LMB administration, headed overwhelmingly by Christians (several from Lee's very own Somang Presbyterian church) were continuing the tradition of the Church in Korea as being a beacon for issues of religious and individual liberty, as well as protesting against oppressive dictatorial regimes.

THE PRESIDENT AND PROTESTANTISM

There were, however, darker manifestations of Lee's firm Christian faith. The South Korean megachurch Christianity of which Lee is an adherent is something of a loud, proud, unashamedly steamrolling juggernaut. Aggressive evangelisation is encouraged, particularly among Protestant denominations – at any given time, there are roughly 11,000 South Korean missionaries spreading the Gospel throughout the world, a figure only exceeded by

Americans – while churches compete quite publicly over which has the largest congregation.[31] These Protestant megachurches unapologetically preach
the pursuit and celebration of material wealth and career successes to
their followers. Such thinking is based on a theological principle known
as *gibok sinang* – 'faith seeking blessings', or the idea that material riches
and temporal successes are divine rewards for one's strong Christian faith.
Accordingly, powerful figures in society are often high-ranking members
within the churches, and vice-versa (Lee himself is a good example: an
ex-CEO of Hyundai and former President, he is also a Somang Church
elder). Big business, power, money, preferentialism, politics and churches are
all intimately intertwined in contemporary South Korea.

This triumphalist, active, highly hands-on approach to 'doing' Christianity is paralleled in the theological preoccupations that predominate in
much, albeit not all, of Korean Protestantism: evangelism, proselytising, a
firm belief in biblical inerrancy and an emphasis on energetic activism.[32] Lee
was, and is, a torch bearer for this forthright form of Christianity (although
the Somang Church plays down the role of evangelisation), defiantly nailing
his religious colours to the mast to woo the Protestant electorate in both the
election to become mayor of Seoul and the subsequent presidential election
(the tactic won him, by some estimates, 80 per cent of the eligible Christian
vote in 2007[33]).

In 2004, while mayor, Lee publicly dedicated the city of Seoul to God, and
subsequently in 2005 hosted and co-organised the Jerusalem Summit Asia
there, a massive pro-Israel gathering of Asian Christians.[34] Upon winning
his party's nomination as presidential candidate in 2007, Lee's second public
appearance was to rapturous applause at the Christian Council of Korea, a
deliberate move designed to make a serious statement to his electorate about
where his priorities lay. When George W. Bush visited the Blue House (the
presidential residence) in 2008, Lee made sure it was Christian prayers that
were said to welcome his guest, and indeed he implemented a general policy
of hosting regular Christian prayer services at the complex.

The result, however, of Lee's brazen endorsement of Protestantism while
in office was the widespread accusation of deepening the religious divisions
in South Korea, by ignoring and marginalising non-Protestant faiths (for

example, by appointing only one Buddhist to his cabinet, versus thirteen Christians).[35] There was a backlash from the Buddhist population: in August 2008, vast numbers took to the street in protest at what they saw, perhaps justifiably, as marginalisation of the ancient religion of the country. Lee was understood to have shamelessly filled his government with his co-religionists, essentially subduing any influence of Korea's religious minorities. Estimates vary, but somewhere between 60,000 and 200,000 Buddhists marched against the administration, including 7,000 monks, protesting against Lee's 'anti-Buddhist bias' and his perceived intention to turn the country into a 'medieval Christian kingdom'.[36] Lee's single-minded, undiplomatic devotion to using his office to promote Protestantism as the foremost Korean religion had the direct and tangible effect of exacerbating existing religious divisions in Korean society.

Lee's administration was further dogged by accusations of shameless cronyism and links to corrupt individuals, which were intertwined with his religious allegiance. Regarding nepotism, there is nothing new in a political leader being accused of making appointments based on personal relationships. What is unique about Lee's particular brand of partiality is that it was based to a strong degree on *ecclesiastical* lines – upon his taking power, a startling number of the country's plum positions were subsequently awarded to tenuously qualified men, simply on the basis that they too attended Lee's own Somang Presbyterian Church, had studied at Korea University and originated from the Youngnam region. The press seized on this, and eventually 'the Somang government' had become a widely used tongue-in-cheek metonym for the Lee administration, while other outlets referred to the 'Ko So Young cabinet'[37] (based on the first syllables of Korea University, Somang Church and Youngnam region respectively).

Compounding this already morally dubious approach was the fact that many of these figures were widely held to have had corrupt business dealings – including Lee himself. Of the fifteen major associates Lee brought with him into government in 2008, thirteen were accused of either tax evasion or violation of real estate laws, and three had to actually withdraw before their confirmation hearings at the National Assembly as a result. Lee even conceded himself, subsequently, that the 'moral standards' he had employed when making these appointments had not measured up to the people's expectations.[38]

Lee himself was hardly spotless. It has since been shown that he showed serious partiality in awarding government contracts to companies with which he had been previously associated, including Hyundai, which was often not the most fitting organisation to take on the projects. It has been estimated that this favouritism by the Lee government knocked 0.21–0.32 per cent off the annual GDP of the country.[39] Lee was also alleged to have been implicated in the BKK stock price manipulation incident of 2007, which saw his close business associate Kim Kyung-joon flee to America with an embezzled $38 million, leaving thousands of investors out of pocket. The charges against Lee were dropped but, nevertheless, on 15 August 2008 (Liberation Day), he took the opportunity to publicly pardon three of South Korea's most powerful businessmen, variously imprisoned on charges of embezzlement, fraud and assault.[40] Legally culpable or not, Lee is clearly a man capable of laying aside his Christian scruples when it suits him.

Lee's heavy personal connection with Protestantism, which in Korea has an aggressively pro-business, anti-communist culture, as well as being attended and often administered by small circles of highly powerful social elites, paved the way for his nepotistically appointed 'Somang government', as well as his association with, and even public pardoning of, some of South Korea's less morally salubrious capitalists. This is a continuation of a wider toxic trend that originated in the Protestant Church of the 1990s, where there were 'many scandals surrounding high-profile clergy and prominent church elders accused of corruption, extravagance, nepotism and hypocrisy'.[41]

CONCLUSION

Frustratingly, we have very little from Lee's own mouth about the specifics of his religious beliefs, perhaps learning from his lengthy, high-level career in business negotiations that it pays to keep one's cards close to one's chest where possible. We are, instead, left to infer much about Lee's convictions from what we do know about South Korean Presbyterianism and Christianity more widely. Nevertheless, there can be little doubt that the ex-CEO, who spent three years volunteering as a humble parking attendant at his Somang church, has a sincere Christian faith; the impact of this faith can be detected in the most courageous and progressive aspects of Lee's politics, but also in some of the least admirable ones.

NOTES

1. In researching this chapter, the author spoke to academics in the fields of South Korean political history, Korean society and Korean Christianity at a number of institutions (Oxford University's Oriental Institute, SOAS, Sheffield University and Kookmin University in Seoul). All agreed that although Lee was undoubtedly a committed and sincere Christian, he had not and did not reveal much about the precise nature of his beliefs. As such, the chapter integrates what is known within a wider perspective of the remarkable story of Korean Christianity.

2. Donald Clark, *Christianity in Modern Korea* (Lanham, MD, University Press of America, 1986), p. 5.

3. Sebastian C. H. Kim and Kirsteen Kim, *A History of Korean Christianity* (New York: Cambridge University Press, 2015), p. 11.

4. Ibid., p. 18.

5. Hyun Sook Foley, 'The Jerusalem of the East', *Christian History*, no. 109, 2014, pp. 47–51.

6. Kim and Kim, *A History of Korean Christianity*, p. 108.

7. 'Korean War fast facts', CNN website, 21 June 2016, http://edition.cnn.com/2013/06/28/world/asia/korean-war-fast-facts (accessed 26 January 2017). The distinct lack of available data from the Northern and Chinese militaries, combined with vast but unrecorded civilian casualties, makes it impossible to give a more precise total death toll.

8. Clark, *Christianity in Modern Korea*, p. 9.

9. Ibid., p. 40.

10. Ibid., p. 43.

11. Ibid., p. 1.

12. 'North Korea', Open Doors website, https://www.opendoorsusa.org/christian-persecution/world-watch-list/north-korea (accessed 26 January 2017).

13. Wi Jo Kang, *Christ and Caesar in Modern Korea: A History of Christianity and Politics* (Albany: State University of New York Press, 1997), p. 156.

14 http://www.forbes.com/sites/dougbandow/2016/10/31/north-koreas-war-on-christianity-the-globes-number-one-religious-persecutor/#59372aad7eab (accessed 7 March 2017).

15. Lee Myung-bak, *The Uncharted Path: An Autobiography* (Naperville, IL: Sourcebooks, 1995), p. 7.

16. Ibid., p. 8.

17. Ibid., p. 9.

18. Sunny Lee, 'A "God-given" president-elect', *Asia Times Online*, 1 February 2008, http://www.atimes.com/atimes/Korea/JB01Dg01.html (accessed 26 January 2017).

19. Lee, *The Uncharted Path*, p. 150.

20. Ibid., p. 223.

21. Kim and Kim, *A History of Korean Christianity*, p. 291.

22. Li Tianchen, 'Confucian Ethics and the Environment', *Culture Mandala*, vol. 6, no.1, 2003, available at http://www.international-relations.com/wbcm6-1/WbLi.htm (accessed 26 January 2017).

23. 17th Presidential Transition Committee, *A Success Story Goes On* (Seoul: Korean Overseas Culture and Information Service, Ministry of Culture, Sports and Tourism, 2008), pp. 127–41.

24. Ian Jeffries, *North Korea, 2009–2012: A Guide to Economic and Political Developments* (Abingdon: Routledge, 2013), p. 631.

25. The name stems from one of Aesop's fables: the Wind and the Sun were competing to see who was the stronger by attempting to make a traveller to remove his cloak – the Wind blew hard, but this only made the traveller wrap himself up more tightly; the Sun, however, bathed him in warm rays, causing the traveller to remove the cloak of his own volition.

26. Victor Cha, *The Impossible State: North Korea, Past and Future* (New York: Ecco, 2012), p. 202.

27. Andrew Wolman, 'South Korea's Response to Human Rights Abuses in North Korea: An Analysis of Policy Options', *AsiaPacific Issues*, no. 110, 2013, p. 5, http://www.eastwestcenter.org/sites/default/files/private/api110.pdf (accessed 27 January 2017).

28. Cha, *The Impossible State*, p. 202.

29. Ibid, p. 4.

30. Jhe Seong Ho, 'North Korean human rights and some urgent tasks for their improvement', Peterson Institute for International Economics website, 29 April 2009, https://piie.com/commentary/speeches-papers/north-korean-human-rights-and-some-urgent-tasks-their-improvement (accessed 27 January 2017).

31. Young-gi Hong, 'Korean Protestantism to the Present Day', in Alister E. McGrath and Darren C. Marks (eds), *The Blackwell Companion to Protestantism* (Malden, MA: Blackwell, 2004).

32. Kim and Kim, *A History of Korean Christianity*, p. 275.

33. Lee, 'A "God-given" president-elect'.

34. http://www.jerusalemsummit.org/eng/index_js_asia_seoul.php (accessed 7 March 2017).

35. Patrick Köllner, 'South Korea in 2008: Domestic Developments and the Economy', in Rüdiger Frank, Jim Hoare, Patrick Köllner and Susan Pares (eds), *Korea Yearbook 2009: Politics, Economy and Society* (Leiden: Brill, 2009), p. 23.

36. Kim and Kim, *A History of Korean Christianity*, p. 298.

37. Uk Heo and Terence Roehrig, *South Korea since 1980* (New York: Cambridge University Press, 2010), p. 71.

38. *Korean Yearbook (2009): Politics, Economy and Society*, p. 19.

39. Lee Jeong-hun, 'Academic paper details cost of President Lee Myung-bak's cronyism', *The Hankyoreh*, 18 January 2016, http://english.hani.co.kr/arti/english_edition/e_national/726680.html (accessed 27 January 2017).

40. Köllner, 'South Korea in 2008', p. 33.

41. Kim and Kim, *A History of Korean Christianity*, p. 284.

FERNANDO LUGO (2008–12)

BEN RYAN

INTRODUCTION

With many of the leaders in this collection there is a debate to be had over which came first, the religious commitment or the policy decisions. Uniquely, when it comes to Fernando Armindo Lugo Méndez (known more commonly simply as Fernando Lugo), there is no debate at all. This is for the simple reason that long before Lugo became President of Paraguay in 2008 or ever had any official political manifesto he had been one of his country's (and arguably South America's) most prominent Catholic bishops.

Lugo's situation is almost unique in modern times, since it is illegal under Canon 285 for Roman Catholic clerics 'to assume public offices which entail a participation in the exercise of civil power'.[1] Since the start of the twentieth century the only Catholic clerics to be heads of government were the fascist Jozef Tiso, who was the President of the short-lived Nazi satellite state of the Slovak Republic until he was hanged in 1945, and Ignaz Seipel, a right-wing Christian democrat who was Chancellor of Austria twice in the 1920s.

Lugo's story, context and politics could not be more different. He was part of the 'Pink Tide' (*Marea Rosa* in Spanish) that saw a succession of populist left-wing leaders, including Evo Morales in Bolivia and Lula in Brazil, elected in Latin America. As bishop of San Pedro he developed a reputation as a radical advocate for the poor.

His presidency would prove short lived; it lasted less than four years before being replaced in what amounted to a legally questionable constitutional coup. In many ways it failed to live up to Lugo's radical and hopeful promises to change Paraguay for the better, though given the situation he inherited that was perhaps inevitable.

This chapter will focus particularly on the development of Lugo before his ill-fated presidency. This is slightly different from the approach taken in most of the other chapters in the book, partly because of Lugo's uniquely interesting pre-political life and partly for two reasons of necessity. The first is that sources on Lugo as a President are limited. He was not in power very long, and Paraguay is not a country that gets significant international press or academic attention. By comparison, the sources on his religious work are rather more extensive. The second is that, although Lugo was only a professional politician for a relatively short period, he spent many years as a bishop in a poor diocese, and it was there that he developed his particular political role. The intersection of his theology and politics is best seen in that period of his life. His policies as President reflect that development – they were not forged in a classic political context, but through a pastoral ministry in one of the poorest parts of Latin America.

PARAGUAY

The country inherited by Lugo as President in 2008 was faced with a number of serious challenges. Paraguay is a small, landlocked country, with a population of under seven million. Of those seven million, more than 1.2 million live in extreme poverty. After its independence from Spain in 1811, the country remained relatively isolated, ruled by a series of military officers and dictators. Its development was severely hampered by a costly war on the Triple Alliance of Argentina, Brazil and Uruguay in 1864. The result had near-genocidal consequences for Paraguay, with estimates that as many as 69 per cent of the population lost their lives.[2]

Political instability became a feature. Between 1904 and 1954 Paraguay had thirty-one Presidents, mostly replaced in armed insurrections. From 1954 to 2008, the country was ruled by a single party, the National Republican Association, better known as the Colorados ('Reds'; the colour has no socialist connotation). For thirty-five of those years it was controlled by Alfredo Stroessner, the longest-serving dictator in South American history. Backed by the USA, Stroessner oversaw some economic progress, but also rampant corruption and widespread human rights abuses. Even after his overthrow in 1989, the Colorados retained power until Lugo's victory in 2008.

Paraguay remains overwhelmingly agrarian, being one of the least urbanised societies in Latin America. Many of the population are little more than serfs – landless peasants forced to work for exploitative landowners. Seventy-seven per cent of Paraguay's land in 2008 was owned by just one per cent of the population.[3] The population is around 85 per cent *Mestizo* (mixed Amerindian and European descent),[4] and is one of the most bilingual populations in the world, with the vast majority speaking both Spanish and Guaraní as joint first languages (though until Lugo, Spanish was used for almost all official functions). Catholicism continues to be by far the biggest religious group, accounting for over 88 per cent of the population.

The dominance of the Catholic Church, combined with the weakness of opposing political parties during the Colorado period, has resulted in the Church being a major political player (even aside from Lugo). Refusals to celebrate San Blas's Day in February (Blas, or Blaise in English, is the patron saint of Paraguay) or the festival of Santa María de Caacupé in December have been used by the Church to publicly sanction governments and have caused significant social stirs.

This was the situation which Lugo inherited: an impoverished, isolated country used to despotic government and endemic corruption in which the Church possessed significant political power as a protest against government.

LUGO'S FAMILY AND UPBRINGING

Lugo's upbringing would not have suggested that he would go on to become the 'bishop of the poor' in a largely rural district, or that he would be the man to finally break the grip of the Colorados on government. By Paraguayan standards, he was brought up in a fairly comfortable, middle class home. Born in 1951, the youngest of seven children, his father was a railway worker and mother a school teacher. It was a committed Catholic household. His family, in one of life's ironies, were all committed Colorados. His father was prominent in the local party structure, as were several of Fernando Lugo's older brothers.

Even more prominent was his uncle, Epifanio Méndez Fleitas. Epifanio was widely famed in Paraguay as a writer, musician, composer and Colorado politician. In the chaotic politics of 1940s Paraguay, he was a key power broker who rose to become police chief in Asunción and president of the Central Bank. The situation did not last, with serious consequences for Lugo's family. Stroessner, always suspicious of non-military politicians and paranoid that his position was under threat, fell out with and then exiled Epifanio in 1956. His name became toxic, not least as he co-ordinated much of the political activity of Stroessner's many exiled enemies abroad. Lugo's father, despite his commitment to the party, was arrested and tortured for his support of Epifanio and his faction. He was denounced at work, arrested and waterboarded so badly that it did permanent damage to his kidneys. Several of Fernando's older siblings were exiled.[5]

Fernando Lugo, for his own protection, was urged to avoid too much public prominence and certainly a Paraguayan political career. Even outside politics his family name and history were held against him. He thrived in his military service and was due to be awarded a prestigious prize as a leading cadet, with the likelihood of a promising career in the military as a reward. The army chiefs, learning of his family, decided it would not be politic to have the nephew of Epifanio Méndez on a stage receiving an award from Stroessner, and gave the prize (and career) to another young man.

With his career hopes dashed Lugo decided to become a teacher, and slowly came to know an order of Catholic priests who had become important local figures.

LUGO THE PRIEST AND LUGO THE 'BISHOP OF THE POOR'

Lugo came to know a number of prominent local priests from the Verbistas order (officially the Divine Word Missionaries or *Societas Verbi Divini* in their Latin name). Though not a particularly rich or prominent order by comparison with the better-known Jesuits, Dominicans or Franciscans, they were well established in Paraguay and across the river from Encarnación, where Lugo was living at the time, in the Argentine city of Posadas. It was as a Verbista that Lugo felt a vocation. He became a novice in 1970, read for a degree and was ordained in 1977. The Verbistas then made a decision that was to make a huge impact on Lugo's politics: after ordination they sent him to Ecuador.

Ecuador was Lugo's first real exposure to the abject treatment of Amerindians by Latin American governments. It was also where he encountered the remarkable bishop of Riobamba, Leonidas Proaño. Proaño, nicknamed 'the bishop in the poncho' or 'the bishop of the Indians', was a champion of the poor and Indians. He was also one of the leading advocates of liberation theology. He was charismatic, idolised by his young priests, and a thorn in the side of the military junta.

LUGO AND LIBERATION THEOLOGY

Lugo, inspired by what he heard from Proaño and his followers, and by what he had seen in Ecuador, became a liberation theologian. The movement was at the height of its prominence in the late 1970s, and the height of its controversy within the Church. At root, liberation theology is a radical Catholic idea that arose after the Second Vatican Council. It is a call to a renewal of the Church lived in solidarity with the poor and the oppressed. Its starting point is the idea that God has a 'preferential option for the poor'.[6] Fundamentally it is a practical theology; it is not meant to be imposed and taught in the academy but lived and experienced alongside the poor – as Jesus lived. Thus Gustavo Gutiérrez, the Peruvian often seen as the father of the movement, described the source of the movement as originating 'among the world's anonymous, whoever may write the books or declarations articulating it'.[7]

Liberation is understood as having a real political and social content to it regarding the emancipation of the poor. In a Latin American context of endemic poverty, that vision took fire among many Catholic priests and laypeople. It was never without criticism. Many liberation theologians drew upon Marxist analysis of structural poverty, going so far as to describe the situation of the poor as being one of 'structural sin'. The Catholic hierarchy, witnessing the Cold War and the plight of Catholicism on its doorstep in central and eastern Europe, was militantly opposed to any hint of socialism and Marxism, which it saw as an atheistic and evil creed. The association of liberation theology with socialism and Marxism was unacceptable to many in the Church. In 1978, Karol Wojtyła would become Pope John Paul II. As a Pole who had witnessed first-hand the effects of communism on a traditional Catholic country, John Paul would countenance no surrender to Marxism and viewed liberation theology as innately dangerous.

More broadly, liberation theology was criticised for making the concerns of the Church too earthly at the expense of traditional Church teaching and piety. The movement was censured by Cardinal Joseph Ratzinger (later Pope Benedict XVI, then the head of the Congregation for the Doctrine of the Faith, the successor to the Inquisition) in an official Church document entitled *Instruction on Certain Aspects of the 'Theology of Liberation'*. In it he declared:

> Faced with the urgency of certain problems, some are tempted to empha-size, unilaterally, the liberation from servitude of an earthly and temporal kind. They do so in such a way that they seem to put liberation from sin in second place, and so fail to give it the primary importance it is due.[8]

Prominent liberation theologians were consistently investigated by the Vatican. Some, including the Brazilian Leonardo Boff, were officially silenced and banned from teaching by the Church, or had their books condemned.

Lugo was at the heart of the movement in Paraguay. He was close friends with many of the leading figures across Latin America, including Boff and Ernesto Cardenal, both of whom would one day attend Lugo's inauguration as President of Paraguay. He did not write many prominent works himself, but he was a rousing and radical speaker who filled his sermons with increasingly politicised calls for liberation and the rights of the poor. His sermons as a priest on his return to Paraguay were sufficiently radical that, combined with his family history, they were recorded by the military and ultimately led to a firm suggestion from the authorities to his Verbista superiors that he be sent out of the country. He went to Rome, completed a second degree and became a far more prominent churchman than he might ever have done had he been forced to stay at home.

POLITICAL BISHOP

By virtue of his status as a prominent liberation theologian Lugo bonded together the roles of political activist and cleric. For Lugo, there is no space between where politics ends and Christianity begins. Authentic Christianity is about liberation and fighting for justice, so that is what Lugo did. His career as a priest is, in effect, also his career as a politician.

So it was that having returned to the country in 1987 and become a bishop in 1994, Lugo started to become a key public figure. In 1996, he told a conference in his diocese that 'the sight of so many families without land or homes, and of children without schooling, health or hope is an injustice that cries to heaven, and demands the full power of our reflection and action'.[9] That basic programme, calling for land, education, healthcare and a new, more hopeful Paraguay, was essentially the same when, a decade later, Lugo laid out his political programme for the presidency. Politics and religion are not divisible in Lugo's vision. He would summarise that, years later, in an interview soon after winning the election:

> I have always strongly maintained that anywhere in the world, anyone who radically accepts the life of Jesus Christ must also live the way he lived. I believe that defending the gospel values of truth against so many lies, justice against so much injustice, and peace against so much violence, is like rowing against the current.[10]

In 1994, he was Paraguay's youngest bishop and had been given the difficult diocese of San Pedro. In 2004, after a decade of toil he was still faced with a diocese of over 380,000 people, 90 per cent of whom were Catholics, and only eighteen priests – in effect, 19,444 Catholics for each priest.[11] Moreover, it was desperately poor.

Lugo's actions were classic for a liberation theologian bishop. First, he encouraged 'basic ecclesial communities' (CEBs in the Spanish acronym). These are small groups of Catholics who gather together alongside parish models. They take part in Bible study, prayer, community work and local campaigning and politics. They are a staple of liberation theology, but also a

practical necessity in areas with a serious shortage of priests. Lugo was an enthusiastic advocate of CEBs from his first days as a bishop.[12] Over the course
of his time in San Pedro, he doubled the number of CEBs in the diocese
and encouraged them in political participation. He also changed the official
language of all church services and businesses from Spanish (the language of
education, politics and formality) to Guaraní (the more common language
of everyday peasant life). He eschewed the bishop's quarters and moved into
a modest house, drove around the diocese on a motorbike and tried to avoid
wearing full clerical garb in favour of more traditional local clothes.

Some of his other moves were even more radical. He withdrew all his
diocesan priestly candidates (trainee priests) from the national seminary and
tried to set one up within the diocese that would be less focused on classic
education and instead see them work and live alongside the poor.[13] It was a
brave move, in keeping with Lugo's theology and politics, but one which, in
this case, sadly failed. A lack of suitable formation directors and the difficulties of making it work in practice doomed the idea.

His political work also became more pronounced and public. The diocese
was largely rural, and there was significant conflict (some of it sporadical-
ly violent and backed by guerrilla groups) between on the one hand, the
(mostly) landless peasants and farmworkers (*campesinos*), mostly Guaraní
speakers who live in *asentamientos*, small villages lacking even basic infrastructure, and on the other, their landowners. Most of the landowners owed
their property to cronyism during the Stroessner years. Almost all were
hugely unpopular. Lugo was generally careful to shy away from calling for
armed uprisings or violence (although he did associate with those who were
less cautious), and campaigned vociferously on the part of the *campesinos*.
His campaigns always returned to the constant refrains of liberation theology
– emancipation and liberation, fighting for the poor and the dispossessed
(particularly Amerindians), and seeing in all of this a deliberate echoing of
the option for the poor as taken by God.

More broadly, he became a constant campaigner, endlessly petitioning
and protesting to get more local funding for infrastructure, education and
healthcare reform from the central government. He fought against corruption and clientelism and worked to hold government-sponsored violence

to account. He denounced the government-sponsored vigilante groups as 'terrorists'.[14] His fame grew, he gained the nickname 'bishop of the poor' or more simply 'El Bueno'. He was now a national figure and cult hero to many of the peasants.

This fame and campaigning spirit, combined with the ongoing weakness of the opposition political parties and the status of the Church for many years as critic of the government, led to Lugo being seen more and more as the official spokesperson for opposition to the Colorado government. He did little to dispel these impressions, calling again and again for the poor to go into the streets and denounce bad politicians. In June 2000, he led a mass protest to demand government work on a major highway that had been allowed to erode.[15] He took an ever greater interest in economics, and in 2001 attended the World Social Forum in Brazil. He could be extremely blunt in his diagnosis of his country and global economics. Commenting on Paraguay's history after independence from Spain, he said, 'New forms of slavery appeared, the English arrived with their capital, their companies, their people.'[16]

Eventually the strain of fighting these political battles alongside his other duties as bishop seems to have taken its toll on Lugo. He suffered with thrombosis, and that was the reason offered in his resignation letter to John Paul II in 2004. A revealing quotation from soon afterwards suggests that what really ailed him was not only physical health but a sense of frustration at being unable to see enough of a practical impact for his work:

> The impotence of not being able to see the institutional way forward, and of not being able to help so many families who had their human rights humiliated, because of the young people who want to study and work and can't because of a lack of money and, on the other hand, observe impotently that the institutions of the state did not have the capacity of giving answers to the needs of the population that I as a pastor would like to have given more dignity.[17]

This quotation gets to the heart of Lugo's theo-political instincts. His faith and theology had led him to radical political demands that seemed to him

to be beyond the abilities of a bishop to address. After a further year of refusing to take on an official political role, but still taking prominent political
positions (notably leading a huge protest against a proposed constitutional
reform that would have dramatically empowered the then President, Nica-
nor Duarte), on Christmas Day 2006 he finally announced he would run for
President. By September 2007, he had formed a seven-party coalition.

VICTORY AGAINST THE ODDS
AND THE LUGO PRESIDENCY

Lugo's faith had not so much shaped his politics as created them from scratch.
His political campaign and presidency were, in terms of policies, identical
to the campaigns he had fought as a liberation theologian and bishop for
years. They were quite simple: agrarian reform, giving dignity to the landless
and exploited, and investment in education, infrastructure and healthcare
to help liberate the poor from the structures that oppressed them. More
broadly, Lugo promised an end to the corruption that permeates every level
of Paraguayan society and a simple message of hope for something better.
The campaign tag line was simply 'Lugo has heart'.

Even with Lugo's undeniable popularity, particularly among the poor,
victory was not a given. The Colorado Party had not held power for over
fifty years by simple good luck. A number of dubious election practices were
reported – including a large number of suspiciously elderly voters who were
registered in marginal constituencies and whole areas being reclassified as if
they were located somewhere else. Moreover, the Colorado Party had for decades cultivated a simple model of clientelism. In a poor country with high
unemployment, the government was directly responsible for more than
200,000 jobs that could only be held by paid-up members of the party. The
financial war chest available was massive, as was a large body of workers reliant
on the party staying in power. Lugo was aided, however, by a split in the Colorados that saw two separate candidates divide the vote, and by the backing of
the largest of the traditional opposition parties, the Liberals (PLRA or blues).

His peculiar status as a priest did lead to a constitutional and legal issue.
The Church for some time refused to recognise Lugo's right to run for office,
which is, as noted, against canon law. He received stern rebukes from the

Vatican that continued for some months. Only after his election was the issue settled, with Pope Benedict XVI sending Lugo a gift, congratulating him and formally recognising that he had a calling to justice and politics. The decision to become a politician received a mixed reception from his fellow bishops, even in Paraguay, with several believing the move to have been reckless.

The inauguration ceremony was a study in Lugo's religion and politics. Shunning a suit, he attended in sandals and a traditional Indian shirt (*ao po'i*), and gave his speech largely in Guaraní. Present among the guests were a number of other leaders of the 'pink tide' of Latin American politics, including Lula of Brazil, Morales of Bolivia and Hugo Chávez of Venezuela, and a number of the great figures of liberation theology, including Leonardo Boff and Ernesto Cardenal.

ASSESSMENT OF TIME IN OFFICE AND FALL FROM GRACE

Lugo's period in office began with extraordinarily high expectations from his supporters. Perhaps they were too high. Lugo inherited a state apparatus with a huge number of government employees, all of whom owed their livelihood to the Colorados. Attempts to eliminate corruption or prompt major reforms given such an embedded opposition were never likely to be easy. Nor, after decades out of power, did the various opposition parties that had backed Lugo have enough experience and competent figures to drive through reforms in critical offices.

There were successes. Healthcare improved, particularly for the poorest. There was a focus on much-needed infrastructure which greatly improved the situation of many of the poor. Lugo also presided over a radical education reform, importing a Cuban educational system and resources through Venezuela, in a deal brokered between himself and Chávez.

Ultimately, however, his work was doomed by four factors. First, there was the sheer scale of the task given the level of poverty, under-investment and resistance from civil servants. Second, despite significant efforts, Lugo was unable to bring in radical agrarian reform fast enough for many of the poor. This issue would ultimately play a major role in his impeachment.

The other two factors were more personal. His health was a problem. In 2010, he was diagnosed with non-Hodgkin's lymphoma, forcing regular treatment in Brazil (Paraguay did not have the facilities to treat him). The illness sapped much of his energy. Finally, he was shaken by a succession of revelations about his personal life. A succession of women, four to date, claimed Lugo was the father of their children. The claims went back years and Lugo has been forced to recognise his paternity of two children. These paternity suits did huge damage to Lugo's moral credibility. As a Catholic priest he had sworn to be celibate, and though a number of Latin American bishops are well known to turn a blind eye to the celibacy of their priests, it was a significant scandal.

He might have been able to survive the reputational damage of those revelations and won further elections, but he was never given the chance. Frustrations at the slow pace of land reform meant that violent clashes between *campesinos* and landowners continued under Lugo; indeed, they continue to this day. One such violent clash, in which seventeen died, was used, along with a number of other charges relating to alleged support for criminal groups, as an excuse to impeach him. He was given only hours to mount a defence, in what was roundly condemned by a number of Latin American heads of state as a constitutional coup, the legality of which has been challenged.

CONCLUSION

This was a sad end to the Lugo presidency, which had promised much to help turn around Paraguay and help the poor. It seems unlikely, even in Latin America, where the Church remains a significant and powerful presence, that we will see another Catholic priest as head of state. Lugo had, and still has (for he has latterly returned to politics as a senator), an unquestionable courage in standing up for the poor and campaigning for their needs.

This courage and vision is founded within Lugo's theology in a more clear and linear sense than for other politicians in this collection. With many Christian leaders it is possible to question which came first – the ideology, or the religious thought to justify and explain that ideology and the resulting policies. With Lugo there is a clear answer to that question. In his years of service as a priest and bishop to Paraguay's poor, the theology undeniably came first. It just so happens that the theology and the political vision were, in Lugo's case, one and the same thing.

Ironically, after years of Lugo feeling that the Church was impotent to help enact the radical change that he felt was necessary for the sake of the poor, within a year of his fall from power it elected a man to the papacy, who more than any previous Pope, sympathises with Lugo's position. Jorge Bergoglio, like Lugo, is a middle-class Latin American who would become a bishop to the poor.[18] His criticisms of unchecked capitalism as 'the dung of the devil'[19] could have come from one of Lugo's firebrand sermons. Pope Francis is not a liberation theologian, at least not of the classic variety, and has always been a wary critic of Marxism. Perhaps Lugo can take heart that, though his presidency did not bear the fruit he had longed for, his Church at least seems to be coming round to his way of thinking.

NOTES

1. Canon 285 on the obligations and rights of clerics from the Code of Canon Law, http:// www.vatican.va/archive/ENG1104/_PY.HTM (accessed 27 January 2017).

2. For the upper estimate see, for example, Thomas L. Whigham and Barbara Potthast, 'The Paraguayan Rosetta Stone: New Insights into the Demographics of the Paraguayan War, 1864–1870', *Latin American Research Review*, vol. 34, no. 1, 1999, pp. 174–86.

3. Toby Stirling Hill, 'Paraguay battles over land rights in the courts and across the airwaves', *The Guardian*, 3 May 2016, https://www.theguardian.com/global-development/2016/ may/03/paraguay-battles-over-land-rights-in-the-courts-and-across-the-airwaves (accessed 27 January 2017).

4. Joel Morales Cruz, *The Histories of the Latin American Church: A Handbook* (Minneapolis: Fortress Press, 2014), p. 457.

5. Their respective fates are mentioned in Richard Gott, 'The red bishop in Paraguay', *London Review of Books*, 21 February 2008.

6. The line is first attributed to Pedro Allupe, when he was superior of the Jesuit order, in a letter of 1968. It would be taken on in the famous conference at Medellín in Colombia in 1968 which is seen by many as the birth of liberation theology. It would become popularised by Gustavo Gutiérrez in the 1971 book *A Theology of Liberation*, which is a key text in the early liberation theology movement.

7. Gustavo Gutiérrez, 'Two Theological Perspectives: Liberation Theology and Progressivist Theology', in Sergio Torres and Virginia Fabella (eds), *The Emergent Gospel: Theology from the Underside of History* (Maryknoll, NY: Orbis, 1978), p. 240.

8. *Instruction on Certain Aspects of the 'Theology of Liberation'*, Congregation for the Doctrine of the Faith, 6 August 1984, available at http://www.vatican.va/roman_curia/congregations/ cfaith/documents/rc_con_cfaith_doc_19840806_theology-liberation_en.html (accessed 27 January 2017).

9. Quoted in 'Paraguay leads way for base communities', *The Tablet*, 17 August 1996.

10. 'Q&A: a bishop with his (sandalled) feet on the ground', Inter Press Service, 2 May 2008, http://www.ipsnews.net/2008/05/qa-a-bishop-with-his-sandalled-feet-on-the-ground (accessed 27 January 2017).

11. Hugh O'Shaughnessy, *The Priest of Paraguay: Fernando Lugo and the Making of a Nation* (London: Zed, 2009), p. 94.

12. In 'Paraguay leads way for base communities', op. cit., he is reported as the host of a major international conference and keynote speaker.

13. Alberto Luna, 'Paraguay: the bishop who would be President', *Thinking Faith*, 4 February 2008, http://www.thinkingfaith.org/articles/20080204_1.htm (accessed 27 January 2017).

14. Quoted in O'Shaughnessy, *The Priest of Paraguay*, p. 97.

15. Ibid., p. 99.

16. Quoted in Gott, 'The red bishop in Paraguay'.

17. Quoted in O'Shaughnessy, *The Priest of Paraguay*, p. 100.

18. See Austen Ivereigh, *The Great Reformer: Francis and the Making of a Radical Pope* (London: Allen and Unwin, 2014).

19 Quoted in 'Unbridled capitalism is the "dung of the devil", says Pope Francis', *The Guardian*, 10 July 2015, https://www.theguardian.com/world/2015/jul/10/poor-must-change-new-colonialism-of-economic-order-says-pope-francis (accessed 27 January 2017).

BARACK OBAMA (2009–17)

SIMON PERFECT

In June 2009, *Newsweek* editor Evan Thomas captured something of the adulation in the air concerning the new President. For him, Obama was saying, 'We're not just parochial, we're not just chauvinistic … in a way Obama's standing above the country, above – above the world, he's sort of God.'[1]

It was this feeling of messianism, his image as America's new prophet, which swept Barack Obama into power. And it was his inevitable inability to live up to that image that led to a collapse of faith in him. Central to this story are his complex personal faith, his deployment of religion to serve his political ends, and a clash between a growing secular left and a revived Religious Right.

Obama has been one of the most vocal Presidents in modern times concerning his religion.[2] But his faith has also been one of the most heavily scrutinised of any President. His 'liberal' theology and social attitudes have been denounced as un-Christian or secularist by opponents. In 2008, internet evangelist Bill Keller brought down hellfire on anyone tainted with Obamaism, saying that any Christians who supported Obama were 'a stench in the nostrils of God!'[3]

He has also been accused of being a Muslim – a rumour which began by drawing on his past as the son of an ex-Muslim and which strengthened as his failures in the Middle East helped lead to the spawning of new jihadist groups. Indeed, the rumour became more popular over the course of his presidency. In 2008, five months before the election, 10 per cent of

Americans thought Obama was a Muslim and 53 per cent a Christian.[4] A CNN/ORC poll in September 2015 found that 39 per cent thought he was a 'Protestant/Christian' and 29 per cent a Muslim.[5] Donald Trump faced criticism in the same month for failing to correct a questioner who said Obama was a Muslim (in 2011 Trump announced he had dispatched investigators to Hawaii to try to disprove that Obama was born in America).[6]

How is it that a man who put so much political energy into affirming his Christianity could be so misunderstood by the American public? 'We have a guy in the Oval Office who we don't know,' said Republican candidate Chris Christie in 2016. 'He's been serving us for seven years and we don't know him.'[7] This chapter explores the reality of Obama's religious narrative, and how he tried to use religion to win him the American people.

A PATCHWORK HERITAGE

Obama is keenly aware of his heritage. He recounts his journey in his two memoirs, *Dreams from My Father* (1995) and *The Audacity of Hope* (2006), emphasising the importance of his interracial and interreligious past to his self-understanding.

Obama was born in Hawaii in 1961. His father, Barack Obama Sr, was a former Muslim from Kenya who had abandoned his faith. His marriage to Obama's white mother, (Stanley) Ann Dunham, was short lived, and Ann was soon remarried, to Lolo Soetoro, an Indonesian Muslim. The two Baracks corresponded but met only once more, when the younger Barack was ten.[8]

In 1967, Ann and Obama went to live with Soetoro in Jakarta. Obama describes Soetoro as following 'a brand of Islam that could make room for the remnants of more ancient animist and Hindu faiths'.[9] In Jakarta Obama attended a Catholic school and, for a year, a predominantly Muslim public elementary school. He returned to Hawaii in 1971 to attend an American school and lived with his maternal grandparents, who in earlier years had belonged to a Unitarian church. Ann, however, remained in Indonesia, forging a career focusing on the country's poor and the status of its women until her death in 1995.[10] In later life, Obama's Indonesian years would provide fuel for his enemies when trying to discredit his Christianity.

It was above all Obama's mother who instilled in him a deep respect for the spirituality of others. Despite her 'professed secularism', for Obama she was 'the most spiritually awakened person that I've ever known'. She exposed him to Buddhist, Shinto and other shrines as much as to Christian services. Her faith was in human dignity and goodness, and the importance of fighting injustice.[11] These principles would come to underpin Obama's own faith.

This out-of-the-ordinary heritage became a tool for pushing politician Obama into the extraordinary. He was black, but more than black; and as an adult he would be Christian, but more than Christian. He presented himself as the symbol of the American melting pot myth, the very embodiment of the post-racial and trans-religious politics he believed America was searching for.

CHICAGO YEARS: PRESIDENT AS PROPHET

Obama's faith journey began when he moved to Chicago in 1985. He became a community organiser in Chicago's South Side, working closely with black churches for three years.[12] It was a transformative time. He began to attend a church, Trinity United Church of Christ, to get closer to the people he sought to help.[13] And gradually the experience of being part of a community, which he had never truly known before, drew him to embrace Christianity.[14]

Trinity offered Obama a tradition in which to root and act upon his deep concern for justice for the poor. The church's pastor, Jeremiah Wright, espoused black liberation theology, insisting that God aligns with the oppressed and powerless.[15] This was also Martin Luther King Jr's tradition. Obama was deeply influenced by this vision of the pastor as prophet, as speaking truth unto power. The black church tradition gave him a narrative of faith as noble struggle and fortified his racial identity. 'I imagined the stories of ordinary black people merging with the stories of David and Goliath, Moses and Pharaoh ... Our trials and triumphs became at once unique and universal, black and more than black.'[16] It was one of Wright's sermons – on the power of faith and hope in spite of pain, on the audacity of hope – that provided the name of Obama's second memoir.[17]

Obama also adopted from the black church tradition the great oratorical device of the jeremiad – the prophetic sermon which laments the state of society and demands moral renewal, before offering a glimpse of a future society in which God has brought about justice. It took a particular form in African American culture, drawing on themes of black protest at racial injustice and messianic liberation.[18] Obama would come to use this device in his speeches, casting himself as King's prophetic heir and calling America to a vision of renewal.

PRESIDENTIAL PRINCIPLES

At heart, Obama's Christianity is community-orientated and is driven by the demand for justice that he encountered at Trinity and in the writings of King. It is liberal on social issues and open to pluralism. In *The Audacity of Hope*, he described his gradual coming to Christianity as a way to systematise, and root in tradition and community, his previously held beliefs about God and human dignity. Christianity became 'a vessel for my beliefs'.[19] Later, however, he would describe his spiritual journey in more evangelical terms, as a born-again conversion.[20] His public rhetoric became more explicitly Christian and more theologically orthodox during his presidency. This reflected both his apparently deepening private faith and his manipulation of its public expression as a political tool.

Humanity's need for God's redemptive grace and Jesus' atonement for humanity's sins were increasingly important themes for Obama as his faith developed during his presidency. His willingness to speak publicly on multiple occasions about Jesus, rather than just about God, showed his confidence in his faith, as much as his recognition of the political importance of using language familiar to evangelicals. (It also stood in contrast to his predecessor – in his eight annual National Prayer Breakfast speeches, George W. Bush didn't mention 'Jesus', 'Christ' or 'Savior' once). At the Easter Prayer Breakfast in 2013, Obama declared that Jesus was 'our Savior, who suffered and died was resurrected, both fully God and also a man'.[21] Such an explicit public admission of Jesus' complete divinity was, however, rare for him. Obama was much more likely to speak of Jesus' resurrection, atonement and his continual presence than specifically of his divinity. Nevertheless, he was most comfortable describing Jesus as a model for ethical behaviour – especially so before the launch of his 2008 election campaign. In a 2004 interview, he said that 'Jesus is an historical figure for me, and he's also a bridge between God and man, in the Christian faith … he serves as that means of us reaching something higher. And he's also a wonderful teacher.'[22] At the time this left Obama open to accusations of denying that Jesus is God.[23]

So it is Jesus' actions, rather than his nature, that are of primary concern to Obama – his praxis (redemptive and ethical) more than his doctrine. The central crux of Obama's faith is that following Jesus demands, above all else, an urgent concern to raise up the poor and oppressed. This is a revival of the ideas of the Social Gospel movement of late nineteenth- and early twenti-eth-century America, which Martin Luther King melded with the prophetic fervour of the black Protestant churches.[24] For Obama, 'we are our brother's keeper and our sister's keeper and our destinies are linked.'[25] He tried to tie this phrase to his presidency, and even named a major White House initia-tive for minority boys and young men after it.[26] In this way Obama sought to justify his overarching economic policies – by linking them to a narrative of collective salvation here on earth.[27]

Tied with this, though, is a concern about the dangers of religious dog-matism and an insistence that doubt is an important part of faith.[28] He has called for critical interpretation when reading the Bible.[29] And in the 2004 interview mentioned above he declared that 'I believe that there are many paths to the same place … I find it hard to believe that my God would consign four-fifths of the world to hell.' His doubts, and his broad religious pluralism, though offensive to many religious conservatives, proved useful for his campaigns. They enabled him to present a vision of America as both Christian and more than Christian.[30] And his upholding, or even celebrat-ing, of doubt and the mystery of God was an important theological tool for building political alliances between people of very different beliefs.

It has been suggested, however, that Obama made a subtle shift during the 2008 presidential race to downplay the scepticism he had proudly described in 2004 and in *The Audacity of Hope*. In *The Audacity of Hope*, for example, he admitted that he was not sure what happens after death.[31] But in a 2008 interview with *Christianity Today*, he said that he believes that 'faith gives me a path to be cleansed of sin and have eternal life'. His stated belief 'in the redemptive death and resurrection of Jesus Christ'[32] was also more akin to orthodox creedal statements than his nervous description of Jesus in 2004.

This may indicate that his faith was deepening by 2008 (or simply that he was more prepared for the question than in 2004) – but it was seen by some conservative commentators as evidence of deceit, and a willingness to mould his faith to suit his audience.[33] In any case, during Obama's first term the evangelical pastor Joel Hunter, one of his spiritual advisors, affirmed that the President was in a period of theological transition, and that he no longer thought all religions are essentially the same or would question the existence of an afterlife. Joshua DuBois, another advisor and pastor, insisted that 'Barack Obama is a born again man who has trusted in Jesus Christ with his whole heart'.[34]

Obama learned, during his presidency, to deal with failure by conceiving it as an integral part of a faith journey that must be honed by struggle. At times this even led him to reconstitute tragic events as part of God's wider, unknowable plan, from which goodness can emerge. He articulated this publicly in June 2015 in his momentous eulogy for the victims of the Charleston shooting. Cody Keenan, Obama's speechwriter, sought to emulate Abraham Lincoln's 1865 second inaugural address.[35] In that speech, Lincoln framed the Civil War as part of God's providence.[36] The night before his eulogy, Obama rewrote the latter half of Keenan's draft and made grace the central theme.[37] The final product was his greatest jeremiad and it brought together the core themes of his faith. 'Oh, but God works in mysterious ways,' he preached, more pastor-in-chief than President. 'God has different ideas. [The killer] didn't know he was being used by God … [He] could never have anticipated the way the families of the fallen would respond … with words of forgiveness.'[38]

REINHOLD NIEBUHR:
PRESIDENT AS PHILOSOPHER

Alongside this theological liberalism is an insistence that politics cannot ignore religion, and that economic and social policies are ultimately moral issues.[39] Obama is heavily influenced on these points by Reinhold Niebuhr (1892–1971), one of the most influential American theologians and ethicists in the twentieth century and the developer of 'Christian realist' thought. At the heart of Niebuhr's thought is an emphasis on the reality of evil, and the fallibility and sinfulness of humanity. He rejects utopianism and the central notion of America's civil religion – the myth of its exceptionalism and messianic destiny. He insists that politicians must pursue ideals and face down evil – but they should do so in a realistic rather than idealistic way, recognising the limitations of power.[40]

Much of this resonates with Obama. Indeed, R. Ward Holder and Peter Josephson argue that Obama's political work has been guided by Niebuhr's Christian realism.[41] Obama takes away from Niebuhr 'the compelling idea that there's serious evil in the world' and that people must recognise their limited ability to defeat it. 'But we shouldn't use that as an excuse for cynicism and inaction.'[42] This is an admission of moral absolutes and a rejection of a liberal relativism, and the challenges of the presidency would confirm the truth of this to him. And yet, the extent to which Obama's actual policies as well as his rhetoric were 'Niebuhrian' continues to be contested by commentators. For example, depending on the context, in his political rhetoric Obama either downplayed American exceptionalism or ramped it up to win electoral points.[43] Obama's electoral slogan – 'Yes, we can!' – may have struck Niebuhr as sheer naïvety and utopianism.

Regardless of how far Obama is Niebuhrian, he stood to gain from portraying himself as such. It served to mould his public image into a mid-point between 'naïve idealism and bitter realism'[44] – into the president-philosopher as much as the president-prophet.

RACE TO THE WHITE HOUSE

After the Democratic Party's defeat in the 2004 election, its leaders concluded that the party needed candidates who could shake it out of its reluctance to talk about faith.[45] Obama, influenced by Niebuhr, agreed. Now Senator of Illinois (2005–08), he threw his hat into the ring.

But his theological roots almost derailed him in early 2008. Journalists unearthed quotes from Jeremiah Wright's past sermons which were politically toxic. '[They want] us to sing "God Bless America". No, no, no, not "God Bless America". God damn America – that's in the Bible – for killing innocent people.'[46] Obama swiftly broke with Wright and sought to push public perceptions of his faith away from the pastor's racialised theology.[47]

But the damage was done. In a poll following the storm, 41 per cent of registered voters said they had a less favourable opinion of Obama due to his association with Wright.[48] Among some commentators, the association between Obama and 'suspect' religion stuck.

This was particularly problematic because Obama's electoral strategy was to a large extent faith based. Electoral victory would depend on stealing the evangelical vote from Republican candidate John McCain. This required an ambitious two-pronged approach. Firstly, he prioritised faith in his campaign more than any Democratic presidential candidate had since Jimmy Carter. Prayers opened and closed his rallies and he gave multiple interviews about his faith. He insisted that the Democrats could be the party of religion.[49] He was helped by McCain's reluctance to discuss his faith or to give his policies religious grounding.[50] Obama, on the other hand, stressed the biblical basis for his policies on poverty, healthcare and immigration[51] – an irony considering his stated objection to politicians resorting to God to justify their politics.[52]

Secondly, he needed to reclaim evangelicalism from the Religious Right. This was pushing for a new religious centre in American politics. Joshua DuBois, the leader of Obama's faith campaign, recognised that many self-defining evangelicals were less conservative (and less white and less wealthy) than the Religious Right. And even among those who were conservative on social issues, like abortion and gay rights, many were sympathetic to Obama's economic policies and his anti-Iraq War stance. Florida megachurch pastor Joel Hunter, for example, was strongly opposed to Obama's pro-choice position on abortion, but lent his support to the campaign because of Obama's demand for action on poverty and climate change. Finding points of commonality above the traditional dividing lines on abortion and gay rights helped Obama to form broad-based religious alliances that McCain could not compete with.[53]

This centrist-coalition approach reflected Obama's core pitch: that America needed a new politics rooted in bipartisanship, and that he was the man who could deliver. His personal faith, as portrayed in his speeches, was the perfect foil for this politics – broad enough to embrace the progressives and conservatives, critical enough to appease the sceptics. His victory was heralded as the beginning of a new and brighter future for America.[54]

RELIGION IN THE OVAL OFFICE:
GAYS, CONDOMS AND EMBRYOS

So, religion helped win the White House for Obama. But religion would also be at the heart of some of some of the biggest battles of his presidency.

Upon entering the White House, Obama created an informal prayer circle with a number of nationally known pastors, some Pentecostal, some politically conservative – reflecting Obama's 'big tent'[55] approach to faith. All were more theologically conservative than Jeremiah Wright.[56] Throughout his presidency Obama received emailed daily devotionals from Joshua DuBois, and he spoke publicly about his prayer routine.[57] But he was less disciplined in attending church – attending a service only eighteen times in his first five years in office.[58] Obama knew from experience that in regularly attending one church he could associate himself too closely with a specific denomination; but his laxity was seen by some as indicating a lack of piety (an accusation that was thrown at Ronald Reagan for his even poorer record of attendance, as mentioned in the chapter on him in this volume – though thrown at him with, perhaps, less vigour).[59]

The Obama administration's main negotiations with religious groups were conducted through its Office of Faith-Based and Neighborhood Partnerships, headed by DuBois until 2013. This office, established under George W. Bush, provides support and federal funding for faith-based and secular civil society initiatives in local communities. Obama strengthened the outfit and used it to realise his vision of local religious groups, motivated by faith, working together on social problems. Many conservatives supported this increased federal aid to faith-based organisations involved in social services provision – though some expressed concerns that religious groups were being encouraged by the programme to follow the administration's own agenda.[60]

Three of Obama's policies in particular dominated his relations with religious groups: abortion, embryo research and gay rights. These were precisely the issues that Obama managed to sideline in his negotiations with religious conservatives in 2008, but they came back with a vengeance. He had always been clear that he was pro-choice on abortion, but sought to win over conservatives by pledging to combat the socioeconomic inequalities that may lead to higher abortion rates.[61] But in 2011, his administration modified Bush's 'conscience clause', which had made it easier for medical professionals to refuse to perform procedures they objected to morally, including in rela- tion to abortion. And in January 2012, the year of the presidential election, the administration announced that all health insurance plans must cover the cost of contraceptives for employees, except for plans offered by churches and seminaries. Faith-based organisations that provided social services for the public (including medical centres) were not covered by the exemptions. Both policies caused uproar among conservative religious organisations, faced with the prospect of having to pay for abortions and contraception. The White House was forced to compromise on the insurance plan, but many Catholic bishops, along with other conservative Christian leaders, continued to protest that the policy was a gross violation of freedom of conscience.[62] Catholic auxiliary bishop James Conley warned that America was becoming an 'atheocracy', while Cardinal Francis George branded the Obama White House 'the most secularist administration in history'.[63]

The President's staunch advocacy of gay rights was another critical issue in 2012. In 2006, Obama had said that he opposed same-sex marriage, but insisted he supported equivalent rights for LGBT couples as for heterosexual ones. He also resorted to the unknowability of God's will to keep his future options open: 'as a Christian' as well as a politician, he was obliged 'to remain open to the possibility that my unwillingness to support gay marriage is mis- guided'.[64] In office, his administration repealed in 2011 the 'Don't ask, don't tell' policy in relation to LGBT people serving in the military, and opposed the Defense of Marriage Act (DOMA), which effectively barred same-sex couples from receiving federal marriage benefits (this was struck down by the Supreme Court in 2013).[65]

In May 2012, in the midst of his election battle against Mitt Romney, Obama announced that he had been persuaded of the rightness of same-sex marriage. Earlier in the week Vice-President Joe Biden had declared his sup- port for gay marriage; Biden's move forced Obama to clarify his position.[66] Strikingly, Obama described his change of heart not only as compatible with his Christian beliefs, but as motivated by them. 'The one thing that I've wrestled with is this gay marriage issue ... when [he and his wife Michelle] think about our faith … at root [what] we think about is not only Christ sacrificing himself on our behalf, but it's also the golden rule, you know?'[67] And in his second inaugural address in 2013, he insisted his policies were demanded by a God of justice. The gays of Stonewall were the blacks of Selma, and Obama painted himself as their new King.[68]

Strikingly, Obama didn't make faith as central a part of his 2012 campaign strategy as he had in 2008. He recognised that many conservative Christians would not be won back by his religious rhetoric. The GOP, meanwhile, found itself in faith-based conundrums of its own with the election of the Mormon Mitt Romney; with many evangelicals suspicious of Mormonism, Republican leaders sought to avoid raising faith issues which might put their candidate in an awkward position.[69] In an ironic twist, while Romney attacked Obama's supposedly secular agenda, the President faced accusations of permitting his supporters to attack Romney as having a suspect, un-Christian faith.[70] In the end, Obama won because of overwhelming support from African Americans, Latinos and religiously unaffiliated whites. But he secured less than 40 per cent of the votes of white Christians.[71]

Polarisation – particularly on Obamacare, gun control and gay marriage – increased dramatically over the course of Obama's second term. Resentment at the President, and a sense that the economy, though growing, was not delivering perceptible improvements to ordinary Americans, spilled out in the October 2014 midterm elections, which the Republicans had successfully framed as a popular referendum on the President's performance. Obama emerged without control of either the Senate or the House, and the GOP was in its strongest position since 1928.[72] Hamstrung, he resorted to executive measures to drive forward his agenda on immigration reform and gun control, leading to accusations of tyranny (in reality, he used these measures far less than Bush or Clinton did).[73]

His abortion and gay marriage positions continued to cause him problems. In February 2015, a few months before the Supreme Court declared same-sex marriage legal across the country, Obama's former senior advisor David Axelrod claimed that the President had always supported same-sex marriage, but had been persuaded to hide his position during his first campaign. The story only confirmed what Obama's opponents had believed all along: that the President lied about his religious beliefs in order to further his agenda.[74] And, in late 2015, Planned Parenthood, a major healthcare group and America's largest abortion provider, was accused of selling foetal parts for profit.[75] Congress Republicans seized on the controversy and tried to pass legislation repealing both Obamacare and federal funding for Planned Parenthood. Though predictably blocked by Obama's veto in January 2016, the bill signalled Republican determination to unravel Obama's signature policies if they won the 2016 race.[76] It also served to define Obama's religion, once again, by the terms of his opponents, reducing his nuanced and complex Christianity to simple standpoints on these specific issues.

To some extent, Obama's 'big tent' faith succeeded in helping him find allies – particularly among liberals, secularists and minority faiths – and gave him a shared language and history with moderate evangelicals, even if they disagreed with his policies. But the loudest voices in the media, often more hardline, were frequently critical. Secularists were irritated by his expansion of federal funding to religious organisations and his emphasis on the importance of faith. For religious conservatives and Republicans, criticising Obama's religion became a political tool for expressing a general anger at his policies, as well as a way of reviving the Religious Right with a narrative that Christian America is in danger. But they also had genuine concerns about the nature of his beliefs. Some resented his use of biblical language to justify what they saw as unbiblical policies. Many considered his Christianity to be the wrong sort – as watered down and unwilling to grapple with hard biblical truths, or as imposing onto Jesus Obama's own liberal socialist agenda – or insisted he is really an atheist (or Muslim). For some, the matter was even more black and white: he was the Antichrist, and he heralded the End Times.[77]

Obama publicly expressed great frustration at the narrative of his 'suspect' religion, and made efforts to emphasise his Christianity in public.[78] He insisted the challenges he faced had deepened his faith and reliance on God, in doing so comparing himself to Lincoln. 'Abe Lincoln said … "I have been driven to my knees many times by the overwhelming conviction that I had no place else to go."'[79]

In his last State of the Union address, delivered in January 2016, Obama called once again for a renewed bipartisanship in politics, and said that 'one of the few regrets' of his presidency was 'that the rancor and suspicion between the parties has gotten worse instead of better'.[80] Here he avoided pointing the finger, but at other times he made it clear he blamed Congress's intransigence for his problems.[81] His calls for a civil politics were in part a repositioning of himself as the rational, clear-headed Moral Man: a Lincoln above the crowd. But they were also a genuine expression of his sadness that he had failed to be the bridge-builder he promised he would be.

GOD ABROAD

Some of the biggest challenges Obama had to face involved God abroad, not at home. He was elected as Democratic candidate in 2008 on an anti-Iraq War platform, calculated to put the biggest distance between himself and his then rival, Hillary Clinton. His primary concerns when taking office were to rebuild America's reputation, extricate itself from the Middle East and orientate itself towards Asia to focus on China and Russia's unchecked influence.[82] In contrast to George W. Bush, who emphasised America's exceptionalism and cast his War on Terror as a great moral (if not divinely sanctioned) struggle,[83] Obama presented himself, and indeed has been interpreted, as taking a Niebuhrian middle way between hardline realism and naïve idealism. He was said to have a non-ideological, 'liberal internationalist approach'[84] to foreign policy, which sought to work in partnership with other nations as the best way to promote America's interests. He combined a results-based pragmatism with a concern to push forward where he could on particular values – human rights, democracy and religious freedom. These were not new values in American foreign policy but ones which he had inherited from his predecessors, including Bush.[85] These would not be the only strands of continuity between Bush and Obama in this acclaimed era of new American international relations.

These themes emerged in two speeches in 2009. In Cairo, Obama proclaimed a historic 'new beginning' in American relations with the Muslim world. He called on Muslim states to promote religious freedom and democracy – but included a cautious disclaimer that 'no system of government can or should be imposed upon one nation by any other'.[86] In Oslo, when collecting his Nobel Peace Prize (an awkward affair for the man engaged in wars in Iraq and Afghanistan), his speech was influenced by Niebuhr's Christian realism. He warned that the non-violence of Gandhi and King 'could not have halted Hitler's armies', and that America's use of its military power to defend itself and others was morally justified. But he also insisted that politicians must not give up on striving for ideals, just because an idealised world can never be reached.[87]

Obama's administration tended to pursue his realist approach. But in practice, his preference for flexibility rather than ideology in foreign policy at times caused confusion and frustration among advisors and commentators. He had some major successes, including his 2015 triumphs of the Iran deal and the Paris agreement on climate change (for which the White House naturally took credit).[88] But he was seen as indecisive in other spheres, including in his responses to the Arab Spring revolutions and in relation to Vladimir Putin.[89] Perhaps most damagingly, he was accused of playing down the threat posed by ISIS (on the day of the San Bernadino shooting, the worst Muslim terrorist attack on US soil since 9/11, he insisted that 'our homeland has never been more protected')[90] and of not doing enough to defend Christians in Iraq and Syria.[91]

Conversely, he also faced criticism from leftists for being too willing to continue the violence in the Middle East. For some, Obama was simply Bush reborn.[92] The 'religious freedom' agenda was attacked as simply being a means by which American influence in the Middle East could be maintained.[93] And Obama's counter-terrorism strategies at home, his failure to close Guantanamo Bay, and his drone policy and the concomitant deaths of hundreds of civilians, caused major strife. In a 2013 speech on national security, he justified drone strikes on utilitarian and just-war grounds, but confessed that the deaths of civilians would haunt him as long as he lived.[94] He was praised for admitting his 'anguish' about the consequences of perpetual war.[95] Yet his willingness to be publicly self-critical (rare for a President) and to speak of his own moral struggle was still seen as a performance, even if based on genuine feeling.[96] It allowed him to clean up his image, catharsis-like, 'without undermining his administration's operational flexibility'[97] in reality.

CONCLUSION

Barack Obama achieved what had been thought impossible – he made the Democratic Party appealing for secularists, liberals and minorities, and moderate evangelicals alike. Perhaps most remarkably, he was able to shift the debate about religion in politics to a higher level than the usual abortion and gay rights division. But it was only for a single, glorious moment. His religious and secular alliance could not be maintained when he began to push his progressive agenda. Despite his talk of humility and the mystery of God's will, he remained convinced, naturally, that his plans were closer to God's than his opponents' were. Ironically, the deeper his Christian faith became, the more America doubted it. And the more America cared about his religion, the more it revealed that it wasn't ready for the post-racial, trans-religious future Obama had promised.

NOTES

1. Quoted in Kyle Drennen, 'Newsweek's Evan Thomas: Obama is "sort of God"', MRC NewsBusters, 5 June 2009, http://www.newsbusters.org/blogs/kyle-drennen/2009/06/05/newsweek-s-evan-thomas-obama-sort-god (accessed 27 January 2017).

2. Greg Jaffe, 'The quiet impact of Obama's Christian faith', *Washington Post*, 22 December 2015, http://www.washingtonpost.com/sf/national/2015/12/22/obama-faith (accessed 27 January 2017).

3. Gary Scott Smith, *Religion in the Oval Office: The Religious Lives of American Presidents* (Oxford: Oxford University Press, 2015), p. 386.

4. David L. Holmes, *The Faiths of the Postwar Presidents: From Truman to Obama* (Athens: University of Georgia Press, 2012), p. 270.

5. CNN/ORC International poll, 4–8 September 2015, p. 15, http://i2.cdn.turner.com/cnn/2015/images/09/12/iranpoll.pdf (accessed 27 January 2017).

6. Ben Jacobs, 'Donald Trump fails to correct questioner who calls Obama Muslim', *The Guardian*, 18 September 2015, http://www.theguardian.com/us-news/2015/sep/18/trump-fails-to-correct-questioner-who-calls-obama-muslim-and-not-even-american; Joshua Green, 'What Donald Trump's birther investigators with find in Hawaii', *The Atlantic*, 12 April 2011, http://www.theatlantic.com/politics/archive/2011/04/what-donald-trumps-birther-investigators-will-find-in-hawaii/237198 (both accessed 27 January 2017).

7. Jonathan Bernstein, 'The Republican obsession with a secret Obama', BloombergView, 5 January 2016, http://www.bloombergview.com/articles/2016-01-05/republicans-obsession-with-a-secret-obama (accessed 27 January 2017).

8. Holmes, *The Faiths of the Postwar Presidents*, pp. 271–5.

9. Barack Obama, *Dreams from My Father: A Story of Race and Inheritance* (Edinburgh: Canongate, 2007), p. 37.

10. Holmes, *The Faiths of the Postwar Presidents*, pp. 273, 276–9.

11. Barack Obama, *The Audacity of Hope: Thoughts on Reclaiming the American Dream* (Edinburgh: Canongate, 2007), pp. 203–6.

12. Christopher Jackson, 'Obama's faith journey', Third Way, January–February 2016, https://thirdway.hymnsam.co.uk/editions/januaryfebruary-2016/features/obama's-faith-journey.aspx (accessed 27 January 2017).

13. Obama, *Dreams from My Father*, pp. 206–8.

14. Obama, *The Audacity of Hope*, pp. 206–8.

15. Jonathan L. Walton, 'Stationed in the King's Court: Evangelicals in the Age of Obama', *Souls: A Critical Journal of Black Politics, Culture and Society*, vol. 16, no. 1–2, 2014, pp. 82–3.

16. Obama, *Dreams from My Father*, p. 294. Here Obama recounts his reaction to Jeremiah Wright's sermon 'The Audacity of Hope'.

17. R. Ward Holder and Peter B. Josephson, *The Irony of Barack Obama: Barack Obama, Reinhold Niebuhr and the Problem of Christian Statecraft* (Farnham, Surrey: Ashgate Publishing Limited), 2012, p. 52.

18. David Howard-Pitney, *The African American Jeremiad: Appeals for Justice in America* (Philadelphia: Temple University Press, 2005), pp. 6–7.

19. Obama, *The Audacity of Hope*, p. 206.

20. As he testified in his speech at the 2011 National Prayer Breakfast, 'I came to know Jesus Christ for myself and embrace Him as my Lord and Savior' ('Remarks by the president at National Prayer Breakfast', White House website, 3 February 2011, https://obamawhitehouse.archives.gov/the-press-office/2011/02/03/remarks-president-national-prayer-breakfast (accessed 27 January 2017)).

21. 'Remarks by the President and Vice President at Easter Prayer Breakfast', White House website, 5 April 2013, https://obamawhitehouse.archives.gov/photos-and-video/video/2013/04/05/easter-prayer-breakfast-2013#transcript (accessed 27 January 2017).

22. Cathleen Falsani, 'Obama on faith: The exclusive interview', The Dude Abides blog, Patheos, http://www.patheos.com/blogs/thedudeabides/obama-on-faith-the-exclusive-interview (accessed 27 January 2017).

23. Holder and Josephson, *The Irony of Barack Obama*, p. 60.

24. John Blake, 'The Gospel according to Obama', Belief blog, 21 October 2012, http://religion.blogs.cnn.com/2012/10/21/to-some-obama-is-the-wrong-kind-of-christian (accessed 27 January 2017).

25. Barack Obama, 'Remarks by the President at 'Christmas in Washington', White House website, 12 December 2010, https://obamawhitehouse.archives.gov/the-press-office/2010/12/13/remarks-president-christmas-washington (accessed 27 January 2017).

26. In 2014, Obama launched the My Brother's Keeper initiative, which aimed 'to address persistent opportunity gaps faced by boys and young men of color and to ensure that all young people can reach their full potential' ('My Brother's Keeper', White House website, https://obamawhitehouse.archives.gov/my-brothers-keeper (accessed 27 January 2017)).

27. Holder and Josephson, *The Irony of Barack Obama*, p. 79.

28. As Obama said in 2004, 'I retain from my childhood and my experiences growing up a suspicion of dogma … I think that religion at its best comes with a big dose of doubt' (Falsani, 'Obama on faith').

29. Barack Obama, 'Call to Renewal: Keynote Address', ObamaSpeeches, 28 June 2006, http://obamaspeeches.com/081-Call-to-Renewal-Keynote-Address-Obama-Speech.htm (accessed 27 January 2017).

30. 'Whatever we once were, we are no longer just a Christian nation; we are also a Jewish nation, a Muslim nation, a Buddhist nation, a Hindu nation, and a nation of nonbelievers', (Obama, 'Call to Renewal'). http://obamaspeeches.com/081-Call-to-Renewal-Keynote-Address-Obama-Speech.htm.

31. Obama, *The Audacity of Hope*, p. 226.

32. Sarah Pulliam and Ted Olsen, 'Q&A: Barack Obama', *Christianity Today*, 23 January 2008, http://www.christianitytoday.com/ct/2008/januaryweb-only/104-32.0.html (accessed 27 January 2017).

33. Alexander LaBrecque, 'Obama's religious ruse: his "conversion"', *American Thinker*, 15 October 2008, http://www.americanthinker.com/articles/2008/10/obamas_religious_ruse_his_conv_1.html (accessed 27 January 2017).

34. Quoted in Stephen Mansfield, 'Religion and the 2012 presidential race, Part I: Is Barack Obama a "born again" Christian?', Huffington Post, 22 May 2012, http://www.huffing-tonpost.com/stephen-mansfield/religion-and-the-2012-presidential-race-obama-born-again_b_1530508.html (accessed 27 January 2017).

35. Michiko Kakutani, 'Obama's eulogy, which found its place in history', *New York Times*, 3 July 2015, http://www.nytimes.com/2015/07/04/arts/obamas-eulogy-which-found-its-place-in-history.html (accessed 27 January 2017).

36. Abraham Lincoln, second inaugural address, 4 March 1865, available at http://www.bartle-by.com/124/pres32.html (accessed 27 January 2017).

37. Kakutani, 'Obama's eulogy, which found its place in history'.

38. Barack Obama, 'Remarks by the president in eulogy for the Honorable Reverend Clementa Pinckney', White House website, 26 June 2015, https://obamawhitehouse.archives.gov/the-press-office/2015/06/26/remarks-president-eulogy-honorable-reverend-clementa-pinckney (accessed 27 January 2017).

39. As Obama declared in a speech in 2006, the notion that people 'should not inject their "personal morality" into public policy debates is a practical absurdity' (Obama, 'Call to Renewal') http://obamaspeeches.com/081-Call-to-Renewal-Keynote-Address-Obama-Speech.htm

40. David Little, *Essays on Religion and Human Rights: Ground to Stand On.* (Cambridge: Cambridge University Press, 2015), pp. 347–8.

41. Holder and Josephson, *The Irony of Barack Obama*, p. 7.

42. Quoted in David Brooks, 'Obama, gospel and verse', *New York Times*, 26 April 2007, http://www.nytimes.com/2007/04/26/opinion/26brooks.html (accessed 27 January 2017).

43. Holder and Josephson, *The Irony of Barack Obama*, pp. 16–17.

44. Brooks, 'Obama, gospel and verse'.

45. Scott Smith, *Religion in the Oval Office*, p. 380.

46. Holmes, *The Faiths of the Postwar Presidents*, p. 297.

47. Ibid., p. 304.

48. Brian Braiker, 'Newsweek poll: Obama loses some ground', *Newsweek*, 26 April 2008, http://europe.newsweek.com/newsweek-poll-obama-loses-some-ground-86357 (accessed 27 January 2017).

49. Holmes, *The Faiths of the Postwar Presidents*, p. 295.

50. Scott Smith, *Religion in the Oval Office*, p. 386.

51. Ibid., p. 383.

52. For example, in 2004 he argued that 'there is an enormous danger on the part of public figures to rationalize or justify their actions by claiming God's mandate' (Falsani, 'Obama on faith').

53. Walton, 'Stationed in the King's Court', pp. 81, 90–91.

54. As Simon Schama put it with starry eyes in January 2009, 'the mere fact of the Obama administration offers a fixed point around which belief in American reinvention can make a credible stand' (Simon Schama, 'The great hope – Barack Obama', *The Independent*, 24 January 2009, http://www.independent.co.uk/news/presidents/simon-schama-the-great-hope-barack-obama-1482927.html (accessed 27 January 2017)).

55. As Stephen Mansfield has described it: see 'Obama's faith fits our times', *USA Today*, 1 June 2009, http://usatoday30.usatoday.com/printedition/news/20090601/column01_st.art.htm (accessed 27 January 2017).

56. Mansfield, 'Religion and the 2012 presidential race, Part I'.

57. Holmes, *The Faiths of the Postwar Presidents*, p. 312.

58. Ashley Parker, 'As the Obamas celebrate Christmas, rituals of faith become less visible', *New York Times*, 28 December 2013, http://www.nytimes.com/2013/12/29/us/as-the-obamas-celebrate-christmas-rituals-of-faith-stay-on-the-sidelines.html (accessed 27 January 2017).

59. Scott Smith, *Religion in the Oval Office*, p. 376.

60. Ibid., pp. 391–2, 414.

61. See 'Saddleback Presidential Candidates Forum', CNN website, 16 August 2008, http://transcripts.cnn.com/TRANSCRIPTS/0808/16/se.02.html (accessed 27 January 2017).

62. In February 2012 the administration decided that the cost of paying for contraceptives for employees would move from religiously affiliated charities and universities to health insurance companies: see Scott Smith, *Religion in the Oval Office*, pp. 394–6, 400.

63. David Gibson, 'Catholic bishops welcome dialogue with Obama as concerns remain', *Salt Lake Tribune*, 19 November 2011, http://archive.sltrib.com/story.php?ref=/sltrib/lifestyle/52932329-80/bishops-religious-dolan-obama.html.cspeliefs (accessed 27 January 2017).

64. Obama, *The Audacity of Hope*, pp. 222–3.

65. DOMA defined marriage as the union of one man and one woman for federal purposes. See Mark Segal, 'It's nice to have President Obama as a friend', *Advocate*, 18 November 2015, http://www.advocate.com/books/2015/11/18/its-nice-have-president-obama-friend (accessed 27 January 2017).

66. Biden subsequently apologised to Obama for forcing the president to announce his support for same-sex marriage before he had planned to. See Tobin Grant, 'President's evolution is over: Obama commits to supporting same-sex marriage', *Christianity Today*, 9 May 2012, http://www.christianitytoday.com/ct/2012/mayweb-only/obama-commits-to-supporting-same-sex-marriage.html; 'AP source: Biden apologizes to Obama over comments', Fox News US website, 10 May 2012, http://www.foxnews.com/us/2012/05/10/ap-source-biden-apologizes-to-obama-over-comments.html (both accessed 27 January 2017).

67. 'Transcript: Robin Roberts ABC News interview with President Obama', ABC News website, 9 May 2012, http://abcnews.go.com/Politics/transcript-robin-roberts-abc-news-interview-president-obama/story?id=16316043 (accessed 27 January 2017).

68. 'We, the people, declare today that the most evident of truths – that all of us are created equal – is the star that guides us still; just as it guided our forebears through Seneca Falls, and Selma, and Stonewall; just as it guided all those men and women, sung and unsung, who left footprints along this great Mall, to hear a preacher say that we cannot walk alone; to hear a King proclaim that our individual freedom is inextricably bound to the freedom of every soul on Earth.' Barack Obama, 'Inaugural address by President Barack Obama', White House website, 21 January 2013, https://obamawhitehouse.archives.gov/the-press-office/2013/01/21/inaugural-address-president-barack-obama (accessed 27 January 2017).

69. Matthew Avery Sutton and Darren Dochuk, 'Introduction' in Sutton and Dochuk, *Faith in the New Millennium: The Future of Religion and American Politics* (Oxford: Oxford University Press, 2016), pp. 2–3.

70. For example, prominent black pastors in Norfolk sought to win back for Obama African Americans who had been alienated by his support for gay marriage, by contrasting his 'Biblical Christianity' with Romney's Mormonism. See Scott Smith, *Religion in the*

Oval Office, p. 402; Douglas MacKinnon, 'Obama must end the attacks on Mormons', *Townhall*, 14 May 2012, http://townhall.com/columnists/douglasmackinnon/2012/05/14/ obama_must_end_the_attacks_on_mormons/page/full (accessed 27 January 2017).

71. Scott Smith, *Religion in the Oval Office*, p. 405.

72. Gary C. Jacobson, 'Obama and Nationalized Electoral Politics in the 2014 Midterm', *Political Science Quarterly*, vol. 130, no. 1, 2015, pp. 1–3.

73. Alexis Simendinger, 'Obama speech will pave way for Dems in '16', *RealClear Politics*, 12 January 2016, http://www.realclearpolitics.com/articles/2016/01/12/obama_speech_will_ pave_way_for_dems_in_16_129289.html (accessed 27 January 2017).

74. In fact, in 1996 Obama had filled out a questionnaire stating that he favoured legalising same-sex marriages and would fight efforts to prohibit them: see Ben Smith, 'Obama backed same-sex marriage in 1996', *Politico*, 13 January 2009, http://www.politico.com/ blogs/ben-smith/2009/01/obama-backed-same-sex-marriage-in-1996-015306 (accessed 27 January 2017). Obama subsequently rejected Axelrod's assertion and insisted that his changes of position were due to genuine introspection on the issue: see Ben Smith, 'Obama defends his legacy: "These are the kinds of things you learn"', *BuzzFeed*, 11 February 2015, http://www.buzzfeed.com/bensmith/buzzfeed-news-interview-president-obama (accessed 27 January 2017). For criticism of Obama's shifting positions on this, see for example Thomas Lifson, 'Axelrod reveals that Obama lied about his "Christian faith"', *American Thinker*, 11 February 2015, http://www.americanthinker.com/blog/2015/02/axelrod_re-veals_that_obama_lied_about_his_christian_faith.html (accessed 27 January 2017).

75. In January 2016 a Texas grand jury cleared Planned Parenthood of misconduct. Instead it charged members of the Center for Medical Progress, which had secretly filmed Planned Parenthood and made the original allegations, of tampering with government records. See 'Filmmakers who targeted Planned Parenthood face charges', BBC News website, 26 January 2016, http://www.bbc.co.uk/news/world-us-canada-35405636 (accessed 27 January 2017).

76. 'House Republicans are ready for their latest, doomed try to kill President Barack Obama's health care law', *US News and World Report*, 2 February 2016, http://www.usnews.com/ news/business/articles/2016-02-02/house-gop-to-vote-to-repeal-obamas-health-care-law (accessed 27 January 2017).

77. Scott Smith, *Religion in the Oval Office*, pp. 412–14.

78. For example, in his speech at the 2011 National Prayer Breakfast, he insisted that when he and his wife Michelle 'hear our faith questioned from time to time', they remind themselves that what ultimately matters is their consciences before God. Obama, 'Remarks by the President at National Prayer Breakfast'.

79. Ibid.

80. Barack Obama, 'Remarks of President Barack Obama – State of the Union address as delivered', White House website, 13 January 2016, https://www.whitehouse.gov/the-press-office/2016/01/12/remarks-president-barack-obama-%E2%80%93-prepared-deliv-ery-state-union-address (accessed 27 January 2017).

81. For example, on the Guantanamo Bay detention camp, he insisted that he had done his best to close it, and that 'there is no justification beyond politics for Congress to prevent us from closing a facility that should have never have been opened' (Barack Obama, 'Obama's speech on drone policy', *New York Times*, 23 May 2013, http://www.nytimes. com/2013/05/24/us/politics/transcript-of-obamas-speech-on-drone-policy.html (accessed 27 January 2017)).

82. Ryan Lizza, 'The consequentialist', *New Yorker*, 2 May 2011, http://www.newyorker.com/ magazine/2011/05/02/the-consequentialist (accessed 27 January 2017).

83. In October 2005 a Palestinian politician claimed that, in 2003, Bush had said that God commanded him to invade Afghanistan and Iraq. A White House spokesperson subsequently denied that the comments had ever been made. See 'Bush God comments "not literal"', BBC News website, 7 October 2005, http://news.bbc.co.uk/1/hi/4320586.stm (accessed 27 January 2017).

84. Gary J. Dorrien, *The Obama Question: A Progressive Perspective* (Lanham, MD: Rowman & Littlefield Publishers Inc., 2012), pp. 14, 125.

85. Andrew Preston, 'America's World Mission in the Age of Obama' in Matthew Avery Sutton and Darren Dochuk, *Faith in the New Millennium: The Future of Religion and American Politics* (Oxford: Oxford University Press, 2016), p. 187.

86. Barack Obama, 'Remarks by the president at Cairo University, 6-04-09', White House website, 4 June 2009, https://obamawhitehouse.archives.gov/the-press-office/remarks-president-cairo-university-6-04-09 (accessed 27 January 2017).

87. Barack Obama, 'Remarks by the president at the acceptance of the Nobel Peace Prize', White House website, 10 December 2009, https://obamawhitehouse.archives.gov/the-press-office/remarks-president-acceptance-nobel-peace-prize (accessed 27 January 2017).

88. Ryan Lizza, 'Hillary vs. Barack, round LXXXVIII', *New Yorker*, 20 December 2015, http://www.newyorker.com/news/news-desk/hillary-clinton-obama-democratic-debate (accessed 27 January 2017).

89. Lizza, 'The consequentialist'.

90. Jim Geraghty, 'Obama's awful year', *National Review*, 14 December 2015, http://www.nationalreview.com/article/428503/obama-worst-year-washington-award-should-go-him (accessed 27 January 2017).

91. Preston, 'America's World Mission in the Age of Obama', pp. 191–2.

92. Ibid., pp. 190–91.

93. For example, see Joseph A. Massad, *Islam in Liberalism* (Chicago: The University of Chicago, 2015).

94. Obama, 'Obama's speech on drone policy'.

95. Jane Mayer, 'Obama's challenge to an endless war', *New Yorker*, 23 May 2013, http://www.newyorker.com/news/daily-comment/obamas-challenge-to-an-endless-war (accessed 27 January 2017).

96. Ross Douthat, 'Obama's artful anguish', *New York Times*, 25 May 2013, http://www.nytimes.com/2013/05/26/opinion/sunday/douthat-obamas-artful-anguish.html (accessed 27 January 2017).

97. Benjamin Wittes, 'The president's speech: a quick and dirty reaction – part 1 (are we at war?)', *Lawfare*, 23 May 2013, https://www.lawfareblog.com/presidents-speech-quick-and-dirty-reaction%E2%80%94part-1-are-we-war (accessed 27 January 2017).

GOODLUCK JONATHAN (2010–15)

MADDY FRY

INTRODUCTION

The erstwhile President of Nigeria, Goodluck Jonathan, not only boasts a middle name that means 'God's wish' (Ebele) but comes from an area of the world saturated by religion. In much of west Africa, Christianity sells – businesses with names like 'Christ-the-Almighty Plumbing' and 'Thank You Jesus Hardware' can be found from Freetown to Cape Town.[1] Although swathes of its population live in considerable deprivation, Nigeria also hosts some of the richest people on earth, due to its vast, some would say ill-managed, oil reserves. Perhaps unsurprisingly, in this part of the world the notion of the 'Prosperity Gospel' – that God wants you to be rich – has flourished. In a country where politics often fails, the divine fills the void.

Few would dispute that Goodluck Jonathan's personal religious convictions seem genuine. In 2014, not long before his campaign for re-election, he embarked on a two-day pilgrimage to Jerusalem, where he met Israeli Prime Minister Benjamin Netanyahu in private, and visited various sites of religious devotion, including the Western Wall, Mount Tabor and Mount Carmel.[2] He also publicly declared his solidarity with Israel after the kidnapping of several Israeli teenagers in 2014, an incident that came not long after 319 schoolgirls were taken by militants from Boko Haram, the violent radical Islamist group with a fondness for unleashing carnage across Nigeria. The

Israeli ambassador spoke openly about his belief that Jonathan's homeland would support the country at the United Nations.[3]

Behind the scenes, those within Jonathan's hierarchy were also well aware of how appeals to his religiosity would be key to gaining any kind of public support within Nigeria. It was therefore in this context that Jonathan's particular brand of Christianity underpinned even the most divergent aspects of his leadership, from his relationship with the country's 'super pastors' – the heads of Nigeria's vast and hugely popular Pentecostal megachurches – to his fondness for claiming his poverty-stricken childhood meant that he grew up without shoes.[4] He is perhaps that most unremarkable of things: a devout Christian in a country where faith is such an overt presence that it gets re-appropriated seamlessly by both the wealthy and the poor.

BIOGRAPHY

Jonathan's origins were hardly gilded. Born in 1957 in Ogbia, a region in southern Nigeria where the local economy revolved largely around farming and fishing, his parents worked as canoe-makers. His notable first name was a result of his father's hope that he would out-live his siblings, most of whom had died in infancy. Indeed, not only did Jonathan do just that, but the moniker 'Goodluck' was often used by his opponents as a wry comment on how he had reached power in the first place, with many suspecting it was through sheer opportunism rather than skill or competence.

Educated at Christian schools, his student career was promising. He gained a bachelor's degree in zoology from the University of Port Harcourt in 1981, before going on to get a master's in fisheries and hydrobiology. He was eventually awarded a PhD in zoology in 1995. He held positions as a teacher and as an educational and an environmental inspector before going on to work for the (now obsolete) government department of the Oil and Minerals Producing Areas Development Commission. He left in 1998 to pursue politics, and went on to marry the civil servant and former teacher Patience Faka, with whom he has two children.[5]

In a country whose political system has become a byword for corruption and economic negligence, the fact that Jonathan's early years in government were uneventful is possibly credit-worthy. He was elected as the deputy governor of his home state of Bayelsa in 1999 as part of the People's Democratic Party (PDP), a position he held until 2005, when the governor he replaced was ousted on corruption charges. Two years later, he became the running mate of Umaru Musa Yar'Adua, the PDP's presidential candidate.[6]

Following the party's election to power in 2007, his activities largely seemed to consist of wrangling with militias in the oil-rich Niger Delta, who were frequently at violent odds with the region's petroleum companies. By comparison, Yar'Adua was unpopular in many areas, having been accused of rigging the election by the heads of the two primary opposition parties, the All Nigeria People's Party and the Action Congress. Despite his attempts at placating the corruption charges by publicly declaring his assets, the rest of Yar'Adua's career was dogged by calls for the election to be invalidated.[7] When he fell ill with what was reported to be a chronic heart condition in 2010, there were calls from much of the electorate for Jonathan to take the reins, and his subsequent death resulted in Jonathan being sworn in. Although questions were raised over how constitutional the process had been, he went on to be victorious in the country's formal elections in 2011, securing 59 per cent of the vote – a figure more believable than his predecessor's claim to have secured support from 70 per cent of the electorate.[8]

IN POWER

Jonathan's election was a deviation from the trend of allowing Nigeria's leadership to be alternately occupied by representatives from the Christian south and the predominantly Muslim north. Jonathan's vow to tackle corruption, improve access to energy and reform the electoral process appeared to have hit home with some voters – yet it didn't prevent riots breaking out over the installation of another southern Christian. Much of the violence was instigated by unemployed young men, particularly from the north, where infrastructure and economic opportunities had long lagged far behind the more prosperous south.[9]

These regional tensions were also compounded by the burgeoning threat from Boko Haram, which had become notorious for meting out mass bombings on the country's Christian population. Barely a year into his presidency, the group publicly demanded that Jonathan renounce his faith and convert to Islam, or else resign his position. If he refused, then Boko Haram would continue with its violent campaigns. Although this rather ostentatious attempt at blackmail was dismissed by the government, it did much to illuminate the stark religious tensions underlying Nigeria's vast population.[10]

Alongside this, one of the most noticeable indicators of the fusion between faith and politics within Nigeria's government was that of Jonathan's relationship with the super pastors. This ranged from seeking blessings from two of the best-known pastors – the general overseer of the Redeemed Christian Church of God, Pastor Enoch Adeboye, and the presiding bishop of the Winners Chapel, Bishop David Oyedepo – by actively seeking their intercessions on his behalf when he ran for re-election in 2015. The fact that Jonathan lost the election appeared not to dent his trust in them; in fact, it would most likely have been seen as a minor detail by many in Nigeria.

As Lagun Akinloye, a political analyst based at the Central Association for Nigerians in the UK, has said, many of these churches function more like a 'business than a religious entity, with the pastors owning private jets, luxury cars and mansions'. In the process, the downtrodden are meant to seek 'help and advice for all things, from finding the right partner/marriage, success in a job search, and trying for a child'.[11] Despite the accusations of exploitation that Nigerian churches are often saddled with, in the eyes of many of the country's faithful, religion works as the great equaliser. In the words of Paul Gifford, former professor of religions and philosophies at the School of Oriental and African Studies and an expert in African Pentecostalism, 'a form of Christianity has now gained acceptance which meets the specifically religious need of combating hostile spiritual forces, on a continent where misfortune is the lot of so many'.[12]

FAITH AND POWER

For many politicians in Europe, personal faith is often regarded as somewhat anomalous and certainly not something to be paraded before the electorate. Yet in Nigeria the existence of God is taken for granted in the same way as gravity, and the language of faith is central, indeed essential, to public rhetoric.

Jonathan's speeches provide vivid evidence of this. While accepting his victory in the 2011 election, he talked of having a 'heart full of gratitude to

Almighty God', predicting a 'new dawn' for Nigeria and laying out a vision of the country's future that implied an inevitable stride towards unified greatness: 'a nation marching towards collective progress in which no one is left behind'. The aim appears to have been to promote Nigeria as some kind of Promised Land bestowed with divine blessings. Jonathan even went so far as to state that he had 'no enemies' – a notable claim for any politician to make, particularly one in a land so riven with divisions that rivalry and strife are an almost universal experience. He ended his victory speech with an exhortation to Nigerians to 'thank our merciful God for this day' and 'continue to pray for God's guidance in the years ahead'.[13] The idea that the Almighty has a personal relationship with the whole nation seemed to be at the heart of his message to a beleaguered electorate.

These biblically influenced rhetorical flourishes were common in Jonathan's successive speeches. When declaring his intention in 2014 to run again for the presidency, he spoke of a divinely sanctioned relationship with ordinary Nigerians, with God having given him the opportunity to bond with them during his leadership. The imagery is saturated with Old Testament idioms, with references comparing the country to powerful birds of prey ('I see a Nigeria where the flames in the eagles will re-kindle, and the falcons will soar higher in victory!'[14]) clearly attempting to convey a spirit of rejuvenation and re-birth. Upon eventually losing the race in 2015, his brief concession ended with an obligatory 'May God Almighty continue to bless the Federal Republic of Nigeria'.[15]

This continued after his tenure as President. His 2016 address at the Bloomberg studios in London contained numerous allusions to the Roman empire, the US constitution and the letters of St Paul. He maintained that within Nigeria 'the great bulwarks of liberty' should be 'inviolable' and that the country should aspire to providing a status for its citizens much like there had been in ancient Rome, where citizenship meant that it did not matter if you were 'rich or poor or even a prisoner'.[16] His speeches, therefore, continued to draw on a rich oral political tradition with its roots in the Bible, laying out a faith-inspired vision for Nigeria that involves peace, prosperity and progress. All the way through his tenure, Jonathan's belief in his unique role as the bringer of a positive destiny supported by God underpinned his proclamations. Although undoubtedly still a noble vision, it was to remain an unfulfilled one under his leadership.

Perhaps this is because another more contentious side to his religiosity was the influence wielded by the intensely conservative attitudes to sexual morality preached by Nigerian churches, with homosexuality, masturbation and oral sex, among other things, being widely condemned.[17] The most obvious example of its influence on Jonathan's leadership was also possibly his most internationally high-profile decision as President, which was to completely outlaw any kind of homosexuality within the country. The bill he introduced in 2014 not only stated that 'only a marriage between a man and a woman shall be recognised as valid in Nigeria'; it forbade any kind of homosexual activity, including belonging to gay groups, publicly being in a same-sex relationship, and gay matrimony of any kind. A fourteen-year prison sentence was promised to any current and future 'deviants'.[18]

Up until this point, Jonathan's premiership had been dogged by accusations of internal corruption, with Nigeria's legacy of mismanagement continuing with suspicions over billions of dollars having been re-appropriated by high-ranking officials.[19] Yet the howls of outrage from human rights groups over Nigeria's new bill were lasting and profound. Amnesty International called it 'discriminatory' and 'catastrophic' for lesbian, gay, bisexual and transgender civilians, while a plethora of the great and the good, from Barack Obama to Desmond Tutu, variously compared the law to those that existed in apartheid-era South Africa which notoriously forbade intermingling between different races.[20]

The bill illustrated a fundamental tension at the heart of how much of Africa and much of the West views the relationship between religion and sexuality. Many Western churches in recent years had sought to incorporate gay and lesbian believers into their congregations just as African countries were doing the opposite, with violence, discrimination and oppression becoming commonplace experiences for many homosexuals, and often sanctioned, unofficially if not officially, by the churches. Yet the reality was that Nigeria was following a trajectory playing out across many parts of the continent. Moreover, Jonathan's approach was mild compared to some; the country currently stands as one of thirty-eight in Africa that enforces severe penalties for homosexual acts,[21] but, unlike Uganda, Nigeria didn't seek to impose a life sentence in prison for being gay.[22] Although some of the heavily Muslim areas of Nigeria have enacted death by stoning for homosexuals, this has yet to be adopted in the country's Christian zones. Furthermore, Jonathan's presidential spokesman Reuben Abati responded to the criticism by claiming that 'more than 90 per cent of Nigerians are opposed to same-sex marriage' and that the law was therefore in sync with 'our cultural and religious beliefs as a people.'[23]

However, some external observers have regarded Jonathan's decision to completely outlaw homosexuality as lacking any serious moral conviction. The strata of religious fundamentalists that are a potent force within the National Assembly, one of the country's main legislative bodies, were people Jonathan was keen to keep on his side. One could also see it as a cynical exercise in dog-whistle politics, with Jonathan attempting to score political points on issues that had the potential to play in his favour – especially in light of how, by this point, his presidency had become beset by domestic failures.

Jonathan had promised a lengthy list of reforms, including addressing the flaws in the country's electoral system and dealing with the unequal distribution of its resources. He made some gains when he negotiated a three-month ceasefire from the militias in the Niger Delta in 2009, yet his legacy by 2014 was defined by broken promises. This included accusations that he had gone against his vow to reverse the mass privatisation of several state-owned companies that had occurred under his predecessor by giving contracts to a line of businesses owned by his family.[24]

The potential insincerity of his stance on gay rights was lent further weight by an interview he gave to Bloomberg in 2016, where he declared that Nigeria might reconsider the ban on homosexual activity:

When it comes to equality, we must all have the same rights as Nigerian citizens. The nation may at the appropriate time revisit the law in the light of deepening debates for all Nigerians and other citizens of the world to be treated equally and without discrimination, and with the clear knowledge that the issue of sexual orientation is still evolving.[25]

According to Lagun Akinloye, this shows that Jonathan's attitude to human sexuality 'is based more on political considerations, as opposed to his own religious or personal beliefs'. His interview at Bloomberg would seem to support this, at the very least giving weight to his religiosity not being completely inflexible. Religious fervour combined with political pragmatism is certainly a rare virtue within many political systems, even if there was less of it in Jonathan's leadership than many outside Nigeria would have liked.

CONCLUSION

In light of this decidedly mixed legacy, many regard the point at which Jonathan withdrew from the leadership as the finest aspect of his political career. His campaign for the 2015 election failed, with the northern Muslim Muhammadu Buhari taking the lead. However, instead of tampering with the constitution or brutalising opposition voters – strategies favoured by previous Nigerian Presidents and still employed by leaders in other parts of the continent – Jonathan conceded defeat, and retreated.[26] Not long after, Jonathan stated that he wished for a Nigeria where people would 'evaluate each other on our merits, rather than our religion or region'.[27] Yet, under Buhari, the old divisions looked set to continue.

One could argue that there was something profoundly Christian about Jonathan's willingness to accept this final, and most potent, of political failures. His tenure was a mixture of cynicism and conviction, rank opportunism and attempts at genuine social reform. In this sense, he was perhaps like many politicians across the globe; yet within his own country, the overt message of both his and successor's career seemed to be that to succeed politically in such an enormous and diverse land, you need faith. Jonathan's clear abundance of it was hopefully of some comfort to him after his somewhat disappointing legacy was consigned to his nation's history.

NOTES

1. Yomi Kazeem, 'In rural Ghana, there's a thin line between your business and your faith', *Quartz Africa*, 2 June 2016, http://qz.com/696751/in-rural-ghana-theres-a-thin-line-between-your-business-and-your-faith (accessed 30 January 2017).

2. Herb Keinon, 'Nigerian president Goodluck Jonathan in Jerusalem on private pilgrimage, meets Netanyahu', *Jerusalem Post*, 26 October 2014, http://www.jpost.com/Christian-News/

Nigerian-President-Goodluck-Jonathan-in-Jerusalem-on-private-pilgrimage-meets-Netan-yahu-379889 (accessed 30 January 2017).

3. Jonny Paul, 'What makes Nigeria Israel's strongest ally in Africa?', Arutz Sheva website, 9 November 2014, http://www.israelnationalnews.com/News/News.aspx/185013#.VZwcR-flVhBd (accessed 30 January 2017).

4. 'Nigeria's Goodluck Jonathan, profile of a defeated president', BBC News website, 31 March 2015, http://www.bbc.com/news/world-africa-12192152 (accessed 30 January 2017).

5. Amy McKenna, 'Goodluck Jonathan', Encyclopaedia Britannica website, 29 May 2015, https://www.britannica.com/biography/Goodluck-Jonathan (accessed 30 January 2017).

6. Ibid.

7. 'Obituary: President Yar'Adua', BBC News website, 6 May 2010, http://news.bbc.co.uk/2/hi/africa/6187249.stm (accessed 30 January 2017).

8. McKenna, 'Goodluck Jonathan'.

9. 'Q&A: Nigeria elections', BBC News website, 22 April 2011, http://www.bbc.com/news/world-africa-12941582 (accessed 30 January 2017).

10. Anissa Haddadi, 'Boko Haram: Nigeria president Goodluck Jonathan should quit and convert to Islam', *International Business Times*, 6 August 2012, http://www.ibtimes.co.uk/boko-haram-nigeria-president-goodluck-jonathan-resign-370695 (accessed 30 January 2017).

11 From an interview with Lagun Akinloye, political analyst and public relations officer for the Central Association for Nigerians in the UK, 10 August 2016.

12. Paul Gifford, 'The Southern Shift of Christianity', in Ciprian Burlacioiu and Adrian Hermann (eds), *Veränderte Landkarten: auf dem Weg zu einer polyzentrischen Geschichte des Weltchristentums – Festschrift für Klaus Koschorke zum 65. Geburtstag* (Wiesbaden: Harrassowitz, 2013), p. 203.

13. 'Full text of President Jonathan's acceptance speech', *CPAfrica*, 29 May 2011, http://www.cp-africa.com/2011/04/19/full-text-of-president-jonathans-acceptance-speech (accessed 30 January 2017).

14. 'Full text of Goodluck Jonathan's declaration speech', Channels Television website, 11 November 2014, https://www.channelstv.com/2014/11/11/full-text-goodluck-jonathans-declaration-speech (accessed 30 January 2017).

15. Beth Hart, 'Jonathan delivers concession speech', *Naij.com*, 2015, https://www.naij.com/413540-jonathan-delivers-concession-speech.html (accessed 30 January 2017).

16. 'Jola Sotubo, 'Full text of ex-president's speech at Bloomberg Studios', Pulse.ng, 6 June 2016, http://pulse.ng/local/goodluck-jonathan-read-full-tet-of-ex-president-s-speech-at-bloomberg-studios-id5118396.html (accessed 30 January 2017).

17. Gifford, 'The Southern Shift', p. 194.

18. 'Nigeria passes law against gay relationships', Al Jazeera website, 13 January 2014, http://www.aljazeera.com/news/africa/2014/01/nigeria-passes-law-banning-gay-marriage-2014113151626685617.html (accessed 30 January 2017).

19. 'Crude tactics', *The Economist*, 30 January 2016, http://www.economist.com/news/middle-east-and-africa/21689584-cheap-oil-causing-currency-crisis-nigeria-banning-imports-no (accessed 30 January 2017).

20. 'Nigeria passes law against gay relationships'.

21. 'Nigeria passes law banning homosexuality', *Daily Telegraph*, 14 January 2014, http://www.telegraph.co.uk/news/worldnews/africaandindianocean/nigeria/10570304/Nigeria-passes-law-banning-homosexuality.html (accessed 30 January 2017).

22. 'Uganda court annuls anti-homosexuality law', BBC News website, 1 August 2014, http://www.bbc.com/news/world-africa-28605400 (accessed 30 January 2017).

23. 'Nigeria passes law against gay relationships'.
24. 'Obituary: President Yar'Adua'.
25. Yinka Ibukun, 'Nigeria's Jonathan says country may revisit law on gay marriage', Bloomb-erg website, 6 June 2016, https://www.bloomberg.com/news/articles/2016-06-06/nigeria-s-jonathan-says-country-may-revisit-law-on-gay-marriage (accessed 30 January 2017).
26. Alexis Okeowo, 'The best thing Goodluck Jonathan ever did was to concede', *New Yorker*, 1 April 2015, http://www.newyorker.com/news/daily-comment/the-best-thing-goodluck-jonathan-ever-did-was-to-concede (accessed 30 January 2017).
27. Sotubo, 'Full text of ex-president's speech at Bloomberg Studios'.

DAVID CAMERON (2010–16)

NICK SPENCER

INTRODUCTION

David Cameron appeared under the British political spotlight almost as abruptly as he left it. He assumed the stage in October 2005, one of four candidates to succeed Michael Howard as the Conservative Party leader, following a general election in which the party made a significant dent in Labour's massive majority but remained firmly in opposition. Cameron was the outsider, some way behind Ken Clarke, Liam Fox and the favourite, David Davis, but a winsome, script-less performance at the Conservative Party conference won over his audience. He was to lead his party for eleven years and his country for six.

LIFE

Cameron was born on 9 October 1966, the third of Ian and Mary Cameron's four children. Ian Cameron, who had been born with severely deformed legs, was a stockbroker, and Mary a justice of the peace. The family lived in Kensington and Chelsea, in London, before moving to an old rectory near Newbury, in Berkshire, after which David was sent to an exclusive prep school and then on to Eton. He went on to study PPE (philosophy, politics and economics) at Oxford University, where he gained a first-class degree and joined the Bullingdon Club, an infamously rich, rowdy dining club for elite public schoolboys. He proceeded to a job in the Conservative Research Department where he worked with his future leadership competitor David

Davis, met his future Chancellor George Osborne and helped brief Prime Minister John Major for the then still bi-weekly Prime Minister's Questions. From politics Cameron moved sideways into PR, working as head of corporate communications for the ITV television company Carlton for seven years, before unsuccessfully contesting the seat of Stafford in the 1997 general election, and then winning Witney, in Oxfordshire, four years later.

Cameron had thus only been in Parliament for four years before he contested the Conservative Party leadership, yet it was precisely this novelty that appealed to his audience. The legacy of Thatcherism, a painful post-Thatcher government marked by scandal and open warfare over Europe, and the force of political nature that was New Labour had left the Tory Party contaminated and seemingly unelectable. Cameron offered a new start. Indeed, in many ways he was the product of New Labour, in the same way as New Labour had been the product of Margaret Thatcher. A young, pragmatic, adaptable, liberal-minded, socially concerned Conservative, he was also father of a severely disabled son, Ivan, who required constant care, and whose needs scythed through the privilege in Cameron's past. When he spoke of how the National Health Service was a lifesaver and what carers meant to people, Cameron knew whereof he spoke, in the process allaying voters' fears about an NHS in Tory hands.

This new, young Tory politician broke the mould of the recent past and won voters over, at least in part. In May 2010 he became the youngest British Prime Minister since 1812 and the first, since the Second World War, of a coalition government.

SPIRITUAL BIOGRAPHY

In the normal run of things, David Cameron would be a borderline candidate for inclusion in this volume. While clearly no atheist, Cameron's Christian faith is, by his repeated admissions, somewhat vague.

His upbringing was unusual not only for its privilege but also because the circles in which he moved saw the establishment and its established church as a honourable part of the national furniture as ever fewer people did the last decades of the twentieth century. He told *Church Times* in April 2014 that his parents 'spent countless hours helping to support and maintain the village church that I grew up next to', a cultural immersion that his time at Eton and Oxford reinforced. In 2008, Cameron borrowed a phrase from his Oxford and Tory Party friend Boris Johnson about how his faith was 'like reception for Magic FM in the Chilterns: it sort of comes and goes'. It was to become the stock phrase for his premiership, much as Alastair Campbell's 'We don't do God' was for Tony Blair's.

Cameron was nothing if not consistent in this view. '[I am] a wishy-washy sort of Christian', he told *Church Times* in May 2011. I do believe in God, he told Dylan Jones in a series of conversations that were subsequently published in book form. 'I always find this difficult,' he went on:

> I'm a typical 'Church of Englander' and I believe that there is a power greater than us and the life and work of Jesus Christ is an important guide to morality and action ... I'm not a literalist [Bible believer] ... I don't have a personal direct line [to God] ... I'm a pretty classic Church of England 'racked-with-doubt-and-scepticism' believer.[1]

'[I think] the idea of a resurrection, a living God, of someone who's still with us, is fantastically important – even if you, as I do, struggle over some of the details,' he told a reception of church leaders at Easter 2011.[2] 'I'm hardly a model church-going, God-fearing Christian,' he wrote in *Premier Christianity* magazine in 2015.[3] 'Like so many others, I'm a bit hazy on the finer points of our faith. But even so, in the toughest of times, my faith has helped me move on and drive forward. It also gives me a gentle reminder every once in a while about what really matters and how to be a better person, father and citizen.'

His personal habit bore out this picture of hazy belief. 'I am a committed – but, I have to say, vaguely practising – Church of England Christian,' he told an audience of academics and ecclesiastical dignitaries in Oxford in 2011, in a remarkable speech to mark the 400th anniversary of the King James Bible, a speech to which we will return. 'I go to church monthly rather than weekly. More than Christmas and Easter but not every week,' he remarked elsewhere.[4] He spoke highly of Mark Abrey, the vicar of his local church, St Nicholas's in Chadlington, who 'look[ed] after' him spiritually in the constituency,[5] and especially after his son Ivan died aged six. '[My] moments of greatest peace' come 'perhaps every other Thursday morning' when I slip into the sung Eucharist at St Mary Abbots. 'I find a little bit of peace and hopefully a bit of guidance', he told a reception in 2014.[6]

At times, this gentle and tentative faith could sound more fervent. 'I'm proud this year to have completed a small pilgrimage, which is I have finally made it to the place where Our Saviour was both crucified and born,' he told the same Easter reception in 2014.[7] 'It's a very special moment the first time you go to the Church of the Holy Nativity', he went on. 'It's a remarkable, extraordinary place, and I think something that will stay with me.'

These were rare moments, however. One biographer, Anthony Seldon, claimed that the Prime Minister was 'institutionally, but not spiritually, religious'. According to Seldon, Cameron 'enjoys the ceremony and rhythm of church services but does not derive profound solace from them ... [and has] a non-doctrinal approach to religion', and although this possibly plays down Cameron's personal connection a little too much, it is a generally fair and valid assessment.[8]

FROM DOING GOD TO MAGIC FM

In spite of this non-doctrinal approach, Cameron's premiership was notable precisely for its willingness to talk about Christianity, religion and faith, a fact that marked him out from his two predecessors, in a way he often pointed out.

This can be seen in the sheer number of Christmas, Easter and latterly Ramadan messages Cameron delivered from Downing Street. Such addresses had, until then, been only occasional affairs; Cameron turned them into a regular tradition. Moreover, whereas this could have been an opportunity for the most toe-curling of platitudes, Cameron was prepared to get quite explicit in his content. For example, while his Christmas 2012 naturally celebrated the Jubilee and the Olympics of that year, it also quoted St John's Gospel,[9] which Cameron used as a basis for paying tribute to British forces then serving overseas. The *New Statesman* observed that the address had an 'unusually Christian tone'.[10] The 2013 message was less biblically explicit (though the prophet Isaiah got a look in[11]) and the 2014 message even less so.

Cameron's Christmas addresses were more than matched by his Easter ones. In April 2011, Cameron's first Easter as Prime Minister, he quoted St

Mark's Gospel and said that Easter reminded us all to 'follow our conscience and ask not what we are entitled to, but what we can do for others'.[12] The following year he quoted St Luke's, in an address that felt still more personal, remarking that 'this is the time when, as Christians, we remember the life, sacrifice and living legacy of Christ', and calling Jesus 'a man of incomparable compassion, generosity, grace, humility and love.'[13]

Cameron also held Easter receptions at No. 10, remarking at the third, in 2013, that when he became Prime Minister, he spotted that 'we were holding receptions for Eid and for Diwali, but we weren't holding a reception for Christians', and adding that 'it's right to have it at Easter, the most important Christian festival, the one that has all the challenges of faith, but really is all about – for me, anyway – the triumph of life over death'.[14] Like his Christmas addresses, Cameron's Easter ones became less obviously biblical as time went on, but the very fact that he marked the moments at all, let alone as biblically and confessionally as he sometimes did, is noteworthy.

Cameron's religious addresses were not limited to Christian festivals. From his first year in office, he also gave an annual message during Ramadan, remarking in 2012, for example, that during this 'hugely important time of prayer and fasting, we are reminded of the importance of charity and compassion', and he linked this to 'the role Britain plays on the international stage to help those less fortunate through our aid budget'.[15] Two years later, he focused on charity and community, saying that 'here in Britain, Muslims are our biggest donors – they give more to charity than any other faith group'.[16]

The likelihood is that Cameron's willingness to talk about Christianity and faith was not – apropos the opening words of this section – *in spite* of Cameron's non-doctrinal approach to religion, but because of it. It seems to have been precisely this somewhat tepid, uncertain and ultimately quite private faith that enabled Cameron to 'do God' in the way he did. Tony Blair couldn't or wouldn't do God because people thought that he took the Christian thing really quite seriously.[17] David Cameron could because they thought he didn't.

CHRISTIAN ACTION IN A CHRISTIAN NATION

If this is the case, it invites the (familiar) question about substance. Was there any content to Cameron's religious agenda? Was it simply an example of a Prime Minister who was alert to the religiously plural nature of his country and willing to respond accordingly? Or, more cynically, an example of a Prime Minister who was willing to tout for votes wherever he might find them?

Such questions are ultimately unanswerable (and the answers often say more about who voices them than who they are talking about) but Cameron's rhetoric and to some extent his policy strongly suggest he was doing more than just playing the psephological game. In particular, there were two ideas – that of Britain as a Christian country, and that which might come under the umbrella of the Big Society – to which he repeatedly returned.

A CHRISTIAN COUNTRY

When asked by Dylan Jones in 2008 whether we should be a Christian country, Cameron replied directly, 'We are a Christian country, it is an important part of our make-up and I don't see any reason to change.' It was a theme to which he repeatedly returned. 'As a Christian country, we must remember what His birth represents: peace, mercy, goodwill and, above all, hope,' he said in his Christmas 2015 message.[18] Values of responsibility, hard work, charity, compassion and pride in working for the common good and honouring the social obligations are Christian values, he said the following Easter, 'and they should give us the confidence to say yes, we are a Christian country and we are proud of it'.[19]

By far his fullest, and most sophisticated, treatment of the topic was in his speech commemorating the 400th anniversary of the King James Bible, given in Oxford in 2011. While this might have been an occasion that never got beyond the bromides concerning that translation's magisterial language and its impact on our literature, Cameron also used his speech to talk of how 'the Bible runs through our political history in a way that is often not properly recognised'. This, he argued, could be found in the subtle interplay of freedom and order.[20] On the one hand, the knowledge that God created man in His own image was 'a game changer for the cause of human dignity and equality': 'When each and every individual is related to a power above all of us ... and when every human being is of equal and infinite importance, created in the very image of God ... we get the irrepressible foundation for equality and human rights.' This, augmented by the fact that the Torah 'placed the first limits on royal power', led to the Bible being at the forefront of the emergence of democracy and the abolition of slavery.

One the other hand, there was the biblical emphasis on political order. 'The history and existence of a constitutional monarchy owes much to a Bible in which kings were anointed and sanctified with the authority of God … a clear emphasis on the respect for royal power and the need to maintain political order.' It was this subtle balance and interplay that had generated Britain's unusual and historically admired parliamentary democracy, under the monarch and under God, and it encouraged Cameron to say baldly, 'We are a Christian country. And we should not be afraid to say so.'

Such an emphasis on Britain's Christianity was further underlined by his unusually tough anti-secular rhetoric. Cameron frequently spoke against the 'secularisation that can sometimes happen in our society'. He pointed out that 'societies do not necessarily become more secular with modernity but rather more plural', and attacked the common secular argument that confessing the Christian nature of a country necessarily undermines other faith positions:

> Those who say being a Christian country is doing down other faiths … simply don't understand that it is easier for people to believe and prac-tise other faiths when Britain has confidence in its Christian identity … Because the tolerance that Christianity demands of our society provides greater space for other religious faiths too. And because many of the values of a Christian country are shared by people of all faiths and indeed by people of no faith at all.

This was an argument made the following year by the Queen, who com-mented in an address at Lambeth Palace at the start of her Jubilee Year that the established church was 'occasionally misunderstood and … commonly under-appreciated' for its public role in 'protect[ing] the free practice of all faiths in this country'.[21] That the Prime Minister and his Queen should be singing so heartily from the same Anglican hymn book seemed entirely appropriate.

Cameron's Christian-nation rhetoric was understood by some to be an attempt to woo back a core constituency he had lost through his gay marriage proposals.[22] His support of this bill was itself something of a conversion. On record for having attacked Tony Blair for 'moving heaven and earth to allow the promotion of homosexuality in our schools'[23] and having voted to retain a version of Section 28 in 2003 (for which he apologised in 2009), Cameron was no life-long gay activist. He had, in his 2006 conference speech, included a paean to marriage that was subsequently interpreted as paving the way for gay marriage, but the precise wording seems to be clearly about civil partnerships, which Cameron himself supported.[24]

However, seemingly out of nowhere (the issue was raised neither in the Conservatives' 2010 manifesto nor in the coalition agreement), Cameron announced his intention to push through the bill in his 2011 conference speech. It was a courageous moment, when his stock with his backbenchers and the wider party was not particularly high, but he carefully placed the issue in the context of commitment and family security, rather than gay rights, and was able therefore to present it as a conservative rather than a progressive piece of legislation. 'I don't support gay marriage despite being a Conservative. I support gay marriage because I'm a Conservative,' he told his conference audience.

Be that as it may, the bill, its sudden and electorally untested genesis, and the way in which Cameron personally drove it home upset a large body of opinion and although some polls suggested there was (nominal) Christian support for the measure, all the mainline churches opposed the measure[25] and the Coalition for Marriage collected several hundred thousand signatures in opposition.

Cameron could have further angered opponents – his coalition partners were indignant at the fact that he gave the issue a free vote, believing that this was not a matter of conscience – but the whole gay marriage debate showed that there were considerable tensions between what Cameron understood by the term 'Christian nation' and what others did.

THE BIG SOCIETY

For all that Cameron was sincere in his discussion of Britain's Christian identity, his Christian-nation rhetoric was, if anything, a vehicle for what he said was his fundamental political mission.

The ideas behind this had a complex and varied genesis. As early as 2006, Cameron speech writer (and Christian) Danny Kruger had written in *Prospect* magazine that Cameron's philosophy circumvented the liberty and equality agendas that had historically defined right and left respectively, in favour of the third revolutionary cry: fraternity.[26] Kruger located Cameron's philosophy 'in what Oliver Letwin had described as "right relationships"' – itself a theologically pregnant term – and although he educed no explicitly Christian content to this philosophy, the ideas and thinkers quoted – a sense of solidarity, the need to trust people, Edmund Burke, T. S. Eliot – were at very least consonant with (a certain strand of) Christian social theory.

At the same time, the Centre for Social Justice think tank, originally set up by the Catholic Iain Duncan Smith, published its substantial *Broken Britain* report, in response to which Cameron commissioned a follow-up report, *Breakthrough Britain*, which commended the idea of a 'welfare society'. A couple of years later, Anglican theologian and philosopher Philip Blond emerged into public consciousness, with a *Prospect* magazine cover story, a book, and then a think tank espousing 'Red Toryism' and being, at least according to the *Daily Telegraph*, 'a driving force behind David Cameron's "Big Society" agenda'.[27]

It was not until 2009, however, when Cameron delivered that year's Hugo Young lecture, arguably the most ambitious and philosophically sophisticated speech in his time on the political front line, that the idea gained a title, by which it was to be respectively known, celebrated and mocked. The 'Big Society' was Cameron's attempt to reform the British political landscape, not simply to roll back the state, as Thatcher had promised, but to use the state (as he stressed in the Hugo Young lecture) to repopulate the exposed shoreline with the richness of voluntary and associational activity that had once characterised national life. Faith groups were absolutely central to this, and Cameron was keen to let them know this. Indeed, very few of his faith speeches are free from this theme. Writing for *Premier Christianity* magazine in 2015 he described himself as an 'unapologetic supporter of the role of faith in this country'.[28] 'Faith-based groups are at the heart of modern social action,' he told his King James audience. 'What we both need more of is evangelism. More belief that we can get out there and actually change people's lives,' he told an Easter reception in 2014.

The link was not just incidental but often explicit. In the 2013 Downing Street Easter reception, musing on the theme of faith, hope and charity, Cameron said he wanted 'to celebrate again what it is that our faith communities do in terms of what I call the Big Society',[29] and he made the same association in his Christmas message that year,[30] and more explosively at the Easter reception the following year:

> People sometimes say … 'You talk about the Big Society; don't you realise this is what the Church has been doing for decades?' And I say yes, absolutely. Jesus invented the Big Society 2,000 years ago, I just want to see more of it and encourage as much of it as possible.[31]

Tying Jesus Christ to such a specific policy idea was simultaneously clever and foolish. Either way, it was guaranteed to get attention.

The theme of faith as social capital had been a significant one in the New Labour years, but it became a linchpin of Cameron's political project.[32] Accordingly, he appointed the first ever minister for faith, Sayeeda Warsi, giving her a voice at the Cabinet table, and allowed the local government minister Eric Pickles to repeatedly counter the Alastair Campbell line, by emphasising that the (then) coalition government did do God.[33]

The Cameron government's free school policy,[34] his stated determination 'to stand up for the rights of Christians to practice their faith' and the willingness to 'change the law so that people can go on saying prayers before council meetings' were part of this broader attempt to enable faith groups to feel more confident and comfortable in delivering public services.[35] This was also what lay behind his anti-secular rhetoric, at one point borrowing the words of Barack Obama in *The Audacity of Hope*, saying that 'in reaction to religious overreach we equate tolerance with secularism, and forfeit the moral language that would help infuse our politics with larger meaning'.[36]

CHURCHES AND THE BIG SOCIETY

Broadly speaking, the initiative was welcomed by churches. Archbishop Rowan Williams was quoted calling the idea 'painfully stale',[37] and Archbishop Vincent Nichols described it as 'lacking a cutting edge. It has no teeth.'[38] However, these (widely reported) comments did not reflect the generally positive response given the idea by both men and their churches. In a detailed speech on the topic, Williams gave it 'two-and-a-half cheers',[39] while the Catholic Church discussed it in depth and appreciatively in a seminar and then a paper on Catholic social teaching and the philosophy behind the Big Society.[40] Similarly, the Von Hügel Institute in Cambridge published a detailed report stating that the Big Society was consonant with a number of key elements within Catholic social teaching, such as personalism, common good and subsidiarity.[41]

The ecclesiastical response was not wholly uncritical. The respective archbishops' criticisms have already been noted, while Tim Stevens, the Bishop of Leicester, gave evidence to the House of Commons Public Administration Select Committee in which he was

> keen to stress the limits of the Church of England's capacity for delivering public services, stating that provision of services by churches 'cannot be an alternative to public service provision across the piece. They cannot deliver the professionalism … the resources … the standards … the consistency, and they should not be expected to.'[42]

Ministers cannot expect 'the Church to behave like a local authority or a Government department' he warned.[43] Charles Wookey, giving evidence on behalf of the Catholic Archbishop of Westminster, concurred, saying that 'as far as the Catholic Church is concerned, we do not want to raise expectations about what religious communities can suddenly do in replacing any kind of state provision'.[44]

These (very real) concerns about capacity aside, however, the Big Society was powerfully consonant with a great deal of Christian social thought, perhaps not entirely surprisingly given some of the influences on its development. Nevertheless, the fact is that the idea died in the first few years of Cameron's first government. When the party unveiled its 2010 election manifesto, the Big Society took centre stage, but it was rarely mentioned in the rest of the 2010 campaign. Launched properly after the election with a speech on 19 July 2010, and relaunched in February 2011 at Somerset House, during which a £200 million Big Society bank, National Citizen Service and 5,000 community organisers were announced, the idea was pushed again in May that year at a further relaunch in Milton Keynes, when ministers were given a day of voluntary service per year to lead by example and it was emphasised that 'the Big Society is not some sort of fluffy add-on to more gritty and more important subjects'.

By that point, however, the idea had by then become inextricably linked up with in the post-crash programme of deficit reduction and austerity, its detractors within government believing Cameron should be focusing his attentions on the hard reality of reducing the deficit and restarting the economy. The widespread rejection of the idea of locally elected mayors in England and a brutally low turnout in elections for police commissioners, both part of the localism programme that ran alongside the Big Society, further undermined the initiative, and it petered out quietly in the final years of the coalition government.

CONCLUSION

There are other elements of Cameron's interaction with things eternal that we might mention, such as his engagement with Islam, particularly vis-à-vis the security agenda that was so important during his premiership.[45] Such an omission notwithstanding, however, we can move towards a tentative conclusion regarding this most recently departed of British political leaders.

Cameron 'did God' in his six years in No. 10 more consistently than any British Prime Minister since Margaret Thatcher, and arguably rather more than she did. That in itself is an interesting point to note. This was partly because he was governing a country where religious faith was growing in prominence and salience as a political issue, and partly because his first administration was informed by an idea, at least in the early years, that positively depended on active religious engagement. But it was also partly precisely because Cameron's own somewhat vague faith allowed him to rush in where more obviously pious leaders feared to tread.

That noted, if it was Cameron's Christian vagueness that enabled him to set out on such religious seas, it was the same vagueness that laid him particularly open to the challenge of playing politics with faith. Indeed, Cameron's very eagerness to denounce secularism, to celebrate the nation's Christianity and to encourage – and make straight the paths for – faith-based social action was precisely the cause for suspicion among many. He seemed almost oddly, almost indecently, keen to do God for someone whose own faith came and went like Magic FM in the Chilterns.

NOTES

1. David Cameron and Dylan Jones, *Cameron on Cameron: Conversations with Dylan Jones* (London: Fourth Estate, 208), pp. 179–180.

2. Michael Ashcroft and Isabel Oakeshott, *Call Me Dave: The Unauthorised Biography of David Cameron* (Biteback Publishing, 2015), p. 402.

3. 'David Cameron's Easter message to Christians', *Premier Christianity*, https://www.premierchristianity.com/Topics/Society/Politics/David-Cameron-s-Easter-Message-to-Christians (accessed 30 January 2017).

4. Cameron and Jones, *Cameron on Cameron*, p. 180.

5. 'Easter reception at Downing Street 2014', Gov.uk, 9 April 2014, https://www.gov.uk/government/speeches/easter-reception-at-downing-street-2014 (accessed 30 January 2017).

6 Quoted in Ashcroft and Oakeshott, *Call Me Dave*, p. 402.

7. Ibid.

8. Anthony Seldon & Peter Snowdon, *Cameron at 10: the inside story 2010–2015* (London: William Collins, 2015), pp. 75, 274.

9. 'The Gospel of John tells us that in this man was life, and that his life was the light of all mankind, and that he came with grace, truth and love. Indeed, God's word reminds us that Jesus was the Prince of Peace' ('Prime minister's Christmas message', Gov.uk, 25 December 2012, https://www.gov.uk/government/news/prime-ministers-christmas-message-2012 (accessed 30 January 2017)).

10. 'Full text: David Cameron's Christmas message', *New Statesman*, 24 December 2012, http://www.newstatesman.com/religion/2012/12/full-text-david-camerons-christmas-message (accessed 30 January 2017).

11. 'PM's Christmas message 2013', Gov.uk, 24 December 2013, https://www.gov.uk/government/news/pms-christmas-message-2013 (accessed 30 January 2017).

12. 'David Cameron's Easter message', Gov.uk, 24 April 2011, https://www.gov.uk/government/news/david-camerons-easter-message (accessed 30 January 2017).

13. 'Prime minister's Easter message', Gov.uk, 3 April 2012, https://www.gov.uk/government/news/prime-ministers-easter-message (accessed 30 January 2017).

14. 'Transcript of prime minister's speech at Downing Street Easter reception', Gov.uk, 21 March 2013, https://www.gov.uk/government/speeches/transcript-of-prime-ministers-speech-at-downing-street-easter-reception (accessed 30 January 2017).

15. 'Prime Minister David Cameron's message for Ramadan', Gov.uk, 20 July 2012, https://www.gov.uk/government/news/prime-minister-david-camerons-message-for-ramadan (accessed 30 January 2017).

16. 'Ramadan 2014: David Cameron's message', Gov.uk, 27 June 2014, https://www.gov.uk/government/news/ramadan-2014-david-camerons-message (accessed 30 January 2017).

17. And also because he learned early on that no matter what a Labour Prime Minister said about the Christian faith not being the possession of the left, he would be reported and/or heard to be saying otherwise.

18. 'Christmas 2015: prime minister's message', Gov.uk, 24 December 2015, https://www.gov.uk/government/news/christmas-2015-prime-ministers-message (accessed 30 January 2017).

19. 'Easter 2016: David Cameron's message', Gov.uk, 27 March 2016, https://www.gov.uk/government/news/easter-2016-david-camerons-message (accessed 30 January 2017).

20. The author cannot help but detect his own book, published that year on that topic, entitled *Freedom and Order: History, Politics and the English Bible* (London: Hodder and Stoughton, 2011) behind this argument. Alas, he has never been able to verify whether this was in fact so.

21. 'A speech by The Queen at Lambeth Palace, 2012', Royal.uk, 15 February 2012. https://www.royal.uk/queens-speech-lambeth-palace-15-february-2012 (accessed 30 January 2017).

22. Tim Montgomerie, 'Cameron's Christmas message described "as the most Christian of its kind from an incumbent prime minister"', *ConservativeHome*, 24 December 2012, http://www.conservativehome.com/thetorydiary/2012/12/cameronchristmasmessage.html (accessed 30 January 2017).

23. Ashcroft, p. 404, quoting Johann Hari, *Attitude*, February 2010.

24. The relevant text reads: 'There's something special about marriage. It's not about religion. It's not about morality. It's about commitment. When you stand up there, in front of your friends and your family, in front of the world, whether it's in a church or anywhere else, what you're doing really means something. Pledging yourself to another means doing something brave and important. You are making a commitment. You are publicly saying: it's not just about me, me, me anymore. It is about we – together, the two of us, through thick and thin. That really matters. *And by the way, it means something whether you're a man and a woman, a woman and a woman or a man and another man. That's why we were right to support civil partnerships, and I'm proud of that.*' (Emphases added.)

25. The Church of England, for example, claimed that the government 'misunderstand[s] the legal nature of marriage in this country. They mistake the form of the ceremony for the institution itself' ('Initial response to government consultation on same-sex marriage', Church of England website, 15 March 2012, https://www.churchofengland.org/media-centre/news/2012/03/initial-response-to-government-consultation-on-same-sex-marriage.aspx (accessed 30 January 2017)).

26. Danny Kruger, 'The right dialectic', *Prospect*, September 2006.

27. Patrick Hennessy, 'Minister backs plan for massive state sell off of assets', *Daily Telegraph*, 13 November 2010, http://www.telegraph.co.uk/news/politics/8131290/Minister-backs-plan-for-massive-state-sell-off-of-assets.html (accessed 30 January 2017).

28. 'David Cameron's Easter message to Christians'.

29. 'Transcript of prime minister's speech at Downing Street Easter reception'.

30. 'PM's Christmas message 2013'.

31. 'Easter reception at Downing Street 2014'.

32. See Daniel Nilsson DeHanas, Therese O'Toole and Nasar Meer, 'Faith and Muslims in Public Policy', in Daniel Singleton (ed.), *Faith with Its Sleeves Rolled Up* (London: FaithAction, 2013): 'In terms of policy, the coalition has to a large degree brought engagement with the faith sector under the banner of Big Society. In this respect, the coalition's emphasis on Christian heritage has been accompanied by a renewal of inter-faith work.'

33. See, for example, 'Uniting our communities: integration in 2013', Gov.uk, 15 January 2013, https://www.gov.uk/government/speeches/uniting-our-communities-integration-in-2013; Eric Pickles, 'A Christian ethos strengthens our nation', *Daily Telegraph*, 12 September 2012, http://www.telegraph.co.uk/news/religion/9538561/A-Christian-ethos-strengthens-our-nation.html (both accessed 30 January 2017).

34. 'Easter reception at Downing Street 2014'.

35. 'Transcript of Prime Minister's speech at Downing Street Easter reception', https://www.gov.uk/government/speeches/transcript-of-prime-ministers-speech-at-downing-street-easter-reception (accessed 7 March 2017).

36. Barack Obama, *The Audacity of Hope: Thoughts on Reclaiming the American Dream* (Edinburgh: Canongate, 2007), p. 39.

37. His full statement was: 'The widespread suspicion that this has been done for opportunistic or money-saving reasons allows many to dismiss what there is of a programme for Big Society initiatives; even the term has fast become painfully stale' ('The government needs to know how afraid people are', *New Statesman*, 9 June 2011, http://www.newstatesman.com/uk-politics/2011/06/long-term-government-democracy (accessed 30 January 2017)).

38. Jonathan Wynne Jones, 'Catholic church: Big Society is failing', *Daily Telegraph*, 16 April 2011, http://www.telegraph.co.uk/news/religion/8456301/Catholic-church-Big-Society-is-failing.html (accessed 30 January 2017).

39. 'How should churches respond to the Big Society', Dr Rowan Williams, 104th Archbishop of Canterbury website, 23 July 2010, http://rowanwilliams.archbishopofcanterbury.org/articles.php/571/how-should-churches-respond-to-the-big-society-rowan-williams (accessed 30 January 2017).

40. John Loughlin, Peter Allott and Richard Crellin, *The UK Government's 'Big Society' Programme and Catholic Social Teaching* (Chelmsford: Matthew James, 2013).

41. Ibid.

42. House of Commons Public Administration Select Committee, *The Big Society*, Seventeenth Report, Session 2010–12, 7 December 2011, HC 902-I, p. 48, available at http://www.publications.parliament.uk/pa/cm201012/cmselect/cmpubadm/902/902.pdf (accessed 31 January 2017). Stevens went on to say that 'what they can do is add value, they can mobilise volunteers, they can support initiatives, and in localities they can do things that are small scale and transformational'.

43. Ibid.

44. House of Commons Public Administration Select Committee, Seventeenth Report of Session 2010–12, *The Big Society*, Para. 136; https://www.publications.parliament.uk/pa/cm201012/cmselect/cmpubadm/902/902.pdf (accessed 7 March 2017). These comments reflect Vincent Nichols's earlier remarks about the idea lacking in teeth, and he went on to say that 'devolving greater power to local authorities should not be used as a cloak for masking central cuts. It is not sufficient for the government, in its localism programme, simply to step back from social need and say this is a local issue.' James Meikle, '"Big society" has no teeth, says Catholic archbishop', *The Guardian*, 17 April 2011; https://www.theguardian.com/world/2011/apr/17/catholic-archbishop-big-society-teeth (accessed 7 March 2017).

45. In one regard, Cameron was notably in tune with his friend and ally Michael Gove's muscular criticism, in his book *Celsius 7/7*, of those willing to accommodate unacceptable Muslim viewpoints (see, for example, his speech at the Munich Security Conference in 2011). Nevertheless, for every rattle of a sabre, there was an olive branch offered, and Cameron often used his Downing Street addresses at Ramadan and Eid to insist that terrorism was an 'assault on Islam, whose good name it perverts' ('Eid 2015: David Cameron's message', Gov.uk, 16 July 2015, https://www.gov.uk/government/news/eid-2015-david-camerons-message (accessed 31 January 2017)) to emphasise the compatibility of Islam with British life, and to highlight the historical precedents for this: '[In] the First World War … more than a million men and boys from India fought with our troops during that conflict and many thousands of them were Muslims. They travelled across the world to fight to defend our freedom, guided and sustained by their bravery, comradeship and, above all, by their faith' ('Ramadan 2014: David Cameron's message').

TONY ABBOTT (2013–15)

GILLIAN MADDEN

INTRODUCTION

Tony Abbott, Australia's most recently removed Prime Minister – at least at the time of writing – was difficult to pin down as a politician. An ideologue and 'conviction politician', Abbott was also given to 'frequent and spectacular' changes of mind.[1] He was not afraid to take unpopular positions on some moral issues, yet was characterised as a pragmatic 'political animal'.[2] As opposition leader, Abbott was adversarial, claiming, 'Oppositions are not there to get legislation through. Oppositions are there to hold the government to account.'[3] His time in office was brief and turbulent, lasting only two years as leader of the conservative Liberal–National coalition before being ousted in a leadership challenge by long-time rival Malcolm Turnbull in September 2015.

The interplay between Abbott's Catholic convictions and his political life has long fascinated the media and public. To appreciate that fascination we will briefly explore some aspects of Abbott's personal history and the world in which he developed his views and commitments, and examine Australian society's attitude to the interface between religion and politics. Finally, we will consider Abbott's approach to three significant issues to understand better the manner and extent of the mingling of his religion and his politics.

ABBOTT'S RELIGIOUS AND POLITICAL FORMATION

Abbott was born in London in 1957 to middle-class Catholic British-Australian parents. When he was three years old, the family returned to Australia and settled on the North Shore, an affluent region of Sydney. Catholicism was a particularly significant influence on Abbott's early life and he regularly attended Mass. The importance of the faith also ran through his education at two of Sydney's most prestigious Catholic boys' schools, St Aloysius' and St Ignatius' colleges.

Abbott has reflected that, alongside his parents, 'the church was the biggest influence on my early life'.[4] His Catholic education infused his worldview with a 'Jesuit ethos', and he appreciated the Jesuit approach to intellectual argument, examining issues from all sides.[5] It was during his time at St Ignatius' that Abbott met Father Emmet Costello, the school chaplain. Costello, a Jesuit with a strong interest in politics, mentored Abbott and gave shape to the idea of politics as a spiritual vocation. Abbott's Catholic upbringing and education would go on to play a significant part in shaping his political outlook, rhetoric and public image.

As a young adult, Abbott's heart became set on holy orders. This aspiration persisted even in the early phases of his political career. As an undergraduate student at the University of Sydney, he was a highly vocal and active member of the Students' Representative Council, where he eventually became president after extensive campaigning. During this time he also got involved with the Democratic Labour Party (DLP) on campus. One of Abbott's greatest political heroes, the staunchly Catholic political organiser B. A. Santamaria, was a founding member and ideologue of the DLP. Santamaria actively oriented the DLP towards Catholic social policies and opposed 'permissiveness'.[6] Given Abbott's dual pursuit of religious and political aspirations, it is not surprising that Santamaria's vision for the party resonated with him. In fact, it was the DLP's support of 'traditional values' that first drew Abbott into politics.[7]

While at Oxford as a Rhodes scholar, Abbott became particularly interested in the writings of the eighteenth-century philosopher Edmund Burke. Although not an explicitly religious source, ideas on the relationship between faith and society in Burke's work impacted on Abbott's approach to morality and duty in public life.[8] He also frequented Campion Hall, a Jesuit institution connected with the university, where he came into contact with a training Jesuit priest, Paul Mankowski, a devout Catholic and a boxer who quickly became another of Abbott's spiritual mentors. Abbott was a vocal supporter of Thatcherite politics while at Oxford, and he has also reflected that his experiences at Queen's College cemented his 'instinctive respect for values and institutions that have stood the test of time'.[9] It is apparent that Abbott's Oxford years served to nurture his politically conservative values as well as his religious aspirations.

On returning from Oxford in 1984, Abbott enrolled at St Patrick's Seminary in Sydney to train for the priesthood. However, he never completed the training, leaving in 1987 after mounting frustrations with the culture and approaches of the seminary. As Abbott reflected in an article for *The Bulletin*, 'three years' grinding struggle to meet the Church's standard was over. But a dream had died, as well – the dream that I could join that splendoured company founded by Christ which has angered, amazed and enthralled the world ever since.'[10]

The comment reveals Abbott's conflicted relationship between his faith, its institutions, and what he saw as his vocation. It demonstrates a high view of the Church, but also a frustration with what Abbott may have seen as an unattainable idealism with regard to what it expected or demanded of him. It points to a felt tension of ideology against pragmatism, a battle that would continue throughout his political life.

Shortly after dropping out of seminary, Abbott redirected his focus to his political career. During his brief stint as a journalist for political magazine *The Bulletin* and broadsheet *The Australian*, Abbott revisited his ambition of a life in politics. He started out as an advisor to the Liberal Party in the early 1990s under John Hewson, who was then the Liberal opposition leader. In 1994, he secured the seat of Warringah on Sydney's prestigious Northern Beaches in a by-election. Over the next four years, he worked his way to the front bench where in 1998 he became minister for employment services, by this time under the leadership of Prime Minister John Howard. Howard took a shine to Abbott, securing him a key role in Cabinet with important portfolios on workplace relations and later health. Over the next few years, Howard became a political mentor to Abbott.

Whereas Abbott's strong Catholic persona and hard stance on controversial issues such as abortion might previously have been thought to exclude him from a chance at party leadership, the recent religious transformation of Australia's political tone and culture under Howard opened up the realm of opportunity.[11] That opportunity came in 2009, when Abbott secured enough party support to become leader of the Liberal Party, winning a three-way leadership challenge against Malcolm Turnbull (later to become Prime Minister himself) and Joe Hockey, a prominent frontbencher.

IN CONTEXT: THE CATHOLIC CHURCH AND POLITICAL CULTURE IN AUSTRALIA

The Catholic Church in Australia that helped to form Abbott's worldview had been developing within the nation's social, political and cultural context for many years.[12] A principal focus in the nineteenth and early twentieth century was the building and propagation of schools, funded solely by the Catholic population and staffed by religious nuns and brothers. By the 1950s, there was a sense of collective self and an attitude, at times belligerent, built on a story of struggling against the odds and succeeding.[13] During the 1960s, Abbott's school years, the Catholic Church globally underwent changes in its self-understanding and its relation to other denominations and religions in the Second Vatican Council.[14] The Jesuits, in particular, focused on the creation and development of 'greater public schools', independent private schools that would educate leaders of Australian society, while arguing articulately for social justice for Aboriginals, the working classes and the destitute. It is not difficult to see how these features of Catholicism in Australia impacted on and shaped the person, rhetoric and actions of Abbott.

The way Abbott's personal faith interplayed with his public role was also reflective of the broader Australian political culture. For the greater part of the last hundred years, Australian politics has been dominated by two major political parties, the Labor Party, typically found on the centre-left, and the Liberal–National coalition on the centre-right. There have been incursions by more minor parties over the years, including the Democratic Labor Party in the 1950s and more recently the Greens, but the two major parties have remained largely entrenched in power. That said, Australia has experienced significant social changes over the last half-century, and waves of immigration have contributed to a distinctive multicultural society. Since 2007, the political tone in Australia has shifted to one of 'constant political warfare' from previous decades of strong stable government, with multiple leadership challenges, a hung parliament and party changes within the course of these few years.[15]

Since the second half of the twentieth century, Australia has made a determined effort to steer away from sectarian politics. Australia does not have a particularly strong history of overtly religious national leaders, and religiously backed moral crusading has not developed. Steve Bruce observes that Australia does not 'exhibit religious beliefs or attitudes that become increasingly popular or important in political action'. He believes that 'the presence of the Anglican Church and the culture of British imperialism absorbed and neutered sectarianism'.[16] As John Warhurst, a prominent Australian academic and emeritus professor at the Australian National University points out, 'Between Chifley's loss in 1949 and when Howard took office in 1996 Australia was led by Prime Ministers (nine of them) who were not observant Christians.'[17]

Howard's prime ministership heralded a new wave of public religiosity in Australian politics, though as Marion Maddox, author of the book *God under Howard*, contends, religious rhetoric in the Australian political arena is targeted not so much at committed churchgoers with established political positions, but rather towards the vicariously religious.[18] That is not to belittle the effect of this shift. Since Howard, religious rhetoric and identification in Australian politics has undoubtedly grown more salient, further reinforced by Kevin Rudd, who gave his Anglican faith a high profile throughout his career in politics.* Nonetheless, the treatment of Abbott's religion in the media demonstrates an underlying cultural tension about the place of a leader's religion in politics.

DOING GOD IN POLITICS
– ENDURING AMBIVALENCE IN RHETORIC

Concerns about Abbott's Catholicism impacting his politics, no doubt compounded by his previous clerical ambitions, earned him the nickname 'Mad Monk'.[19] Abbott's pejorative nickname became journalistic shorthand for the

---

* See pp. 191–203.

prevalence of his personal faith in his public life. It points to the sometimes uncomfortable relationship between the two, and the media's wariness of religious convictions being inappropriately applied. In some policy areas, such as abortion, marriage and stem cell research, Abbott's background and commitments did seem to affect his stance. Other areas in which one might expect those to have made a difference include asylum seeker policy and the environment. Here the focus will be Abbott's positions on asylum seekers, abortion and the environment. While these are not the only areas where his faith might have had some bearing, they help to indicate the significance and the complexity of the interplay between Abbott's religious beliefs and his political roles.

In a speech delivered in June 2010 to the Australian Christian Lobby (ACL), Abbott stated that 'faith has influenced my life but it does not, and I believe should not, shape my politics'. Six years earlier, Abbott had addressed the Adelaide University Democratic Club with a speech he had titled 'The Ethical Responsibilities of a Christian Politician'. Here, Abbott argued that a 'Christian politician faces the double test of not only being an effective politician but also a credible Christian'.[20] Between these speeches, Abbott appeared to equivocate on the importance and role of his faith in his public life. He first acknowledged that his Christian principles were integral to his political identity, and were open for scrutiny in the public domain. Later, he seemed to retreat from this claim, seeking to forge a clearer distinction between his personal ideology and political role.

These contradictory statements might indicate an internal grappling by Abbott to reconcile the tension of being a Catholic and a politician within a secular Australian context, a context that requires political solutions that are public and practical for the many. Alternatively, it may be that Abbott was not as clear in himself about the outworking of his religious faith in the political domain as some might have expected. It is, of course, easier to expound high moral principles as one's beliefs than it is to demonstrate in action that one truly holds those principles.

On a less generous view, Abbott's rhetorical inconsistency may suggest a kind of political pragmatism that was willing to deploy religion as a tool to further its aims, but only when it was not politically disadvantageous to do so. Perhaps Abbott did not want to be held to the demands of religious standards he enunciated, as was the case with Kevin Rudd.[21] Abbott, by distancing his political positions from his personal religious views, avoided giving as clear a set of moral criteria on which he was prepared to be assessed.

ASYLUM SEEKERS

Whatever the reasons for Abbott's attempts to distance his personal faith from his politics, these efforts were not entirely effective. In August 2013, a letter signed by more than 400 Jesuit school students was sent to Abbott and several other Jesuit-educated federal politicians concerning the government's asylum seeker policy. The letter offered a stinging critique of Abbott's betrayal of Jesuit values and 'lack of moral courage', trading 'human lives for political expediency'.[22]

The shorthand for Abbott's government policy objective on asylum seekers was to 'stop the boats'. Abbott often used this phrase himself, both in the campaign rhetoric leading up to the 2011 election and while in office. In more depth, 'Operation Sovereign Borders', the coalition's 2013 policy document on asylum seekers, sought to restore temporary protection visas for those found to be refugees, establish off-shore processing on Nauru and Manus Island, and organise a military-led border control programme involving turning back boats carrying asylum seekers where it would be safe to do so.[23] This is clearly a strongly deterrent approach that framed the issue primarily as a matter of border security.

Abbott was prepared to invoke Christian principles in speaking about asylum seekers on ABC Radio in 2012, though not as one might expect:

> I don't think it's a very Christian thing to come in by the back door rather than the front door ... I think the people we accept should be coming the right way and not the wrong way ... if you jump the queue, if you take yourself and your family on a leaky boat, that's doing the wrong thing, not the right thing, and we shouldn't encourage it.[24]

Julian Burnside, a prominent Australian barrister and human rights advocate, criticised the statement, pointing out that 'it is entirely appropriate that [Abbott] should consider the matter from the perspective of Christian teaching, given that he trained for the priesthood', but that he 'should know, better than most politicians, that the Christian doctrine he claims to understand and espouse emphasises the message of welcoming and protecting the stranger'.[25]

ABORTION

Abbott was prepared for his religious convictions to make him a figurehead for some controversial and politically unpopular stances. In 2004, he attracted widespread media attention when he expressed dismay at the number of terminated pregnancies in Australia and labelled abortion 'the easy way out'.[26] However, Abbott maintained a refusal to drive changes in abortion legislation, despite the possibility that such changes may have better aligned with his own conservative persuasion on the issue. On this point, he insisted that as party leader he did not 'have the luxury of personal views' to justify political decisions.[27] In his piece for *Quarterly Essay* on Abbott, David Marr portrayed him as a man fundamentally conflicted between his morals and politics. For Marr, if Abbott was tested, the 'political animal' triumphed.[28]

Abbott's mentor, B. A. Santamaria, was highly vocal on social issues.[29] Motivated by his vision to integrate Catholic-informed social principles and structures into Australian society, Santamaria did not fear political unpopularity.[30] Abbott admired 'Santa' for 'the courage that kept him going as an advocate for unfashionable truths', and sought to model his own politics on this pattern.[31]

In 2004, as health minister, Abbott reignited political debate on abortion with his 'Ethical Responsibilities' speech, quoted above. In 2006, a conscience vote regarding the abortion drug RU-486 was held in the Australian Federal Parliament. Abbott supported the existing powers of the minister of health to veto its administration, in keeping with his social conservatism and religious beliefs. During parliamentary debates, Senator Kerry Nettle directly attacked Abbott's stance on abortion, criticising its apparent religious motivations by wearing a T-shirt with the slogan 'Mr Abbott, get your rosaries off my ovaries'.[32] While Abbott did not alter his position on abortion, his address to the ACL possibly indicated a desire to distance his religious commitments from some of his political positions.

ENVIRONMENTAL POLICY

This distancing was particularly clear in Abbott's approach to environmental policy. Shortly after the 2011 election, Abbott's government repealed Australia's three-year-old carbon tax, which had levied companies emitting large amounts of carbon dioxide into the atmosphere. It also controversially abolished the Climate Commission, an independent government body established in 2011 that served to conduct research and provide information about environmental issues related to climate change (the commission later relaunched as the Climate Council, a non-government organisation). Under Abbott, the government also approved plans for the expansion of coal terminals around the Great Barrier Reef, which was subsequently declared by the World Heritage Committee to be in danger. In 2014, he appointed a climate change sceptic to lead a review into Australia's renewable energy targets. The federal budget released that year confirmed spending cuts to a range of environmental programmes.

These policy shifts deprioritised environmental issues such as climate change on the national agenda. While Abbott, like any Prime Minister, did not single-handedly shape policies, his approach to environmental responsibility was somewhat at odds with the published positions of the Catholic Church in Australia. Informed by Catholic social teaching, which includes care for our 'common home' as one of its foci, the Church submits that a 'human-induced accelerated climate change suggests a lack of understanding for the integrity and the cycles of nature. It raises serious moral and spiritual questions, not just for Catholics but for all Australian citizens and leaders, and calls for change in our way of life.'[33] Whereas on other issues Abbott was willing to bring his faith into his politics, it was not the case on this matter.

CONCLUSION

How did Abbott go about 'doing God' in Australian politics? On one side, the interaction between his Catholic convictions and his responsibilities as a politician was at many points unresolved, sometimes insufficiently examined and inconsistently applied, as seen in the varying policy tacks above. On the other, despite its inconsistencies, his devout faith was evidently at play as he progressed his political career. It was present as he was forming his social and political ideologies, as it was in his mentorship under John Howard. Abbott understood himself as a 'Christian politician', and recognised the challenges inherent in such a position. He was prepared to stand by his religiously informed convictions on certain controversial issues that may have come at a political cost. He was loyal to his party and his conservative brand of politics, and to the impulse of his religious convictions.

Abbott was obviously aware of the difficulties of bringing religion into political decision making and rhetoric, and his shortcomings in this domain may have been symptomatic of wider unresolved tensions in Australian political culture about the place of religion in politics. Abbott's comments on faith and politics, as well as political actions that were necessarily informed by his personal views, portray a man who was confronted by the secularity of the social and political world in which he was working. Even while recognising the centrality of his Christian faith and beliefs for giving substance and motivation to much of his career, he was also protective of his religious faith, seeking to shelter it from the gaze of those who might not appreciate its meaning and worth to him.

In the public view, Abbott's way of relating his faith and politics was idiosyncratic, and for that reason difficult to demarcate. Was he the passionate ideologue willing to stand by unpopular opinions? Or was he rather the 'political animal', opting for expediency? In attempting to resolve this apparent contradiction we hit upon the tension for any political leader doing God, and certainly all of those examined in this collection, of balancing principles and pragmatism. It is a challenge relating religious convictions to public life, and as success in each domain is measured differently it is hard to do both well. Still, the Christian faith impels its followers to work out their faith beyond the private sphere, and as such it is fitting for political leaders of faith to acknowledge that their religious commitments do have a significant bearing on their public life. It may sometimes be operating in the background, informing an ideological stance, but never jettisoned from one's overall political approach. In Abbott's case, much more of the interplay between his faith and his politics remained hidden than was actually revealed, explicated on conservative 'moral' issues but on other policy issues only half acknowledged or gestured towards. As to living in the tension between personal faith and public life, between religiously informed ideology and necessary political pragmatism, Abbott provides a striking example.

NOTES

1. Waleed Aly, 'Inside Tony Abbott's Mind', *The Monthly*, July 2013, https://www.themonthly.com.au/issue/2013/july/1372600800/waleed-aly/inside-tony-abbotts-mind (accessed 31 January 2017).

2. David Marr, 'Political Animal: The Making of Tony Abbott', *The Monthly*, September 2012, https://www.themonthly.com.au/issue/2012/september/1347234466/david-marr/political-animal-making-tony-abbott (accessed 31 January 2017).

3. 'Comment: oppositions are not there to get legislation through', SBS website, 11 December 2013, http://www.sbs.com.au/news/article/2013/12/11/comment-oppositions-are-not-there-get-legislation-through (accessed 31 January 2017).

4. Tony Abbott, *Battlelines* (Carlton, VIC: Melbourne University Press, 2009), p. 8.

5. Ibid.

6. Cathy Madden, 'The Democratic Labor Party an overview', Parliament of Australia website, 18 July 2011, http://www.aph.gov.au/About_Parliament/Parliamentary_Departments/Parliamentary_Library/pubs/BN/2011-2012/DPLOverview (accessed 31 January 2017).

7. Abbott, *Battlelines*, p. 10.

8. Louis Nowra, 'The whirling dervish: on Tony Abbott', *The Monthly*, February 2010, https://www.themonthly.com.au/monthly-essays-louis-nowra-whirling-dish-tony-abbott-2250 (accessed 31 January 2017).

9. Andy Beckett, 'Tony Abbott at Oxford: fighter, networker, Thatcherite', *The Guardian*, 16 August 2013, http://www.theguardian.com/world/2013/aug/16/tony-abbott-at-oxford-university (accessed 31 January 2017).

10. Quoted in Marr, 'Political Animal'.

11. Marion Maddox, *God under Howard: The Rise of the Religious Right in Australian Politics* (Crows Nest, NSW: Allen and Unwin, 2005).

12. For example, consider the influence of Catholics in the early development of the labour unions in Australia, and also the rise, in Melbourne, of 'The Movement' to counter communism and, in Sydney, the less extreme decision to remain within Labor (Gerard Henderson, *Mr Santamaria and the Bishops*, Studies in the Christian Movement 7 (Manly, NSW: St Patrick's College, 1982)).

13. James Franklin, *Catholic Values and Australian Realities* (Ballan, VIC: Connor Court, 2006).

14. Pope John XXIII called the council in 1959. Some 2,300 bishops from 116 countries took part. The meetings of the council occurred in ten-week sessions each year from 1962 to 1965.

15. Gregory Melleuish, 'Canada and Australia share a political culture of conflict', *The Conversation*, 16 March 2015, http://theconversation.com/canada-and-australia-share-a-political-culture-of-conflict-37881 (accessed 31 January 2017).

16. Steve Bruce, *Conservative Protestant Politics* (Oxford: Oxford University Press, 1998), p. 190.

17. John Warhurst, 'The religious beliefs of Australia's prime ministers', *Eureka Street*, 11 November 2010, http://www.eurekastreet.com.au/article.aspx?aeid=24159 (accessed 31 January 2017).

18. Marion Maddox, 'God under Gillard: religion and politics in Australia', ABC Religion and Ethics website, 10 November 2011, http://www.abc.net.au/religion/articles/2011/11/10/3360973.htm (accessed 31 January 2017). Grace Davie in *Religion in Britain: A Persistent Paradox*, 2nd ed. (Chichester: Wiley Blackwell, 2015) explains, 'By vicarious is meant the notion of religion performed by an active minority but on behalf of a larger number, who (implicitly at least) not only understand, but appear to approve of what a minority are doing' (p. 6).

19. Noel Turnbull, 'Come in Spinner: is there anything original in politics?', *Crikey*, 26 November 2012, http://www.crikey.com.au/2012/11/26/come-in-spinner-is-there-anything-original-in-politics (accessed 31 January 2017).

20. Tony Abbott, 'Speech notes: The Ethical Responsibilities of a Christian Politician', 16 March 2004, p. 3, available at http://rodneyolsen.net/wp-content/uploads/2004/03/04mar16_ethicalresp_politician.pdf (accessed 31 January 2017).

21. Rudd set out his own religious convictions regarding asylum seekers in an article for *The Monthly* in 2006, esteeming the theologian and active opponent of Nazi Germany Dietrich Bonhoeffer. Entitled 'Faith in Politics', in it Rudd expounded the Christian ideal of caring for the 'vulnerable stranger in our midst'. When the Labor Party, led by Rudd, introduced a hard-line policy towards asylum seekers, criticisms were directed not only to the policy's content, but also to the evident betrayal by Rudd of his own religious convictions.

22. Michael Gordon, 'Tony Abbott's old school hits out at asylum seeker stance as "betraying moral values"', *Sydney Morning Herald*, 21 August 2013, http://www.smh.com.au/federal-politics/federal-election-2013/tony-abbotts-old-school-hits-out-at-asylum-seeker-stance-as-betraying-moral-values-20130821-2savt.html (accessed 31 January 2017).

23. The Coalition's Operation Sovereign Borders Policy', July 2013, https://www.asrc.org.au/wp-content/uploads/2013/07/Operation-Sovereign-Borders_FINAL-Sept-2013.pdf (accessed 7 March 2017).

24. Quoted in Julian Burnside, 'Boat people un-Christian? Wrong, Mr Abbott', ABC News website, 11 July 2012, http://www.abc.net.au/news/2012-07-11/burnside-an-unchristian-view-of-asylum-seekers/4123872 (accessed 31 January 2017).

25. Ibid.

26. Abbott, 'Speech notes: The Ethical Responsibilities of a Christian Politician', p. 5.

27 'No U-turn on abortion: Abbott' by Katharine Murphy, *Sydney Morning Herald*, 21 October 2011, http://www.smh.com.au/national/no-uturn-on-abortion-abbott-20111020-1mac5.html (accessed 7 March 2017).

28. David Marr, *'Power Trip' Rudd v. Abbott 'Political Animal': Two Classic Quarterly Essays* (Collingwood, VIC: Black Inc., 2013), pp. 311–12.

29 .Bernadette Tobin, 'B.A. Santamaria: Aeolian Australian', Quadrant Online, https://quadrant.org.au/magazine/2016/07-08/b-santamaria-aeolian-australian/ (accessed 7 March 2017).

30. Bruce Duncan and Greg Sheridan, 'Remembering Bob Santamaria', *Sydney Papers*, vol. 13, no. 3, 2001, pp. 186–99.

31. Abbott, *Battlelines*, p. 11.

32. 'I'll wear ovaries T-shirt again: Nettle', *Sydney Morning Herald*, 10 February 2006, http://www.smh.com.au/news/national/ill-wear-ovaries-tshirt-againnettle/2006/02/10/1139465826319.html (accessed 31 January 2017).

33. 'Climate Change: Our Responsibility to Sustain God's Earth', Catholic Church in Australia, 19 November 2005, https://www.catholic.org.au/organisation-documents/catholic-earthcare-australia-1/318-bishops-position-paper-on-climate-change-1/file (accessed 31 January 2017).

THERESA MAY (2016–)

NICK SPENCER

INTRODUCTION

In the brief Conservative Party, and therefore prime ministerial, leadership contest in the summer of 2016, the former Tory Chancellor Kenneth Clarke was caught on camera, with a live microphone, making unguarded comments about one of the frontrunners, Theresa May. Theresa, he told his interlocutor, Malcolm Rifkind, was good at her job but a 'bloody difficult woman'. Still, he went on, 'you and I worked for Margaret Thatcher'.

The comparison, which is unlikely to have done May much harm in the contest, was an obvious one to make. Apart from both being Tories, women and formidable – or 'bloody difficult' – both were Oxford educated, both were/are renowned for their appetite for hard work and both were/are practising Christians.

Their Christianity, however, divides at least as much as it unites them. Margaret Thatcher was unashamedly public about her faith, rooting her political outlook in her religious one, and unafraid to assume the pulpit when the occasion demanded, or even when it didn't. May, on the other hand, is rather more circumspect, not only about her faith but also her personal life. That, plus the fact that at the time of writing she had only been in post for six months – having arrived there via a vigorous but short-lived bout of Tory bloodletting which allowed her to circumvent the usual media scrutiny of private and personal details – means that she is, as yet, a difficult subject to speak of with any certainty. We don't know much about Theresa May's faith because we don't yet know much about Theresa May. 'What's my vision for Britain? My philosophy? My approach?' she asked an expectant Tory party conference in October 2016, most of whom had no real idea.

BIOGRAPHY

Theresa Brasier was born in Eastbourne on 1 October 1956, to Zaidee Mary and the Rev. Hubert Brasier, a Church of England vicar. The family later moved to Oxfordshire and she gained a place at a local grammar school, which then became Wheatley Park Comprehensive School during her time there, and thereafter a place at St Hugh's College, Oxford, to study geography, during which time she met her husband Philip May. After graduation, May went to work in the City of London, first at the Bank of England and then at the Association for Payment Clearing Services, where she ended up head of the European Affairs Unit.

May cherished electoral ambitions from her early years – friends from childhood recall her speaking of an ambition to be the nation's first female Prime Minister – and, in 1986, she was elected as a local councillor in Merton, south London, serving there for a decade and eventually becoming deputy leader. She first stood for Parliament in the safe Labour seat of North West Durham in 1992, and then again in a by-election for Barking in east London in 1994, where she polled fewer than 2,000 votes and suffered under the cloud of the unpopular and divided Conservative government of the time.

She finally won a parliamentary seat, for Maidenhead, in 1997, and was taken onto the front bench shortly after, first as shadow education secretary, then shadow transport secretary. Following a spell in 2002–03 as Conservative Party chair, she was appointed shadow culture secretary, shadow leader of the House of Commons and shadow work and pensions secretary, before she became home secretary in the 2010 coalition government.

May was an unexpected home secretary – the position was thought to be Chris Grayling's, who had shadowed the brief in opposition – but she remained there for longer than anyone else in modern times. Her time at the Home Office was dominated by running battles with the police (so to speak) over reform, a more authoritarian approach to data gathering and surveillance, and, above all, immigration, which she pledged but failed to reduce. Her time there showed her to be competent and tough but prepared – in the notorious example of sending vans around London telling illegal immigrants to go home or face arrest – to countenance efforts that were ineffective and morally questionable.[1]

PRIVATE LIFE

May's private life is indeed private. Months after her acceding to the highest office in the land, political pundits were still asking who she was and what she stood for.

This is partly as a result of her having been a political outsider, both, it appears, through temperament and through circumstance. She first came to public notice in 2002 for exposing her party, at its conference, to the fact that it was widely known as 'the nasty party'. Criticised by some for publicly acknowledging this harsh truth, May had positioned herself as having enough perspective, honesty and toughness to see and admit what others did not.

That 'nasty' Tory 'brand' was detoxified, to some degree, over the next decade by David Cameron, but May was never part of Cameron's inner circle and remained an outsider. According to the memoir of his time in the coalition government, the former Liberal Democrat minister David Laws wrote about how May 'would frequently clash with George Osborne over immigration ... rarely got on anything but badly with Michael Gove... [and she and] Cameron seemed to view each other with mutual suspicion'. She had particular reputation for straight dealing and toughness. According to Laws, following a 'difficult' meeting with May, the then Deputy Prime Minister, Nick Clegg, admitted that he had 'grown to rather like' her despite the fact that 'she's a bit of an Ice Maiden and has no small talk whatsoever'.[2] This reputation did, however, earn her respect rather than enemies, a respect that was augmented by a widespread sense that she listened to people and worked very hard, being, according to her Labour shadow at the Home Office, Yvette Cooper, 'steady and serious [and] authoritative in parliament'.[3]

PRIVATE FAITH

May has said on several occasions – although admittedly not as many as Margaret Thatcher – that she owed a lot to her father. Hubert Brasier was the son of a regimental sergeant-major and a former parlour maid. He trained at the College of the Resurrection at Mirfield, Yorkshire, and was chaplain of All Saints' Hospital, Eastbourne, when May was born. The family subsequently moved to Oxfordshire so that he could take up the post of vicar of Enstone with Heythrop, and then Wheatley in 1970. According to the *Financial Times*, parish records and interviews with former members of his congregation reveal an image of 'a local vicar whose seriousness, conservatism, High Anglican beliefs and steadfast devotion to duty left an indelible imprint on his only child'.[4]

May has underlined much of this. She told a Conservative campaign video in 2016 that 'my father encouraged me to, whatever job I did, just go get on with it and do my best,' and said to Andrew Marr at the start of the 2016 Conservative Party conference that what she learned from her parents 'was a very strong belief in public service and in always trying to understand what you need to do for other people'. She has, however, been somewhat more circumspect about her father's politics, not so much denying his Conservatism as emphasising how his pastoral role was very deliberately an inclusive one. Thus, she told Marr that, as a clergyman, her father

> took a very simple view. He was the clergyman for the whole of his parish. He was the local vicar and it wasn't right for him to set out what his politics were, because he should be appealing [to] and working with everyone in his parish ... He wanted to ensure that nobody felt that he was somebody he couldn't approach.

Critics will naturally point out that this was precisely the image May was trying to cast over her new administration and that there may well have been a bit of retrospective reimagining going on here, but there are sufficient similar recollections (albeit from nearly half a century ago: May's father was killed in a road accident in 1981) to suggest that there is truth in her claims.

May's early life naturally revolved around the parish. She attended her father's church and taught some Sunday school classes there, even going back to attend the annual meeting of the parochial church council when she had left for Oxford (which was, admittedly, not far away). She insisted that her father never 'imposed' his Christianity on her as a child and her parents 'always said to me, that obviously they would very much like it if I were a regular churchgoer and so forth but they weren't going to force me to go'.[5] One of the two hymns May chose when a guest on the BBC Radio 4 programme *Desert Island Discs* was entitled Lingua Gloriosi Corporis Mysterium (sometimes sung as English the hymn 'Of the glorious body telling', the words originally written by St Thomas Aquinas), of which she said, 'It comes from a hymn which sometimes, if my father, mother and I were just alone in the church, we would just kneel down and sing.'

As a consequence of this parental latitude, she attended 'of my own choosing', the result being that, unlike some friends who were clergy daughters but who felt under more compulsion and therefore 'kicked over the traces', she remained and remains a practising Anglican. 'I do call myself a Christian, and I am still a practising member of the Church of England,' she told *High Profiles*.[6] It was a faith that she grew into. There was never any 'blinding flash' or 'point in time at which I can say I decided to be a Christian'. Rather, there was 'a positive process' in 'accepting' the strong, family 'Christian faith' within which she grew up. The Christian faith is 'part of who I am and therefore how I approach things ... [it] helps to frame my thinking and my approach'. When asked by the *Sunday Times* about how she dealt with the toughness and moral challenges of office, she replied, 'I suppose there is something in terms of faith, I am a practising member of the Church of England and so forth, [and] that lies behind what I do.'[7] The 'and so forth' is masterful, an almost perfectly Anglican parenthesis.

POLITICAL FAITH

Pinpointing how that faith frames May's political life is somewhat harder, however, and her statements on the matter tend towards the general. When asked by *High Profiles* in 2003 – still the most detailed and acute profile of her beliefs – what lasting values being brought up a vicar's daughter instilled in her, May said that it was 'the value of service to others, always wanting to help others to make a difference to their lives'. She cited her father (in the way that Gordon Brown and Margaret Thatcher were usually comfortable doing with theirs), in May's case for the fact that 'his job wasn't just doing services on Sunday mornings' but for being 'very good at visiting people in the village'. After he died (in the same year May's mother passed away), May remembered people from a previous parish remarking on how he had touched their life enormously, despite the fact that 'they had never darkened the doors of the church'.

Such a model might have led her politically left or right, but May has indicated how her Christianity in fact led her to Conservatism. Reaching political maturity in the 1970s, she was faced with 'a clear-cut choice between Conservatism and socialism', and although there were plenty at the time who put forward a forceful 'Christian moral argument' for socialism, she felt that the left and, in particular, 'its extreme form, communism' denied the value of the individual and was therefore less consonant with Christian beliefs: 'it actually isn't based on what I would call "Christianity"'. By contrast, she believed that Conservatism offered a better recognition of 'the value of the individual' but also of 'their relationship with others in society and their need to contribute to a society, to be part of that greater thing'.

This second, corrective point seems important to May because she acknowledged that the back end of the Thatcher/Major years – being the time when she twice failed in her attempt at getting a seat – was a difficult period in which the value of the individual *as individual* had been taken too far. In the first instance, from the time that Margaret Thatcher took the Tory reins in the mid-1970s, there had been, in May's view,

a very real need to release the energies and abilities of individuals and to give them that opportunity to blossom, to shine, to do what they wanted to do, rather than feeling that the state was stopping them from (if you like) being able to achieve what they wanted to achieve.

This was textbook Thatcherism, as was May's ensuing comment that it was 'very important to release that dead hand of state control'. However, albeit with some carefully chosen caveats, May claims that by the end of this four-term period in office, 'rightly or wrongly, people felt [we] just promoted the individual without promoting the community and realising their role in society as a whole'.

May's opening parenthesis in that statement carefully disguises the extent to which she thinks 'people' were right or wrong in holding this impression but the very fact she raised this popular concern marks her off from the ideologically purer Thatcherites, as does her claim that it was precisely that perception that lost the Tories the 1997 election.[8] Whether it was on account of this ideological discomfort with an unencumbered liberal view of the individual drifting away from a more visibly Christian view of the relation-ally embedded individual, or whether it was because she felt with particular pointedness the bleakness of the Tories' exile to the political wilderness in 1997 – when people seriously spoke of the possibility of there not being another Conservative administration in their lifetime, possibly ever – May became one of the party's modernisers, most visibly in her 2002 conference speech.

The *High Profiles* interview, coming more or less at this point, gestured to the direction in which May wanted to take the party, which, she gently suggested, had been where the party had always been truest to itself. 'Com-passionate, or caring, Conservatism – whatever phrase one attaches to it', she claimed, 'is that it is actually, if you like, core Conservatism.' This was a po-litical philosophy that rejected the kind of government that 'denies people's ability to find how they want to be and to make decisions for themselves, their families and their local communities', but at the same time was actively involved in giving 'people a helping hand to help themselves and others'. She went on:

> We've always been a party that believed that, while we should be releasing the abilities and energies of individuals, people do have a place within society and we should always ensure that the government provides a safety net for those who can't help themselves and, for a whole variety of reasons, find themselves in particular difficulties.

This was a vision in which government, although warned off any ideas that it could run the economy, is not, in itself, a problem to be overcome.

This idea of government as enabling mutual service across society dovetails well with what May appears to have taken from Christianity. 'Our approach is not just about freeing individuals, it's about freeing communities as well', not least communities like the Church:

> To me, the Christian faith is not just about the moral issues but about ena-
> bling people to be individuals, while recognising that 'no man is an island'.
> We are interlinked with others and have a role to play in giving service to
> others and improving (if you like) the common good by what we do.

This was the role that Christianity played in her politics – underpinning the sense of mutual rights and responsibilities, and exercising those responsibilities through practical service. It was also, she hinted, the way in which the Church would itself be renewed within society, responding to the spiritual thirst:

> Some of the churches I've been involved in have been very lively and have
> had a lot of people, and it has often started because they offer activities and
> that sort of thing and then people start to feel comfortable coming in and
> they probably know they want something else in life

May may have parted company with the more individualistic path taken by Thatcher's heirs, but she also parted company with the more socially conservative tone that marked Thatcher's own view, just as she did from Thatcher's own more public, and somewhat more muscular, Christianity. If she rejected new Tory hyper-individualism, she also rejected old-school Tory moralising.

When asked by *High Profiles* whether she thought as a nation we were becoming 'spiritually bankrupt', her reply was tentative. She agreed that maybe there was 'a real issue that a lot of people [were] yearning for something more spiritual in their lives but don't find a way of achieving that', but she went on to say firstly that 'there is a genuine question about the extent to which politicians are in the business of imposing moral values on people', and secondly that 'there are issues for the church, as well, in how it presents itself and offers that to people'. It was a typically guarded response, which simultaneously acknowledged a spiritual need in society and insinuated that neither politicians nor ecclesiastics were ideally placed to do anything about it. The Conservatives' much-mocked 'Back to Basics' campaign from the 1990s had been sealed in concrete and buried deep underground.

IN POWER

At the time of writing, May was still on prime ministerial honeymoon, the real impact – indeed the real nature – of Brexit still to reveal itself. And yet, her first few months in power indicated, albeit only rhetorically at that stage, a definite change in tone and direction for the government.

Her Downing Street speech as the newly appointed Prime Minister, which borrowed liberally from her opening address in the brief leadership campaign, struck a distinctly different note, as did her first conference speech as premier. In the first instance, the style of government under May appears to have changed from the informality of the Blair years and the cliqueyness of the Cameron ones, with cabinet members claiming that there is now more discussion, more consultation and more formality, although with the same defined hierarchy of recent administrations.[9]

More substantially, the underlying ideas and objectives seemed to have shifted too. 'The central tenet of my belief is that there is more to life than individualism and self-interest,' she told her conference audience.[10] 'We applaud success ... but we also value something else: the spirit of citizenship ... We form families, communities, towns, cities, counties and nations [and] have a responsibility to one another,' she said, a responsibility that government also shares.

This was a major theme. 'We are a country built on the bonds of family, community, citizenship ... of strong institutions and a strong society', and one that she linked back to her upbringing: 'the country of my parents, who instilled in me a sense of public service and of public servants everywhere

who want to give something back'. Hers was a vision of the priority of civil
society, whose health and security government is mandated to serve, 'to
encourage and nurture those relationships, networks and institutions' and
'to step up to correct injustices and tackle unfairness where it can'. It was
a speech in which the individual, when s/he featured, was almost always
positioned in some kind of relational network:[11]

> The state exists to provide what individual people ... cannot ... I want
> Britain to be a country in which every child has access to a good school
> place that's right for that individual child ... We saw how individual suc-
> cess was powered by collective effort ... Work coaches are giving individu-
> al advice to each claimant, helping them take control of their own lives ...
> That helps each individual contribute what they can'

Alternatively, s/he appeared in an altogether more negative guise: 'No individual tycoon and no single business, however rich, has succeeded on their
own ... there is more to life than individualism and self-interest.'[12]

Moreover, the rhetoric appeared to carry through into some surprising
specificity: workers' rights and their representation on company boards (a
proposal soon to be watered down); a willingness for the state to step in 'to
repair' free markets 'when they aren't working as they should'; 'a new industrial strategy';[13] attacks on the kind of boss 'who earns a fortune but doesn't
look after your staff'; and the aggressive pursuit of anyone – 'accountant, a
financial adviser or a middleman' – who 'helps people to avoid what they
owe to society'. It was the kind of speech that might have been delivered by
Ed Miliband, the previous Labour Party leader, although it would have been
greeted in a very different way by much of the press.[14]

Without ever abandoning the core creeds of individual worth and opportunity, which May stressed had brought her into politics, it was a speech
located in a clear commitment to relationally rooted individuals,[15] served by
a positive vision of 'the good that government can do',[16] and all framed as a
rejection of 'the ideological templates provided by the socialist left and the
libertarian right', without ever daring to utter a phrase like 'the middle' or

'third way'. *The Economist* wasn't very enthusiastic.[17] *The Guardian*'s Polly
Toynbee searched for reasons to dislike it.[18] And her colleague Giles Fraser,
the paper's resident vicar, gave it 'two cheers'.

CONCLUSION

The question we might like to pose, by way of conclusion, is how far any of
what we see in Prime Minister May is traceable to her Christian convictions.
The apparent consonance between the two, in so far as we can accurately
identify it, suggests the answer might be a great deal, but that is liable to
get Theresa May wrong, just as it is liable to get the relationship between
the Almighty and the mighty wrong. Politicians, not least leading ones in
modern, plural democracies, tend not to construct their political edifices
simply according to their spiritual blueprints.

May is an instinctively private individual and politician. Writing a matter
of months after her arrival in No. 10, the *Guardian* columnist Martin Kettle
observed, rightly, that she is not an economic liberal like Thatcher, nor a social
liberal like Cameron. Indeed, 'liberalism of any kind seems almost a marginal
consideration in her thinking and her policy making', and although these were
clearly still early days, he ventured that 'May's speeches, both before and after
becoming Prime Minister, are unified by post-liberal thinking'.[19]

The content of this analysis seems right, but the framing wrong, af-
fording May a degree of philosophical and ideological coherence that
never appears to have animated, or bothered, her. May is a politician with
strong views rather than a strong ideology, and those views were seemingly
shaped by her Christian upbringing and faith. That Christianity gives her,
in her own words, 'a moral backing to what I do, and I would hope that
the decisions I take are taken on the basis of my faith'. It is a faith, she
went on to say in interview, that '"informs" those decisions', a phrase that
she immediately went on to apologise for, for being 'terribly jargonistic'.[20]
Christianity 'helps to frame my thinking and my approach,' she told *Desert
Island Discs*, before going on to say that it is 'right that we don't flaunt these
things here in British politics'. In this regard at the very least, May practises what
she preaches.

NOTES

1. Alan Travis, '"Go home" vans resulted in 11 people leaving Britain, says report', *The Guardian*, 31 October 2013, https://www.theguardian.com/uk-news/2013/oct/31/go-home-vans-11-leave-britain (accessed 31 January 2017).

2. David Laws, *Coalition: The Inside Story of the Conservative–Liberal Democrat Coalition* (Biteback Publishing, 2016), p. 274. David Cameron is supposed to have agreed wholeheartedly, saying, 'She's exactly like that with me too.'

3 Yvette Cooper, 'Theresa May helped to divide Britain. She won't heal it', *The Guardian*, 7 July 2016, https://www.theguardian.com/commentisfree/2016/jul/07/theresa-may-britain-tory-candidate (accessed 7 March 2017).

4. 'The making of May: her faith and father shaped British PM's core', *Financial Times*, 2 October 2016.

5 'Looking Right', http://highprofiles.info (accessed 7 March 2017). This is probably the most detailed and revealing interview on May's beliefs to date.

6. 'Looking Right', http://highprofiles.info

7. Eleanor Mills, 'The interview: Theresa May', *Sunday Times*, 27 November 2016, http://www.thetimes.co.uk/magazine/the-sunday-times-magazine/the-interview-theresa-may-hmpgom2lg (accessed 31 January 2017).

8. While that may be true, is it also true to say that after nearly eighteen years in power, faced with the eruption of New Labour, and when even the *Daily Telegraph* abandoned the Tory Party, nothing short of a miracle would have won them the 1997 election.

9. Laura Kuenssberg, 'How government is changing under Theresa May', BBC News website, 19 September 2016, http://www.bbc.co.uk/news/uk-politics-37408893 (accessed 31 January 2017).

10. 'Prime Minister: the good that government can do', http://press.conservatives.com (accessed 31 January 2017).

11. The two exceptions are her statements that 'it is the fabric of our free society – the order, the stability, the equality and the individual freedom – that we all love and respect', and that 'for more than 1,000 years this country has led the world on protecting individual freedoms'.

12. See also her more tangential reference to 'individuals who prey on vulnerable men and women ... where innocent people were murdered by a radicalised individual'.

13. 'Identifying the industries that are of strategic value to our economy and supporting and promoting them through policies on trade, tax, infrastructure, skills, training, and research and development.'

14. It is a curiosity that May was praised by the tabloids for much of what she said, whereas Miliband would have been unlikely to be so lauded. This could be because commentators would have feared Miliband's rhetoric was a disguise for a more radically left-wing agenda, whereas many presumably thought that in May's instance it was PR for a more radically right-wing one. More cynically, it may simply be because some sections of the press would oppose the Labour Party even if it started to take its cue from Milton Friedman.

15. 'If you believe you're a citizen of the world, you're a citizen of nowhere. You don't understand what the very word "citizenship" means.'

16. 'The state exists to provide what individual people, communities and markets cannot.'

17. 'May's revolutionary conservatism', *The Economist*, 5 October 2016, http://www.economist.com/news/britain/21708223-britains-new-prime-minister-signals-new-illiberal-direction-country (accessed 31 January 2017).

18. 'The stirring sermon delivered by the vicar's daughter, a homily on morality, social justice and fairness that could have come from Labour (bar the anti-immigration riffs). What party doesn't pitch for "everyone", "one nation", "the many not the few"?' ('Will Theresa May's speech appeal beyond Tory conference? Our panel's verdict', *The Guardian*, 5 October 2016, https://www.theguardian.com/commentisfree/2016/oct/05/theresa-may-speech-tory-conference-panel-verdict (accessed 31 January 2017).

19. Martin Kettle, 'Brexit was a revolt against liberalism. We've entered a new political era', *The Guardian*, 15 September 2016, https://www.theguardian.com/commentisfree/2016/sep/15/brexit-liberalism-post-liberal-age (accessed 31 January 2017).

20 'Looking Right', http://highprofiles.info

DONALD TRUMP (2017–)

NICK SPENCER

There are many reasons why Donald Trump should not be in this volume.[1] Mr Trump had been US President for a matter of weeks at the time of writing. Prior to that, he had never held public office of any kind. He is not known for his interest in theology, the Church or religion. His statements about faith, not least his own faith, have been infrequent and vague.

And yet, Trump is insistent that he believes in God, loves the Bible and has a good relationship with the Church. He made some loud Christian noises on the campaign trail and garnered a remarkable level of support among (white, evangelical) Christians. His first days in office have been marked by political appointments and policy gestures calculated to appeal to the 'Religious Right'. Simply to dismiss Trump's faith talk would be to dismiss Trump, and 2016 showed that that is a mistake.

BIOGRAPHY

Donald John Trump was born in New York in 1946, the fourth child and second son of Frederick Christ Trump, the son of German immigrants, and Mary Anne Trump, née MacLeod, who had been born on the Scottish island of Lewis.

Frederick and Mary Anne were a wealthy couple, having made money through real estate; when he died in 1999, Frederick left a (much-contested) will of nearly $300 million. The family lived in New York and Donald attended the New York Military Academy from the age of thirteen, although managed to avoid combat in Vietnam. He went on to study economics at the University of Pennsylvania and to work in the family real estate company, then called Elizabeth Trump & Son, before taking over control in 1971 (his older brother showing little interest in business).

The company, which he renamed the Trump Organization, would be famously successful and unsuccessful. A number of real estate deals in Manhattan and New York would turn the company into a multi-billion-dollar enterprise, and over the years Trump would add numerous hotels, golf courses and casinos to his portfolio. However, many of his enterprises would be declared bankrupt – six times in total between 1991 and 2009 – and, although Trump himself never personally filed for bankruptcy, leaked tax returns from the mid-1990s reported enormous business losses which meant that he was able to escape paying income tax for much of the next two decades.

Alongside his business affairs, Trump developed a powerful media presence, primarily through the US reality TV programme *The Apprentice*, which proved enormously popular and financially rewarding, a role Trump left in 2015 to pursue his political ambitions.

Those ambitions were famously dismissed as fantastical and outrageous by many people during the Republican primaries and in the early stages of the presidential campaign. Donald Trump had never held any public office at any level, a deficiency he turned into a virtue in the light of the widespread public disaffection with 'Washington'. He had no long-standing allegiance to any particular party or political ideology. He showed few signs of grasping, or wanting to grasp, geo-political details, openly disputed with the intelligence services, refused to confirm he would accept the result of the election if he lost, and generally exhibited such a profound lack of experience and interest as to cause fifty former national security officials to sign a letter saying he was 'not qualified to be president and commander-in-chief … [and] would put at risk our country's national security and well-being'.[2]

Over and above this professional inexperience were the personal flaws he revealed on the campaign trail and, in particular, an attitude to women that could be bluntly misogynistic.

Trump married the Czech-born American businesswoman Ivana Zelníčková in 1977, with whom he had three children. They divorced fourteen years later when it emerged that Trump was having an affair with Marla Maples. Trump and Maples then married in 1993 but split six years later, after which Trump remarried again, this time to Melania Knauss, a Slovenian-born American model, with whom he has one child.

Throughout his marriages Trump was dogged by multiple accusations of sexual misconduct – numbers vary but certainly exceed a dozen. He dismissed these as political smears but did little to help his image when he implied that Fox News' Megyn Kelly asked him a tough question during a TV debate because she was menstruating,[3] and was then revealed, on a ten-year-old recording, boasting about sexual harassment. 'I moved on her, and I failed,' he told radio and television host Billy Bush, talking about TV host Nancy O'Dell. 'I did try and fuck her. She was married ... And I moved on her very heavily ... I moved on her like a bitch. But I couldn't get there. And she was married.'[4] In case this wasn't candid and revealing enough of his character, he went on to tell his friend, 'You know, I'm automatically attracted to beautiful – I just start kissing them. It's like a magnet... When you're a star, they let you do it. You can do anything... Grab 'em by the pussy. You can do anything.'

Such views were complemented by his mockery of Serge Kovaleski, a reporter with arthrogryposis, or congenital joint contractures (something Trump subsequently denied doing); his description of Mexican immigrants as criminals and rapists; and his blanket hostility toward and interdiction of Muslims entering America. Although he received nearly three million fewer votes than Hillary Clinton, he won 56 per cent of electors in the Electoral College and took the oath of office on 20 January 2017.

SPIRITUAL BIOGRAPHY

According to Michael Gove, the first British journalist to conduct an interview with the new President, Donald Trump is less influenced by religion than any President since Richard Nixon.[5] While the analysis of Presidents in this book would support that verdict, it would be wrong to assume that this meant that Trump is unfamiliar with, indifferent to, or, still less, hostile to Christianity.

Trump's parents were Presbyterians, who attended Marble Collegiate Church in Manhattan. Part of the Reform Church in America, Marble Collegiate

Church is best known for being one of the oldest continuous congregations in America, having been founded in 1628, and for its mid-century pastor Norman Vincent Peale. Peale headed up the church for over half a century from 1932, speaking to congregations that could number in the thousands, many drawn there by his book *The Power of Positive Thinking*. This was a fairly normal example of the self-help genre, but one that was driven to abnormal success – it remained on *the New York Times* bestseller list for over three years – by the way it managed to blend 'worldliness with godliness', resulting in 'an easy-to-follow theology that preached self-confidence as a life philosophy'.[6]

Both the book and its author were criticised by theologians and church leaders at the time for a partial, materialistic and egocentric understanding of Christianity in which the individual assumed centre stage, sin was replaced by negativity, redemption by optimism, and Jesus Christ tacked on as something of an afterthought. Positive thinking was deemed vaguely cultish, evasive and morally thin. It was, however, rather popular.

Trump knew Peale as a child, attended his church for several years and retained a connection with him into his adult life, Peale marrying Trump and Ivana in 1977. Trump would latterly refer to Peale with admiration, remarking at the Iowa Family Leadership Summit in 2015 that he still now remembered Peale's sermons: 'He would bring real-life situations, modern-day situations into the sermon. And you could listen to him all day long. When you left the church, you were disappointed that it was over.'[7]

Peale's influence was not total. Peale was married for sixty-three years, led a scandal-free life and condemned the 1952 Democratic presidential candidate Adlai Stevenson II as unfit for office on account of his being divorced (a condemnation that elicited Stevenson's memorable riposte: 'Speaking as a Christian, I find Saint Paul appealing and Saint Peale appalling'). However else Peale's Christianity influenced Trump, it wasn't in his attitude to marriage, divorce or women.

In as far as Peale did influence Trump – one cannot dismiss the possibility that there was simply a happy coincidence between the pastor's message and Trump's natural worldview – we see in Trump's faith a similar egocentric confidence – a kind of 'moral therapeutic deism'[8] – rather than anything one might identify as informed by Christian doctrine or orthodoxy.

In his book, *Think Like a Billionaire*, Trump wrote that if God 'ever wanted an apartment in Trump Tower, I would immediately offer my best luxury suite at a very special price'.[9] This reads like quite a good joke, not least as the preceding phrase tells his reader 'for the record I do not think I am God'. However, his ensuing words – 'I believe God is everywhere and in all of us, and I want every decision I make to reflect well on me when it's time for me to go to that big boardroom in the sky. When I get permanently fired by the ultimate boss, I want the elevator to heaven to go up, not down' – suggest that the billionaire was being serious, and could imagine God incarnated in a cut-price penthouse suite rather than a Bethlehem stable.

He went into more detail, of sorts, in an interview with *The Brody File*.[10] 'I believe in God. I am Christian,' he told David Brody, a journalist for the Christian Broadcasting Network. 'I think The Bible is certainly, it is THE book ... I've had a good relationship with the church over the years. I think religion is a wonderful thing.' When pressed about whether he went to church, he said he went 'as much as I can', although what this actually meant was not entirely clear. 'Always on Christmas. Always on Easter. Always when there's a major occasion. And during the Sundays. I'm a Sunday church person. I'll go when I can.'

A further, if slightly idiosyncratic, illustration of the nature of his faith was in his revelation that he was sent Bibles by many people. Being based in Manhattan, he hadn't the space to keep all his mail but he refused, out of respect, to bin the Bibles he received. 'There's no way I would ever throw anything, to do anything negative to a Bible, so what we do is we keep all of the Bibles.'

Respecting the Bible was not the same as knowing it, however, and questions of – and about – Trump's knowledge and understanding followed him around the campaign trail. Having said that it was his favourite book, ahead of his own *Art of the Deal*, he refused to name a favourite Bible verse, telling Bloomberg Television that he didn't want 'to get into specifics', and leading some critics to doubt whether he knew any.[11] A few months later, when asked the same question, he replied that it was 'an eye for an eye',[12] a revealing, if odd, choice of Bible verse for a Christian, given Christ's abrogation of the command. He subsequently said he liked the book of Proverbs and in particular 'the chapter "never bend to envy"', which doesn't appear to exist.[13]

More significantly, Trump pooh-poohed the idea that he needed to repent or ask God for forgiveness for his actions. 'I am not sure I have. I just go on and try to do a better job from there ... if I do something wrong, I think, I just try and make it right. I don't bring God into that picture. I don't.'[14] Quoting chapter and verse is a pretty superficial, party-game way of identifying someone's Christianity. Hearing them reject the need for repentance is somewhat more substantial. While this attitude may have been in keeping with Norman Vincent Peale's positive thinking (and even then it may have been stretching it somewhat), it is harder to square with the famously blunt but oft-quoted New Testament verse, 'If we claim to be without sin, we deceive ourselves and the truth is not in us.'[15]

CHRISTIAN SUPPORT

Given Trump's patchy and idiosyncratic knowledge of the Bible, his marital and sexual history and his disavowal of the need for repentance, one would have assumed that America's Christians, and in particular the country's large and influential evangelical constituency – for whom biblical knowledge, sexual propriety and personal repentance are conspicuously important – would have found little reason to support Donald Trump.

At first, they did not. Prominent evangelicals, like James Dobson of Focus on the Family, threw their weight behind Senator Ted Cruz. Anti-abortion women released an open letter entitled 'Pro-Life Women Sound the Alarm: Donald Trump Is Unacceptable'.[16] According to the Pew Research Center, as late as April 2016, only a third (34 per cent) of Americans who attended religious services weekly said that Trump was the preferred Republican nominee, whereas well over half (57 per cent) were Trump 'skeptics ... having not expressed support for Trump as the GOP nominee in any of the three surveys' (December 2015, March 2016 and April 2016).[17] One profile said confidently that those 'for whom religion is the central thing in their lives will likely be more put off by him than those whose connection to Christianity is more limited'.[18]

It made sense at the time but turned out to be a dreadful prediction. Trump's Christian constituency began to swell when he achieved the nomination, and swelled further when it became clear that he would be standing

against Hillary Clinton. Nomination secured, Trump released a long list
of evangelical advisors, not, his press release made clear, because they had
formally agreed to support him, but rather because he wanted to endorse
them: 'The board represents Donald J. Trump's endorsement of those diverse
issues important to Evangelicals and other Christians and his desire to have
access to the wise counsel of such leaders as needed.'[19] It was reminiscent of
Reagan's address to the national convention of the Religious Roundtable in
1980, though without Reagan's cinematic charm.*

Trump's support began to grow. Richard Land, seminary president and
Southern Baptist leader, joined the advisory board, on the grounds that it
was his 'spiritual obligation and responsibility to speak biblical truth in love
to all who will listen', though did not endorse Trump.[20] Popular author,
speaker and radio host Eric Metaxas lent his support. James Dobson came
round to the cause. Jerry Falwell Jr, president of Liberty University and son
of late Moral Majority founder Jerry Falwell, was a long-standing and vocal
supporter.[21]

Much of this support was transparently because Trump was the not-
Hillary candidate, Hillary Clinton animating a spectacular fear and loathing
among millions in America who would have voted for pretty much any
human being in history to prevent her acceding to the Oval Office.

For others, however, Trump was a genuine and sincere born-again believer,
albeit one who had much to learn of the faith. 'I believe he really made a
commitment,' James Dobson said, adding that 'he's a baby Christian ... You
got to cut him some slack.'[22] Falwell said that Trump 'lives a life of loving and
helping others as Jesus taught in the Great Commandment'.[23] Most prominently, pastor and evangelist Paula White, who was credited with leading
Trump to faith and who delivered a prayer at his inauguration, insisted that
'I have heard Mr Trump verbally acknowledge his faith in Jesus Christ for the
forgiveness of his sins through prayer'.[24] 'I know that President-elect Trump
has a personal relationship with the Lord Jesus Christ,' she added on the eve
of the inauguration. 'We've had in-depth conversations about God', although
she too acknowledged that he 'doesn't speak what I call "Christianese"'.[25]

---

*   See p. 17.

Christian, indeed even evangelical, support was not ubiquitous. When Jerry Falwell Jr voiced his support, over 2,000 students from his university signed a petition opposing the Republican candidate. Nearly eighty evangelical leaders signed a petition in October declaring that 'Mr Trump has fueled white American nationalism with xenophobic appeals and religious intolerance at the expense of gospel values, democratic principles, and important international relationships'.[26] Russell Moore of the Southern Baptist Convention's Ethics and Religious Liberty Commission said that 'for evangelicals to support Donald Trump would mean tossing aside everything that evangelicals have previously said about character matters and about human dignity.'[27]

Most substantially, Andy Crouch, formerly editor of *Christianity Today*, wrote a scathing critique of Donald in a pre-election article, which was hardly uncritical of Hillary Clinton. Trump's obsession with wealth, success and the self, and his 'vile and crude boasting about sexual conquest', exemplified precisely what St Paul urged the early Colossian Christians to avoid: 'sexual immorality, impurity, lust, evil desires, and greed, which is idolatry'. Crouch's words to Trump-supporting evangelicals were not much more emollient:

> Enthusiasm for a candidate like Trump gives our neighbours ample reason to doubt that we believe Jesus is Lord. They see that some of us are so self-interested, and so self-protective, that we will ally ourselves with someone who violates all that is sacred to us – in hope, almost certainly a vain hope given his mendacity and record of betrayal, that his rule will save us.[28]

If not quite voices crying in a wilderness, such evangelical complaints went unheard or unheeded. According to the Pew Forum, 58 per cent of Protestants voted for Trump (versus 39 per cent who voted for Clinton), as did 81 per cent of white evangelicals – a higher proportion than had done for George W. Bush in 2004.

IN POWER

A week may be a long time in politics, but a month is not long enough to judge the theo-politics of a new President.

Opinions of what we should expect of Trump from the nature of his appointments vary. Some, like Michael Gove, have argued that Trump has 'tended to appoint people on the basis of either business expertise or military expertise … rather than coming from particular traditions'.[29] Others, like Michelle Goldberg in the *New York Times*, have insisted that 'for all his flagrant sinfulness, he's assembling a near-theocratic administration, his cabinet full of avowed enemies of church–state separation'.[30]

For all that this verdict is marred by the 'theocratic' hyperbole so favoured by liberal critics, it is clear that, however thin Trump's own loyalty to the Republican Party is, his is clearly a Republican administration, staffed by people with views on issues like abortion, sexual ethics, taxation, education, faith and evolution that Democrats and secularists (and some Christians) do not like. Some appointments, like Rex Tillerson as Secretary of State (who, as head of Exxon Mobil, acknowledged anthropogenic climate change and, as head of the Scouts, opened its membership to gay youth) may not quite fit the stereotype. Others – like Steve Bannon, formerly of Breitbart News, now White House chief strategist, Mike Pompeo, as CIA director, or the Vice-President himself, Mike Pence, a Catholic altar boy turned evangelical – fulfil every liberal fear.

Whether Trump's libertinism makes him 'the perfect Trojan Horse for conservative values', as Michelle Goldberg put it, is too early to tell. What his first few weeks in power do show is a willingness to pursue conservative causes that are more reflective of Trump's supporters than of Trump himself.

Not long after inauguration day, the President reinstated the so-called 'gag rule', preventing those NGOs that receive American state funding from conducting, or offering information about, abortions, a rule introduced by Ronald Reagan in 1984 and treated as a political football by incoming Republican and Democrat administrations ever since. Shortly after that, Mike Pence spoke to the March for Life in Washington, DC, the highest-ranking official to appear at this annual pro-life event.[31] Trump has also made promises to defund Planned Parenthood, America's single largest abortion provider.

These are all classic Religious Right moves but it is worth recalling that one of the few 'Did he say that?' moments in his presidential campaign from which Trump rowed back was his off-the-cuff statement that there should be some form of punishment for women who have abortions were the practice to become illegal in the US.[32] This achieved the remarkable feat of uniting (in opposition) both pro-life and pro-choice campaigners, something that many thought impossible, but it also underlined how little thought-through was Trump's own view on this issue. In this regard, the early pro-life noises made by his administration seem to reflect less the President's carefully considered views on the issue, still less his long-standing faith-based commitments, as they did for someone like Ronald Reagan or George W. Bush, but more those of the support base that brought him into power and to which he is happy to give space and support.

More authentically Trump, as evidenced in the earliest weeks of his presidency, is another aspect of Norman Vincent Peale's Christianity heretofore not mentioned: its fiercely patriotic spirit.

Preaching and writing during the Cold War, Peale's Christianity, like that of Whittaker Chambers, who proved such an influence on Ronald Reagan, was loudly patriotic, seeing in America's Christianity a sign of divine favour and responsibility against the totalitarian godlessness of Soviet Communism. Trump arrived in the White House at a time in which, for all their recently heightened tensions, relations between America and Russia were on a different scale than in Peale's time. Nevertheless, these rather different conditions notwithstanding, a similarly patriotic tone suffused both Trump's campaign – 'Make American Great Again' – and his first days in office.

This was well seen in his inaugural address. The speech was comparatively brief, at sixteen minutes and a little over 1,400 words, but mentioned 'America', 'American' or 'Americans' thirty-four times. Trump promised that 'from this moment on, it's going to be America First'. He said that they would rebuild the country 'with American hands and American labour', that 'every decision on trade, on taxes, on immigration, on foreign affairs, will be made to benefit American workers and American families'. He ended with the rousing, repetitive, rallying cry, 'Together, We Will Make America Strong Again. We Will Make America Wealthy Again. We Will Make America Proud Again. We Will Make America Safe Again. And, Yes, Together, We Will Make America Great Again.'[33]

This resolute focus shifted the address from being patriotic, which all inaugurals are by definition, to being straightforwardly nationalistic, a fact underlined by his declaration that the day of his inauguration should be a 'national day of patriotic devotion'. The theologian Stanley Hauerwas was not alone in picking up the significance of that last word, writing in the *Washington Post*, 'Patriotic devotion? Christians are devoted to God, not to any nation.'[34]

Trump's address was, in fact, no more biblically or theologically saturated than previous inaugurals, although the ceremony was symbolically heavily Christian, with a record six separate prayers spoken and with Trump being sworn in on two Bibles (his mother's to him and the Lincoln Bible). The speech itself contained only one reference to the Bible (Psalm 133:1): 'The Bible tells us, "how good and pleasant it is when God's people live together in unity"' – significantly deployed against potential prejudice – although even here the biblical register was seamlessly elided with the patriotic one, Trump introducing his scriptural quote with the words, 'When you open your heart to patriotism, there is no room for prejudice.'

Hauerwas, an acute critic of nationalised Christianity at any time, wrote that the address was 'a stunning example of idolatry', pervaded by the sense that salvation lay in the power, potential and unity of the nation. Trump's statement that 'at the bedrock of our politics will be a total allegiance to the United States of America and through our loyalty to our country we will recover loyalty to each other' is, Hauerwas wrote, 'clearly a theological claim that offers a kind of salvation'. Similarly, his insistence that America would be 'protected by the great men and women of our military and law enforcement and, most importantly, we are protected by God' was uncomplicatedly God-on-our-side material. While it is hard to think of a single inaugural address that would have escaped Hauerwas's condemnation – the blurring of patriotism, providence and (usually Protestant) Christianity having marked American self-identity since era of the Founding Fathers[35] – Trump's speech was a particularly egregious example of this tendency.

The extent to which Trump's theo-nationalistic rhetoric finds its way into his politics is, at the time of writing, yet to be seen. On-shoring jobs after a decade of seeing them move to China and elsewhere will be a challenge, but one that is a better indication of economic policy than theological stance. More telling is the ongoing and rather messy saga involving the much-promised wall with Mexico and badly implemented travel ban from seven predominantly Muslim countries.

There is good evidence that these actions were precisely the kind of thing that earned Trump his popularity, not least among Christian voters. It has garnered him less support among Christians elsewhere. Louis Sako of Baghdad, Iraq's Catholic Chaldean Patriarch, criticised the travel ban as 'a trap' that would 'feed tensions with our Muslim fellow citizens', saying that 'every reception policy that discriminates [between] the persecuted and suffering on religious grounds ultimately harms the Christians of the East'.[36]

Rather more prominent is Pope Francis's view of Trump, a subject of much media interest. While some have speculated that the two global figures in fact share a similar iconoclastic style,[37] they use it to different ends. The Pope has made several not-so-oblique criticisms of Trump's wall-building, Muslim-banning policies, and went as far as to remark, on a trip back from Mexico, that 'a person who thinks only about building walls, wherever they may be, and not building bridges, is not Christian'.[38] Trump, for his part, has not judged the Pope as beyond criticism, saying on his Facebook page that 'if and when the Vatican is attacked by ISIS ... I can promise you that the Pope would have only wished and prayed that Donald Trump would have been President because this would not have happened'.[39]

Popes and Presidents have not always got on. Pope John Paul II fell out with President George W. Bush over the Iraq War, and with President Clinton before him over abortion, and didn't even see eye-to-eye with President Reagan over defence policy. There is nothing, in principle, unprecedented about Donald Trump and Pope Francis's running spat. However, the fact that the dispute is over Trump's signature policy and has erupted so early in his administration – indeed, it surfaced nearly a year before Trump assumed office – underlines the significance and seriousness of the dispute and crystallises neatly the difference between someone who looks after Bibles and someone who reads them.

CONCLUSION

One of the earliest appearances of any new President is at the National Prayer Breakfast, held annually in Washington, DC, on the first Thursday of February every year since 1953. Trump duly spoke at the breakfast, as had his eleven immediate predecessors. He began by thanking a number of friends and participants and then by having a dig at Arnold Schwarzenegger as his replacement on *The Apprentice*:

> When I ran for President, I had to leave the show ... And they hired a big, big movie star – Arnold Schwarzenegger – to take my place. And we know how that turned out. The ratings went right down the tubes. It's been a total disaster ... And I want to just pray for Arnold, if we can, for those ratings, okay?[40]

He went on say that 'most importantly today, I want to thank the American people', adopting an approach that firmly underlined Hauerwas's criticism of his nationalised Christianity. 'No one has inspired me more in my travels than the families of the United States military,' he said, before quoting John 15:13 ('Greater love hath no man than this: that a man lay down his life for his friends').[41] 'Our freedom is won by their sacrifice, and our security has been earned with their sweat and blood and tears. God has blessed this land to give us such incredible heroes and patriots.' This was not all Trump said in his address – he spoke of religious freedom, of the 'faith [that] lives on in my heart every single day', of how America would succeed 'as long as our most vulnerable citizens ... have a path to success' – but it serves as a good cipher for Trump's faith.

Although the Prayer Breakfast address is one of the few occasions on which Presidents can be openly and unapologetically pious, piety was in short supply on this occasion. Jesus, for example, was conspicuous by his absence in Trump's words, the Bible was thin on the ground, and doctrine was absent or, if present, distorted.

By contrast, the reference to *The Apprentice*, although perhaps a mistake to dwell on for too long, felt cheap, trivial and egocentric, especially in the context. The simplistic way in which geo-politics and government were understood – 'the world is in trouble, but we're going to straighten it out' – suggested a Manichean worldview of light versus dark, good versus evil, similar to that of which George W. Bush was often accused. And the manner in which Trump proposed it should be 'straightened' – 'it will be stopped

... It may not be pretty for a little while ... All nations have a duty to work together to confront [violence] and to confront it viciously, if we have to' – indicates a willingness to resort to force – indeed, 'vicious' force – that felt singularly misplaced, ill-chosen and deaf to the Christian context.

But the clearest indication of Trump's faith lay in his identification, of a piece with much of his campaigning and inaugural rhetoric, of nation with salvation. 'America is a nation of believers,' he remarked, among which Trump insistently numbers himself. Such insistence notwithstanding, however, Trump's belief is more comfortable when focused on himself and on his country than it is with Christian doctrine, practice or Christ himself.

NOTES

1   I would like to thank Rachel Fidler for her helpful research in preparing this chapter at short notice.

2   Adam Kelsey, '50 Former National Security Officials Say Trump 'Not Qualified to Be President', ABC News, 8 April 2016, http://abcnews.go.com/Politics/50-national-security-officials-trump-qualified-president/story?id=41215597

3   'You could see there was blood coming out of her eyes, blood coming out of her – whatever', he told CNN after the debate. Harriet Alexander, 'Donald Trump says Megyn Kelly's tough questioning was due to menstruation', *Daily Telegraph*, 8 August 2015, http://www.telegraph.co.uk/news/worldnews/us-election/11791693/Donald-Trump-says-Megyn-Kellys-tough-questioning-was-due-to-menstruation.html

4   'Transcript: Donald Trump's Taped Comments About Women', *New York Times*, 8 October 2016, https://www.nytimes.com/2016/10/08/us/donald-trump-tape-transcript.html?_r=0

5   James Macintyre, 'Exclusive Michael Gove Interview: On Trump Quitting Early, Not Talking To Cameron And Being A Flawed Christian', Christian Today, 23 February 2017, http://www.christiantoday.com/article/exclusive.michael.gove.interview.on.trump.quitting.early.not.talking.to.cameron.and.being.a.flawed.christian/104960.htm

6   Gwenda Blair, 'How Norman Vincent Peale Taught Donald Trump to Worship Himself', *Politico*, 6 October 2016, http://www.politico.com/magazine/story/2015/10/donald-trump-2016-norman-vincent-peale-213220

7   Tamara Keith, 'Trump Crowd Size Estimate May Involve "The Power Of Positive Thinking"', NPR, 22 January 2017, http://www.npr.org/2017/01/22/510655254/trump-crowd-size-estimate-may-involve-the-power-of-positive-thinking

8   The phrase derives from Christian Smith and Melinda Lundquist Denton, *Soul Searching: The Religious and Spiritual Lives of American Teenagers* (Oxford: Oxford University Press, 2005).

9   Donald Trump, *Trump: Think Like a Billionaire* (Ballantine Books Inc.; reissue edition, 9 December 2005), p. xii.

10 David Brody, 'Exclusive: Donald Trump to Brody File: "I believe in God. I am Christian."', http://www1.cbn.com/thebrodyfile/archive/2011/04/11/exclusive-donald-trump-to-brody-file-i-believe-in-god

11 Max Ehrenfreund, 'Trump: "The Bible means a lot to me, but I don't want to get into

specifics"', *Washington Post*, 27 August 2015, https://www.washingtonpost.com/news/wonk/wp/2015/08/27/trump-the-bible-means-a-lot-to-me-but-i-dont-want-to-get-into-specifics/?utm_term=.1ceaef997a4f

12 Carey Lodge, 'What Do We Know About Trump's Faith?', Christian Today, 9 November 2016; http://www.christiantoday.com/article/what.do.we.know.about.trumps.faith/100219.htm

13 Ibid. See also Jenna Johnson, 'Donald Trump likes that Proverbs verse that might not exist', *Washington Post*, 16 September 2015; https://www.washingtonpost.com/news/post-politics/wp/2015/09/16/donald-trump-likes-that-proverbs-verse-that-might-not-exist/?utm_term=.a5fa1ec31535

14 Eugene Scott, 'Trump believes in God, but hasn't sought forgiveness', CNN, 19 July 2015, http://edition.cnn.com/2015/07/18/politics/trump-has-never-sought-forgiveness/

15 1 John 1:8.

16 https://www.sba-list.org/home/pro-life-women-sound-the-alarmdonald-trump-is-unacceptable

17 Gregory Smith, 'Churchgoing Republicans, once skeptical of Trump, now support him', Pew Forum, 21 July 2016, http://www.pewresearch.org/fact-tank/2016/07/21/churchgoing-republicans-once-skeptical-of-trump-now-support-him/

18 David Stebenne, 'Donald Trump's Religious Background and the 2016 Presidential Election', Huffington Post, 19 September 2016, http://www.huffingtonpost.com/david-stebenne/donald-trumps-religious-b_b_11072346.html

19 'Trump Campaign announces evangelical executive advisory board', 21 June 2016, https://www.donaldjtrump.com/press-releases/trump-campaign-announces-evangelical-executive-advisory-board

20 Richard Land, 'Why I Joined Donald Trump's Evangelical Executive Advisory Board', Christian Post, 22 June 2016, http://www.christianpost.com/news/why-i-joined-donald-trump-evangelical-executive-advisory-board-165499/

21 Kate Shellnutt and Sarah Eekhoff Zylstra, 'Who's Who of Trump's "Tremendous" Faith Advisers', *Christianity Today*, 22 June 2016, http://www.christianitytoday.com/ct/2016/june-web-only/whos-who-of-trumps-tremendous-faith-advisors.html

22 Eric Bradner, 'Trump aide mum on Dobson's assertion Trump is a "baby Christian"', 26 June 2016, http://edition.cnn.com/2016/06/26/politics/donald-trump-james-dobson-baby-christian/

23 Kate Shellnutt and Sarah Eekhoff Zylstra, 'Who's Who of Trump's "Tremendous" Faith Advisers', *Christianity Today*, 22 June 2016, http://www.christianitytoday.com/ct/2016/june-web-only/whos-who-of-trumps-tremendous-faith-advisors.html

24 'Paula White on Donald Trump's Christian Faith', Christian Post, 8 June 2016, http://www.christianpost.com/news/paula-white-on-donald-trumps-christian-faith-exclusive-interview-166205/

25 Noah Weilandjan, 'Paula White, Trump's Spiritual Adviser, Says He Has "a Hunger for God"', *New York Times*, 19 January 2017, https://www.nytimes.com/2017/01/19/us/trumps-pastor-paula-white.html?_r=0

26 A Declaration by American Evangelicals Concerning Donald Trump, https://www.change.org/p/donald-trump-a-declaration-by-american-evangelicals-concerning-donald-trump

27 Quoted in Terry Eastland, 'The Religion of Trump', Weekly Standard, 25 January 2016, http://www.weeklystandard.com/the-religion-of-trump/article/2000601

28 Andy Crouch, 'Speak Truth to Trump', *Christianity Today*, 10 October 2016, http://www.christianitytoday.com/ct/2016/October-web-only/speak-truth-to-trump.html?start=1

29 Macintyre, 'Exclusive Michael Gove Interview', op. cit.

30 Michelle Goldberg, 'Donald Trump, the Religious Right's Trojan Horse', *New York Times*, 27 January 2017.

31 Michelle Hackman, 'Vice President Mike Pence Addresses "March for Life" Anti-abortion Rally', *Wall Street Journal*, 27 January 2017, https://www.wsj.com/articles/vice-president-mike-pence-to-speak-at-march-for-life-antiabortion-march-1485528430

32 Jessica Glenza, 'Donald Trump retracts call for women who have abortions to be "punished"', *The Guardian*, 31 March 2016, https://www.theguardian.com/us-news/2016/mar/30/donald-trump-women-abortions-punishment

33 https://www.whitehouse.gov/inaugural-address

34 Stanley Hauerwas, 'Christians, don't be fooled: Trump has deep religious convictions', *Washington Post*, 27 January 2017, https://www.washingtonpost.com/news/acts-of-faith/wp/2017/01/27/christians-dont-be-fooled-trump-has-deep-religious-convictions/?utm_term=.f385bb06e15e

35 See Daniel L. Dreisbach, *Reading the Bible with the Founding Fathers* (Oxford: OUP, 2017)

36 Carol Glatz, 'Iraqi patriarch: Fast track for Christian refugees will fuel tensions', Crux, 30 January 2017, https://cruxnow.com/global-church/2017/01/30/iraqi-patriarch-fast-track-christian-refugees-will-fuel-tensions/ See also Tom Malinowski, 'Donald Trump's Phony Compassion for Christians', *New York Times*, 5 February 2017, https://www.nytimes.com/2017/02/05/opinion/donald-trumps-phony-compassion-for-christians.html?_r=2

37 See Matthew Schmitz, 'What Donald Trump and Pope Francis actually have in common', *Washington Post*, 19 February 2016, https://www.washingtonpost.com/news/acts-of-faith/wp/2016/02/19/what-donald-trump-and-pope-francis-actually-have-in-common/?utm_term=.1e977aee0bd2

38 Ben Jacobs, 'Donald Trump calls Pope Francis "disgraceful" for questioning his faith', *The Guardian*, 18 February 2016, https://www.theguardian.com/us-news/2016/feb/18/donald-trump-pope-francis-christian-wall-mexico-border See also, from a year later, Jacopo Barigazzi, 'Pope Francis: Donald Trump of the left', *Politico*, 24 January 2017, http://www.politico.eu/article/francis-and-trump-populist-pope-vs-populist-president/

39 https://www.donaldjtrump.com/press-releases/donald-j.-trump-response-to-the-pope

40 https://www.whitehouse.gov/the-press-office/2017/02/02/remarks-president-trump-national-prayer-breakfast

41 This is oddly and presumably accidentally reminiscent of the Christianity that many Anglican padres reported finding in the First World War trenches, with their belief that dying in battle for your country automatically ensures an afterlife in heaven.

CONCLUSION

NICK SPENCER

Thatcher, Blair, Brown, Cameron, May: it is striking how many recent British Prime Ministers feature in this volume. Indeed, since the end of the 1970s, only John Major is absent. The same is the case for the US – Reagan, Clinton, Bush, Obama, Trump – although that trend is perhaps less surprising and more questionable. Australia – with Howard, Rudd and Abbott – offers similar evidence, and if France elects François Fillon in 2017, after Nicolas Sarkozy failed to secure his party's nomination, it too may be bucking its secular tradition. A devout German Chancellor has dominated European politics for the last ten years, and a resurgent Russia is unthinkable without a publicly Orthodox Vladimir Putin. Eastern European politics too has become acutely aware of 'Christian heritage' issues latterly, epitomised in this collection by Viktor Orbán. And all this is before we cast the net over Central and South America, sub-Saharan Africa and even, as we see here in Lee Myung-bak, parts of Asia.

No less striking is how recent Christian premiers compare with their immediate predecessors. Although John Howard did not create the religious shift in Australian politics single handedly – both Paul Keating and even Bob Hawke were influential in this[1] – Australian politics took a noticeable turn on his watch. The public resurgence and rhetorical renaissance of Christian politics in America under (Jimmy Carter and) Ronald Reagan are well attested. And, in Britain, Harold Macmillan was the only devoutly Christian

Prime Minister between the end of the Second World War and 1980, compared with the two or three or four since.

One has to be slightly careful here. After the war, Western politics often simply assumed its Christianity. Whether in the Christian Democratic parties that dominated continental Europe in the post-war decades, or the Christian socialism that underpinned many British Labour parliamentarians, or the unassuming Anglicanism of post-war Tories, or widespread Christian assumptions of both Republican and Democrat parties in the US, Christian politics was part of the post-war furniture. We have not gone from zero to sixty on the dial of Christian politics. Nevertheless, the presence and prevalence of Christian leaders, not least in some of the world's most secular, plural and 'modern' countries, remains noteworthy. The idea that 'secularisation' would purge politics of religious commitment is surely misguided.

If faith remains a potent presence at the highest level of politics, however, one might be excused for asking what difference it actually makes. The figures in this volume have been notably diverse in their political views. What, after all, unites Margaret Thatcher and Gordon Brown, John Howard and Kevin Rudd, Lee Myung-bak and Fernando Lugo, Vladimir Putin and Barack Obama? The answer is very little, at least politically speaking. The leaders discussed in these pages stretch from the hard left (Lugo) through the left (Brown), the centre-left (Blair, Rudd, Obama), the centre-right (Merkel, Sarkozy, Cameron) to the right (Thatcher, Reagan, Howard, Bush, Abbott). Others are harder to classify and even these classifications are questionable, pinned as they are to a left–right scale that is tasked with the impossible job of explaining all political difference. However else we might want to summarise them, the essays in this volume show that the political directions in which political leaders have taken their faith are many and varied. The wonder is that they all claim affinity with and roots in the same religion. Indeed, one wonders at times whether it is the same religion.

Such incredulity invites a completely different response. If the religious soil in which these leaders sink their political roots results in such radically different political programmes, perhaps those roots are actually very shallow.

Maybe, in other words, the ideology is a front, and the religion mere electoral sheen.

The problem with this conclusion – despite the fact that it is thrown about with abandon (usually as an accusation) – is that it is somewhat difficult to sustain. Almost all political leaders are accused of putting their faith on for the cameras, some – such as Clinton, Putin, Orbán, Obama, and Trump – particularly so. Moreover, in a number of contexts – US, Russia, Hungary – it is relatively easy to see what political capital might be gained from such a public faith. However, to take these established facts and then generalise that such public professions are simply cynical attempts at vote winning is to go too far too fast. In the first place, a number of figures covered in these pages – Mandela, Blair, Merkel, Brown and May for example – clearly preferred to do the opposite and take their faith *off* for the cameras. Second, some of those who did talk about their faith in a surprisingly candid or public way, such as Nicolas Sarkozy or perhaps Tony Abbott, had little to gain and quite a bit to lose (not least the accusation of hypocrisy) in doing so. Third, most obviously, even when a politician did have something to gain from their public Christianity, that doesn't necessarily mean they were faking it. Only the most boneheaded of critics would accuse many of the leaders discussed here of 'doing God' *just* for show. Who, after all, thinks that Thatcher, McAleese, Rudd, Jonathan, Lugo or Lee didn't actually believe what they said they believed? Only in those cases where the personal faith of the leader is open to question *and* there is clear political capital to be made out of a public profession of their faith – Orbán for example, Putin perhaps, Clinton maybe, Trump certainly – does the 'pure hypocrisy' accusation gain credibility, and even then it may say as much about the accuser as the accused.

• • •

We are left, therefore, in an uncomfortable middle ground. We cannot trace a simple line from the Christian faith to a political agenda, but nor can we pretend no such lines exist and that all the faith stuff is mere window dressing, moral bouquets that make the stench of realpolitik more tolerable. So, does Christianity make any coherent difference?

The best answer to this begins not with the politics but with the politician. It is striking how, time and time again in this volume, politicians have claimed that their Christian faith informed them personally with a commitment to public service or to the common good or to hope or to deeper wells of moral energy or to a sense of justice that transcended the ephemera of daily politics. In other words, Christianity shaped them before it shaped their politics.

One might justly claim that they would say that, wouldn't they? Duty, hope, morality, justice: who is going to complain about those? If Christian faith fosters such personal virtues among politicians, then it must, by definition, be a good, and any residual public concern about believing politicians will be obviated. While there may be something in this, it does demand some pretty deeply entrenched scepticism. Perhaps a few of the political leaders featured in this book do indeed draw a sense of personal duty, or hope, or morality, or justice from their faith. It's just possible that some of them are telling the truth.

What they clearly don't draw from their Christian faith is an unambiguous or incontrovertible political vision. This is not a new problem. In a study of the political use of the Bible within English (latterly British) history, published to mark the 400th anniversary of the publication of the King James translation,[2] I argued that, more often than not, those who looked to the Bible for political answers were able to come up with more or less anything they wanted. This was often due less to cynicism than to circumstance. When the Anglo-Saxons read the Bible through the lens of a warrior culture and found examples of heroic bravery, they were not being any more cynical than when socially marginal Baptists read it in the seventeenth century and found ideas of toleration. Similarly, when Enlightenment-influenced evangelicals read the Bible in the eighteenth century and found ideas of emancipation, they were being no more manipulative than the working-class Christian radicals who read it in the nineteenth century and found an uncompromising criticism of the New Poor Law. Everyone reads sacred texts from somewhere, and where you read it from shapes much of what you read.

As with history, so with geography: Christian politics looks different from, say, the (Hungarian) former margins of the Ottoman empire than it does from the recently humbled but now resurgent (Russian) seat of the Third Rome; or the slums of Ecuador and Paraguay; or the painfully (and religiously) divided culture of South Africa; or the painfully (and religiously) unstable ones of Liberia and Nigeria; or the leadenly secularised halls of French power; or the democratically stable but often fiscally challenged states of the UK or Australia; or the democratically still stable but religiously polarised culture of the US. The fact that any one of these countries can itself produce a wide variety of Christian leaders – sometimes politically diametrically opposed from one another – clearly shows that context and circumstance do not *dictate* political theology. But only a fool would imagine that they don't *influence* it.

In the aforementioned study of the Bible and politics in the UK, I argued that the Bible contains two powerful, distinct and apparently conflicting political impulses. The first of these is to political freedom (both the *negative* freedom from political constraints[3] and the *positive* freedom to enable the fulfilment of inherent human potential)[4] and the second is towards political order. Hence the book's title: *Freedom and Order*.

While allowing for the fact that no politician is wholly informed by a single ideology and that even the ideologically fiercest have to pay attention to circumstance, compromise and, in democracies, the messy business of representation, it seems that these twin impulses towards freedom and order describe much of the theo-political variation we have seen in this collection. Thus Margaret Thatcher, Ronald Reagan, John Howard, George W. Bush, and to a different extent Angela Merkel and Lee Myung-bak, derived from their biblical reflections a commitment, sometimes an overwhelming commitment, to freedom of the negative kind. By contrast, Bill Clinton, Tony Blair, Gordon Brown, Kevin Rudd, Fernando Lugo, Barack Obama and even, if early signs are anything to go by, Theresa May all take from their Christianity a more interventionist approach, which corresponds to freedom of a positive kind. If there are figures who adhere more tightly to the biblical impulse to order – much rarer today than would have been the case in the past – they can best be seen in this collection by Vladimir Putin and Viktor

Orbán, although the instability of their political contexts naturally oriented Ellen Johnson Sirleaf and Goodluck Jonathan in this direction also. Other figures are less easy to compartmentalise for various reasons, whether it be on account of their philosophical rather than theological approach (as with Václav Havel), their determined circumspection (as with Nelson Mandela) or their generally non-ideological stance (as with David Cameron).

The obvious criticism to this – that it's a remarkable coincidence that these people's theological commitments are so similar to their political ideology – is also a silly criticism. We are unlikely to find anyone, let alone any political leader, whose religious beliefs are opposed to their political ones. Theological beliefs inform and reform political (and social) ones, as political and social ones do for theology. There is an element of chicken and egg in the discussion of theology and politics.

The Christian commitments of the various leaders represented here may well have influenced their emerging political vision, in the same way as their upbringing and personality and the times through which they lived undoubtedly did. But when that political vision was formed, it was only natural for the leader in question to derive from their faith that which affirmed and confirmed that political vision. Thus, *pace* the interpretations above, it's not that Christian political leaders are formed only by their Christian political roots or that, conversely, those roots are simply shallow and superficial. Rather it is that, having had their political vision formed (in part) by their faith, political leaders subsequently draw from theological soil only those nutrients that sanction their now-established political visions. Faith might be the ground on which political visions grow but, after a while, it is used primarily to support and sustain those visions, and not to reform or challenge them.

•   •   •

This view is supported by the fact that virtually none of the figures in these pages have reflected long and deep on the political significance of their theological beliefs. Beyond Havel's philosophical cogitations, Lugo's training for the priesthood, Abbott's Catholic-flavoured reflections on Burke, and Rudd's essay on what Christian politics is, no one in this volume has engaged in any sustained theological reflection on politics. There has been plenty of general orientation and informing of views, but little evidence of political theology per se.

This should, in theory, calm jittery secular horses, not least among those liberals who see in theologically informed politics a subversion of the open, rational, discursive processes that underpin democratic liberty. Not only do devout political leaders not take their instructions straight from the Pope, or from 'fundamentalist' 'literal' readings of the Bible – a caricature the like of which we saw in Angela Eagle's fringe speech in the introduction – but they don't even really take them from their theology, or at least not in any direct command-and-control way.

This will reassure many people, and rightly so. If leadership is a (delicate) balance between ideology, representation and circumstance, any leader who takes his or her cues unduly from only the first of these – whether it be a religious or secular ideology – is liable to undermine the public good. But in the case of Christianity, this reassurance comes with a health warning. The last twenty years have seen a remarkable rise in what is known as 'populism' across Western, particularly European, democracies. Most of these populist movements have been of the political right, many have been fuelled by fears of migration and Islam, and quite a few have adopted Christian images and vocabulary to justify themselves and attract supporters. The Northern League in Italy, the Austrian Freedom Party, the Swiss People's Party, the Law and Justice Party in Poland, and Hungary's Fidesz and its Justice and Life Party, to name only the most prominent, have made a vigorous defence, albeit in different contexts, of their country's (and the continent's) Christian culture, its Christian values, its Christian heritage and its Christian people. They have forcefully defended Christian symbols, particularly the cross, Christian practices (like prayer) and Christian churches. And they have usually done this in direct and often aggressive opposition to the values of liberalism, multiculturalism and, especially, Islam.

This isn't a problem confined to Christianity. In their book on the subject of 'how populists hijack religion', Nadia Marzouki, Duncan McDonnell and Olivier Roy point out that in France, with its embedded secularism, and in the Netherlands, with its deep tradition of (a kind of) liberal toleration, populist parties, like the National Front, the Pim Fortuyn List and the

Dutch Party for Freedom, have eschewed Christianity as a vehicle for their exclusionary politics. With a curious twist on the usual picture, secularism and liberalism are being deployed there as a means of attacking minorities.

Nevertheless, this is a problem that is more serious for Christianity simply because Christianity arouses passions that secularism and liberalism tend not to. The depth, colour, history, omnipresence, coherence and power of Christianity in Europe make it a political force to be reckoned with, which is precisely what these populist parties seek to do. It is a striking fact, therefore, as Marzouki, McDonnell and Roy repeatedly stress in their analysis, that 'most populists tend to be secular themselves, and do not consider Christianity as a faith, but rather as an identity. They place Christendom above Christianity.' Moreover, 'when evoking the Christian identities of their nations, populist leaders tend to refer to symbols such as the cross than to theological dogma'.[5]

Thus, in Italy the Northern League's 'defence of "the Christian people" focuses more on symbols and the question of "who belongs" (and does not belong) than on Christian beliefs'.[6] The Austrian Freedom Party's 'inclusion of religion in [its] programme … is to be understood as a populist mobilisation strategy rather than an indicator of adherence to a faith'.[7] In populist Hungary, 'God is not presented as a symbol of universal religious identity, as understood in the New Testament or explained in the speeches of Pope Francis, but as "the God of the Hungarians", in its particularistic, tribal, paganised political understanding'.[8]

It is no accident, therefore, that the principal and principled opposition to this kind of religious-flavoured populism has often come from the churches themselves, which have gone into battle against these bastardised forms of Christian identity armed primarily with actual Christian beliefs.[9] Thus, in Switzerland, the Swiss People's Party 'found itself at odds with the country's principal Churches … which considered a ban on minarets contrary to the principle of religious freedom'.[10] In the UK, every mainstream church has spoken out vigorously against the BNP and the English Defence League, the General Synod of the Church of England even going as far as to vote to ban clergy from belonging to the BNP. In a 'rather explicit' press statement responding to the Austrian People's Party's official 'endorsement' of Christianity in their 1997 party manifesto, 'the Austrian Conference of Bishops declared that they did not want to be used in an instrumental way by the [party]'.[11]

Moreover, fascinatingly, such polling as exists on the subject suggests that the more theologically informed voters are, the more likely they are to see through the Christian identity smokescreen raised by the populists. According to a 2010 poll in France, for example, 'only 5 per cent of French Evangelicals vote for the *Front National*, as opposed to 38 per cent of traditional Lutherans in Alsace'. Similarly, although polls indicate that the church-going Catholic vote for the Front National has risen slightly, 'it still remains a minority both among FN voters and among Catholic voters ... the Catholic vote for the FN is below that of the general population'.[12] It seems, Marzouki, McDonnell and Roy conclude, that 'the more the individual insists on "faith" versus "identity", the less likely he or she is to vote for populists'.[13] The outlier here, as it is in so many ways, seems to be the US, where the evangelical support for Trump discussed in the last chapter suggests that professing a Christian *faith* can co-exist happily with claiming the 'rights' of a Christian *identity*.

If this analysis is right, it suggests that the best defence against superficial, content-lite Christian *identity* politics is theologically informed, content-heavy Christian *belief* politics. Anxious liberals fret about too much 'belief' in politics, for fear it will deafen leaders to the demands of circumstance or the responsibilities of representation: the believing politician heeds God, or the Pope, or the Scriptures rather than his or her electorate or constitutional mandate. But the emergence of populism over recent decades has underlined that neither circumstance nor representation is exactly morally uncomplicated. Whereas the rallying cry of the democratic Enlightenment was that representation was the solution to the problem posed by belief, today we might suggest that belief is a solution to some of the problems currently posed by representation. Contrary to the kind of scare stories with which this book opened, Christian belief can be an instrument of political stability and reason, casting doubt over simplistic, majoritarian politics especially when such politics is coloured and even justified by Christian vocabulary and identity.

Ultimately, the best argument for the Christian faith in politics, and indeed the reason why no single coherent political programme emerges from the collection of figures in this book, is a version of this point. Christian belief contests the politics of Christian identity that we have seen emerge in Europe over recent decades. But, in a sense, Christian belief contests *all* politics, its vision of human flourishing and the ethical claims it makes of people being so demanding that no political leader or political programme can fully satisfy them. Any politician who imagines they can tame and control the faith comfortably for their political ends is going to be disappointed. Christian belief is always, unreasonably, asking for more, and holding politicians to standards that precious few can satisfy. As Tony Abbott said, the 'Christian politician faces the double test of not only being an effective politician but also a credible Christian'.[14] It's a double test that they are, in effect, condemned to fail, but we should be grateful that so many are prepared even to try.

NOTES

1. See Roy Williams, *In God They Trust? The Religious Beliefs of Australia's Prime Ministers, 1901–2013* (Australia: Bible Society, 2013).

2. Nick Spencer, *Freedom and Order: History, Politics and the English Bible* (London: Hodder and Stoughton, 2011).

3. Ideas of negative freedom were derived from a wide variety of sources: the story of the Exodus, the supreme icon of political liberation in the Old Testament; the conditions placed upon kings in the Torah; the origins of Israelite kingship in all its ambiguity; the various tales of wicked Old Testament kings who angered God and were (sometimes) punished for their sins; and the subservience of all kings before the King of Kings, who would one day judge them for the way in which they discharged the divinely set obligations of their office.

4. These came from a similar variety of biblical sources. The divine judgment that implicitly limited royal authority also presented kings with the duty to secure the safety, peace, justice and common wealth of their people. The frequent injunctions in the Old Testament to care for society's most vulnerable – the poor, the widow, the orphan, the alien – were repeatedly used as a yardstick against which rulers were measured. When Christ told his audience in Matthew 25 that whatever they did 'unto one of the least of these my brethren' – the hungry, the thirsty, the stranger, the naked, the prisoner – they did for him, he emphasised in the strongest possible terms the imperative of caring for the vulnerable. Perhaps most influentially, the creation story of Genesis 1 told how 'God created man in his own image', an idea that did more than any other to underline human equality and dignity. The duty to secure that dignity did not rest with the king alone, of course, but he bore much of its responsibility. The condition of the weakest of his people reflected directly on his standing before God.

5. Nadia Marzouki, Duncan McDonnell and Olivier Roy, *Saving the People: How Populists Hijack Religion* (London: Hurst, 2016), p. 186.

6. Ibid., p. 27.

7. Ibid., p. 45.

8. Ibid., p. 146.

9. It should be noted that this is not a universal response, and there are examples of prominent clerics and of churches, sometimes smaller, newer or more independent, which have endorsed the Christian identity rhetoric of right-wing populists.

10. Marzouki et al., *Saving the People*, p. 60.

11. Ibid., p. 41.

12. Ibid., p. 88.

13. Ibid., p. 200.

14. Tony Abbott, 'Speech notes: The Ethical Responsibilities of a Christian Politician', 16 March 2004, p. 3, http://rodneyolsen.net/wp-content/uploads/2004/03/04mar16_ethical-resp_politician.pdf (accessed 31 January 2017).